Praise for *Building Secure and Reliable Systems*

It is very hard to get practical advice on how to build and operate trustworthy infrastructure at the scale of billions of users. This book is the first to really capture the knowledge of some of the best security and reliability teams in the world, and while very few companies will need to operate at Google's scale many engineers and operators can benefit from some of the hard-earned lessons on securing wide-flung distributed systems. This book is full of useful insights from cover to cover, and each example and anecdote is heavy with authenticity and the wisdom that comes from experimenting, failing and measuring real outcomes at scale. It is a must for anybody looking to build their systems the correct way from day one.

—Alex Stamos, Director of the Stanford Internet Observatory and former CISO of Facebook and Yahoo

This book is a rare treat for industry veterans and novices alike: instead of teaching information security as a discipline of its own, the authors offer hard-wrought and richly illustrated advice for building software and operations that actually stood the test of time. In doing so, they make a compelling case for reliability, usability, and security going hand-in-hand as the entirely inseparable underpinnings of good system design.

—Michał Zalewski, VP of Security Engineering at Snap, Inc. and author of The Tangled Web *and* Silence on the Wire

This is the "real world" that researchers talk about in their papers.

—JP Aumasson, CEO at Teserakt and author of Serious Cryptography

Google faces some of the toughest security challenges of any company, and they're revealing their guiding security principles in this book. If you're in SRE or security and curious as to how a hyperscaler builds security into their systems from design through operation, this book is worth studying.

—*Kelly Shortridge, VP of Product Strategy at Capsule8*

If you're responsible for operating or securing an internet service: caution! Google and others have made it look too easy. It's not. I had the privilege of working with these book authors for many years and was constantly amazed at what they uncovered and their extreme measures to protect our users' data. If you have such responsibilities yourself, or if you're just trying to understand what it takes to protect services at scale in the modern world, study this book. Nothing is covered in detail—there are other references for that—but I don't know anywhere else that you'll find the breadth of pragmatic tips and frank discussion of tradeoffs.

—*Eric Grosse, former VP of Security Engineering at Google*

Building Secure and Reliable Systems

Best Practices for Designing, Implementing, and Maintaining Systems

Heather Adkins, Betsy Beyer, Paul Blankinship, Piotr Lewandowski, Ana Oprea, and Adam Stubblefield

Beijing · Boston · Farnham · Sebastopol · Tokyo

Building Secure and Reliable Systems

by Heather Adkins, Betsy Beyer, Paul Blankinship, Piotr Lewandowski, Ana Oprea, and Adam Stubblefield

Published by O'Reilly Media, Inc., 1005 Gravenstein Highway North, Sebastopol, CA 95472.

O'Reilly books may be purchased for educational, business, or sales promotional use. Online editions are also available for most titles (*https://oreilly.com*). For more information, contact our corporate/institutional sales department: 800-998-9938 or *corporate@oreilly.com*.

Acquisitions Editor: John Devins
Development Editor: Virginia Wilson
Production Editor: Kristen Brown
Copyeditor: Rachel Head
Proofreader: Sharon Wilkey

Indexer: WordCo, Inc.
Interior Designer: David Futato
Cover Designer: Karen Montgomery
Illustrators: Jenny Bergman and Rebecca Demarest

March 2020:   First Edition

Revision History for the First Edition
2020-03-11:   First Release

See *https://oreilly.com/catalog/errata.csp?isbn=9781492083122* for release details.

978-1-492-08312-2

[LSI]

To Susanne, whose strategic project management and passion for reliability and security kept this book on track!

Table of Contents

Part IV. Maintaining Systems

Part V.   Organization and Culture

Foreword by Royal Hansen

For years, I've wished that someone would write a book like this. Since their publication, I've often admired and recommended the Google Site Reliability Engineering (SRE) books—so I was thrilled to find that a book focused on security and reliability was already underway when I arrived at Google, and am only too happy to contribute in a small way to the process. Ever since I began working in the tech industry, across organizations of varying sizes, I've seen people struggling with the question of how security should be organized: Should it be centralized or federated? Independent or embedded? Operational or consultative? Technical or governing? The list goes on....

When the SRE model (*https://oreil.ly/OZvsg*), and SRE-like versions of DevOps, became popular, I noticed that the problem space SRE tackles exhibits similar dynamics to security problems. Some organizations have combined these two disciplines into an approach called "DevSecOps."

Both SRE and security have strong dependencies on classic software engineering teams. Yet both differ from classic software engineering teams in fundamental ways:

- Site Reliability Engineers (SREs) and security engineers tend to break and fix, as well as build.
- Their work encompasses operations, in addition to development.
- SREs and security engineers are specialists, rather than classic software engineers.
- They are often viewed as roadblocks, rather than enablers.
- They are frequently siloed, rather than integrated in product teams.

SRE created a role and responsibilities specific to a set of skills, which we can see as analogous to the role of security engineer. SRE also created an implementation model that connects teams, and this seems to be the next step that the security community needs to take. For many years, my colleagues and I have argued that security should be a first-class and embedded quality of software. I believe that embracing an SRE-inspired approach is a logical step in that direction.

Since arriving at Google, I've learned more about how the SRE model was established here, how SRE implements DevOps philosophies, and how SRE and DevOps have evolved. Meanwhile, I've been translating my IT security experience in the financial services industry to the technical and programmatic security capabilities at Google. These two sectors are not unrelated, but each has its own history worth understanding. At the same time, enterprises are at a critical point where cloud computing, various forms of machine learning, and a complicated cybersecurity landscape are together determining where an increasingly digital world is going, how quickly it will get there, and what risks are involved.

As my understanding of the intersection between security and SRE has deepened, I've become even more certain that it's important to more thoroughly integrate security practices into the full lifecycle of software and data services. The nature of the modern hybrid cloud—much of which is based on open source software frameworks that offer interconnected data and microservices—makes tightly integrated security and resilience capabilities even more important.

The operational and organizational approaches to security in large enterprises have varied dramatically over the past 20 years. The most prominent instantiations include fully centralized chief information security officers and core infrastructure operations that encompass firewalls, directory services, proxies, and much more—teams that have grown to hundreds or thousands of employees. On the other end of the spectrum, federated business information security teams have either the line of business or technical expertise required to support or govern a named list of functions or business operations. Somewhere in the middle, committees, metrics, and regulatory requirements might govern security policies, and embedded Security Champions might either play a relationship management role or track issues for a named organizational unit. Recently, I've seen teams riffing on the SRE model by evolving the embedded role into something like a site security engineer, or into a specific Agile scrum role for specialist security teams.

For good reasons, enterprise security teams have largely focused on confidentiality. However, organizations often recognize data integrity and availability to be equally important, and address these areas with different teams and different controls. The SRE function is a best-in-class approach to reliability. However, it also plays a role in the real-time detection of and response to technical issues—including security-related attacks on privileged access or sensitive data. Ultimately, while engineering teams are often organizationally separated according to specialized skill sets, they have a common goal: ensuring the quality and safety of the system or application.

In a world that is becoming more dependent upon technology every year, a book about approaches to security and reliability drawn from experiences at Google and across the industry can be an important contribution to the evolution of software development, systems management, and data protection. As the threat landscape evolves, a dynamic and integrated approach to defense is now a basic necessity. In my previous roles, I looked for a more formal exploration of these questions; I hope that a variety of teams inside and outside of security organizations find this discussion useful as approaches and tools evolve. This project has reinforced my belief that the topics it covers are worth discussing and promoting in the industry—particularly as more organizations adopt DevOps, DevSecOps, SRE, and hybrid cloud architectures along with their associated operating models. At a minimum, this book is another step in the evolution and enhancement of system and data security in an increasingly digital world.

— Royal Hansen, Vice President,
Security Engineering

Foreword by Michael Wildpaner

At their core, both Site Reliability Engineering and Security Engineering are concerned with keeping a system usable. Issues like broken releases, capacity shortages, and misconfigurations can make a system unusable (at least temporarily). Security or privacy incidents that break the trust of users also undermine the usefulness of a system. Consequently, system security is top of mind for SREs.

On the design level, security has become a highly dynamic property of distributed systems. We've come a long way from passwordless accounts on early Unix-based telephony switches (nobody had a modem to dial into them, or so people thought), static username/password combinations, and static firewall rules. These days, we instead use time-limited access tokens and high-dimensional risk assessment at millions of requests per second. Granular cryptography of data in flight and at rest, combined with frequent key rotation, makes key management an additional dependency of any networking, processing, or storage system that deals with sensitive information. Building and operating these infrastructure security software systems requires close collaboration between the original system designers, security engineers, and SREs.

The security of distributed systems has an additional, more personal, meaning for me. From my university days until I joined Google, I had a side career in offensive security with a focus on network penetration testing. I learned a lot about the fragility of distributed software systems and the asymmetry between system designers and operators versus attackers: the former need to protect against all possible attacks, while an attacker needs to find only a single exploitable weakness.

Ideally, SRE is involved in both significant design discussions and actual system changes. As one of the early SRE Tech Leads of Gmail, I started seeing SREs as one of the best lines of defense (and in the case of system changes, quite literally the last line of defense) in preventing bad design or bad implementations from affecting the security of our systems.

Google's two books about SRE—*Site Reliability Engineering* and *The Site Reliability Workbook*—relate the principles and best practices of SRE, but don't go into details about the intersection of reliability and security. This book fills that gap, and also has the space to dive deeper into security-focused topics.

For many years at Google, we've been pulling aside engineers and giving them "the talk"—a conversation about how to responsibly handle the security of our systems. But a more formal treatment of how to design and operate secure distributed systems is long overdue. In this way, we can better scale this previously informal collaboration.

Security is at the forefront of finding new classes of attacks and immunizing our systems against the varied threats in today's networked environments, while SRE plays a major role in preventing and remediating such issues. There's simply no alternative to pushing for reliability *and* security as integral parts of the software development lifecycle.

— *Michael Wildpaner, Senior Director,*
Site Reliability Engineering

Preface

Can a system ever truly be considered reliable if it isn't fundamentally secure? Or can it be considered secure if it's unreliable?

Successfully designing, implementing, and maintaining systems requires a commitment to the full system lifecycle. This commitment is possible only when security and reliability are central elements in the architecture of systems. Yet both are often afterthoughts, considered only after an incident occurs, resulting in expensive and sometimes difficult improvements.

Security by design (*https://oreil.ly/-46BV*) is increasingly important in a world where many products are connected to the internet, and where cloud technologies are becoming more prevalent. The more we come to rely on those systems, the more reliable they need to be; the more trust we place in their security, the more secure they need to be.

Systems

In this book we talk generally about *systems*, which is a conceptual way of thinking about the groups of components that cooperate to perform some function. In our context of systems engineering, these components typically include pieces of software running on the processors of various computers. They may also include the hardware itself, as well as the processes by which people design, implement, and maintain the systems. Reasoning about the behavior of systems can be difficult, since they're prone to complex emergent behaviors.

Why We Wrote This Book

We wanted to write a book that focuses on integrating security and reliability directly into the software and system lifecycle, both to highlight technologies and practices that protect systems and keep them reliable, and to illustrate how those practices interact with each other. The aim of this book is to provide insights about system design, implementation, and maintenance from practitioners who specialize in security and reliability.

We'd like to explicitly acknowledge that some of the strategies this book recommends require infrastructure support that simply may not exist where you're currently working. Where possible, we recommend approaches that can be tailored to organizations of any size. However, we felt that it was important to start a conversation about how we can all evolve and improve existing security and reliability practices, as all the members of our growing and skilled community of professionals can learn a lot from one another. We hope other organizations will also be eager to share their successes and war stories with the community. As ideas about security and reliability evolve, the industry can benefit from a diverse set of implementation examples. Security and reliability engineering are still rapidly evolving fields. We constantly find conditions and cases that cause us to revise (or in some cases, replace) previously firmly held beliefs.

Who This Book Is For

Because security and reliability are everyone's responsibility, we're targeting a broad audience: people who design, implement, and maintain systems. We're challenging the dividing lines between the traditional professional roles of developers, architects, Site Reliability Engineers (SREs) (*https://oreil.ly/EVa7K*), systems administrators, and security engineers. While we'll dive deeply into some subjects that might be more relevant to experienced engineers, we invite you—the reader—to try on different hats as you move through the chapters, imagining yourself in roles you (currently) don't have and thinking about how you could improve your systems.

We argue that everyone should be thinking about the fundamentals of reliability and security from the very beginning of the development process, and integrating those principles early in the system lifecycle. This is a crucial concept that shapes this entire book. There are many lively active discussions in the industry about security engineers becoming more like software developers, and SREs and software developers becoming more like security engineers.[1] We invite you to join in the conversation.

When we say "you" in the book, we mean the reader, independent of a particular job or experience level. This book challenges the traditional expectations of engineering roles and aims to empower you to be responsible for security and reliability throughout the whole product lifecycle. You shouldn't worry about using all of the practices

---

[1] See, for example, Dino Dai Zovi's "Every Security Team Is a Software Team Now" talk (*https://oreil.ly/Wap7b*) at Black Hat USA 2019, Open Security Summit's DevSecOps track (*https://oreil.ly/_PAzE*), and Dave Shackleford's "A DevSecOps Playbook" SANS Analyst paper (*https://oreil.ly/_Wmcx*).

described here in your specific circumstances. Instead, we encourage you to return to this book at different stages of your career or throughout the evolution of your organization, considering whether ideas that didn't seem valuable at first might be newly meaningful.

A Note About Culture

Building and adopting the widespread best practices we recommend in this book requires a culture that is supportive of such change. We feel it is essential that you address the culture of your organization in parallel with the technology choices you make to focus on both security and reliability, so that any adjustments you make are persistent and resilient. In our opinion, organizations that don't embrace the importance of both security and reliability need to change—and revamping the culture of an organization in itself often demands an up-front investment.

We've woven technical best practices throughout the book and we support them with data, but it's not possible to include data-backed cultural best practices. While this book calls out approaches that we think others can adapt or generalize, every organization has a distinct and unique culture. We discuss how Google has tried to work within its culture, but this may not be directly applicable to your organization. Instead, we encourage you to extract your own practical applications from the high-level recommendations we've included in this book.

How to Read This Book

While this book includes plenty of examples, it's not a cookbook. It presents Google and industry stories, and shares what we've learned over the years. Everyone's infrastructure is different, so you may need to significantly adapt some of the solutions we present, and some solutions may not apply to your organization at all. We try to present high-level principles and practical solutions that you can implement in a way that suits your unique environment.

We recommend you start with Chapters 1 and 2, and then read the chapters that most interest you. Most chapters begin with a boxed preface or executive summary that outlines the following:

- The problem statement
- When in the software development lifecycle you should apply these principles and practices
- The intersections of and/or tradeoffs between reliability and security to consider

Within each chapter, topics are generally ordered from the most fundamental to the most sophisticated. We also call out deep dives and specialized subjects with an alligator icon.

This book recommends many tools or techniques considered to be good practice in the industry. Not every idea will be suitable for your particular use case, so you should evaluate the requirements of your project and design solutions adapted to your particular risk landscape.

While this book aims to be self-contained, you will find references to *Site Reliability Engineering* (*https://oreil.ly/SRE-book-toc*) and *The Site Reliability Workbook* (*https://oreil.ly/SRE-workbook-TOC*), where experts from Google describe how reliability is fundamental to service design. Reading these books may give you a deeper understanding of certain concepts but is not a prerequisite.

We hope you enjoy this book, and that some of the information in these pages can help you improve the reliability and security of your systems.

Conventions Used in This Book

The following typographical conventions are used in this book:

Italic
> Indicates new terms, URLs, email addresses, filenames, and file extensions.

`Constant width`
> Used for program listings, as well as within paragraphs to refer to program elements such as variable or function names, databases, data types, environment variables, statements, and keywords.

`Constant width bold`
> Shows commands or other text that should be typed literally by the user. Also used for emphasis within program listings.

`Constant width italic`
> Shows text that should be replaced with user-supplied values or by values determined by context.

 This element signifies a general note.

This icon indicates a deep dive.

O'Reilly Online Learning

 For more than 40 years, *O'Reilly Media* has provided technology and business training, knowledge, and insight to help companies succeed.

Our unique network of experts and innovators share their knowledge and expertise through books, articles, conferences, and our online learning platform. O'Reilly's online learning platform gives you on-demand access to live training courses, in-depth learning paths, interactive coding environments, and a vast collection of text and video from O'Reilly and 200+ other publishers. For more information, please visit *https://oreilly.com*.

How to Contact Us

Please address comments and questions concerning this book to the publisher:

O'Reilly Media, Inc.
1005 Gravenstein Highway North
Sebastopol, CA 95472
800-998-9938 (in the United States or Canada)
707-829-0515 (international or local)
707-829-0104 (fax)

We have a web page for this book, where we list errata, examples, and any additional information. You can access this page at *https://oreil.ly/buildSecureReliableSystems*.

Email *bookquestions@oreilly.com* to comment or ask technical questions about this book.

For more information about our books, courses, conferences, and news, see our website at *https://www.oreilly.com*.

Find us on Facebook: *https://facebook.com/oreilly*

Follow us on Twitter: *https://twitter.com/oreillymedia*

Watch us on YouTube: *https://www.youtube.com/oreillymedia*

Acknowledgments

This book is the product of the enthusiastic and generous contributions of about 150 people, including authors, tech writers, chapter managers, and reviewers from engineering, legal, and marketing. The contributors span 18 time zones throughout the Americas, Europe, and Asia-Pacific, and more than 10 offices. We'd like to take a moment to thank everyone who isn't already listed on a per-chapter basis.

As the leaders of Google Security and SRE, Gordon Chaffee, Royal Hansen, Ben Lutch, Sunil Potti, Dave Rensin, Benjamin Treynor Sloss, and Michael Wildpaner were the executive sponsors within Google. Their belief in a project that focuses on integrating security and reliability directly into the software and system lifecycle was essential to making this book happen.

This book would never have come to be without the drive and dedication of Ana Oprea. She recognized the value a book like this could have, initiated the idea at Google, evangelized it to SRE and Security leaders, and organized the vast amount of work necessary to make it happen.

We'd like to recognize the people who contributed by providing thoughtful input, discussion, and review. In chapter order, they are:

- Chapter 1, *The Intersection of Security and Reliability*: Felipe Cabrera, Perry The Cynic, and Amanda Walker
- Chapter 2, *Understanding Adversaries*: John Asante, Shane Huntley, and Mike Koivunen
- Chapter 3, *Case Study: Safe Proxies*: Amaya Booker, Michał Czapiński, Scott Dier, and Rainer Wolafka
- Chapter 4, *Design Tradeoffs*: Felipe Cabrera, Douglas Colish, Peter Duff, Cory Hardman, Ana Oprea, and Sergey Simakov
- Chapter 5, *Design for Least Privilege*: Paul Guglielmino and Matthew Sachs
- Chapter 6, *Design for Understandability*: Douglas Colish, Paul Guglielmino, Cory Hardman, Sergey Simakov, and Peter Valchev
- Chapter 7, *Design for a Changing Landscape*: Adam Bacchus, Brandon Baker, Amanda Burridge, Greg Castle, Piotr Lewandowski, Mark Lodato, Dan Lorenc, Damian Menscher, Ankur Rathi, Daniel Rebolledo Samper, Michee Smith, Sampath Srinivas, Kevin Stadmeyer, and Amanda Walker
- Chapter 8, *Design for Resilience*: Pierre Bourdon, Perry The Cynic, Jim Higgins, August Huber, Piotr Lewandowski, Ana Oprea, Adam Stubblefield, Seth Vargo, and Toby Weingartner
- Chapter 9, *Design for Recovery*: Ana Oprea and JC van Winkel

- Chapter 10, *Mitigating Denial-of-Service Attacks*: Zoltan Egyed, Piotr Lewandowski, and Ana Oprea
- Chapter 11, *Case Study: Designing, Implementing, and Maintaining a Publicly Trusted CA*: Heather Adkins, Betsy Beyer, Ana Oprea, and Ryan Sleevi
- Chapter 12, *Writing Code*: Douglas Colish, Felix Gröbert, Christoph Kern, Max Luebbe, Sergey Simakov, and Peter Valchev
- Chapter 13, *Testing Code*: Douglas Colish, Daniel Fabian, Adrien Kunysz, Sergey Simakov, and JC van Winkel
- Chapter 14, *Deploying Code*: Brandon Baker, Max Luebbe, and Federico Scrinzi
- Chapter 15, *Investigating Systems*: Oliver Barrett, Pierre Bourdon, and Sandra Raicevic
- Chapter 16, *Disaster Planning*: Heather Adkins, John Asante, Tim Craig, and Max Luebbe
- Chapter 17, *Crisis Management*: Heather Adkins, Johan Berggren, John Lunney, James Nettesheim, Aaron Peterson, and Sara Smollet
- Chapter 18, *Recovery and Aftermath*: Johan Berggren, Matt Linton, Michael Sinno, and Sara Smollett
- Chapter 19, *Case Study: Chrome Security Team*: Abhishek Arya, Will Harris, Chris Palmer, Carlos Pizano, Adrienne Porter Felt, and Justin Schuh
- Chapter 20, *Understanding Roles and Responsibilities*: Angus Cameron, Daniel Fabian, Vera Haas, Royal Hansen, Jim Higgins, August Huber, Artur Janc, Michael Janosko, Mike Koivunen, Max Luebbe, Ana Oprea, Andrew Pollock, Laura Posey, Sara Smollett, Peter Valchev, and Eduardo Vela Nava
- Chapter 21, *Building a Culture of Security and Reliability*: David Challoner, Artur Janc, Christoph Kern, Mike Koivunen, Kostya Serebryany, and Dave Weinstein

We'd also like to especially thank Andrey Silin for his guidance throughout the book.

The following reviewers provided valuable insight and feedback to guide us along the way: Heather Adkins, Kristin Berdan, Shaudy Danaye-Armstrong, Michelle Duffy, Jim Higgins, Rob Mann, Robert Morlino, Lee-Anne Mulholland, Dave O'Connor, Charles Proctor, Olivia Puerta, John Reese, Pankaj Rohatgi, Brittany Stagnaro, Adam Stubblefield, Todd Underwood, and Mia Vu. A special thanks to JC van Winkel for performing a book-level consistency review.

We are also grateful to the following contributors, who supplied significant expertise or resources, or had some otherwise excellent effect on this work: Ava Katushka, Kent Kawahara, Kevin Mould, Jennifer Petoff, Tom Supple, Salim Virji, and Merry Yen.

External directional review from Eric Grosse helped us strike a good balance between novelty and practical advice. We very much appreciate his guidance, along with the thoughtful feedback we received from industry reviewers for the whole book: Blake Bisset, David N. Blank-Edelman, Jennifer Davis, and Kelly Shortridge. The in-depth reviews of the following people made each chapter better targeted to an external audience: Kurt Andersen, Andrea Barberio, Akhil Behl, Alex Blewitt, Chris Blow, Josh Branham, Angelo Failla, Tony Godfrey, Marco Guerri, Andrew Hoffman, Steve Huff, Jennifer Janesko, Andrew Kalat, Thomas A. Limoncelli, Allan Liska, John Looney, Niall Richard Murphy, Lukasz Siudut, Jennifer Stevens, Mark van Holsteijn, and Wietse Venema.

We would like to extend a special thanks to Shylaja Nukala and Paul Blankinship, who generously committed the time and skills of the SRE and security technical writing teams.

Finally, we'd like to thank the following contributors who worked on content that doesn't appear directly in this book: Heather Adkins, Amaya Booker, Pierre Bourdon, Alex Bramley, Angus Cameron, David Challoner, Douglas Colish, Scott Dier, Fanuel Greab, Felix Gröbert, Royal Hansen, Jim Higgins, August Huber, Kris Hunt, Artur Janc, Michael Janosko, Hunter King, Mike Koivunen, Susanne Landers, Roxana Loza, Max Luebbe, Thomas Maufer, Shylaja Nukala, Ana Oprea, Massimiliano Poletto, Andrew Pollock, Laura Posey, Sandra Raicevic, Fatima Rivera, Steven Roddis, Julie Saracino, David Seidman, Fermin Serna, Sergey Simakov, Sara Smollett, Johan Strumpfer, Peter Valchev, Cyrus Vesuna, Janet Vong, Jakub Warmuz, Andy Warner, and JC van Winkel.

Thanks also to the O'Reilly Media team—Virginia Wilson, Kristen Brown, John Devins, Colleen Lobner, and Nikki McDonald—for their help and support in making this book a reality. Thanks to Rachel Head for a fantastic copyediting experience!

Finally, the book's core team would also like to personally thank the following people:

From Heather Adkins

I'm often asked how Google stays secure, and the shortest answer I can give is that the diverse qualities of its people are the linchpin in Google's ability to defend itself. This book is reflective of that diversity, and I am sure that in my lifetime I shall discover no greater set of defenders of the internet than Googlers working together as a team. I personally owe an especially enormous debt of gratitude to Will, my wonderful husband (+42!!), to my Mom (Libby), Dad (Mike), and brother (Patrick), and to Apollo and Orion for inserting all those typos. Thank you to my team and colleagues at Google for tolerating my absences during the writing of this book and for your fortitude in the face of immense adversaries; to Eric Grosse, Bill Coughran, Urs Hölzle, Royal Hansen, Vitaly Gudanets, and Sergey Brin for their guidance, feedback, and the occasional raised eyebrow over the past 17+ years; and to my dear friends and colleagues (Merry,

Max, Sam, Lee, Siobhan, Penny, Mark, Jess, Ben, Renee, Jak, Rich, James, Alex, Liam, Jane, Tomislav, and Natalie), especially r00t++, for your encouragement. Thank you, Dr. John Bernhardt, for teaching me so much; sorry I didn't finish the degree!

From Betsy Beyer

To Grandmother, Elliott, Aunt E, and Joan, who inspire me every single day. Y'all are my heroes! Also, to Duzzie, Hammer, Kiki, Mini, and Salim, whose positivity and sanity checks have kept me sane!

From Paul Blankinship

First, I want to thank Erin and Miller, whose support I rely on, and Matt and Noah, who never stop making me laugh. I want to express my gratitude to my friends and colleagues at Google—especially my fellow technical writers, who wrestle with concepts and language, and who need to simultaneously be both experts *and* advocates for naive users. Immense appreciation goes to the other authors of this book—I admire and respect each of you, and it is a privilege to have my name associated with yours.

From Susanne Landers

To all the contributors to this book, I can't say how honored I feel to have been part of this journey! I wouldn't be where I am today without a few special folks: Tom for finding the right opportunity; Cyrill for teaching me everything I know today; Hannes, Michael, and Piotr for inviting me to join the most amazing team ever (Semper Tuti!). To you all who take me for coffee (you know who you are!), life would be incredibly boring without you. To Verbena, who probably shaped me more than any other human being ever could, and most importantly, to the love of my life for your unconditional support and our most amazing and wonderful children. I don't know how I deserve you all, but I'll do my very best.

From Piotr Lewandowski

To everyone who leaves the world a better place than how they found it. To my family for their unconditional love. To my partner for sharing her life with me, for better or worse. To my friends for the joy they bring into my life. To my coworkers for being easily the best part of my job. To my mentors for their ongoing trust; I wouldn't be part of this book without their support.

From Ana Oprea

To the little one who will be born just as the book is going to print. Thank you to my husband, Fabian, who supported me and made it possible to work on this and many more things, while building a family. I'm grateful that my parents, Ica and Ion, have understanding that I am far away. This project is proof that there can be no progress without an open, constructive feedback loop. I was only able to lead the book based on the experience I've gained in the past years, which is thanks to my manager, Jan, and the whole developer infrastructure team, who trusted me to focus my work at the intersection of security, reliability, and development. Last but not least, I want to express my gratitude to the supportive community of BSides: Munich and MUC:SEC, which have been a formative place that I learn from continuously.

From Adam Stubblefield
    Thanks to my wife, my family, and all my colleagues and mentors over the years.

Introductory Material

If you asked your customers to name their favorite features of your products, it's unlikely that their lists would begin with security and reliability. Both features are often hidden in their expectations: if they're working well, your customers don't notice them.

We believe that security and reliability *should* be top priorities for any organization. Ultimately, few people want to use a product that's not secure and reliable, so these aspects provide differentiating business value.

Part I of this book highlights the large overlap between practices that are fundamental to secure and reliable systems, and tradeoffs you might have to make between the two. We then provide high-level guidance on your potential adversaries: how they might act, and how their actions might affect the lifecycle of your systems.

CHAPTER 1

The Intersection of Security and Reliability

By Adam Stubblefield, Massimiliano Poletto,
and Piotr Lewandowski
with David Huska and Betsy Beyer

On Passwords and Power Drills

On September 27, 2012, an innocent Google-wide announcement caused a series of cascading failures in an internal service. Ultimately, recovering from these failures required a power drill.

Google has an internal password manager that allows employees to store and share secrets for third-party services that don't support better authentication mechanisms. One such secret is the password to the guest WiFi system on the large fleet of buses that connect Google's San Francisco Bay Area campuses.

On that day in September, the corporate transportation team emailed an announcement to thousands of employees that the WiFi password had changed. The resulting spike in traffic was far larger than the password management system—which had been developed years earlier for a small audience of system administrators—could handle.

The load caused the primary replica of the password manager to become unresponsive, so the load balancer diverted traffic to the secondary replica, which promptly failed in the same way. At this point, the system paged the on-call engineer. The engineer had no experience responding to failures of the service: the password manager was supported on a best-effort basis, and had never suffered an outage in its five years of existence. The engineer attempted to restart the service, but did not know that a restart required a hardware security module (HSM) smart card.

These smart cards were stored in multiple safes in different Google offices across the globe, but not in New York City, where the on-call engineer was located. When the service failed to restart, the engineer contacted a colleague in Australia to retrieve a smart card. To their great dismay, the engineer in Australia could not open the safe because the combination was stored in the now-offline password manager. Fortunately, another colleague in California had memorized the combination to the on-site safe and was able to retrieve a smart card. However, even after the engineer in California inserted the card into a reader, the service still failed to restart with the cryptic error, "The password could not load any of the cards protecting this key."

At this point, the engineers in Australia decided that a brute-force approach to their safe problem was warranted and applied a power drill to the task. An hour later, the safe was open—but even the newly retrieved cards triggered the same error message.

It took an additional hour for the team to realize that the green light on the smart card reader did not, in fact, indicate that the card had been inserted correctly. When the engineers flipped the card over, the service restarted and the outage ended.

Reliability and security are both crucial components of a truly trustworthy system, but building systems that are both reliable and secure is difficult. While the requirements for reliability and security share many common properties, they also require different design considerations. It is easy to miss the subtle interplay between reliability and security that can cause unexpected outcomes. The password manager's failure was triggered by a reliability problem—poor load-balancing and load-shedding strategies—and its recovery was later complicated by multiple measures designed to increase the security of the system.

The Intersection of Security and Privacy

Security and privacy are closely related concepts. In order for a system to respect user privacy, it must be fundamentally secure and behave as intended in the presence of an adversary. Similarly, a perfectly secure system doesn't meet the needs of many users if it doesn't respect user privacy. While this book focuses on security, you can often apply the general approaches we describe to achieve privacy objectives, as well.

Reliability Versus Security: Design Considerations

In designing for reliability and security, you must consider different risks. The primary reliability risks are nonmalicious in nature—for example, a bad software update or a physical device failure. Security risks, however, come from adversaries who are actively trying to exploit system vulnerabilities. When designing for reliability, you assume that some things will go wrong at some point. When designing for security, you must assume that an adversary could be trying to make things go wrong at any point.

As a result, different systems are designed to respond to failures in quite different ways. In the absence of an adversary, systems often fail *safe* (or *open*): for example, an electronic lock is designed to remain open in case of power failure, to allow safe exit through the door. Fail safe/open behavior can lead to obvious security vulnerabilities. To defend against an adversary who might exploit a power failure, you could design the door to fail *secure* and remain closed when not powered.

Reliability and Security Tradeoff: Redundancy

In designing for reliability, you often need to add redundancy to systems. For instance, many electronic locks fail secure but accept a physical key during power failures. Similarly, fire escapes provide a redundant exit path for emergencies. While redundancy increases reliability, it also increases the attack surface. An adversary need only find a vulnerability in one path to be successful.

Reliability and Security Tradeoff: Incident Management

The presence of an adversary can also affect methods of collaboration and the information that's available to responders during an incident. Reliability incidents benefit from having responders with multiple perspectives who can help find and mitigate the root cause quickly. By contrast, you'll often want to handle security incidents with the smallest number of people who can fix the problem effectively, so the adversary isn't tipped off to the recovery effort. In the security case, you'll share information on a *need-to-know* basis. Similarly, voluminous system logs may inform the response to an incident and reduce your time to recovery, but—depending on what is logged— those logs may be a valuable target for an attacker.

Confidentiality, Integrity, Availability

Both security and reliability are concerned with the confidentiality, integrity, and availability of systems, but they view these properties through different lenses. The key difference between the two viewpoints is the presence or lack of a malicious adversary. A reliable system must not breach confidentiality accidentally, like a buggy chat system that misdelivers, garbles, or loses messages might. Additionally, a secure system must prevent an active adversary from accessing, tampering with, or destroying confidential data. Let's take a look at a few examples that demonstrate how a reliability problem can lead to a security issue.

Confidentiality, integrity, and availability have traditionally been considered fundamental attributes of secure systems and are referred to as the *CIA triad*. While many other models extend the set of security attributes beyond these three, the CIA triad has remained popular over time. Despite the acronym, this concept is not related to the Central Intelligence Agency in any way.

Confidentiality

In the aviation industry, having a push-to-talk microphone stuck in the transmit position (*https://oreil.ly/QXg1F*) is a notable confidentiality problem. In several well-documented cases, a stuck mike has broadcast private conversations between pilots in the cockpit, which represents a breach of confidentiality. In this case, no malicious adversary is involved: a hardware reliability flaw causes the device to transmit when the pilot does not intend it to.

Integrity

Similarly, data integrity compromise need not involve an active adversary. In 2015, Google Site Reliability Engineers (SREs) noticed that the end-to-end cryptographic integrity checks on a few blocks of data were failing. Because some of the machines that processed the data later demonstrated evidence of uncorrectable memory errors, the SREs decided to write software that exhaustively computed the integrity check for every version of the data with a single-bit flip (a 0 changed to a 1, or vice versa). That way, they could see if one of the results matched the value of the original integrity check. All errors indeed turned out to be single-bit flips, and the SREs recovered all the data. Interestingly, this was an instance of a security technique coming to the rescue during a reliability incident. (Google's storage systems also use noncryptographic end-to-end integrity checks, but other issues prevented SREs from detecting the bit flips.)

Availability

Finally, of course, availability is both a reliability and a security concern. An adversary might exploit a system's weak spot to bring the system to a halt or impair its operation for authorized users. Or they might control a large number of devices spread around the world to perform a classic distributed denial-of-service (DDoS) attack, instructing the many devices to flood a victim with traffic.

Denial-of-service (DoS) attacks are an interesting case because they straddle the areas of reliability and security. From a victim's point of view, a malicious attack may be indistinguishable from a design flaw or a legitimate spike in traffic. For example, a 2018 software update (*https://redd.it/9iivc5*) caused some Google Home and Chromecast devices to generate large synchronized spikes in network traffic as the devices adjusted their clocks, resulting in unexpected load on Google's central time service. Similarly, a major breaking news story or other event that prompts millions of people to issue near-identical queries can look very much like a traditional application-level DDoS attack. As shown in Figure 1-1, when a magnitude 4.5 earthquake hit the San Francisco Bay Area in the middle of the night in October 2019, Google infrastructure serving the area was hit with a flood of queries.

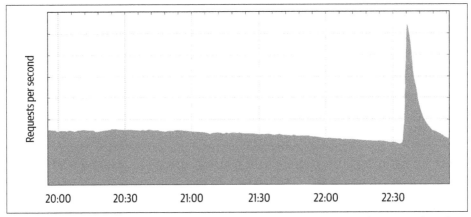

Figure 1-1. Web traffic, measured in HTTP requests per second, reaching Google infrastructure serving users in the San Francisco Bay Area when a magnitude 4.5 earthquake hit the region on October 14, 2019

Reliability and Security: Commonalities

Reliability and security—unlike many other system characteristics—are emergent properties of a system's design. Both are also difficult to bolt on after the fact, so you should ideally take both into account from the earliest design stages. They also require ongoing attention and testing throughout the entire system lifecycle, because it is easy for system changes to inadvertently affect them. In a complex system, reliability and security properties are often determined by the interaction of many components, and an innocuous-looking update to one component may end up affecting the reliability or security of the entire system in a way that may not be evident until it causes an incident. Let's examine these and other commonalities in more detail.

Invisibility

Reliability and security are mostly invisible when everything is going well. But one of the goals of reliability and security teams is to earn and keep the trust of customers and partners. Good communication—not only in times of trouble, but also when things are going well—is a solid foundation for this trust. It is important that the information be—to the greatest degree possible—honest and concrete, and free of platitudes and jargon.

Unfortunately, the inherent invisibility of reliability and security in the absence of emergencies means that they're often seen as costs that you can reduce or defer without immediate consequences. However, the costs of reliability and security failures can be severe. According to media reports, data breaches (*https://oreil.ly/QJuBm*) may have led to a $350 million reduction in the price Verizon paid to acquire Yahoo!'s internet business in 2017. In the same year, a power failure (*https://oreil.ly/vyXAE*) caused key computer systems to shut down at Delta Airlines and resulted in almost 700 flight cancellations and thousands of delays, reducing Delta's flight throughput for the day by approximately 60%.

Assessment

Because it's not practical to achieve perfect reliability or security, you can use risk-based approaches to estimate the costs of negative events, as well as the up-front and opportunity costs of preventing these events. However, you should measure the probability of negative events differently for reliability and security. You can reason about the reliability of a composition of systems and plan engineering work according to desired error budgets,[1] at least in part because you can assume independence of failures across the individual components. The security of such a composition is more difficult to assess. Analyzing a system's design and implementation can afford some level of assurance. Adversarial testing—simulated attacks typically performed from the perspective of a defined adversary—can also be used to evaluate a system's resistance to particular kinds of attacks, the effectiveness of attack detection mechanisms, and the potential consequences of attacks.

Simplicity

Keeping system design as simple as possible is one of the best ways to improve your ability to assess both the reliability and the security of a system. A simpler design reduces the attack surface, decreases the potential for unanticipated system interactions, and makes it easier for humans to comprehend and reason about the system. Understandability is especially valuable during emergencies, when it can help responders mitigate symptoms quickly and reduce mean time to repair (MTTR). Chapter 6 elaborates on this topic and discusses strategies such as minimizing attack surfaces and isolating responsibility for security invariants into small, simple subsystems that can be reasoned about independently.

---

1 For more information on error budgets, see Chapter 3 in the SRE book.

Evolution

No matter how simple and elegant the initial design, systems rarely remain unchanged over time. New feature requirements, changes in scale, and evolution of the underlying infrastructure all tend to introduce complexity. On the security side, the need to keep up with evolving attacks and new adversaries can also increase system complexity. Additionally, pressure to meet market demands can lead system developers and maintainers to cut corners and accumulate technical debt. Chapter 7 addresses some of these challenges.

Complexity often accumulates inadvertently, but this can lead to tipping-point situations where a small and apparently innocuous change has major consequences for a system's reliability or security. A bug that was introduced in 2006 and discovered almost two years later in the Debian GNU/Linux version of the OpenSSL library provides one notorious example (*https://oreil.ly/OIX0b*) of a major failure caused by a small change. An open source developer noticed that Valgrind, a standard tool for debugging memory problems, was reporting warnings about memory used prior to initialization. To eliminate the warnings, the developer removed two lines of code. Unfortunately, this caused OpenSSL's pseudo-random number generator to only be seeded with a process ID, which on Debian at the time defaulted to a number between 1 and 32,768. Brute force could then easily break cryptographic keys.

Google has not been immune to failures triggered by seemingly innocuous changes. For example, in October 2018, YouTube was down (*https://oreil.ly/CpxXL*) globally for more than an hour because of a small change in a generic logging library. A change intended to improve the granularity of event logging looked innocent to both its author and the designated code reviewer, and it passed all tests. However, the developers didn't fully realize the impact of the change at YouTube scale: under production load, the change quickly caused YouTube servers to run out of memory and crash. As the failures shifted user traffic toward other, still healthy servers, cascading failures brought the entire service to a halt.

Resilience

Of course, a memory utilization problem should not have caused a global service outage. Systems should be designed to be resilient under adverse or unexpected circumstances. From the reliability perspective, such circumstances are often caused by unexpectedly high load or component failures. Load is a function of the volume and the average cost of requests to the system, so you can achieve resilience by shedding some of the incoming load (processing less) or reducing the processing cost for each request (processing more cheaply). To address component failures, system design should incorporate redundancy and distinct failure domains so that you can limit the impact of failures by rerouting requests. Chapter 8 discusses these topics further, and Chapter 10 goes into depth on DoS mitigations in particular.

However resilient a system's individual components might be, once it becomes sufficiently complex, you cannot easily demonstrate that the entire system is immune to compromise. You can address this problem in part using defense in depth and distinct failure domains. *Defense in depth* is the application of multiple, sometimes redundant, defense mechanisms. *Distinct failure domains* limit the "blast radius" of a failure and therefore also increase reliability. A good system design limits an adversary's ability to exploit a compromised host or stolen credentials in order to move laterally or to escalate privilege and affect other parts of the system.

You can implement distinct failure domains by compartmentalizing permissions or restricting the scope of credentials. For example, Google's internal infrastructure supports credentials that are explicitly scoped to a geographic region. These types of features can limit the ability of an attacker who compromises a server in one region to move laterally to servers in other regions.

Employing independent encryption layers for sensitive data is another common mechanism for defense in depth. For example, even though disks provide device-level encryption, it's often a good idea to also encrypt the data at the application layer. This way, even a flawed implementation of an encryption algorithm in a drive controller won't be sufficient to compromise the confidentiality of protected data if an attacker gains physical access to a storage device.

While the examples cited so far hinge on external attackers, you must also consider potential threats from malicious insiders. Although an insider may know more about potential abuse vectors than an external attacker who steals an employee's credentials for the first time, the two cases often don't differ much in practice. The *principle of least privilege* can mitigate insider threats. It dictates that a user should have the minimal set of privileges required to perform their job at a given time. For example, mechanisms like Unix's sudo support fine-grained policies that specify which users can run which commands as which role.

At Google, we also use multi-party authorization to ensure that sensitive operations are reviewed and approved by specific sets of employees. This multi-party mechanism both protects against malicious insiders and reduces the risk of innocent human error, a common cause of reliability failures. Least privilege and multi-party authorization are not new ideas—they have been employed in many noncomputing scenarios, from nuclear missile silos to bank vaults. Chapter 5 discusses these concepts in depth.

From Design to Production

Security and reliability considerations should be kept in mind when translating even a solid design into a fully deployed production system. Starting with the development of the code, opportunities exist to spot potential security and reliability issues through code reviews, and even to prevent entire classes of problems by using common frameworks and libraries. Chapter 12 discusses some of these techniques.

Before deploying a system, you can use testing to ensure that it functions correctly both in normal scenarios and in the edge cases that typically impact reliability and security. Whether you use load testing to understand the behavior of a system under a flood of queries, fuzzing to explore the behavior on potentially unexpected inputs, or specialized tests to ensure that cryptographic libraries aren't leaking information, testing plays a critical role in gaining assurance that the system you've actually built matches your design intentions. Chapter 13 covers these approaches in depth.

Finally, some approaches to actually deploying code (see Chapter 14) can limit security and reliability risk. For example, canaries and slow rollouts can prevent you from breaking the system for all users simultaneously. Similarly, a deployment system that accepts only code that's been properly reviewed can help to mitigate the risk of an insider pushing a malicious binary to production.

Investigating Systems and Logging

So far we have focused on design principles and implementation approaches to prevent both reliability and security failures. Unfortunately, it is usually impractical or too expensive to attain perfect reliability or security. You must assume that preventive mechanisms will fail, and craft a plan to detect and recover from failures.

As we discuss in Chapter 15, good logging is the foundation of detection and failure preparedness. In general, the more complete and detailed your logs, the better—but this guideline has some caveats. At sufficient scale, log volume poses a significant cost, and analyzing logs effectively can become difficult. The YouTube example from earlier in this chapter illustrates that logging can also introduce reliability problems. Security logs pose an additional challenge: logs typically should not contain sensitive information, such as authentication credentials or personally identifiable information (PII), lest the logs themselves become attractive targets for adversaries.

Crisis Response

During an emergency, teams must work together quickly and smoothly because problems can have immediate consequences. In the worst case, an incident can destroy a business in minutes. For example, in 2014 an attacker put the code-hosting service Code Spaces out of business in a matter of hours by taking over the service's administrative tools and deleting all of its data, including all backups (*https://oreil.ly/ dYXkG*). Well-rehearsed collaboration and good incident management are critical for timely responses in these situations.

Organizing crisis response is challenging, so it's best to have a plan in place before an emergency occurs. By the time you discover an incident, the clock may have been ticking for some time. In any case, responders are operating under stress and time pressure, and (at least initially) with limited situational awareness. If an organization is large and the incident requires 24/7 response capabilities or collaboration across time zones, the need to maintain state across teams and to hand off incident management at the boundaries of work shifts further complicates operations. Security incidents also typically entail tension between the impulse to involve all essential parties versus the need—often driven by legal or regulatory requirements—to restrict information sharing on a need-to-know basis. Moreover, the initial security incident may be just the tip of the iceberg. The investigation might grow beyond company boundaries or involve law enforcement agencies.

During a crisis, it is essential to have a clear chain of command and a solid set of checklists, playbooks, and protocols. As discussed in Chapters 16 and 17, Google has codified crisis response (*https://oreil.ly/NVSXJ*) into a program called Incident Management at Google (IMAG), which establishes a standard, consistent way to handle all types of incidents, from system outages to natural disasters, and organize an effective response. IMAG was modeled on the US government's Incident Command System (ICS) (*https://oreil.ly/uSpFn*), a standardized approach to the command, control, and coordination of emergency response among responders from multiple government agencies.

When not faced with the pressure of an ongoing incident, responders typically negotiate long intervals with little activity. During these times, teams need to keep individuals' skills and motivation sharp and improve processes and infrastructure in preparation for the next emergency. Google's Disaster Recovery Testing program (DiRT) (*https://oreil.ly/hoBK3*) regularly simulates various internal system failures and forces teams to cope with these types of scenarios. Frequent offensive security exercises test our defenses and help identify new vulnerabilities. Google employs IMAG even for small incidents, which further prompts us to regularly exercise emergency tools and processes.

Recovery

Recovering from a security failure often requires patching systems to fix a vulnerability. Intuitively, you want that process to happen as quickly as possible, using mechanisms that are exercised regularly and are therefore decently reliable. However, the capability to push changes quickly is a double-edged sword: while this capability can help close vulnerabilities quickly, it can also introduce bugs or performance issues that cause a lot of damage. The pressure to push patches quickly is greater if the vulnerability is widely known or severe. The choice of whether to push fixes slowly—and therefore to have more assurance that there are no inadvertent side effects, but risk that the vulnerability will be exploited—or to do so quickly ultimately comes down to a risk assessment and a business decision. For example, it may be acceptable to lose some performance or increase resource usage to fix a severe vulnerability.

Choices like this underscore the need for reliable recovery mechanisms that allow us to roll out necessary changes and updates quickly without compromising reliability, and that also catch potential problems before they cause a widespread outage. For example, a robust fleet recovery system needs to have a reliable representation of every machine's current and desired state, and also needs to provide backstops to ensure that state is never rolled back to an obsolete or unsafe version. Chapter 9 covers this and many other approaches, and Chapter 18 discusses how to actually recover systems once an event has occurred.

Conclusion

Security and reliability have a lot in common—both are inherent properties of all information systems that are tempting to initially sacrifice in the name of velocity, but costly to fix after the fact. This book aims to help you address inevitable challenges related to security and reliability early on, as your systems evolve and grow. Alongside engineering efforts, each organization has to understand the roles and responsibilities (see Chapter 20) that contribute to building a culture of security and reliability (Chapter 21) in order to persist sustainable practices. By sharing our experiences and lessons learned, we hope to enable you to avoid paying a bigger price further down the road by adopting some of the principles described here sufficiently early in the system lifecycle.

We wrote this book with a broad audience in mind, with the goal that you will find it relevant regardless of the stage or scope of your project. While reading it, keep the risk profile of your project in mind—operating a stock exchange or a communication platform for dissidents has a drastically different risk profile than running a website for an animal sanctuary. The next chapter discusses the classes of adversaries and their possible motivations in detail.

CHAPTER 2

Understanding Adversaries

By Heather Adkins and David Huska
with Jen Barnason

In August 1986, Clifford Stoll, a systems administrator at Lawrence Livermore Laboratory, stumbled upon a seemingly benign accounting error that led to a 10-month search for someone stealing government secrets from the United States.[1] Largely considered to be the first public example of its kind, Stoll spearheaded an investigation that laid bare the specific tactics, techniques, and procedures (TTPs) the adversary used to achieve their goals. Through careful study, the investigation team was able to construct a picture of how the attacker targeted and siphoned data out of protected systems. Many system designers have incorporated lessons that arose from Stoll's seminal article describing the team's efforts, "Stalking the Wily Hacker."

In March 2012, Google responded to an unusual power outage at one of its Belgian datacenters that ultimately led to local data corruption. Investigation revealed that a cat had damaged a nearby external power supply, triggering a series of cascading failures in the building's power systems. By studying how complex systems fail in similar ways, Google has been able to adopt resilient design practices when suspending, burying, and submerging cables around the world.

Understanding a system's adversaries is critical to building resilience and survivability for a wide variety of catastrophes. In the reliability context, adversaries usually operate with benign intent and take abstract form. They might exist as routine

---

1 Stoll documented the attack in an article in *Communications of the ACM*, "Stalking the Wily Hacker" (*https:// oreil.ly/JaC0B*), and the book *The Cuckoo's Egg: Tracking a Spy Through the Maze of Computer Espionage* (Gallery Books). Both are good resources for anyone designing secure and reliable systems, as their findings are still relevant today.

hardware failures or cases of overwhelming user interest (so-called "success disasters"). They could also be configuration changes that cause systems to behave in unexpected ways, or fishing vessels that accidentally sever undersea fiber-optic cables. By contrast, adversaries in the security context are human; their actions are calculated to affect the target system in an undesirable way. Despite these contrasting intents and methods, studying reliability and security adversaries is important for understanding how to design and implement resilient systems. Without this knowledge, anticipating the actions of a Wily Hacker or a Curious Cat would be quite challenging.

In this chapter, we deep dive on security adversaries to help specialists in diverse fields develop an adversarial mindset. It may be tempting to think of security adversaries through the lens of popular stereotypes: attackers in dark basements with clever nicknames and potentially shady behaviors. While such colorful characters certainly exist, anyone with time, knowledge, or money can undermine the security of a system. For a small fee, anyone can purchase software that enables them to take over a computer or mobile phone to which they have physical access. Governments routinely buy or build software to compromise the systems of their targets. Researchers often probe the safety mechanisms of systems to understand how they work. Therefore, we encourage you to maintain an objective perspective about who is attacking a system.

No two attacks—or attackers—are the same. We recommend taking a look at Chapter 21 for a discussion of the cultural aspects of dealing with adversaries. Predicting future security catastrophes is mostly a guessing game, even for knowledgeable security experts. In the following sections, we present three frameworks to understand attackers that we've found helpful over the years, exploring the potential motives of people attacking systems, some common attacker profiles, and how to think about attackers' methods. We also provide illustrative (and hopefully entertaining) examples within the three frameworks.

Attacker Motivations

Security adversaries are first and foremost human (at least for the time being). Therefore, we can consider the purpose of attacks through the eyes of the people who carry them out. Doing so may better equip us to understand how we should respond, both proactively (during system design) and reactively (during incidents). Consider the following attack motivations:

Fun

> To undermine the security of a system for the sheer joy of knowing it can be done.

Fame
> To gain notoriety for showing off technical skills.

Activism
> To make a point or broadcast a message—typically, a political viewpoint—widely.

Financial gain
> To make money.

Coercion
> To get a victim to knowingly do something they don't want to do.

Manipulation
> To create an intended outcome or change behavior—for example, by publishing false data (misinformation).

Espionage
> To gain information that might be valuable (spying, including industrial espionage). These attacks are often performed by intelligence agencies.

Destruction
> To sabotage a system, destroy its data, or just take it offline.

An attacker might be a financially motivated vulnerability researcher, government espionage agent, and criminal actor all at the same time! For example, in June 2018 the US Department of Justice indicted Park Jin Hyok, a North Korean citizen accused of participating in a wide variety of activities (*https://oreil.ly/mVluG*) on behalf of his government, including creating the infamous 2017 WannaCry Ransomware (used for financial gain), the 2014 compromise of Sony Pictures (intended to coerce Sony into not releasing a controversial movie, and ultimately harming the company's infrastructure), and the compromise of electric utilities (presumably for espionage or destructive purposes). Researchers have also observed government attackers using the same malware leveraged in nation-state attacks to pilfer electronic money (*https://oreil.ly/0SRdz*) in video games for personal gain.

When designing systems, it's important to keep these diverse motivations in mind. Consider an organization that is processing money transfers on behalf of its customers. If we understand why an attacker might be interested in this system, we can design the system more securely. A good example of possible motivations in this case can be seen in the activities of a group of North Korean government attackers (including Park) who allegedly attempted to steal millions of dollars (*https://oreil.ly/u4cJV*) by breaking into banking systems and exploiting the SWIFT transaction system to transfer money out of customer accounts.

Attacker Profiles

We can better understand attacker motivations by taking the people themselves into account: who they are, whether they perform attacks for themselves or for someone else, and their general interests. In this section, we outline some *profiles* of attackers, indicating how they relate to a system designer and including a few tips for protecting your systems from these types of attackers. For the sake of brevity, we've taken some liberties with generalizations, but remember: no two attacks or attackers are the same. This information is meant to be illustrative rather than definitive.

Early Hacking

MIT is considered to be the birthplace of the term *hacking*, which dates back to the 1950s, when this activity spawned from innocent pranks. These benign origins have led some to differentiate "hacking" and "attacking" into separate notions of nonmalicious and malicious behavior. We continue this tradition throughout this book. The MIT hacker community today operates by a loose set of ethics documented in the MIT Mind and Hand Book (*https://handbook.mit.edu/hacking*).

Hobbyists

The first computer hackers were *hobbyists*—curious technologists who wanted to understand how systems worked. In the process of taking computers apart or debugging their programs, these "hackers" discovered flaws that the original system designers hadn't noticed. Generally speaking, hobbyists are motivated by their thirst for knowledge; they hack for fun, and can be allies to developers looking to build resilience into a system. More often than not, hobbyists abide by personal ethics about not harming systems and don't cross boundaries into criminal behavior. By leveraging insight into how these hackers think about problems, you can make your systems more secure.

Vulnerability Researchers

Vulnerability researchers use their security expertise professionally. They enjoy finding security flaws as full-time employees, part-time freelancers, or even accidentally as average users who stumble across bugs. Many researchers participate in Vulnerability Reward Programs, also known as *bug bounties* (see Chapter 20).

Vulnerability researchers are typically motivated to make systems better, and can be important allies to organizations seeking to secure their systems. They tend to operate within a set of predictable disclosure norms that set expectations between system owners and researchers about how vulnerabilities are discovered, reported, fixed, and discussed. Researchers operating under these norms avoid inappropriately accessing data, causing harm, or breaking the law. Typically, operating outside these norms invalidates the possibility of getting a reward and may qualify as criminal behavior.

Relatedly, *Red Teams* and penetration testers attack targets with the permission of the system owner, and may be hired explicitly for these exercises. Like researchers, they look for ways to defeat system security with a focus on improving security and operate within a set of ethical guidelines. For more discussion on Red Teams, see Chapter 20.

Governments and Law Enforcement

Government organizations (for example, law enforcement agencies and intelligence agencies) may hire security experts to gather intelligence, police domestic crime, commit economic espionage, or complement military operations. By now, most national governments have invested in fostering security expertise for these purposes. In some cases, governments may turn to talented students fresh out of school, reformed attackers who have spent time in jail, or notable luminaries in the security industry. While we can't cover these types of attackers extensively here, we provide a few examples of their most common activities.

Intelligence gathering

Intelligence gathering is probably the most publicly discussed government activity that employs people who know how to break into systems. In the past few decades, traditional spying techniques, including signals intelligence (SIGINT) and human intelligence (HUMINT), have modernized with the advent of the internet. In one famous example from 2011, the security company RSA was compromised (*https://oreil.ly/Es3PA*) by an adversary many experts associate with China's intelligence apparatus (*https://oreil.ly/DuLZV*). The attackers compromised RSA to steal cryptographic seeds for their popular two-factor authentication tokens. Once they had these seeds, the attackers didn't need physical tokens to generate one-time authentication credentials to log in to the systems of Lockheed Martin, a defense contractor that builds technology for the US military. Once upon a time, breaking into a company like Lockheed would have been performed by human operatives onsite—for example, by bribing an employee or having a spy hired at the firm. The advent of systems intrusion, however, has enabled attackers to use more sophisticated electronic techniques to obtain secrets in new ways.

Military purposes

Governments may break into systems for military purposes—what specialists often refer to as *cyber warfare* or *information warfare*. Imagine that a government wants to invade another country. Could they somehow attack the target's air defense systems and trick them into not recognizing an inbound air force? Could they shut down their power, water, or banking systems?[2] Alternatively, imagine that a government wants to prevent another country from building or obtaining a weapon. Could they remotely and stealthily disrupt their progress? This scenario supposedly happened in Iran in the late 2000s, when attackers illicitly introduced a modularized piece of software onto the control systems of centrifuges used to enrich uranium. Dubbed *Stuxnet* (*https://oreil.ly/WNu9A*) by researchers, this operation reportedly intended to destroy the centrifuges and halt Iran's nuclear program.

Policing domestic activity

Governments may also break into systems to police domestic activity. In a recent example, NSO Group, a cybersecurity contractor, sold software to various governments that allowed private surveillance of communications between people without their knowledge (through the remote monitoring of mobile phone calls). Reportedly, this software was intended to surveil terrorists and criminals—relatively noncontroversial targets. Unfortunately, some of NSO Group's government customers have also used the software to listen in on journalists and activists, in some cases leading to harassment, arrest, and even possibly death.[3] The ethics of governments using these capabilities against their own people is a hotly debated topic, especially in countries without strong legal frameworks and proper oversight.

Protecting your systems from nation-state actors

System designers should carefully consider whether they could be the target of a nation-state actor. To this end, you need to understand activities carried out by your organization that may be attractive to these actors. Consider a technology company that builds and sells microprocessor technology to a military branch of the government. It's possible that other governments would also be interested in having those chips, and may resort to stealing their designs via electronic means.

Your service may also have data that a government wants but that is otherwise difficult for it to obtain. Generally speaking, intelligence agencies and law enforcement value personal communications, location data, and similar types of sensitive personal information. In January 2010, Google announced (*https://oreil.ly/d3C-z*) it had witnessed a sophisticated targeted attack from China (dubbed "Operation Aurora" by researchers) against its corporate infrastructure that is now widely understood to have been aimed at long-term access to Gmail accounts. Storing the personal

---

2 As an example of how complicated this space can be, not all attackers in such conflicts are part of an organized military. For example, Dutch attackers reportedly compromised the US military during the Persian Gulf War (1991) and offered stolen information to the Iraqi government (*https://oreil.ly/7eNxW*).

3 NSO Group's activities have been researched and documented by The CitizenLab, a research and policy laboratory based at the Munk School of Global Affairs & Public Policy, University of Toronto. For an example, see *https://oreil.ly/IqDN_*.

---

information of customers, especially private communications, can raise the risk that an intelligence or law enforcement agency would be interested in your systems.

Sometimes you might be a target without realizing it. Operation Aurora wasn't limited to large tech companies—it affected at least 20 victims in a variety of finance, technology, media, and chemical sectors. These organizations were both large and small, and many did not consider themselves at risk of a nation-state attack.

Consider, for example, an app that aims to provide athletes with data tracking analytics, including where they cycle or run. Would this data be an attractive target to an intelligence agency? Analysts looking at a public heatmap created by the fitness tracking company Strava considered this exact question in 2018 when they noticed that the locations of secret military bases in Syria were revealed (*https://oreil.ly/N1g_X*) when US troops used the service to track their workouts.

System designers should also be aware that governments can typically deploy significant resources to obtain access to data that they're interested in. Mounting a defense against a government that's interested in your data might require far and above the resources your organization can dedicate to implementing security solutions. We recommend that organizations take the long view with regard to building security defenses by investing early in protecting their most sensitive assets, and by having a continued rigorous program that can apply new layers of protections over time. An ideal outcome is forcing an adversary to expend a significant amount of their resources to target you—increasing their risk of being caught—so that their activities can be revealed to other possible victims and government authorities.

Activists

Hacktivism is the act of using technology to call for social change. This term is loosely applied to a wide variety of online political activities, from the subversion of government surveillance to the malicious disruption of systems.[4] For the purpose of thinking about how to design systems, we consider the latter case here.

Hacktivists have been known to *deface* websites—that is, replace normal content with a political message. In one example from 2015 (*https://oreil.ly/fZAD-*), the Syrian Electronic Army—a collective of malicious actors operating in support of the regime of Bashar al-Assad—took over a content distribution network (CDN) that served web traffic for *www.army.mil*. The attackers were then able to insert a pro-Assad message subsequently seen by visitors to the website. This kind of attack can be very embarrassing for website owners and can undermine user trust in the site.

---

4 There is some debate about who coined this term and what it means, but it became widely used after 1996 when it was adopted by Hacktivismo (*https://oreil.ly/oWzO8*), a group associated with the Cult of the Dead Cow (cDc).

Other hacktivist attacks may be far more destructive. For example, in November 2012 the decentralized, international hacktivist group Anonymous[5] took numerous Israeli websites offline (*https://oreil.ly/Btovx*) through denial-of-service attacks. As a result, anyone visiting the affected websites experienced slow service or an error. Distributed denial-of-service attacks of this nature send the victim a flood of traffic from thousands of compromised machines distributed across the world. Brokers of these so-called botnets often provide this sort of capability for purchase online, making the attacks common and easy to carry out. On the more serious end of the spectrum, attackers may even threaten to destroy or sabotage systems entirely, inspiring some researchers to label them cyberterrorists.

Unlike other types of attackers, hacktivists are usually vocal about their activity and often take credit publicly. This can manifest itself in numerous ways, including posting on social media or destroying systems. Activists involved in such attacks may not even be very technically savvy. This can make predicting or defending against hacktivism difficult.

Protecting your systems from hacktivists

We recommend thinking about whether your business or project is involved in controversial topics that may draw the attention of activists. For example, does your website allow users to host their own content, like blogs or videos? Does your project involve a politically oriented issue like animal rights? Do activists use any of your products, such as a messaging service? If the answer to any of these questions is "yes," you may need to consider very robust, layered security controls that ensure your systems are patched against vulnerabilities and resilient to DoS attacks, and that your backups can restore a system and its data quickly.

Criminal Actors

Attack techniques are used to carry out crimes that closely resemble their nondigital cousins—for example, committing identity fraud, stealing money, and blackmail. *Criminal actors* have a wide range of technical abilities. Some may be sophisticated and write their own tools. Others may purchase or borrow tools that other people build, relying on their easy, click-to-attack interfaces. In fact, *social engineering*—the act of tricking a victim into aiding you in the attack—is highly effective despite being at the lowest end of difficulty. The only barriers to entry for most criminal actors are a bit of time, a computer, and a little cash.

Presenting a full catalog of the kinds of criminal activities that occur in the digital realm would be impossible, but we provide a few illustrative examples here. For

---

5 Anonymous is a moniker that a wide variety of people use for hacktivist (and other) activities. It may (or may not) refer to a single person or a collective of related persons, depending on the situation.

example, imagine that you wanted to predict merger and acquisition activities so you could time certain stock trades accordingly. Three criminal actors in China had this exact idea in 2014–2015 and made a few million dollars (*https://oreil.ly/F8pga*) by stealing sensitive information from unsuspecting law firms.

In the past 10 years, attackers have also realized that victims will hand over money when their sensitive data is threatened. *Ransomware* is software that holds a system or its information hostage (usually by encrypting it) until the victim makes a payment to the attacker. Commonly, attackers infect victim machines with this software (which is often packaged and sold to attackers as a toolkit) by exploiting vulnerabilities, by packaging the ransomware with legitimate software, or by tricking the user into installing it themselves.

Criminal activity does not always manifest as overt attempts to steal money. *Stalkerware*—spying software that's often sold for as little as $20—aims to gather information about another person without their knowledge. The malicious software is introduced onto a victim's computer or mobile phone either by tricking the victim into installing it or via direct installation by an attacker with access to the device. Once in place, the software can record video and audio. Since stalkerware is often used by people close to the victim (*https://oreil.ly/xvpFp*), such as a spouse, this kind of trust exploitation can be devastatingly effective.

Not all criminal actors work for themselves. Companies, law firms, political campaigns, cartels, gangs, and other organizations hire malicious actors for their own purposes. For example, a Colombian attacker (*https://oreil.ly/5sOcj*) claimed he was hired to assist a candidate in the 2012 presidential race in Mexico and other elections throughout Latin America by stealing opposition information and spreading misinformation. In a stunning case from Liberia, an employee of Cellcom, a mobile phone service provider, reportedly hired an attacker (*https://oreil.ly/aSCRX*) to degrade the network of its rival cellular service provider, Lonestar. These attacks disrupted Lonestar's ability to serve its customers, causing the company to lose significant amounts of revenue.

Protecting your systems from criminal actors

When designing systems to be resilient against criminal actors, keep in mind that these actors tend to gravitate toward the easiest way to meet their goals with the least up-front cost and effort. If you can make your system resilient enough, they may shift their focus to another victim. Therefore, consider which systems they might target, and how to make their attacks expensive. The evolution of Completely Automated Public Turing test (CAPTCHA) systems is a good example of how to increase the cost of attacks over time. CAPTCHAs are used to determine whether a human or an automated bot is interacting with a website—for example, during a login. Bots are often a sign of malicious activity, so being able to determine if the user is human can be an important signal. Early CAPTCHA systems asked humans to validate slightly distorted letters or numbers that bots had a difficult time recognizing. As the bots became more sophisticated, CAPTCHA implementers began using distortion pictures and object recognition. These tactics aimed to significantly increase the cost of attacking CAPTCHAs over time.[6]

Automation and Artificial Intelligence

In 2015, the US Defense Advanced Research Projects Agency (DARPA) announced the Cyber Grand Challenge contest (*https://oreil.ly/3ySRv*) to design a cyber-reasoning system that could self-learn and operate without human intervention to find flaws in software, develop ways to exploit these flaws, and then patch against the exploitations. Seven teams participated in a live "final event" and watched their fully independent reasoning systems attack each other from the comfort of a large ballroom. The first-place team succeeded in developing such a self-learning system!

The success of the Cyber Grand Challenge suggests that it's likely at least some attacks in the future could be executed without humans directly at the controls. Scientists and ethicists ponder whether fully sentient machines might be capable enough to learn how to attack each other. The notion of autonomous attack platforms is also prompting the need for increasingly automated defenses, which we predict will be an important area of research for future system designers.

Protecting your systems from automated attacks

To withstand the onslaught of automated attacks, developers need to consider resilient system design by default, and be able to automatically iterate the security posture of their systems. We cover many of these topics in this book, such as automated configuration distribution and access justifications in Chapter 5; automated build, test, and deployment of code in Chapter 14; and handling DoS attacks in Chapter 8.

Insiders

Every organization has *insiders*: current or former employees who are trusted with internal access to systems or proprietary knowledge. *Insider risk* is the threat posed by such individuals. A person becomes an *insider threat* when they are able to perform actions that cover a wide range of malicious, negligent, or accidental scenarios that

---

6 The race to increase the effectiveness of CAPTCHA techniques continues, with newer advancements using behavioral analysis of users as they interact with the CAPTCHA. reCAPTCHA (*https://oreil.ly/C8BXL*) is a free service you can use on your website. For a relatively recent overview of the research literature, see Chow Yang-Wei, Willy Susilo, and Pairat Thorncharoensri. 2019. "CAPTCHA Design and Security Issues." In *Advances in Cyber Security: Principles, Techniques, and Applications*, edited by Kuan-Ching Li, Xiaofeng Chen, and Willy Susilo, 69–92. Singapore: Springer.

could result in harm to the organization. Insider risk is a large topic that could fill the pages of several books. To help system designers, we cover the topic briefly here by considering three general categories, as outlined in Table 2-1.

Table 2-1. General categories of insiders and examples

First-party insiders	Third-party insiders	Related insiders
Employees	Third-party app developers	Friends
Interns	Open source contributors	Family
Executives	Trusted content contributors	Roommates
Board directors	Commercial partners	
	Contractors	
	Vendors	
	Auditors	

Intersection of Reliability and Security: Effects of Insiders

When it comes to protecting against adversaries, reliability and security intersect most when you're designing systems to be resilient against insiders. This intersection is largely due to the privileged access insiders have to your systems. Most reliability incidents stem from actions taken by an insider who often doesn't realize how they're impacting the system—for example, by introducing faulty code or an errant configuration change. On the security side, if an attacker can take over an employee's account, then the attacker can act maliciously against your systems as if they were that insider. Any permissions or privileges you assign to your insiders become available to an attacker.

When designing systems to be both reliable and secure, it's best practice to consider both well-intended insiders who might make mistakes and attackers who might take over an employee account. For example, if you have a database with sensitive customer information that's critical to your business, you likely want to prevent employees from accidentally deleting the database while performing maintenance work. You also want to protect database information from an attacker that hijacks an employee's account. Techniques for least privilege, outlined in Chapter 5, protect against both reliability and security risks.

First-party insiders

First-party insiders are people brought into the fold for a specific purpose—usually to participate directly in meeting business objectives. This category includes employees who directly work for the company, executives, and members of the board who make critical company decisions. You can probably think of other people who fall into the category too. Insiders with first-party access to sensitive data and systems make up the majority of news stories about insider risk. Take the case of the engineer working for General Electric (*https://oreil.ly/hiKqf*) who was indicted in April 2019 on charges of stealing proprietary files, embedding them into photos using steganographic software (in order to conceal their theft), and sending them to his personal email account. Prosecutors allege that his goal was to enable him and his business partner in China to produce low-cost versions of GE's turbomachines and sell them to the Chinese government. Stories like this are prevalent throughout high-tech firms that produce next-generation technology.

Access to personal data can also be tempting to insiders with voyeuristic tendencies, people who want to seem important for having privileged access, and even people who want to sell such information. In an infamous case from 2008 (*https://oreil.ly/Em5wF*), several hospital workers were fired from UCLA Medical Center after inappropriately looking at the files of patients, including high-profile celebrities. As more and more consumers sign up for social networking, messaging, and banking services, protecting their data from inappropriate employee access is more important than ever.

Some of the most radical stories of insider risk involve disgruntled insiders. In January 2019, a man who had been fired for poor performance was convicted of deleting 23 of his former employer's virtual servers (*https://oreil.ly/7avdj*). The incident lost the company key contracts and significant revenue. Almost any company that's been around for a while has similar stories. Because of the dynamics of employment relationships, this risk is unavoidable.

The preceding examples cover scenarios in which someone with malicious intent affects the security of systems and information. However, as some examples earlier in the book illustrate, first-party insiders can also impact the reliability of systems. For example, the previous chapter discusses a string of unfortunate insider actions in the design, operation, and maintenance of a password storage system that prevented SREs from accessing credentials in an emergency. As we'll see, anticipating the mistakes that insiders can introduce is vital to guaranteeing system integrity.

Third-party insiders

With the rise of open source software and open platforms, it's increasingly likely that an insider threat may be someone whom few people (or no one) in your organization have ever met. Consider the following scenario: your company has developed a new library that's helpful for processing images. You decide to open source the library and accept code change lists from the public. In addition to company employees, you now have to consider open source contributors as insiders. After all, if an open source contributor on the other side of the world whom you've never met submits a malicious change list, they can harm people using your library.

Similarly, open source developers rarely have the ability to test their code in all environments where it might be deployed. Additions to the codebase might introduce unpredictable reliability issues, such as unanticipated performance degradations or hardware compatibility issues. In this scenario, you'd want to implement controls ensuring that all submitted code is thoroughly reviewed and tested. For more details on best practices in this area, see Chapters 13 and 14.

You should also think carefully about how you extend a product's functionality via application programming interfaces (APIs). Suppose your organization develops a human resources platform with a third-party developer API so companies can easily extend the functionality of your software. If the third-party developer has privileged or special access to the data, they may now be an insider threat. Carefully consider the access you're providing through the API, and what the third party can do once they have access. Can you limit the impact these extended insiders have on system reliability and security?

Related insiders

It's not uncommon to implicitly trust the people we live with, but these relationships are often overlooked by system designers when designing secure systems.[7] Consider a situation in which an employee takes their laptop home over the weekend. Who has access to that device when it's unlocked on the kitchen table, and what impact could they have, either maliciously or unintended? Telecommuting, working from home, and late-night pager duty are increasingly common for technology workers. When considering your insider risk threat model, be sure to use a broad definition of "workplace" that also includes the home. The person behind the keyboard may not always be the "typical" insider.

Determining Insider Intent

If a system goes offline because of the actions of an insider, and they claim their actions were an accident, do you believe them? The answer to this question can be difficult to determine, and in extreme cases of negligence, it may be impossible to conclusively confirm or rule out. Such cases often require working with expert investigators, such as your organization's legal department, human resources, and perhaps even law enforcement. First and foremost, when designing, running, and maintaining your systems, plan for both malicious and unintended actions, and assume you may not always know the difference.

---

7 For an example of considering how security and privacy features are impacted by domestic partner abuse, see Matthews, Tara et al. 2017. "Stories from Survivors: Privacy & Security Practices When Coping with Intimate Partner Abuse." *Proceedings of the 2017 CHI Conference on Human Factors in Computing Systems*: 2189–2201. *https://ai.google/research/pubs/pub46080*.

Threat modeling insider risk

Numerous frameworks exist for modeling insider risk, ranging from simple to highly topic-specific, sophisticated, and detailed. If your organization needs a simple model to get started, we have successfully used the framework in Table 2-2. This model is also adaptable to a quick brainstorming session or fun card game.

Table 2-2. Framework for modeling insider risk

Actor/Role	Motive	Actions	Target
Engineering	Accidental	Data access	User data
Operations	Negligent	Exfiltration (theft)	Source code
Sales	Compromised	Deletions	Documents
Legal	Financial	Modifications	Logs
Marketing	Ideological	Injections	Infrastructure
Executives	Retaliatory	Leak to press	Services
	Vanity		Financials

First, establish a list of *actors/roles* present in your organization. Attempt to think of all the *actions* that may cause harm (including accidents) and potential *targets* (data, systems, etc.). You can combine items from each category to create many scenarios. Here are some examples to get you started:

- An *engineer* with access to *source code* is unsatisfied with their performance review and *retaliates* by injecting a malicious backdoor into production that steals *user data*.

- An *SRE* with access to the website's SSL *encryption keys* is approached by a stranger and is *strongly encouraged* (for example, via threats to their family) to hand over sensitive material.

- A *financial analyst* preparing the *company financials* is working overtime and *accidentally* modifies the *final yearly revenue numbers* by a factor of 1,000%.

- An *SRE's child* uses their parent's laptop at home and installs a game bundled with *malware* that locks the computer and *prevents the SRE from responding* to a serious outage.

Threat Modeling Mistakes

Sometimes people just make mistakes—to err is human. For around 40 minutes on January 31, 2009, Google Search displayed an ominous warning—"This site may harm your computer"—to every user, for every search! This warning is normally reserved for search results that link to a website that's either compromised or hosting malware. The root cause (*https://oreil.ly/Jua6_*) of this issue was very simple: a "/" had been implicitly (and accidentally!) added to the system's list of sites known to install malicious software in the background, which matched every website on the planet.

Given sufficient time working with systems, everyone is likely to encounter some version of this horror story. These mistakes can be caused by working late at night without enough sleep, typos, or simply encountering unforeseen functionality in the system. When designing secure and reliable systems, remember that humans make mistakes, and consider how to prevent them. An automated check on whether "/" was added to the configuration would have prevented the aforementioned outage!

Designing for insider risk

This book presents many design strategies for security that are applicable to protecting against insider risk and malicious "outside" attackers. When designing systems, you must consider that whoever has access to a system or its data could be any of the attacker types outlined in this chapter. Therefore, the strategies for detecting and mitigating both types of risk are similar.

We have found a few concepts to be particularly effective when thinking about insider risk:

Least privilege
> Granting the fewest privileges necessary to perform job duties, both in terms of scope and duration of access. See Chapter 5.

Zero trust
> Designing automated or proxy mechanisms for managing systems so that insiders don't have broad access that allows them to cause harm. See Chapter 3.

Multi-party authorization
> Using technical controls to require more than one person to authorize sensitive actions. See Chapter 5.

Business justifications
> Requiring employees to formally document their reason for accessing sensitive data or systems. See Chapter 5.

Auditing and detection
> Reviewing all access logs and justifications to make sure they're appropriate. See Chapter 15.

Recoverability
> The ability to recover systems after a destructive action, like a disgruntled employee deleting critical files or systems. See Chapter 9.

Attacker Methods

How do the threat actors we've described carry out their attacks? Knowing the answer to this question is critical for understanding how someone might compromise your systems and, in turn, how you can protect them. Understanding how attackers operate can feel like complex magic. Trying to predict what any particular attacker might do on any given day is unfeasible because of the variety of attack methods available. There is no way for us to present every possible method here, but thankfully, developers and system designers can leverage an increasingly large repository of examples and frameworks to wrap their heads around this problem. In this section, we discuss a few frameworks for studying attacker methods: threat intelligence, cyber kill chains, and TTPs.

Threat Intelligence

Many security firms produce detailed descriptions of attacks they've seen in the wild. This *threat intelligence* can help system defenders understand how real attackers are working every day and how to repel them. Threat intelligence comes in multiple forms, each serving a different purpose:

- *Written reports* describe how attacks occurred and are especially useful for learning about the progression and intent of an attacker. Such reports are often generated as a result of hands-on response activities and may vary in quality depending on the expertise of the researchers.

- *Indicators of compromise* (IOCs) are typically finite attributes of an attack, such as the IP address where an attacker hosted a phishing website or the SHA256 checksum of a malicious binary. IOCs are often structured using a common format[8] and obtained through automated feeds so they can be used to programmatically configure detection systems.

---

8 For example, many tools are incorporating the Structure Threat Information eXpression (STIX) language to standardize the documentation of IOCs that can be traded between systems using services like the Trusted Automated eXchange of Indicator Information (TAXII) project (*https://github.com/TAXIIProject*).

- *Malware reports* provide insight into the capabilities of attacker tools and can be a source of IOCs. These reports are generated by experts in *reverse engineering* binaries, usually using standard tools of the trade such as IDA Pro or Ghidra. Malware researchers also use these studies to cross-correlate unrelated attacks according to their common software attributes.

Acquiring threat intelligence from a reputable security firm—preferably one with customer references—can help you better understand the observed activities of attackers, including attacks affecting peer organizations in your industry. Knowing what kinds of attacks organizations similar to yours are facing can provide an early warning of what you might face someday. Many threat intelligence firms also publicly release yearly summary and trend reports for free.[9]

Cyber Kill Chains™

One way of preparing for attacks is to lay out all the possible steps that an attacker may have to take to achieve their goals. Some security researchers use formalized frameworks like the Cyber Kill Chain[10] to analyze attacks this way. These kinds of frameworks can help you plot the formal progression of an attack alongside defensive controls to consider. Table 2-3 shows the stages of a hypothetical attack relative to some defensive layers.

Table 2-3. Cyber Kill Chain of a hypothetical attack

Attack stage	Attack example	Example defenses
Reconnaissance: Surveilling a target victim to understand their weak points.	Attacker uses a search engine to find the email addresses of employees at a target organization.	Educate employees about online safety.
Entry: Gaining access to the network, systems, or accounts necessary to carry out the attack.	Attacker sends phishing emails to employees that lead to compromised account credentials. The attacker then signs in to the organization's virtual private network (VPN) service using those credentials.	Use two-factor authentication (such as security keys) for the VPN service. Only permit VPN connections from organization-managed systems.
Lateral movement: Moving between systems or accounts to gain additional access.	Attacker remotely logs in to other systems using the compromised credentials.	Permit employees to log in to only their own systems. Require two-factor authentication for login to multiuser systems.

---

9 Notable examples include the annual Verizon Databreach Investigations Report (*https://oreil.ly/x3hfo*) and CrowdStrike's annual Global Threat Report (*https://oreil.ly/i1GOs*).

10 The Cyber Kill Chain (*https://oreil.ly/L0u6I*), conceived (and trademarked) by Lockheed Martin, is an adaptation of traditional military attack structures. It defines seven stages of cyberattacks, but we've found this can be adapted; some researchers simplify it to four or five key stages, as we've done here.

Attack stage	Attack example	Example defenses
Persistence: Ensuring ongoing access to compromised assets.	Attacker installs a backdoor on the newly compromised systems that provides them with remote access.	Use application whitelisting that permits only authorized software to run.
Goals: Taking action on attack goals.	Attacker steals documents from the network and uses the remote access backdoor to exfiltrate them.	Enable least privileged access to sensitive data and monitoring of employee accounts.

Tactics, Techniques, and Procedures

Methodically categorizing attacker TTPs is an increasingly common way of cataloging attack methods. Recently, MITRE has developed the ATT&CK framework (*https://attack.mitre.org*) to instrument this idea more thoroughly. In short, the framework expands each stage of the cyber kill chain into detailed steps and provides formal descriptions of how an attacker could carry out each stage of an attack. For example, in the Credential Access stage, ATT&CK describes how a user's *.bash_history* may contain accidentally typed passwords that an attacker could obtain by simply reading the file. The ATT&CK framework lays out hundreds (potentially thousands) of ways attackers can operate so that defenders can build defenses against each attack method.

Risk Assessment Considerations

Understanding potential adversaries, who they are, and which methods they might use can be complex and nuanced. We have found the following considerations important when assessing the risk posed by various attackers:

You may not realize you're a target.
> It may not be immediately obvious that your company, organization, or project is a potential target. Many organizations, despite being small or not involved in handling sensitive information, can be leveraged to carry out attacks. In September 2012, Adobe—a company best known for software that enables content creators—disclosed that attackers had penetrated its networks (*https://oreil.ly/R4-8A*) with the express intent to digitally sign their malware using the company's official software signing certificate. This enabled the attackers to deploy malware that appeared legitimate to antivirus and other security protection software. Consider whether your organization has assets that an attacker would be interested in, either for direct gain or as part of a larger attack on someone else.

Attack sophistication is not a true predictor of success.
> Even if an attacker has a lot of resources and skills, don't assume that they'll always choose the most difficult, expensive, or esoteric means to achieve their goals. Generally speaking, attackers choose the simplest and most cost-effective methods of compromising a system that meet their goals. For example, some of

the most prominent and impactful intelligence gathering operations rely on basic phishing (*https://oreil.ly/11AyT*)—tricking a user into handing over their password. For this reason, when designing your systems, be sure to cover the simple basics of security (like using two-factor authentication) before worrying about esoteric and exotic attacks (like firmware backdoors).

Don't underestimate your adversary.

Don't assume that an adversary can't procure the resources to carry out an expensive or difficult attack. Consider carefully how much your adversary is willing to spend. The extraordinary tale of the NSA implanting backdoors in Cisco hardware by intercepting shipments en route to customers illustrates the lengths that well-funded and talented attackers will go to achieve their goals.[11] However, keep in mind that these types of cases are very much the exception rather than the norm.

Attribution is hard.

In March 2016, researchers uncovered a new type of ransomware—a malicious program that renders data or systems unavailable until the victim pays a ransom —which they named Petya. Petya appeared to be financially motivated. A year later, researchers discovered a new piece of malware that shared many elements of the original Petya program. Dubbed NotPetya (*https://oreil.ly/DGYDx*), the new malware spread globally very quickly, but was primarily found on systems in Ukraine on the eve of a Ukrainian holiday. To deliver NotPetya, attackers compromised a company that made products explicitly for the Ukrainian market and abused their software distribution mechanism to infect victims. Some researchers believe that this attack was carried out by a Russian state-sponsored actor in order to target Ukraine.

This example shows that motivated attackers can hide their motives and identity in creative ways—in this case, by disguising themselves as something potentially more benign. Since the identity and intent of attackers may not always be well understood, we recommend that you focus on how attackers work (their TTPs) before worrying about who they are specifically.

Attackers aren't always afraid of being caught.

Even if you manage to track an attacker's location and identity, the criminal system (especially internationally) may make it difficult to hold them legally accountable for their actions. This is especially true for nation-state actors working directly for a government that may be unwilling to extradite them for criminal prosecution.

---

11 Greenwald, Glenn. 2014. *No Place to Hide: Edward Snowden, the NSA, and the U.S. Surveillance State.* New York: Metropolitan Books, 149.

Conclusion

All security attacks can be traced back to a motivated person. We've covered some common attacker profiles to help you identify who may want to target your services and why, allowing you to prioritize your defenses accordingly.

Assess who might want to target you. What are your assets? Who buys your products or services? Could your users or their actions motivate attackers? How do your defensive resources compare to the offensive resources of your potential adversaries? Even when facing a well-funded attacker, the information in the rest of this book can help make you a more expensive target, possibly removing the economic incentive for an attack. Don't overlook the smaller, less conspicuous adversary—anonymity, location, ample time, and the difficulty of prosecution can all be advantages to an attacker, allowing them to cause you disproportionately large amounts of damage. Consider your insider risk, as all organizations face both malicious and nonmalicious potential threats from insiders. The elevated access granted to insiders allows them to inflict significant damage.

Stay current on the threat intelligence issued by security firms. While a multistep attack methodology can be effective, it also provides multiple contact points where you can detect and prevent an attack. Be mindful of complex attack strategies, but don't forget that simple, unsophisticated attacks like phishing can be painfully effective. Don't underestimate your adversaries or your own value as a target.

Designing Systems

Part II focuses on the most cost-effective way to implement security and reliability requirements: as early as possible in the software development lifecycle, when designing systems.

Although product design should ideally incorporate security and reliability from the start, much of the security- and reliability-related functionality you'll develop will likely be added to an existing product. Chapter 3 provides an example of how we've made already-operating systems at Google safer and less prone to outages. You can retrofit your systems with many similar enhancements, and they will be much more effective when paired with some of the design principles that follow.

Chapter 4 considers the natural tendency to defer dealing with security and reliability concerns at the expense of sustained velocity. We argue that functional and nonfunctional requirements don't necessarily need to be at odds.

If you're wondering where to begin integrating security and reliability principles into your systems, Chapter 5—which discusses how to evaluate access based upon risk—is an excellent place to start. Chapter 6 then looks at how you can analyze and understand your systems through invariants and mental models. In particular, the chapter recommends using a layered system architecture built on standardized frameworks for identity, authorization, and access control.

To respond to a shifting risk landscape, you need to be able to change your infrastructure frequently and quickly while also maintaining a highly reliable service. Chapter 7 presents practices that let you adapt to short-, medium-, and long-term changes, as well as unexpected complications that might arise as you run a service.

The guidelines mentioned thus far will have limited benefits if a system cannot withstand a major malfunction or disruption. Chapter 8 discusses strategies for keeping a system running during an incident, perhaps in a degraded mode. Chapter 9 approaches systems from the perspective of fixing them after breakage. Finally, Chapter 10 presents one scenario in which reliability and security intersect, and illustrates some cost-effective mitigation techniques for DoS attacks at each layer of the service stack.

CHAPTER 3

Case Study: Safe Proxies

By Jakub Warmuz and Ana Oprea
with Thomas Maufer, Susanne Landers, Roxana Loza,
Paul Blankinship, and Betsy Beyer

Imagine that an adversary wants to deliberately disrupt your systems. Or perhaps a well-intentioned engineer with a privileged account makes a far-reaching change by mistake. Since you understand your systems well, and they're designed for least privilege and recovery, the impact to your environment is limited. When investigating and performing incident response, you can identify the root cause of the issues and take appropriate action.

Does this scenario seem representative of your organization? It's possible that not all your systems fit this picture, and that you need a way to make a running system safer and less prone to outages. Safe proxies are one method to do just that.

Safe Proxies in Production Environments

In general, proxies provide a way to address new reliability and security requirements without requiring substantial changes to deployed systems. Rather than modifying an existing system, you can simply use a proxy to route connections that would have otherwise gone directly to the system. The proxy can also include controls to meet your new security and reliability requirements. In this case study, we examine a set of *safe proxies* we use at Google to limit the ability of privileged administrators to accidentally or maliciously cause issues in our production environment.

Safe proxies are a framework that allows authorized persons to access or modify the state of physical servers, virtual machines, or particular applications. At Google, we use safe proxies to review, approve, and run risky commands without establishing an SSH connection to systems. Using these proxies, we can grant fine-grained access to debug issues or can rate limit machine restarts. Safe proxies represent a single entry point between networks and are key instruments that enable us to do the following:

- Audit every operation in the fleet
- Control access to resources
- Protect production from human mistakes at scale

Zero Touch Prod (*https://oreil.ly/_4rAo*) is a project at Google that requires every change in production to be made by automation (instead of humans), prevalidated by software, or triggered through an audited breakglass mechanism.[1] Safe proxies are among the set of tools we use to achieve these principles. We estimate that ~13% of all Google-evaluated outages could have been prevented or mitigated with Zero Touch Prod.

In the safe proxy model, displayed in Figure 3-1, instead of talking to the target system directly, clients talk to the proxy. At Google, we enforce this behavior by restricting the target system to accept only calls from the proxy through a configuration. This configuration specifies which application-layer remote procedure calls (RPCs) can be executed by which client roles through access control lists (ACLs). After checking the access permissions, the proxy sends the request to be executed via the RPC to the target systems. Typically, each target system has an application-layer program that receives the request and executes it directly on the system. The proxy logs all requests and commands issued by the systems it interacts with.

We've found multiple benefits to using proxies to manage systems, whether the client is a human, automation, or both. Proxies provide the following:

- A central point to enforce multi-party authorization (MPA),[2] where we make the access decisions for requests that interact with sensitive data
- Administrative usage auditing, where we can track when a given request was performed and by whom
- Rate limiting, where changes like a system restart take effect gradually, and we can potentially restrict the blast radius of a mistake

---

1 A breakglass mechanism is one that can bypass policies to allow engineers to quickly resolve outages. See "Breakglass" on page 67.

2 MPA requires that an additional user approve an action before it is allowed to take place. See "Multi-Party Authorization (MPA)" on page 81.

- Compatibility with closed-source third-party target systems, where we control the behavior of components (that we cannot modify) through additional functionality in the proxy
- Continuous improvement integration, where we add security and reliability enhancements to the central proxy point

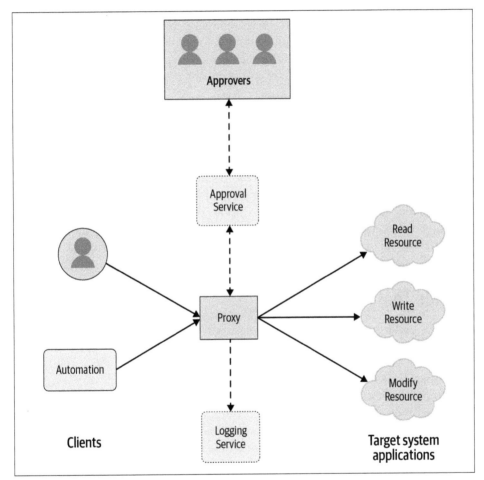

Figure 3-1. Safe proxy model

Proxies also have some downsides and potential pitfalls:

- Increased cost, in terms of maintenance and operational overhead.
- A single point of failure, if either the system itself or one of its dependencies is unavailable. We mitigate this situation by running multiple instances to increase redundancy. We make sure that all of our system's dependencies have an

acceptable service level agreement (SLA), and that the team operating each of the dependencies has a documented emergency contact.

- A policy configuration for access control, which can be a source of errors itself. We guide users to make the right choices by providing templates or automatically generating settings that are secure by default. When creating such templates or automation, we follow the design strategies presented throughout Part II.

- A central machine that an adversary could take control of. The aforementioned policy configuration requires the system to forward the identity of the client and executes any actions on behalf of the client. The proxy itself doesn't give high privileges because no request is executed under a proxy role.

- Resistance to change, as users may wish to connect directly to production systems. To reduce friction imposed by the proxy, we work closely with engineers to make sure they can access the systems through a breakglass mechanism during emergencies. We discuss such topics in more detail in Chapter 21.

Since the main use case for the safe proxy is to add security and reliability capabilities related to access control, the interfaces exposed by the proxy should use the same external APIs as the target system. As a result, the proxy doesn't affect the overall user experience. Assuming the safe proxy is transparent, it can simply forward traffic after performing some pre- and postprocessing for validation and logging. The next section discusses one specific instantiation of a safe proxy that we use at Google.

Google Tool Proxy

Googlers perform the majority of administrative operations using command-line interface (CLI) (*https://oreil.ly/7qk8Q*) tools. Some of these tools are potentially dangerous—for example, certain tools can turn off a server. If such a tool specifies an incorrect scope selector, a command-line invocation can accidentally stop several service frontends, resulting in an outage. It would be difficult and expensive to track every CLI tool, ensure that it performs centralized logging, and make certain that sensitive actions have further protections. To address this issue, Google created a *Tool Proxy*: a binary that exposes a generic RPC method that internally executes the specified command line through a fork and exec. All invocations are controlled through a policy, logged for auditing, and have the ability to require MPA.

Using the Tool Proxy achieves one of the main goals of Zero Touch Prod: making production safer by not allowing humans to directly access production. Engineers are not able to run arbitrary commands directly on servers; they need to contact the Tool Proxy instead.

We configure who is allowed to take which actions by using a fine-grained set of policies that carry out the authorization for the RPC method. The policy in Example 3-1 allows a member of group:admin to run the latest version of the borg CLI with any parameter after someone from group:admin-leads approves the command. The Tool Proxy instances are typically deployed as Borg jobs (*https://oreil.ly/ks1HD*).

Example 3-1. Google Tool Proxy Borg policy

```
config = {
  proxy_role = 'admin-proxy'
  tools = {
    borg = {
      mpm = 'client@live'
      binary_in_mpm = 'borg'
      any_command = true
      allow = ['group:admin']
      require_mpa_approval_from = ['group:admin-leads']
      unit_tests = [{
        expected = 'ALLOW'
        command = 'file.borgcfg up'
      }]
    }
  }
}
```

The policy in Example 3-1 allows an engineer to run a command to stop a Borg job in production from their workstation by using a command like the following:

```
$ tool-proxy-cli --proxy_address admin-proxy borg kill ...
```

This command sends an RPC to the proxy at the specified address, which initiates the following chain of events, as shown in Figure 3-2:

1. The proxy logs all RPCs and checks performed, providing an easy way to audit previously run administrative actions.

2. The proxy checks the policy to ensure the caller is in group:admin.

3. Since this is a sensitive command, MPA is triggered and the proxy waits for an authorization from a person in group:admin-leads.

4. If granted approval, the proxy executes the command, waits for the result, and attaches the return code, stdout, and stderr to the RPC response.

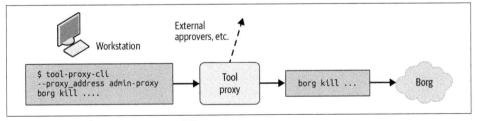

Figure 3-2. Tool Proxy usage workflow

The Tool Proxy requires a small change to the development workflow: engineers need to prepend their commands with `tool-proxy-cli --proxy_address`. To ensure privileged users don't circumvent the proxy, we modified the server to allow only administrative actions to `admin-proxy` and to deny any direct connections outside of breakglass situations.

Conclusion

Using safe proxies is one way to add logging and multi-party authorization to a system. Proxies can thus help make your systems more secure and more reliable. This approach can be a cost-effective option for an existing system, but will be much more resilient if paired with other design principles described in Part II. As we discuss in Chapter 4, if you're starting a new project, you should ideally build your system architecture using frameworks that integrate with logging and access control modules.

CHAPTER 4

Design Tradeoffs

By Christoph Kern
with Brian Gustafson, Paul Blankinship, and Felix Gröbert

Security and reliability needs often seem difficult to reconcile with a project's feature and cost requirements. This chapter covers the importance of reviewing your system's security and reliability needs as early as possible in the software design phase.

We start by talking about the connection between system constraints and product features, then provide two examples—a payment processing service and a microservices framework—that demonstrate some common security and reliability tradeoffs. We conclude with a discussion about the natural tendency to defer security and reliability work, and how early investment in security and reliability can lead to sustained project velocity.

So you're going to build a (software) product! You'll have lots of things to think about in this complex journey from devising high-level plans to deploying code.

Typically, you'll start out with a rough idea of what the product or service is going to do. This might, for example, take the form of a high-level concept for a game, or a set of high-level business requirements for a cloud-based productivity application. You'll also develop high-level plans for how the service offering will be funded.

As you delve into the design process and your ideas about the shape of the product become more specific, additional requirements and constraints on the design and implementation of the application tend to emerge. There'll be specific requirements for the functionality of the product, and general constraints, such as development and operational costs. You'll also come upon requirements and constraints for security and reliability: your service will likely have certain availability and reliability requirements, and you might have security requirements for protecting sensitive user data handled by your application.

Some of these requirements and constraints may be in conflict with each other, and you'll need to make tradeoffs and find the right balance between them.

Design Objectives and Requirements

The feature requirements for your product will tend to have significantly different characteristics than your requirements for security and reliability. Let's take a closer look at the types of requirements you'll face when designing a product.

Feature Requirements

Feature requirements, also known as *functional requirements*,[1] identify the primary function of a service or application and describe how a user can accomplish a particular task or satisfy a particular need. They are often expressed in terms of *use cases, user stories*, or *user journeys (https://oreil.ly/yFvEU)*—sequences of interactions between a user and the service or application. *Critical requirements* are the subset of feature requirements that are essential to the product or service. If a design does not satisfy a critical requirement or critical user story, you don't have a viable product.

Feature requirements are typically the primary drivers for your design decisions. After all, you're trying to build a system or service that satisfies a particular set of needs for the group of users you have in mind. You often have to make tradeoff decisions between the various requirements. With that in mind, it is useful to distinguish critical requirements from other feature requirements.

Usually, a number of requirements apply to the entire application or service. These requirements often don't show up in user stories or individual feature requirements. Instead, they're stated once in centralized requirements documentation, or even implicitly assumed. Here's an example:

All views/pages of the application's web UI must:
- Follow common visual design guidelines
- Adhere to accessibility guidelines
- Have a footer with links to privacy policy and ToS (Terms of Service)

---

1 For a more formal treatment, see The MITRE Systems Engineering Guide (*https://oreil.ly/ful41*) and ISO/IEC/IEEE 29148-2018(E) (*https://oreil.ly/GD6cY*).

Nonfunctional Requirements

Several categories of requirements focus on general attributes or behaviors of the system, rather than specific behaviors. These *nonfunctional requirements* are relevant to our focus—security and reliability. For example:

- What are the exclusive circumstances under which someone (an external user, customer-support agent, or operations engineer) may have access to certain data?

- What are the service level objectives (SLOs) (*https://oreil.ly/EJNnj*) for metrics such as uptime or 95th-percentile and 99th-percentile response latency? How does the system respond under load above a certain threshold?

When balancing requirements, it can be helpful to simultaneously consider requirements in areas beyond the system itself, since choices in those areas can have significant impact on core system requirements. Those broader areas include the following:

Development efficiency and velocity
Given the chosen implementation language, application frameworks, testing processes, and build processes, how efficiently can developers iterate on new features? How efficiently can developers understand and modify or debug existing code?

Deployment velocity
How long does it take from the time a feature is developed to the time this feature is available to users/customers?

Features Versus Emergent Properties

Feature requirements usually exhibit a fairly straightforward connection between the requirements, the code that satisfies those requirements, and tests that validate the implementation. For example:

Specification
A user story or requirement might stipulate how a signed-in user of an application can view and modify the personal data associated with their user profile (such as their name and contact information).

Implementation
A web or mobile application based on this specification would typically have code that very specifically relates to that requirement, such as the following:

- Structured types to represent the profile data

- UI code to present and permit modification of the profile data

- Server-side RPC or HTTP action handlers to query the signed-in user's profile data from a data store, and to accept updated information to be written to the data store

Validation

Typically, there'd be an integration test that essentially walks through the specified user story step by step. The test might use a UI test driver to fill out and submit the "edit profile" form and then verify that the submitted data appears in the expected database record. There are likely also unit tests for individual steps in the user story.

In contrast, nonfunctional requirements—like reliability and security requirements—are often much more difficult to pin down. It would be nice if your web server had an `--enable_high_reliability_mode` flag, and to make your application reliable you'd simply need to flip that flag and pay your hosting or cloud provider a premium service fee. But there is no such flag, and no specific module or component in any application's source code that "implements" reliability.

Reliability and Security as Emergent Properties of System Design

Reliability is primarily an *emergent property* of the design of your system, and indeed the design of your entire development, deployment, and operations workflow. Reliability emerges from factors such as these:

- How your overall service is broken into components, such as microservices

- How your service's availability relates to the availability/reliability of its dependencies, including service backends, storage, and the underlying platform

- What mechanisms components use to communicate (such as RPCs, message queues, or event buses), how requests are routed, and how load balancing and load shedding are implemented and configured

- How unit testing, end-to-end functional testing, production readiness reviews (PRRs) (*https://oreil.ly/P0JdF*), load testing, and similar validation activities are integrated in your development and deployment workflow

- How the system is monitored (*https://oreil.ly/F_iBb*), and whether available monitoring, metrics, and logs provide the information necessary to detect and respond to anomalies and failures

Similarly, the overall security posture of your service does not arise from a single "security module." Rather, it is an emergent property of many aspects of the way your system and operational environment are designed, including but not limited to these:

- How the larger system is decomposed into subcomponents, and the trust relationships between those components

- The implementation languages, platforms, and application/service frameworks on which the application is developed

- How security design and implementation reviews, security testing, and similar validation activities are integrated into your software development and deployment workflow

- The forms of security monitoring, audit logging, anomaly detection, and other tools that are available to your security analysts and incident responders

Finding the right balance among these many design objectives is difficult. Sound decisions often require a lot of experience, and even well-reasoned design decisions can turn out to be incorrect in hindsight. Chapter 7 discusses how to prepare for the inevitable need to revise and adapt.

Example: Google Design Document

Google uses a design document template to guide new feature design and to collect feedback from stakeholders before starting an engineering project.

The template sections pertaining to reliability and security considerations remind teams to think about the implications of their project and kick off the production readiness or security review processes if appropriate. Design reviews sometimes happen multiple quarters before engineers officially start thinking about the launch stage.

Google's Design Document Template

Here are the reliability- and security-related sections of the Google design document template:

Scalability
How does your system scale? Consider both data size increase (if applicable) and traffic increase (if applicable).

Consider the current hardware situation: adding more resources might take much longer than you think, or might be too expensive for your project. What initial resources will you need? You should plan for high utilization, but be aware that using more resources than you need will block expansion of your service.

Redundancy and reliability
Discuss how the system will handle local data loss and transient errors (e.g., temporary outages), and how each affects your system.

Which systems or components require data backup? How is the data backed up? How is it restored? What happens between the time data is lost and the time it's restored?

In the case of a partial loss, can you keep serving? Can you restore only missing portions of your backups to your serving data store?

Dependency considerations

What happens if your dependencies on other services are unavailable for a period of time?

Which services must be running in order for your application to start? Don't forget subtle dependencies like resolving names using DNS or checking the local time.

Are you introducing any dependency cycles, such as blocking on a system that can't run if your application isn't already up? If you have doubts, discuss your use case with the team that owns the system you depend on.

Data integrity

How will you find out about data corruption or loss in your data stores?

What sources of data loss are detected (user error, application bugs, storage platform bugs, site/replica disasters)?

How long will it take to notice each of these types of losses?

What is your plan to recover from each of these types of losses?

SLA requirements

What mechanisms are in place for auditing and monitoring the service level guarantees of your application?

How can you guarantee the stated level of reliability?

Security and privacy considerations

Our systems get attacked regularly. Think about potential attacks relevant for this design and describe the worst-case impact it would have, along with the countermeasures you have in place to prevent or mitigate each attack.

List any known vulnerabilities or potentially insecure dependencies.

If, for some reason, your application doesn't have security or privacy considerations, explicitly state so and why.

Once your design document is finalized, file a quick security design review. The design review will help avoid systemic security issues that can delay or block your final security review.

Balancing Requirements

Because the attributes of a system that satisfy security and reliability concerns are largely emergent properties, they tend to interact both with implementations of feature requirements and with each other. As a result, it's particularly difficult to reason about tradeoffs involving security and reliability as a standalone topic.

Cost of Adding Reliability and Security to Existing Systems

The emergent nature of security and reliability means that design choices related to these considerations are often fairly fundamental, and similar in nature to basic architectural choices like whether to use a relational or NoSQL database for storage, or whether to use a monolithic or microservices architecture. It's usually difficult to "bolt on" security and reliability to an existing system that wasn't designed from the outset with these concerns in mind. If a system lacks well-defined and understandable interfaces between components and contains a tangled set of dependencies, it likely will have lower availability and be prone to bugs with security consequences (see Chapter 6). No amount of testing and tactical bug-fixing will change that.

Accommodating security and reliability requirements in an existing system often requires significant design changes, major refactorings, or even partial rewrites, and can become very expensive and time-consuming. Furthermore, such changes might have to be made under time pressure in response to a security or reliability incident— but making significant design changes to a deployed system in a hurry comes with a significant risk of introducing additional flaws. It's therefore important to consider security and reliability requirements and corresponding design tradeoffs from the early planning phases of a software project. These discussions should involve security and SRE teams, if your organization has them.

This section presents an example that illustrates the kinds of tradeoffs you might have to consider. Some parts of this example delve quite deeply into technical details, which aren't necessarily important in and of themselves. All of the compliance, regulatory, legal, and business considerations that go into designing payment processing systems and their operation aren't important for this example either. Instead, the purpose is to illustrate the complex interdependencies between requirements. In other words, the focus isn't on the nitty-gritty details about protecting credit card numbers, but rather the thought process that goes into designing a system with complex security and reliability requirements.

Example: Payment Processing

Imagine that you're building an online service that sells widgets to consumers.[2] The service's specification includes a user story stipulating that a user can pick widgets from an online catalog by using a mobile or web application. The user can then purchase the chosen widgets, which requires that they provide details for a payment method.

Security and reliability considerations

Accepting payment information introduces significant security and reliability considerations for the system's design and organizational processes. Names, addresses, and credit card numbers are sensitive personal data that require special safeguards[3] and can subject your system to regulatory standards, depending on the applicable jurisdiction. Accepting payment information may also bring the service in scope for compliance with industry-level or regulatory security standards such as PCI DSS (*https://www.pcisecuritystandards.org*).

A compromise of this sensitive user information, especially personally identifiable information (PII), can have serious consequences for the project and even the entire organization/company. You might lose the trust of your users and customers, and lose their business as a result. In recent years, legislatures have enacted laws and regulations placing potentially time-consuming and expensive obligations on companies affected by data breaches. Some companies have even gone entirely out of business because of a severe security incident, as noted in Chapter 1.

In certain scenarios, a higher-level tradeoff at the product design level might free the application from processing payments—for example, perhaps the product can be recast in an advertising-based or community-funded model. For the purposes of our example, we'll stick with the premise that accepting payments is a critical requirement.

---

2 For the purposes of the example, it's not relevant what exactly is being sold—a media outlet might require payments for articles, a mobility company might require payments for transportation, an online marketplace might enable the purchase of physical goods that are shipped to consumers, or a food-ordering service might facilitate the delivery of takeout orders from local restaurants.

3 See, for example, McCallister, Erika, Tim Grance, and Karen Scarfone. 2010. NIST Special Publication 800-122, "Guide to Protecting the Confidentiality of Personally Identifiable Information (PII)." *https://oreil.ly/T9G4D*.

Using a third-party service provider to handle sensitive data

Often, the best way to mitigate security concerns about sensitive data is to not hold that data in the first place (for more on this topic, see Chapter 5). You may be able to arrange for sensitive data to never pass through your systems, or at least design the systems to not persistently store the data.[4] You can choose from various commercial payment service APIs to integrate with the application, and offload handling of payment information, payment transactions, and related concerns (such as fraud countermeasures) to the vendor.

Benefits. Depending on the circumstances, using a payment service may reduce risk and the degree to which you need to build in-house expertise to address risks in this area, instead relying on the provider's expertise:

- Your systems no longer hold the sensitive data, reducing the risk that a vulnerability in your systems or processes could result in a data compromise. Of course, a compromise of the third-party vendor could still compromise your users' data.

- Depending on the specific circumstances and applicable requirements, your contractual and compliance obligations under payment industry security standards may be simplified.

- You don't have to build and maintain infrastructure to protect the data at rest in your system's data stores. This could eliminate a significant amount of development and ongoing operational effort.

- Many third-party payment providers offer countermeasures against fraudulent transactions and payment risk assessment services. You may be able to use these features to reduce your payment fraud risk, without having to build and maintain the underlying infrastructure yourself.

On the flip side, relying on a third-party service provider introduces costs and risks of its own.

Costs and nontechnical risks. Obviously, the provider will charge fees. Transaction volume will likely inform your choice here—beyond a certain volume, it's probably more cost-effective to process transactions in-house.

You also need to consider the engineering cost of relying on a third-party dependency: your team will have to learn how to use the vendor's API, and you might have to track changes/releases of the API on the vendor's schedule.

---

4 Note that whether or not this is appropriate may depend on regulatory frameworks your organization is subject to; these regulatory matters are outside the scope of this book.

Reliability risks. By outsourcing payment processing, you add an additional dependency to your application—in this case, a third-party service. Additional dependencies often introduce additional failure modes. In the case of third-party dependencies, these failure modes may be partially out of your control. For example, your user story "user can buy their chosen widgets" may fail if the payment provider's service is down or unreachable via the network. The significance of this risk depends on the payment provider's adherence to the SLAs (*https://oreil.ly/KZ03g*) that you have with that provider.

You might address this risk by introducing redundancy into the system (see Chapter 8)—in this case, by adding an alternate payment provider to which your service can fail over. This redundancy introduces cost and complexity—the two payment providers most likely have different APIs, so you must design your system to be able to talk to both, along with all the additional engineering and operational costs, plus increased exposure to bugs or security compromises.

You could also mitigate the reliability risk through fallback mechanisms on your side. For example, you might insert a queueing mechanism into the communication channel with the payment provider to buffer transaction data if the payment service is unreachable. Doing so would allow the "purchase flow" user story to proceed during a payment service outage.

However, adding the message queueing mechanism introduces extra complexity and may introduce its own failure modes. If the message queue is not designed to be reliable (for example, it stores data in volatile memory only), you can lose transactions—a new risk surface. More generally, subsystems that are exercised only in rare and exceptional circumstances can harbor hidden bugs and reliability issues.

You could choose to use a more reliable message queue implementation. This likely involves either an in-memory storage system that is distributed across multiple physical locations, again introducing complexity, or storage on persistent disk. Storing the data on disk, even if only in exceptional scenarios, reintroduces the concerns about storing sensitive data (risk of compromise, compliance considerations, etc.) that you were trying to avoid in the first place. In particular, some payment data is never even allowed to hit disk, which makes a retry queue that relies on persistent storage difficult to apply in this scenario.

In this light, you may have to consider attacks (in particular, attacks by insiders) that purposely break the link with the payment provider in order to activate local queueing of transaction data, which may then be compromised.

In summary, you end up encountering a security risk that arose from your attempt to mitigate a reliability risk, which in turn arose because you were trying to mitigate a security risk!

Security risks. The design choice to rely on a third-party service also raises immediate security considerations.

First, you're entrusting sensitive customer data to a third-party vendor. You'll want to choose a vendor whose security stance is at least equal to your own, and will have to carefully evaluate vendors during selection and on an ongoing basis. This is not an easy task, and there are complex contractual, regulatory, and liability considerations that are outside the scope of this book and which should be referred to your counsel.

Second, integrating with the vendor's service may require you to link a vendor-supplied library into your application. This introduces the risk that a vulnerability in that library, or one of its transitive dependencies, may result in a vulnerability in *your* systems. You may consider mitigating this risk by sandboxing the library[5] and by being prepared to quickly deploy updated versions of it (see Chapter 7). You can largely avoid this concern by using a vendor that does not require you to link a pro-prietary library into your service (see Chapter 6). Proprietary libraries can be avoided if the vendor exposes its API using an open protocol like REST+JSON, XML, SOAP, or gRPC.

You may need to include a JavaScript library in your web application client in order to integrate with the vendor. Doing so allows you to avoid passing payment data through your systems, even temporarily—instead, payment data can be sent from a user's browser directly to the provider's web service. However, this integration raises similar concerns as including a server-side library: the vendor's library code runs with full privileges in the web origin of your application.[6] A vulnerability in that code or a compromise of the server that's serving that library can lead to your application being compromised. You might consider mitigating that risk by sandboxing payment-related functionality in a separate web origin or sandboxed iframe. How-ever, this tactic means that you need a secure cross-origin communications mecha-nism, again introducing complexity and additional failure modes. Alternatively, the payment vendor might offer an integration based on HTTP redirects, but this can result in a less smooth user experience.

Design choices related to nonfunctional requirements can have fairly far-reaching implications in areas of domain-specific technical expertise: we started out discussing a tradeoff related to mitigating risks associated with handling payment data, and ended up thinking about considerations that are deep in the realm of web platform security. Along the way, we also encountered contractual and regulatory concerns.

---

5 See, e.g., the Sandboxed API (*https://oreil.ly/fx86y*) project.

6 For more on this subject, see Zalewski, Michał. 2011. *The Tangled Web: A Guide to Securing Modern Web Applications.* San Francisco, CA: No Starch Press.

Managing Tensions and Aligning Goals

With some up-front planning, you can often satisfy important nonfunctional requirements like security and reliability without having to give up features, and at reasonable cost. When stepping back to consider security and reliability in the context of the entire system and development and operations workflow, it often becomes apparent that these goals are very much aligned with general software quality attributes.

Example: Microservices and the Google Web Application Framework

Consider the evolution of a Google-internal framework for microservices and web applications. The primary goal of the team creating the framework was to streamline the development and operation of applications and services for large organizations. In designing this framework, the team incorporated the key idea of applying static and dynamic *conformance checks* to ensure that application code adheres to various coding guidelines and best practices. For example, a conformance check verifies that all values passed between concurrent execution contexts are of immutable types—a practice that drastically reduces the likelihood of concurrency bugs. Another set of conformance checks enforces isolation constraints between components, which makes it much less likely that a change in one component/module of the application results in a bug in another component.

Because applications built on this framework have a fairly rigid and well-defined structure, the framework can provide out-of-the-box automation for many common development and deployment tasks—from scaffolding for new components, to automated setup of continuous integration (CI) environments, to largely automated production deployments. These benefits have made this framework quite popular among Google developers.

What does all this have to do with security and reliability? The framework development team collaborated with SRE and security teams throughout the design and implementation phases, ensuring that security and reliability best practices were woven into the fabric of the framework—not just bolted on at the end. The framework takes responsibility for handling many common security and reliability concerns. Similarly, it automatically sets up monitoring for operational metrics and incorporates reliability features like health checking and SLA compliance.

For example, the framework's web application support handles most common types of web application vulnerabilities.[7] Through a combination of API design and code conformance checks, it effectively prevents developers from accidentally introducing

---

7 See, e.g., the OWASP Top 10 (*https://oreil.ly/O0kva*) and CWE/SANS TOP 25 Most Dangerous Software Errors (*https://oreil.ly/Fm6IJ*).

many common types of vulnerabilities in application code.[8] With respect to these types of vulnerabilities, the framework goes beyond "security by default"—rather, it takes full responsibility for security, and actively ensures that any application based on it is not affected by these risks. We discuss how this is accomplished in more detail in Chapters 6 and 12.

Reliability and Security Benefits of Software Development Frameworks

A robust and commonly used framework with built-in reliability and security features is a win-win scenario: developers adopt the framework because it simplifies application development and automates common chores, making their daily work easier and more productive. The framework provides a common feature surface where security engineers and SREs can build new functionality, creating opportunities for improved automation and accelerating overall project velocity.

At the same time, building on this framework results in inherently more secure and reliable systems, because the framework automatically takes care of common security and reliability concerns. It also makes security and production readiness reviews much more efficient: if a software project's continuous builds and tests are green (indicating that its code complies with framework-level conformance checks), you can be quite confident that it's not affected by the common security concerns already addressed by the framework. Similarly, by stopping releases when the error budget (*https://oreil.ly/t0fnj*) is consumed, the framework's deployment automation ensures that the service adheres to its SLA; see Chapter 16 in the SRE workbook. Security engineers and SREs can use their time to focus on more interesting design-level concerns. Finally, bug fixes and improvements in code that is part of a centrally maintained framework are automatically propagated to applications whenever they are rebuilt (with up-to-date dependencies) and deployed.[9]

Aligning Emergent-Property Requirements

The framework example illustrates that, contrary to common perception, security- and reliability-related goals are often well aligned with other product goals—especially code and project health and maintainability and long-term, sustained project

---

8 See Kern, Christoph. 2014. "Securing the Tangled Web." *Communications of the ACM* 57(9): 38–47. doi: 10.1145/2643134.

9 At Google, software is typically built from the HEAD of a common repository, which causes all dependencies to be updated automatically with every build. See Potvin, Rachel, and Josh Levenberg. 2016. "Why Google Stores Billions of Lines of Code in a Single Repository." *Communications of the ACM* 59(7): 78–87. *https://oreil.ly/jXTZM.*

velocity. In contrast, attempting to retrofit security and reliability goals as a late add-on often leads to increased risks and costs.

Priorities for security and reliability can also align with priorities in other areas:

- As discussed in Chapter 6, system design that enables people to effectively and accurately reason about invariants and behaviors of the system is crucial for security and reliability. Understandability is also a key code and project health attribute, and a key support for development velocity: an understandable system is easier to debug and to modify (without introducing bugs in the first place).

- Designing for recovery (see Chapter 9) allows us to quantify and control the risk introduced by changes and rollouts. Typically, the design principles discussed here support a higher rate of change (i.e., deployment velocity) than we could achieve otherwise.

- Security and reliability demand that we design for a changing landscape (see Chapter 7). Doing so makes our system design more adaptable and positions us not only to swiftly address newly emerging vulnerabilities and attack scenarios, but also to accommodate changing business requirements more quickly.

Initial Velocity Versus Sustained Velocity

There's a natural tendency, especially in smaller teams, to defer security and reliability concerns until some point in the future ("We'll add in security and worry about scaling after we have some customers"). Teams commonly justify ignoring security and reliability as early and primary design drivers for the sake of "velocity"—they're concerned that spending time thinking about and addressing these concerns will slow development and introduce unacceptable delays into their first release cycle.

It's important to make a distinction between *initial velocity* and *sustained velocity*. Choosing to not account for critical requirements like security, reliability, and maintainability early in the project cycle may indeed increase your project's velocity early in the project's lifetime. However, experience shows that doing so also usually *slows you down significantly* later.[10] The late-stage cost of retrofitting a design to accommodate requirements that manifest as emergent properties can be *very* substantial. Furthermore, making invasive late-stage changes to address security and reliability risks can in itself introduce even more security and reliability risks. Therefore, it's important to embed security and reliability in your team culture early on (for more on this topic, see Chapter 21).

---

10 See the discussion of tactical programming versus strategic programming in Ousterhout, John. 2018. *A Philosophy of Software Design*. Palo Alto, CA: Yaknyam Press. Martin Fowler (*https://oreil.ly/Lc2eY*) makes similar observations.

The early history of the internet,[11] and the design and evolution of the underlying protocols such as IP, TCP, DNS, and BGP, offers an interesting perspective on this topic. Reliability—in particular, survivability of the network even in the face of outages of nodes[12] and reliability of communications despite failure-prone links[13]—were explicit and high-priority design goals of the early precursors of today's internet, such as ARPANET.

Security, however, is not mentioned much in early internet papers and documentation. Early networks were essentially closed, with nodes operated by trusted research and government institutions. But in today's open internet, this assumption does not hold at all—many types of malicious actors are participating in the network (see Chapter 2).

The internet's foundational protocols—IP, UDP, and TCP—have no provision to authenticate the originator of transmissions, nor to detect intentional, malicious modification of data by an intermediate node in the network. Many higher-level protocols, such as HTTP or DNS, are inherently vulnerable to various attacks by malicious participants in the network. Over time, secure protocols or protocol extensions have been developed to defend against such attacks. For example, HTTPS augments HTTP by transferring data over an authenticated, secure channel. At the IP layer, IPsec (https://oreil.ly/Bie7A) cryptographically authenticates network-level peers and provides data integrity and confidentiality. IPsec can be used to establish VPNs over untrusted IP networks.

However, widely deploying these secure protocols has proven to be rather difficult. We're now approximately 50 years into the internet's history, and significant commercial usage of the internet began perhaps 25 or 30 years ago—yet there is still a substantial fraction of web traffic that does not use HTTPS.[14]

For another example of the tradeoff between initial and sustained velocity (in this case from outside the security and reliability realm), consider Agile development processes (https://oreil.ly/upg-w). A primary goal of Agile development workflows is to increase development and deployment velocity—in particular, to reduce the latency between feature specification and deployment. However, Agile workflows typically

---

11 See RFC 2235 (https://oreil.ly/UIlV6) and Leiner, Barry M. et al. 2009. "A Brief History of the Internet." *ACM SIGCOMM Computer Communication Review* 39(5): 22–31. doi:10.1145/1629607.1629613.

12 Baran, Paul. 1964. "On Distributed Communications Networks." *IEEE Transactions on Communications Systems* 12(1): 1–9. doi:10.1109/TCOM.1964.1088883.

13 Roberts, Lawrence G., and Barry D. Wessler. 1970. "Computer Network Development to Achieve Resource Sharing." *Proceedings of the 1970 Spring Joint Computing Conference*: 543–549. doi:10.1145/1476936.1477020.

14 Felt, Adrienne Porter, Richard Barnes, April King, Chris Palmer, Chris Bentzel, and Parisa Tabriz. 2017. "Measuring HTTPS Adoption on the Web." *Proceedings of the 26th USENIX Conference on Security Symposium*: 1323–1338. https://oreil.ly/G1A9q.

rely on reasonably mature unit and integration testing practices and a solid continuous integration infrastructure, which require an up-front investment to establish, in exchange for long-term benefits to velocity and stability.

More generally, you can choose to prioritize initial project velocity above all else—you can develop the first iteration of your web app without tests, and with a release process that amounts to copying tarballs to production hosts. You'll probably get your first demo out relatively quickly, but by your third release, your project will quite possibly be behind schedule and saddled with technical debt.

We've already touched on alignment between reliability and velocity: investing in a mature continuous integration/continuous deployment (CI/CD) workflow and infrastructure supports frequent production releases with a managed and acceptable reliability risk (see Chapter 7). But setting up such a workflow requires some up-front investment—for example, you will need the following:

- Unit and integration test coverage robust enough to ensure an acceptably low risk of defects for production releases, without requiring major human release qualification work
- A CI/CD pipeline that is itself reliable
- A frequently exercised, reliable infrastructure for staggered production rollouts and rollbacks
- A software architecture that permits decoupled rollouts (*https://oreil.ly/8E04K*) of code and configurations (e.g., "feature flags")

This investment is typically modest when made early in a product's lifecycle, and it requires only incremental effort by developers to maintain good test coverage and "green builds" on an ongoing basis. In contrast, a development workflow with poor test automation, reliance on manual steps in deployment, and long release cycles tends to eventually bog down a project as it grows in complexity. At that point, retrofitting test and release automation tends to require a lot of work all at once and might slow down your project even more. Furthermore, tests retrofitted to a mature system can sometimes fall into the trap of exercising the current buggy behavior more than the correct, intended behavior.

These investments are beneficial for projects of all sizes. However, larger organizations can enjoy even more benefits of scale, as you can amortize the cost across many projects—an individual project's investment then boils down to a commitment to use centrally maintained frameworks and workflows.

When it comes to making security-focused design choices that contribute to sustained velocity, we recommend choosing a framework and workflow that provide secure-by-construction defense against relevant classes of vulnerabilities. This choice can drastically reduce, or even eliminate, the risk of introducing such vulnerabilities during ongoing development and maintenance of your application's codebase (see Chapters 6 and 12). This commitment generally doesn't involve significant up-front investment—rather, it entails an incremental and typically modest ongoing effort to adhere to the framework's constraints. In return, you drastically reduce your risk of unplanned system outages or security response fire drills throwing deployment schedules into disarray. Additionally, your release-time security and production readiness reviews are much more likely to go smoothly.

Conclusion

It's not easy to design and build secure and reliable systems, especially since security and reliability are primarily emergent properties of the entire development and operations workflow. This undertaking involves thinking about a lot of rather complex topics, many of which at first don't seem all that related to addressing the primary feature requirements of your service.

Your design process will involve numerous tradeoffs between security, reliability, and feature requirements. In many cases, these tradeoffs will at first appear to be in direct conflict. It might seem tempting to avoid these issues in the early stages of a project and "deal with them later"—but doing so often comes at significant cost and risk to your project: once your service is live, reliability and security are not optional. If your service is down, you may lose business; and if your service is compromised, responding will require all hands on deck. But with good planning and careful design, it is often possible to satisfy all three of these aspects. What's more, you can do so with modest additional up-front cost, and often with a reduced total engineering effort over the lifetime of the system.

CHAPTER 5

Design for Least Privilege

By Oliver Barrett, Aaron Joyner, and Rory Ward
with Guy Fischman and Betsy Beyer

The *principle of least privilege* says that users should have the minimum amount of access needed to accomplish a task, regardless of whether the access is from humans or systems. These restrictions are most effective when you add them at the beginning of the development lifecycle, during the design phase of new features. Unnecessary privilege leads to a growing surface area for possible mistakes, bugs, or compromise, and creates security and reliability risks that are expensive to contain or minimize in a running system.

In this chapter, we discuss how to classify access based on risk and examine best practices that enforce least privilege. A configuration distribution example demonstrates the tradeoffs these practices entail in real-world environments. After detailing a policy framework for authentication and authorization, we take a deep dive into advanced authorization controls that can mitigate both the risk of compromised accounts and the risk of mistakes made by on-call engineers. We conclude by acknowledging tradeoffs and tensions that might arise when designing for least privilege. In an ideal world, the people using a system are well-intentioned and execute their work tasks in a perfectly secure way, without error. Unfortunately, reality is quite different. Engineers may make mistakes, their accounts may be compromised, or they may be malicious. For these reasons, it's important to design systems for *least privilege*: systems should limit user access to the data and services required to do the task at hand.

Companies often want to assume their engineers have the best intentions, and rely on them to flawlessly execute Herculean tasks. This isn't a reasonable expectation. As a thought exercise, think about the damage you could inflict to your organization if you *wanted* to do something evil. What could you do? How would you do it? Would you be detected? Could you cover your tracks? Or, even if your intentions were good, what's the worst mistake you (or someone with equivalent access) could make? When debugging, responding to an outage, or performing emergency response, how many ad hoc, manual commands used by you or your coworkers are one typo or copy-paste fail away from causing or worsening an outage?

Because we can't rely on human perfection, we must assume that any possible bad action or outcome can happen. Therefore, we recommend designing the system to minimize or eliminate the impact of these bad actions.

Even if we generally trust the humans accessing our systems, we need to limit their privilege and the trust we place in their credentials. Things can and will go wrong. People will make mistakes, fat-finger commands, get compromised, and fall for phishing emails. Expecting perfection is an unrealistic assumption. In other words—to quote an SRE maxim—hope is not a strategy.

Concepts and Terminology

Before we dive into best practices for designing and operating an access control system, let's establish working definitions for some particular terms of art used in the industry and at Google.

Least Privilege

Least privilege is a broad concept that's well established in the security industry. The high-level best practices in this chapter can lay the foundations of a system that grants the least privilege necessary for any given task or action path. This goal applies to the humans, automated tasks, and individual machines that a distributed system comprises. The objective of least privilege should extend through all authentication and authorization layers of the system. In particular, our recommended approach rejects extending implicit authority to tooling (as illustrated in "Worked Example: Configuration Distribution" on page 74) and works to ensure that users don't have ambient authority (*https://oreil.ly/fF_EA*)—for example, the ability to log in as root—as much as practically possible.

Zero Trust Networking

The design principles we discuss begin with *zero trust networking*—the notion that a user's network location (being within the company's network) doesn't grant any privileged access. For example, plugging into a network port in a conference room does not grant more access than connecting from elsewhere on the internet. Instead, a system grants access based on a combination of user credentials and device credentials—what we know about the user and what we know about the device. Google has successfully implemented a large-scale zero trust networking model via its BeyondCorp program (*https://oreil.ly/8x9OJ*).

Zero Touch

The SRE organization at Google is working to build upon the concept of least privilege through automation, with the goal of moving to what we call *Zero Touch* interfaces. The specific goal of these interfaces—like Zero Touch Production (ZTP), described in Chapter 3, and Zero Touch Networking (ZTN)—is to make Google safer and reduce outages by removing direct human access to production roles. Instead, humans have indirect access to production through tooling and automation that make predictable and controlled changes to production infrastructure. This approach requires extensive automation, new safe APIs, and resilient multi-party approval systems.

Classifying Access Based on Risk

Any risk reduction strategy comes with tradeoffs. Reducing the risk introduced by human actors likely entails additional controls or engineering work, and can introduce tradeoffs to productivity; it may increase engineering time, process changes, operational work, or opportunity cost. You can help limit these costs by clearly scoping and prioritizing what you want to protect.

Not all data or actions are created equal, and the makeup of your access may differ dramatically depending on the nature of your system. Therefore, you shouldn't protect all access to the same degree. In order to apply the most appropriate controls and avoid an all-or-nothing mentality, you need to classify access based on impact, security risk, and/or criticality. For example, you likely need to handle access to different types of data (publicly available data versus company data versus user data versus cryptographic secrets) differently. Similarly, you likely need to treat administrative APIs that can delete data differently than service-specific read APIs.

Your classifications should be clearly defined, consistently applied, and broadly understood so people can design systems and services that "speak" that language. Your classification framework will vary based on the size and complexity of your system: you may need only two or three types that rely on ad hoc labeling, or you may need a robust and programmatic system for classifying parts of your system (API groupings, data types) in a central inventory. These classifications may apply to data stores, APIs, services, or other entities that users may access in the course of their work. Ensure that your framework can handle the most important entities within your systems.

Once you've established a foundation of classification, you should consider the controls in place for each. You need to consider several dimensions:

- Who should have access?
- How tightly should that access be controlled?
- What type of access does the user need (read/write)?
- What infrastructure controls are in place?

For example, as shown in Table 5-1, a company may need three classifications: *public*, *sensitive*, and *highly sensitive*. That company might categorize security controls as *low risk*, *medium risk*, or *high risk* by the level of damage the access can allow if granted inappropriately.

Table 5-1. Example access classifications based on risk

	Description	Read access	Write access	Infrastructure access[a]
Public	Open to anyone in the company	Low risk	Low risk	High risk
Sensitive	Limited to groups with business purpose	Medium/high risk	Medium risk	High risk
Highly sensitive	No permanent access	High risk	High risk	High risk

[a] Administrative ability to bypass normal access controls. For example, the ability to reduce logging levels, change encryption requirements, gain direct SSH access to a machine, restart and reconfigure service options, or otherwise affect the availability of the service(s).

Intersection of Reliability and Security: Permissions

From a reliability perspective, you might start with infrastructure controls, as you want to make sure unauthorized actors can't shut down jobs, change ACLs, and misconfigure services. However, keep in mind that from a security perspective, reading sensitive data can often be just as damaging: overly broad read permissions can lead to a mass data breach.

Your goal should be to construct an access framework from which you can apply appropriate controls with the right balance of productivity, security, and reliability. Least privilege should apply across all data access and actions. Working from this foundational framework, let's discuss how to design your systems with the principles and controls for least privilege.

Best Practices

When implementing a least privilege model, we recommend several best practices, detailed here.

Small Functional APIs

> Make each program do one thing well. To do a new job, build afresh rather than complicate old programs by adding new "features."
>
> —McIlroy, Pinson, and Tague (1978)[1]

As this quote conveys, Unix culture centers around small and simple tools that can be combined. Because modern distributed computing evolved from the single time-shared computing systems of the 1970s into planet-wide network-connected distributed systems, the authors' advice still rings true more than 40 years later. To adapt this quote to the current computing environment, one might say, "Make each API endpoint do one thing well." When building systems with an eye toward security and reliability, avoid open-ended interactive interfaces—instead, design around small functional APIs. This approach allows you to apply the classic security principle of least privilege and grant the minimum permissions necessary to perform a particular function.

What exactly do we mean by *API*? Every system has an API: it is simply the user interface the system presents. Some APIs are very large (such as the POSIX API[2] or the Windows API[3]), some are relatively small (such as memcached[4] and NATS[5]), and some are downright tiny (such as the World Clock API (*http://worldclockapi.com*), TinyURL,[6] and the Google Fonts API[7]). When we talk about the API of a distributed system, we simply mean the sum of all the ways you can query or modify its internal

---

1 McIlroy, M.D., E.N. Pinson, and B.A. Tague. 1978. "UNIX Time-Sharing System: Foreword." *The Bell System Technical Journal* 57(6): 1899–1904. doi:10.1002/j.1538-7305.1978.tb02135.x.

2 POSIX stands for Portable Operating System Interface, the IEEE standardized interface provided by most Unix variants. For a general overview, see Wikipedia (*https://oreil.ly/4vLTI*).

3 The Windows API includes the familiar graphical elements, as well as the programming interfaces like DirectX (*https://oreil.ly/TnmPu*), COM (*https://oreil.ly/PzTUF*), etc.

4 Memcached (*https://memcached.org*) is a high-performance, distributed memory object caching system.

5 NATS (*https://oreil.ly/baCc4*) is an example of a basic API built on top of a text protocol, as opposed to a complex RPC interface like gRPC.

6 The TinyURL.com API isn't well documented, but it is essentially a single GET URL that returns the shortened URL as the body of the response. This is a rare example of a mutable service with a tiny API.

7 The Fonts API (*https://oreil.ly/-Z4F4*) simply lists the fonts currently available. It has exactly one endpoint.

state. API design has been well covered in computing literature;[8] this chapter focuses on how you can design and safely maintain secure systems by exposing API endpoints with few well-defined primitives. For example, the input you evaluate might be CRUD (Create, Read, Update, and Delete) operations on a unique ID, rather than an API that accepts a programming language.

In addition to the user-facing API, pay careful attention to the administrative API. The administrative API is equally important (arguably, more important) to the reliability and security of your application. Typos and mistakes when using these APIs can result in catastrophic outages or expose huge amounts of data. As a result, administrative APIs are also some of the most attractive attack surfaces for malicious actors.

Administrative APIs are accessed only by internal users and tooling, so relative to user-facing APIs, they can be faster and easier to change. Still, after your internal users and tooling start building on any API, there will still be a cost to changing it, so we recommend carefully considering their design. Administrative APIs include the following:

- Setup/teardown APIs, such as those used to build, install, and update software or provision the container(s) it runs in

- Maintenance and emergency APIs, such as administrative access to delete corrupted user data or state, or to restart misbehaving processes

Does the size of an API matter when it comes to access and security? Consider a familiar example: the POSIX API, one of our previous examples of a very large API. This API is popular because it is flexible and familiar to many people. As a production machine management API, it is most often used for relatively well-defined tasks such as installing a software package, changing a configuration file, or restarting a daemon.

Users often perform traditional Unix[9] host setup and maintenance via an interactive OpenSSH session or with tools that script against the POSIX API. Both approaches expose the entire POSIX API to the caller. It can be difficult to constrain and audit a user's actions during that interactive session. This is especially true if the user is

---

8 A good starting point is Gamma, Erich et al. 1994. *Design Patterns: Elements of Reusable Object-Oriented Software.* Boston, MA: Addison-Wesley. See also Bloch, Joshua. 2006. "How to Design a Good API and Why It Matters." *Companion to the 21st ACM SIGPLAN Symposium on Object-Oriented Programming Systems, Languages, and Applications:* 506–507. doi:10.1145/1176617.1176622.

9 Although we use Unix hosts as an example, this pattern is not unique to Unix. Traditional Windows host setup and management follows a similar model, where the interactive exposure of the Windows API is typically via RDP instead of OpenSSH.

maliciously attempting to circumvent the controls, or if the connecting workstation is compromised.

Can't I Just Audit the Interactive Session?

Many simple approaches to auditing, such as capturing the commands executed by bash or wrapping an interactive session in script(1), may seem sufficient and quite comprehensive. However, these basic logging options for interactive sessions are similar to locks on the doors of a house: they only keep the honest people honest. Unfortunately, an attacker who is aware of their existence can easily bypass most of these types of basic session auditing.

As a simple example, an attacker might bypass bash command history logging by opening an editor like vim and executing commands from within the interactive session (e.g., :!/bin/evilcmd). This simple attack also complicates your ability to inspect the typescript log output by script(1), because the output will be muddied by the visual control characters that vim and ncurses use to display the visual editing environment. Stronger mechanisms, like capturing some or all syscalls to the kernel's audit framework, are available, but it's worth understanding the shortcomings of naive approaches, and the difficulty in implementing stronger approaches.

You can use various mechanisms to limit the permissions granted to the user via the POSIX API,[10] but that necessity is a fundamental shortcoming of exposing a very large API. Instead, it's better to reduce and decompose this large administrative API into smaller pieces. You can then follow the principle of least privilege to grant permission only to the specific action(s) required by any particular caller.

> The exposed POSIX API should not be confused with the OpenSSH API. It is possible to leverage the OpenSSH protocol and its authentication, authorization, and auditing (AAA) controls without exposing the entire POSIX API; for example, using git-shell (*https://oreil.ly/gN12-*).

Breakglass

Named after fire alarm pulls that instruct the user to "break glass in case of emergency," a *breakglass mechanism* provides access to your system in an emergency situation and bypasses your authorization system completely. This can be useful for

---

10 Popular options include running as an unprivileged user and then encoding allowed commands via sudo, granting only the necessary capabilities(7) (*https://oreil.ly/7Zf70*), or using a framework like SELinux.

recovering from unforeseen circumstances. For more context, see "Graceful Failure and Breakglass Mechanisms" on page 74 and "Diagnosing Access Denials" on page 73.

Auditing

Auditing primarily serves to detect incorrect authorization usage. This can include a malicious system operator abusing their powers, a compromise of a user's credentials by an external actor, or rogue software taking unexpected actions against another system. Your ability to audit and meaningfully detect the signal in the noise is largely dependent on the design of the systems you're auditing:

- How granular is the access control decision being made or bypassed? (*What? Where?*)
- How clearly can you capture the metadata associated with the request? (*Who? When? Why?*)

The following tips will help in crafting a sound auditing strategy. Ultimately, your success will also depend on the culture associated with auditing.

Collecting good audit logs

Using small functioning APIs (as discussed in "Small Functional APIs" on page 65) provides the largest single advantage to your auditing ability. The most useful audit logs capture a granular series of actions, such as "pushed a config with cryptographic hash 123DEAD...BEEF456" or "executed <x> command." Thinking about how to display and justify your administrative actions to your customers can also help make your audit logs more descriptive, and thus more useful internally. Granular audit log information enables strong assertions about what actions the user did or did not take, but be sure to focus on capturing the *useful* parts of the actions.

Exceptional circumstances require exceptional access, which requires a strong culture of auditing. If you discover that the existing small functional API surfaces are insufficient to recover the system, you have two options:

- Provide breakglass functionality that allows a user to open an interactive session to the powerful and flexible API.
- Allow the user to have direct access to credentials in a way that precludes reasonable auditing of their usage.

In either of these scenarios, you may be unable to build a granular audit trail. Logging that the user opened an interactive session to a large API does not meaningfully tell you what they did. A motivated and knowledgeable insider can trivially bypass many solutions that capture session logs of interactive sessions, such as recording bash command history. Even if you can capture a full session transcript, effectively auditing it may be quite difficult: visual applications using ncurses need to be replayed to be human-readable, and features such as SSH multiplexing can further complicate capturing and understanding the interleaved state.

The antidote to overly broad APIs and/or frequent breakglass use is to foster a culture that values careful auditing. This is critical both for reliability reasons and security reasons, and you can use both motivations to appeal to the responsible parties. Two pairs of eyes help avoid typos and mistakes, and you should always safeguard against unilateral access to user data.

Ultimately, the teams building the administrative APIs and automation need to design them in a way that facilitates auditing. Anyone who regularly accesses production systems should be incentivized to solve these problems collaboratively and to understand the value of a good audit log. Without cultural reinforcement, audits can become rubber stamps, and breakglass use can become an everyday occurrence, losing its sense of importance or urgency. Culture is the key to ensuring that teams choose, build, and use systems in ways that support auditing; that these events occur only rarely; and that audit events receive the scrutiny they deserve.

Choosing an auditor

Once you have collected a good audit log, you need to choose the right person to inspect the (hopefully rare) recorded events. An auditor needs to have both the right context and the right objective.

When it comes to context, an auditor needs to know what a given action does, and ideally why the actor needed to perform that action. The auditor will therefore usually be a teammate, a manager, or someone familiar with the workflows that require that action. You'll need to strike a balance between sufficient context and objectivity: while an internal reviewer might have a close personal relationship with the person who generated the audit event and/or want the organization to succeed, an external private auditor may want to continue to be hired by an organization.

Choosing an auditor with the right objective depends on the purpose of the audit. At Google, we perform two broad categories of auditing:

- Audits to ensure best practices are being followed
- Audits to identify security breaches

Generally speaking, "best practice" audits support our reliability objectives. For example, an SRE team might choose to audit breakglass events from the last week's on-call shift during a weekly team meeting. This practice provides a cultural peer pressure to use and improve smaller service administrative APIs, rather than using a breakglass mechanism to access a more flexible emergency-use API. Widely scoped breakglass access often bypasses some or all safety checks, exposing the service to a higher potential for human error.

Google typically distributes breakglass reviews down to the team level, where we can leverage the social norming that accompanies team review. Peers performing the review have context that enables them to spot even very well-disguised actions, which is key to preventing internal abuses and thwarting malicious insiders. For example, a peer is well equipped to notice if a coworker repeatedly uses a breakglass action to access an unusual resource that they likely don't actually need. This type of team review also helps identify shortcomings in administrative APIs. When breakglass access is required for a specific task, it often signals a need to provide a safer or more secure way to perform that task as part of the normal API. You can read more about this subject in Chapter 21.

At Google we tend to centralize the second type of audit, as identifying external security breaches benefits from a broad view of the organization. An advanced attacker may compromise one team, and then use that access to compromise another team, service, or role. Each individual team may not notice a couple of anomalous actions, and doesn't have the cross-team view to connect the dots between different sets of actions.

A central auditing team may also be equipped to build extra signaling and add code for additional audit events that aren't widely known. These types of tripwires can be especially useful in early detection, but you may not want to share their implementation details widely. You may also need to work with other departments in your organization (such as Legal and HR), to ensure that auditing mechanisms are appropriate, properly scoped, and documented.

We at Google associate structured data with audit log events using *structured justification*. When an event that generates an audit log occurs, we can associate it with a structured reference such as a bug number, ticket number, or customer case number. Doing so allows us to build programmatic checks of the audit logs. For example, if support personnel look at a customer's payment details or other sensitive data, they can associate that data to a particular customer case. Therefore, we can ensure that the observed data belongs to the customer that opened the case. It would be much harder to automate log verification if we relied upon free-text fields. Structured justification has been key to scaling our auditing efforts—it provides a centralized auditing team context that's critical to effective auditing and analysis.

Testing and Least Privilege

Proper testing is a fundamental property of any well designed system. Testing has two important dimensions with regard to least privilege:

- Testing *of* least privilege, to ensure that access is properly granted only to necessary resources
- Testing *with* least privilege, to ensure that the infrastructure for testing has only the access it needs

Testing of least privilege

In the context of least privilege, you need to be able to test that well-defined user profiles (i.e., data analyst, customer support, SRE) have enough privileges to perform their role, but no more.

Your infrastructure should let you do the following:

- Describe what a specific user profile needs to be able to do in their job role. This defines the minimal access (APIs and data) and the type of access (read or write, permanent or temporary) they need for their role.
- Describe a set of scenarios in which the user profile attempts an action on your system (i.e., read, bulk read, write, delete, bulk delete, administer) and an expected result/impact on your system.
- Run these scenarios and compare the actual result/impact against the expected result/impact.

Ideally, to prevent adverse effects on production systems, these are tests that run before code or ACL changes. If test coverage is incomplete, you can mitigate overly broad access via monitoring of access and alerting systems.

Testing with least privilege

Tests should allow you to verify the expected read/write behavior without putting service reliability, sensitive data, or other critical assets at risk. However, if you don't have proper test infrastructure in place—infrastructure that accounts for varied environments, clients, credentials, data sets, etc.—tests that need to read/write data or mutate service state can be risky.

Consider the example of pushing a configuration file to production, which we'll return to in the next section. As your first step in designing a testing strategy for this configuration push, you should provide a separate environment keyed with its own credentials. This setup ensures that a mistake in writing or executing a test won't impact production—for example, by overwriting production data or bringing down a production service.

Alternately, let's say you're developing a keyboard app that allows people to post memes with one click. You want to analyze users' behavior and history so you can automatically recommend memes. Lacking a proper test infrastructure, you instead need to give data analysts read/write access to an entire set of raw user data in production to perform analysis and testing.

Proper testing methodology should consider ways to restrict user access and decrease risk, but still allow the data analysts to perform the tests they need to do their job. Do they need write access? Can you use anonymized data sets for the tasks they need to perform? Can you use test accounts? Can you operate in a test environment with anonymized data? If this access is compromised, what data is exposed?

Security and Reliability Tradeoff: Test Environments

Instead of building out a test infrastructure that faithfully mirrors production, time and cost considerations may tempt you to use special test accounts in production so changes don't impact real users. This strategy may work in some situations, but can muddy the waters when it comes to your auditing and ACLs.

You can approach test infrastructure by starting small—don't let perfect be the enemy of good. Start by thinking about ways you can most easily

- Separate environments and credentials
- Limit the types of access
- Limit the exposure of data

Initially, perhaps you can stand up short-lived tests on a cloud platform instead of building out an entire test infrastructure stack. Some employees may need only read or temporary access. In some cases, you may also be able to use representative or anonymized data sets.

While these testing best practices sound great in theory, at this point, you may be getting overwhelmed by the potential cost of building out a proper test infrastructure. Getting this right isn't cheap. However, consider the cost of *not* having a proper test infrastructure: Can you be certain that every test of critical operations won't bring down production? Can you live with data analysts having otherwise avoidable privileges to access sensitive data? Are you relying on perfect humans with perfect tests that are perfectly executed?

It's important to conduct a proper cost–benefit analysis for your specific situation. It may not make sense to initially build the "ideal" solution. However, make sure you build a framework people will use. People need to perform testing. If you don't provide an adequate testing framework, they'll test in production, circumventing the controls you put in place.

Diagnosing Access Denials

In a complex system, where least privilege is enforced and trust must be earned by the client via a third factor, multi-party authorization, or another mechanism (see "Advanced Controls" on page 81), policy is enforced at multiple levels and at a fine granularity. As a result, policy denials can also happen in complex ways.

Consider the case in which a sane security policy is being enforced, and your authorization system denies access. One of three possible outcomes might occur:

- The client was correctly denied and your system behaved appropriately. Least privilege has been enforced, and all is well.
- The client was correctly denied, but can use an advanced control (such as multi-party authorization) to obtain temporary access.
- The client believes they were incorrectly denied, and potentially files a support ticket with your security policy team. For example, this might happen if the client was recently removed from an authorized group, or if the policy changed in a subtle or perhaps incorrect way.

In all cases, the caller is blind to the reason for denial. But could the system perhaps provide the client with more information? Depending on the caller's level of privilege, it can.

If the client has no or very limited privileges, the denial should remain blind—you probably don't want to expose information beyond a 403 Access Denied error code (or its equivalent), because details about the reasons for a denial could be exploited to gain information about a system and even to find a way to gain access. However, if the caller has certain minimal privileges, you can provide a token associated with the denial. The caller can use that token to invoke an advanced control to obtain temporary access, or provide the token to the security policy team through a support channel so they can use it to diagnose the problem. For a more privileged caller, you can provide a token associated with the denial *and* some remediation information. The caller can then attempt to self-remediate before invoking the support channel. For example, the caller might learn that access was denied because they need to be a member of a specific group, and they can then request access to that group.

There will always be tension between how much remediation information to expose and how much support overload the security policy team can handle. However, if you expose too much information, clients may be able to reengineer the policy from the denial information, making it easier for a malicious actor to craft a request that uses the policy in an unintended way. With this in mind, we recommend that in the early stages of implementing a zero trust model, you use tokens and have all clients invoke the support channel.

Graceful Failure and Breakglass Mechanisms

Ideally, you'll always be dealing with a working authorization system enforcing a sane policy. But in reality, you might run into a scenario that results in large-scale incorrect denials of access (perhaps due to a bad system update). In response, you need to be able to circumvent your authorization system via a breakglass mechanism so you can fix it.

When employing a breakglass mechanism, consider the following guidelines:

- The ability to use a breakglass mechanism should be highly restricted. In general, it should be available only to your SRE team, which is responsible for the operational SLA of your system.
- The breakglass mechanism for zero trust networking should be available only from specific locations. These locations are your *panic rooms*, specific locations with additional physical access controls to offset the increased trust placed in their connectivity. (The careful reader will notice that the fallback mechanism for zero trust networking, a strategy of distrusting network location, is…trusting network location—but with additional physical access controls.)
- All uses of a breakglass mechanism should be closely monitored.
- The breakglass mechanism should be tested regularly by the team(s) responsible for production services, to make sure it functions when you need it.

When the breakglass mechanism has successfully been utilized so that users regain access, your SREs and security policy team can further diagnose and resolve the underlying problem. Chapters 8 and 9 discuss relevant strategies.

Worked Example: Configuration Distribution

Let's turn to a real-world example. Distributing a configuration file to a set of web servers is an interesting design problem, and it can be practically implemented with a small functional API. The best practices for managing a configuration file are to:

1. Store the configuration file in a version control system.
2. Code review changes to the file.
3. Automate the distribution to a canary set first, health check the canaries, and then continue health checking all hosts as you gradually push the file to the fleet

of web servers.[11] This step requires granting the automation access to update the configuration file remotely.

There are many approaches to exposing a small API, each tailored to the function of updating the configuration of your web servers. Table 5-2 summarizes a few APIs you may consider, and their tradeoffs. The sections that follow explain each tactic in more depth.

Table 5-2. APIs that update web server configuration and their tradeoffs

	POSIX API via OpenSSH	Software update API	Custom OpenSSH ForceCommand	Custom HTTP receiver
API surface	Large	Various	Small	Small
Preexisting[a]	Likely	Yes	Unlikely	Unlikely
Complexity	High	High	Low	Medium
Ability to scale	Moderate	Moderate, but reusable	Difficult	Moderate
Auditability	Poor	Good	Good	Good
Can express least privilege	Poor	Various	Good	Good

[a] This indicates how likely or unlikely it is that you already have this type of API as part of an existing web server deployment.

POSIX API via OpenSSH

You can allow the automation to connect to the web server host via OpenSSH, typically connecting as the local user the web server runs as. The automation can then write the configuration file and restart the web server process. This pattern is simple and common. It leverages an administrative API that likely already exists, and thus requires little additional code. Unfortunately, leveraging the large preexisting administrative API introduces several risks:

- The role running the automation can stop the web server permanently, start another binary in its place, read any data it has access to, etc.

- Bugs in the automation implicitly have enough access to cause a coordinated outage of all of the web servers.

- A compromise of the automation's credentials is equivalent to a compromise of all of the web servers.

---

11 *Canarying* a change is rolling it out to production slowly, beginning with a small set of production endpoints. Like a canary in a coal mine, it provides warning signals if something goes wrong. See Chapter 27 in the SRE book for more.

Software Update API

You can distribute the config as a packaged software update, using the same mechanism you use to update the web server binary. There are many ways to package and trigger binary updates, using APIs of varying sizes. A simple example is a Debian package (*.deb*) pulled from a central repository by a periodic apt-get called from cron. You might build a more complex example using one of the patterns discussed in the following sections to trigger the update (instead of cron), which you could then reuse for both the configuration and the binary. As you evolve your binary distribution mechanism to add safety and security, the benefits accrue to your configuration, because both use the same infrastructure. Any work done to centrally orchestrate a canary process, coordinate health checking, or provide signatures/provenance/auditing similarly pays dividends for both of these artifacts.

Sometimes the needs of binary and configuration update systems don't align. For example, you might distribute an IP deny list in your configuration that needs to converge as quickly as is safely practical, while also building your web server binary into a container. In this case, building, standing up, and tearing down a new container at the same rate you want to distribute configuration updates may be too expensive or disruptive. Conflicting requirements of this type may necessitate two distribution mechanisms: one for binaries, another for configuration updates.

For many more thoughts on this pattern, see Chapter 9.

Custom OpenSSH ForceCommand

You can write a short script to perform these steps:

1. Receive the configuration from STDIN.
2. Sanity check the configuration.
3. Restart the web server to update the configuration.

You can then expose this command via OpenSSH by tying particular entries in an *authorized_keys* file with the ForceCommand option.[12] This strategy presents a very small API to the caller, which can connect via the battle-hardened OpenSSH protocol, where the only available action is to provide a copy of the configuration file.

---

12 ForceCommand is a configuration option to constrain a particular authorized identity to run only a single command. See the *sshd_config* manpage (*https://oreil.ly/4ruSh*) for more details.

Logging the file (or a hash of it[13]) reasonably captures the entire action of the session for later auditing.

You can implement as many of these unique key/ForceCommand combinations as you like, but this pattern can be hard to scale to many unique administrative actions. While you can build a text-based protocol on top of the OpenSSH API (such as git-shell (*https://oreil.ly/k4igi*)), doing so starts down the path of building your own RPC mechanism. You're likely better off skipping to the end of that road by building on top of an existing framework such as gRPC (*https://grpc.io*) or Thrift (*https://thrift.apache.org*).

Custom HTTP Receiver (Sidecar)

You can write a small sidecar daemon—much like the ForceCommand solution, but using another AAA mechanism (e.g., gRPC with SSL, SPIFFE (*https://spiffe.io*), or similar)—that accepts a config. This approach doesn't require modifying the serving binary and is very flexible, at the expense of introducing more code and another daemon to manage.

Custom HTTP Receiver (In-Process)

You could also modify the web server to expose an API to update its config directly (*https://oreil.ly/hu7yg*), receiving the config and writing it to disk. This is one of the most flexible approaches, and bears a strong similarity to the way we manage configuration at Google, but it requires incorporating the code into the serving binary.

Tradeoffs

All but the large options in Table 5-2 provide opportunities to add security and safety to your automation. An attacker may still be able to compromise the web server's role by pushing an arbitrary config; however, choosing a smaller API means that the push mechanism won't implicitly allow that compromise.

You may be able to further design for least privilege by signing the config independently from the automation that pushes it. This strategy segments the trust between roles, guaranteeing that if the automation role pushing the configuration is compromised, the automation cannot also compromise the web server by sending a malicious config. To recall McIlroy, Pinson, and Tague 's advice, designing each piece

---

13 At scale, it may be impractical to log and store many duplicate copies of the file. Logging the hash allows you to correlate the config back to the revision control system, and detect unknown or unexpected configurations when auditing the log. As icing on the cake, and if space allows, you may wish to store rejected configurations to aid a later investigation. Ideally, all configs should be signed, indicating they came from the revision control system with a known hash, or rejected.

of the system to perform one task and perform that task well allows you to isolate trust.

The more granular control surface presented by a narrow API also allows you to add protection against bugs in the automation. In addition to requiring a signature to validate the config, you can require a bearer token[14] from a central rate limiter, created independently of your automation and targeted to each host in the rollout. You can very carefully unit test this general rate limiter; if the rate limiter is independently implemented, bugs affecting the rollout automation likely won't simultaneously affect it. An independent rate limiter is also conveniently reusable, as it can rate limit the config rollout of the web server, the binary rollout of the same server, reboots of the server, or any other task to which you wish to add a safety check.

A Policy Framework for Authentication and Authorization Decisions

authentication [noun]: verifying the **identity** of a user or process

authorization [noun]: evaluating if a request from a specific authenticated party **should be permitted**

The previous section advocates designing a narrow administrative API for your service, which allows you to grant the least amount of privilege possible to achieve a given action. Once that API exists, you must decide how to control access to it. Access control involves two important but distinct steps.

First, you must *authenticate* who is connecting. An authentication mechanism can range in complexity:

Simple: Accepting a username passed in a URL parameter
  Example: */service?username=admin*

More complex: Presenting a preshared secret
  Examples: WPA2-PSK, an HTTP cookie

Even more complex: Complex hybrid encryption and certificate schemes
  Examples: TLS 1.3, OAuth

Generally speaking, you should prefer to reuse an existing strong cryptographic authentication mechanism to identify the API's caller. The result of this authentication decision is commonly expressed as a username, a common name, a "principal," a

---

14 A *bearer token* is just a cryptographic signature, signed by the rate limiter, which can be presented to anyone with the rate limiter's public key. They can use that public key to validate that the rate limiter has approved this operation, during the validity window of the token.

"role," and so on. For purposes of this section, we use *role* to describe the inter-changeable result of authentication.

Next, your code must make a decision: is this role *authorized* to perform the requested action? Your code may consider many attributes of the request, such as the following:

The specific action being requested
    Examples: URL, command being run, gRPC method

Arguments to the requested action
    Examples: URL parameters, `argv`, gRPC request

The source of the request
    Examples: IP address, client certificate metadata

Metadata about the authenticated role
    Examples: geographic location, legal jurisdiction, machine learning evaluation of risk

Server-side context
    Examples: rate of similar requests, available capacity

The rest of this section discusses several techniques that Google has found useful to improve upon, and scale up, the basic requirements of authentication and authorization decisions.

Using Advanced Authorization Controls

An access control list for a given resource is a familiar way to implement an authorization decision. The simplest ACL is a string matching the authenticated role, often combined with some notion of grouping—for example, a group of roles, such as "administrator," which expands to a larger list of roles, such as usernames. When the service evaluates the incoming request, it checks whether the authenticated role is a member of the ACL.

More complex authorization requirements, such as multi-factor authorization (MFA) or multi-party authorization (MPA), require more complex authorization code (for more on three-factor authorization and MPA, see "Advanced Controls" on page 81). In addition, some organizations may have to consider their particular regulatory or contractual requirements when designing authorization policies.

This code can be difficult to implement correctly, and its complexity can rapidly compound if many services each implement their own authorization logic. In our experience, it's helpful to separate the complexities of authorization decisions from core API design and business logic with frameworks like the AWS (*https://aws.amazon.com/iam*) or GCP (*https://cloud.google.com/iam*) Identity & Access

Management (IAM) offerings. At Google, we also extensively use a variation of the GCP authorization framework for internal services.[15]

The security policy framework allows our code to make simple checks (such as "Can X access resource Y?") and evaluate those checks against an externally supplied policy. If we need to add more authorization controls to a particular action, we can simply change the relevant policy configuration file. This low overhead has tremendous functionality and velocity benefits.

Investing in a Widely Used Authorization Framework

You can enable authentication and authorization changes at scale by using a shared library to implement authorization decisions, and by using a consistent interface as widely as possible. Applying this classic modular software design advice in the security sphere yields surprising benefits. For example:

- You can add support for MFA or MPA to all service endpoints with a single library change.

- You can then implement this support for a small percentage of the actions or resources in all services with a single configuration change.

- You can improve reliability by requiring MPA for all actions that allow a potentially unsafe action, similar to a code review system. This process improvement can improve security against insider risk threats (for more about types of adversaries, see Chapter 2) by facilitating fast incident response (by bypassing revision control system and code review dependencies) without allowing broad unilateral access.

As your organization grows, standardization is your friend. A uniform authorization framework facilitates team mobility, as more people know how to code against and implement access controls with a common framework.

Avoiding Potential Pitfalls

Designing a complex authorization policy language is difficult. If the policy language is too simplistic, it won't achieve its goal, and you'll end up with authorization decisions spread across both the framework's policy and the primary codebase. If the policy language is too general, it can be very hard to reason about. To mitigate these concerns, you can apply standard software API design practices—in particular, an iterative design approach—but we recommend proceeding carefully to avoid both of these extremes.

---

15 Our internal variant supports our internal authentication primitives, avoids some circular dependency concerns, etc.

Carefully consider how the authorization policy is shipped to (or with) the binary. You may want to update the authorization policy, which will plausibly become one of the most security-sensitive pieces of configuration, independently of the binary. For additional discussion about configuration distribution, see the worked example in the previous section, Chapters 9 and 14 in this book, Chapter 8 in the SRE book, and Chapters 14 and 15 in the SRE workbook.

Application developers will need assistance with the policy decisions that will be encoded in this language. Even if you avoid the pitfalls described here and create an expressive and understandable policy language, more often than not it will still require collaboration between application developers implementing the administrative APIs and security engineers and SREs with domain-specific knowledge about your production environment, to craft the right balance between security and functionality.

 # Advanced Controls

While many authorization decisions are a binary yes/no, more flexibility is useful in some situations. Rather than requiring a strict yes/no, an escape valve of "maybe," paired with an additional check, can dramatically ease the pressures on a system. Many of the controls described here can be used either in isolation or in combination. Appropriate usage depends on the sensitivity of the data, the risk of the action, and existing business processes.

Multi-Party Authorization (MPA)

Involving another person is one classic way to ensure a proper access decision, fostering a culture of security and reliability (see Chapter 21). This strategy offers several benefits:

- *Preventing mistakes* or unintentional violations of policy that may lead to security or privacy issues.
- *Discouraging bad actors* from attempting to perform malicious changes. This includes both employees, who risk disciplinary action, and external attackers, who risk detection.
- *Increasing the cost of the attack* by requiring either compromise of at least one other person or a carefully constructed change that passes a peer review.
- *Auditing past actions* for incident response or postmortem analysis, assuming the reviews are recorded permanently and in a tamper-resistant fashion.
- *Providing customer comfort*. Your customers may be more comfortable using your service knowing that no single person can make a change by themselves.

MPA is often performed for a broad level of access—for example, by requiring approval to join a group that grants access to production resources, or the ability to act as a given role or credential. Broad MPA can serve as a valuable breakglass mechanism, to enable very unusual actions that you may not have specific workflows for. Where possible, you should try to provide more granular authorization, which can provide stronger guarantees of reliability and security. If the second party approves an action against a small functional API (see "Small Functional APIs" on page 65), they can have much more confidence in precisely what they are authorizing.

Potential Pitfalls

Make sure that approvers have enough context to make an informed decision. Does the information provided clearly identify who is doing what? You may need to specify config parameters and targets in order to reveal what a command is doing. This may be particularly important if you're displaying approval prompts on mobile devices and have limited screen space for details.

Social pressure around approvals may also lead to bad decisions. For example, an engineer might not feel comfortable rejecting a suspicious request if its issued by a manager, a senior engineer, or someone standing over their desk. To mitigate these pressures, you can provide the option to escalate approvals to a security or investigations team after the fact. Or, you might have a policy that all (or a percentage) of a certain type of approval are independently audited.

Before building a multi-party authorization system, make sure the technology and social dynamics allow someone to say no. Otherwise, the system is of little value.

Three-Factor Authorization (3FA)

In a large organization, MPA often has one key weakness that can be exploited by a determined and persistent attacker: all of the "multiple parties" use the same centrally managed workstations. The more homogeneous the fleet of workstations, the more likely it is that an attacker who can compromise one workstation can compromise several or even all of them.

A classic method to harden the fleet of workstations against attack is for users to maintain two completely separate workstations: one for general use, such as browsing the web and sending/receiving emails, and another more trusted workstation for communicating with the production environment. In our experience, users ultimately want similar sets of features and capabilities from those workstations, and maintaining two sets of workstation infrastructure for the limited set of users whose credentials require this increased level of protection is both expensive and difficult to sustain over time. Once this issue is no longer top of mind for management, people are less incentivized to maintain the infrastructure.

Mitigating the risk that a single compromised platform can undermine all authorization requires the following:

- Maintaining at least two platforms
- The ability to approve requests on two platforms
- (Preferably) The ability to harden at least one platform

Considering these requirements, another option is to require authorization from a hardened mobile platform for certain very risky operations. For simplicity and convenience, you can only allow RPCs to be originated from fully managed desktop workstations, and then require three-factor authorization from the mobile platform. When a production service receives a sensitive RPC, the policy framework (described in "A Policy Framework for Authentication and Authorization Decisions" on page 78) requires cryptographically signed approval from the separate 3FA service. That service then indicates that it sent the RPC to the mobile device, it was shown to the originating user, and they acknowledged the request.

Hardening mobile platforms is somewhat easier than hardening general-purpose workstations. We've found that users are generally more tolerant of certain security restrictions on mobile devices, such as additional network monitoring, allowing only a subset of apps, and connecting through a limited number of HTTP endpoints. These policies are also quite easy to achieve with modern mobile platforms.

Once you have a hardened mobile platform on which to display the proposed production change, you have to get the request to that platform and display it to the user. At Google, we reuse the infrastructure that delivers notifications to Android phones to authorize and report Google login attempts to our users. If you have the luxury of a similar hardened piece of infrastructure lying around, it might be useful to extend it to support this use case, but failing that, a basic web-based solution is relatively easy to create. The core of a 3FA system is a simple RPC service that receives the request to be authorized and exposes the request for authorization by the trusted client. The user requesting the 3FA-protected RPC visits the web URL of the 3FA service from their mobile device, and is presented with the request for approval.

It is important to distinguish what threats MPA and 3FA protect against, so you can decide on a consistent policy about when to apply them. MPA protects against unilateral insider risk as well as against compromise of an individual workstation (by requiring a second internal approval). 3FA protects against broad compromise of internal workstations, but does not provide any protection against insider threats when used in isolation. Requiring 3FA from the originator and simple web-based

MPA from a second party can provide a very strong defense against the combination of most of these threats, with relatively little organizational overhead.

3FA Is Not 2FA (or MFA)

Two-factor authentication (2FA) is a well-discussed subset of multi-factor authentication. It is specifically the attempt to combine "something you know" (a password) with "something you have" (an application or hardware token that produces cryptographic proof of presence), to form a strong authentication decision. For more on 2FA, see the case study "Example: Strong second-factor authentication using FIDO security keys" on page 133.

The key difference is that 3FA is attempting to provide stronger *authorization* of a specific request, not stronger *authentication* of a specific user. While we acknowledge that the 3 in *3FA* is a bit of a misnomer (it's approval from a second platform, not a third platform), it's a helpful shorthand that your "3FA device" is the mobile device that adds additional authorization for some requests beyond your first two factors.

Business Justifications

As mentioned in "Choosing an auditor" on page 69, you can enforce authorization by tying access to a structured business justification, such as a bug, incident, ticket, case ID, or assigned account. But building the validation logic may require additional work, and may also require process changes for the people staffing on-call or customer service.

As an example, consider a customer service workflow. In an anti-pattern sometimes found in small or immature organizations, a basic and nascent system may give customer service representatives access to all customer records, either for efficiency reasons or because controls don't exist. A better option would be to block access by default, and to only allow access to specific data when you can verify the business need. This approach may be a gradient of controls implemented over time. For example, it may start by only allowing access to customer service representatives assigned an open ticket. Over time, you can improve the system to only allow access to specific customers, and specific data for those customers, in a time-bound fashion, with customer approval.

When properly configured, this strategy can provide a strong authorization guarantee that access was appropriate and properly scoped. Structured justifications allow the automation to require that Ticket #12345 isn't a random number typed in to satisfy a simple regular expression check. Instead, the justification satisfies a set of access policies that balance operational business needs and system capabilities.

Security and Reliability Tradeoff: System Usability

If it's too difficult for engineers to find an approver every time they want to perform an action with elevated privileges, they'll develop potentially dangerous behaviors. For example, they might work around enforced best practices by providing generic business justifications (like "Team foo needed access") that don't fulfill a functional requirement. Patterns of generic justifications should trigger alarm signals in the auditing system.

Temporary Access

You can limit the risk of an authorization decision by granting temporary access to resources. This strategy can often be useful when fine-grained controls are not available for every action, but you still want to grant the least privilege possible with the available tooling.

You can grant temporary access in a structured and scheduled way (e.g., during on-call rotations, or via expiring group memberships) or in an on-demand fashion where users explicitly request access. You can combine temporary access with a request for multi-party authorization, a business justification, or another authorization control. Temporary access also creates a logical point for auditing, since you have clear logging about users who have access at any given time. It also provides data about where temporary access occurs so you can prioritize and reduce these requests over time.

Temporary access also reduces ambient authority. This is one reason that administrators favor sudo or "Run as Administrator" over operating as the Unix user *root* or Windows Administrator accounts—when you accidentally issue a command to delete all the data, the fewer permissions you have, the better!

Proxies

When fine-grained controls for backend services are not available, you can fall back to a heavily monitored and restricted proxy machine (or *bastion*). Only requests from these specified proxies are allowed to access sensitive services. This proxy can restrict dangerous actions, rate limit actions, and perform more advanced logging.

For example, you may need to perform an emergency rollback of a bad change. Given the infinite ways a bad change can happen, and the infinite ways it can be resolved, the steps required to perform a rollback may not be available in a predefined API or a tool. You can give a system administrator the flexibility to resolve an emergency, but introduce restrictions or additional controls that mitigate the risk. For example:

- Each command may need peer approval.
- An administrator may only connect to relevant machines.
- The computer that an administrator is using may not have access to the internet.
- You can enable more thorough logging.

As always, implementing any of these controls comes with an integration and operational cost, as discussed in the next section.

Tradeoffs and Tensions

Adopting a least privilege access model will definitely improve your organization's security posture. However, you must offset the benefits outlined in the previous sections against the potential cost of implementing that posture. This section considers some of those costs.

Increased Security Complexity

A highly granular security posture is a very powerful tool, but it's also complex and therefore challenging to manage. It is important to have a comprehensive set of tooling and infrastructure to help you define, manage, analyze, push, and debug your security policies. Otherwise, this complexity may become overwhelming. You should always aim to be able to answer these foundational questions: "Does a given user have access to a given service/piece of data?" and "For a given service/piece of data, who has access?"

Impact on Collaboration and Company Culture

While a strict model of least privilege is likely appropriate for sensitive data and services, a more relaxed approach in other areas can provide tangible benefits.

For example, providing software engineers with broad access to source code carries a certain amount of risk. However, this is counterbalanced by engineers being able to learn on the job according to their own curiosity and by contributing features and bug fixes outside of their normal roles when they can lend their attention and expertise. Less obviously, this transparency also makes it harder for an engineer to write inappropriate code that goes unnoticed.

Including source code and related artifacts in your data classification effort can help you form a principled approach for protecting sensitive assets while benefiting from visibility into less sensitive assets, which you can read more about in Chapter 21.

Quality Data and Systems That Impact Security

In a zero trust environment that is the underpinning of least privilege, every granular security decision depends on two things: the policy being enforced and the context of the request. *Context* is informed by a large set of data—some of it potentially dynamic—that can impact the decision. For example, the data might include the role of the user, the groups the user belongs to, the attributes of the client making the request, the training set fed into a machine learning model, or the sensitivity of the API being accessed. You should review the systems that produce this data to ensure that the quality of security-impacting data is as high as possible. Low-quality data will result in incorrect security decisions.

Impact on User Productivity

Your users need to be able to accomplish their workflows as efficiently as possible. The best security posture is one that your end users don't notice. However, introducing new three-factor and multi-party authorization steps may impinge on user productivity, especially if users must wait to be granted authorization. You can minimize user pain by making sure the new steps are easy to navigate. Similarly, end users need a simple way to make sense of access denials, either through self-service diagnosis or fast access to a support channel.

Impact on Developer Complexity

As the model for least privilege is adopted across your organization, developers must conform to it. The concepts and policies must be easily consumable by developers who aren't particularly security-savvy, so you should provide training materials and thoroughly document your APIs.[16] As they navigate the new requirements, give developers easy and fast access to security engineers for security reviews and general consulting. Deploying third-party software in this environment requires particular care, as you may need to wrap software in a layer that can enforce the security policy.

Conclusion

When designing a complex system, the least privilege model is the most secure way to ensure that clients have the ability to accomplish what they need to do, but no more. This is a powerful design paradigm to protect your systems and your data from malicious or accidental damage caused by known or unknown users. Google has spent significant time and effort implementing this model. Here are the key components:

---

16 See "A Policy Framework for Authentication and Authorization Decisions" on page 78.

- A comprehensive knowledge of the functionality of your system, so you can classify different parts according to the level of security risk each holds.

- Based on this classification, a partitioning of your system and access to your data to as fine a level as possible. Small functional APIs are a necessity for least privilege.

- An authentication system for validating users' credentials as they attempt to access your system.

- An authorization system that enforces a well-defined security policy that can be easily attached to your finely partitioned systems.

- A set of advanced controls for nuanced authorization. These can, for example, provide temporary, multi-factor, and multi-party approval.

- A set of operational requirements for your system to support these key concepts. At a minimum, your system needs the following:
  - The ability to audit all access and to generate signals so you can identify threats and perform historical forensic analysis
  - The means to reason about, define, test, and debug your security policy, and to provide end-user support for this policy
  - The ability to provide a breakglass mechanism when your system does not behave as expected

Making all these components work in a way that is easy for users and developers to adopt, and that does not significantly impact their productivity, also requires an organizational commitment to making adoption of least privilege as seamless as possible. This commitment includes a focused security function that owns your security posture and interfaces with users and developers through security consulting, policy definition, threat detection, and support on security-related issues.

While this can be a large undertaking, we strongly believe it is a significant improvement over existing approaches to security posture enforcement.

CHAPTER 6

Design for Understandability

By Julien Boeuf, Christoph Kern, and John Reese
with Guy Fischman, Paul Blankinship, Aleksandra Culver,
Sergey Simakov, Peter Valchev, and Douglas Colish

In order to have confidence in your system's security posture and its ability to reach its service level objectives (SLOs), you need to manage the system's complexity: you must be able to meaningfully reason about and understand the system, its components, and their interactions. The degree to which a system is understandable can vary drastically across different properties. For example, it may be easy to understand a system's behavior under high loads, but difficult to understand the system's behavior when it encounters specially crafted (malicious) inputs.

This chapter discusses system understandability as it pertains to every stage of the system lifecycle. We start by discussing how to analyze and understand your systems according to invariants and mental models. We show that a layered system architecture using standardized frameworks for identity, authorization, and access control can help you design for understandability. After deep diving into the topic of security boundaries, we discuss how software design—especially the use of application frameworks and APIs—can significantly impact your ability to reason about security and reliability properties.

For the purposes of this book, we define a system's *understandability* as the extent to which a person with relevant technical background can accurately and confidently reason about both of the following:

- The operational behavior of the system
- The system's invariants, including security and availability

Why Is Understandability Important?

Designing a system to be understandable, and maintaining that understandability over time, requires effort. Generally, this effort is an investment that's repaid in the form of sustained project velocity (as discussed in Chapter 4). More specifically, an understandable system has concrete benefits:

Decreases the likelihood of security vulnerabilities or resilience failures
Whenever you modify a system or software component—for example, when you add a feature, fix a bug, or change configuration—there's an inherent risk that you might accidentally introduce a new security vulnerability or compromise the system's operational resilience. The less understandable the system, the more likely it is that the engineer who's modifying it will make a mistake. That engineer might misunderstand the existing behavior of the system, or may be unaware of a hidden, implicit, or undocumented requirement that conflicts with the change.

Facilitates effective incident response
During an incident, it's vital that responders can quickly and accurately assess damage, contain the incident, and identify and remediate root causes. A complex, difficult-to-understand system significantly hinders that process.

Increases confidence in assertions about a system's security posture
Assertions about a system's security are typically expressed in terms of *invariants*: properties that must hold for *all possible* behaviors of the system. This includes how the system behaves in response to unexpected interactions with its external environment—for example, when the system receives malformed or maliciously crafted inputs. In other words, the system's behavior in response to a malicious input must not violate a required security property. In a difficult-to-understand system, it is hard or sometimes impossible to verify with a high degree of confidence that such assertions hold. Testing is often insufficient to demonstrate that a "for all possible behaviors" property holds—testing typically exercises the system for only a relatively small fraction of possible behaviors that correspond to typical or expected operation.[1] You usually need to rely on abstract reasoning about the system to establish such properties as invariants.

---

1 Automated fuzz testing, especially if combined with instrumentation and coverage guidance, can in some cases explore a larger fraction of possible behaviors. This is discussed in detail in Chapter 13.

System Invariants

A *system invariant* is a property that is always true, no matter how the system's environment behaves or misbehaves. The system is *fully responsible* for ensuring that a desired property is in fact an invariant, even if the system's environment misbehaves in arbitrarily unexpected or malicious ways. That environment includes everything that you don't have direct control over, from nefarious users who hit your service frontend with maliciously crafted requests to hardware failures that result in random crashes. One of our main goals in analyzing a system is to determine whether specific desired properties are actually invariants.

Here are some examples of desired security and reliability properties of a system:

- Only authenticated and properly authorized users can access a system's persistent data store.
- All operations on sensitive data in a system's persistent data store are recorded in an audit log in accordance with the system's auditing policy.
- All values received from outside a system's trust boundary are appropriately validated or encoded before being passed to APIs that are prone to injection vulnerabilities (e.g., SQL query APIs or APIs for constructing HTML markup).
- The number of queries received by a system's backend scales relative to the number of queries received by the system's frontend.
- If a system's backend fails to respond to a query after a predetermined amount of time, the system's frontend gracefully degrades (*https://oreil.ly/bLTJN*)—for example, by responding with an approximate answer.
- When the load on any component is greater than that component can handle, in order to reduce the risk of cascading failure, that component will serve overload errors (*https://oreil.ly/7eJtF*) rather than crashing.
- A system can only receive RPCs from a set of designated systems and can only send RPCs to a set of designated systems.

If your system allows behaviors that violate a desired security property—in other words, if the stated property isn't actually an invariant—then the system has a security weakness or vulnerability. For example, imagine that property 1 from the list is not true for your system because a request handler is missing access checks, or because those checks were implemented incorrectly. You now have a security vulnerability that could permit an attacker to access your users' private data.

Similarly, suppose your system does not satisfy the fourth property: under some circumstances, the system generates an excessive number of backend requests for each incoming frontend request. For example, perhaps the frontend generates multiple retries in quick succession (and without an appropriate backoff mechanism) if a backend request fails or takes too long. Your system has a potential availability weakness: once the system reaches this state, its frontend could completely overwhelm the backend and make the service unresponsive, in a kind of self-inflicted denial-of-service scenario.

Analyzing Invariants

When analyzing whether a system meets a given invariant, there's a tradeoff between the potential harm caused by violations of that invariant and the amount of effort you spend in meeting the invariant and verifying that it actually holds. On one end of the spectrum, that effort might involve running a few tests and reading parts of the source code to look for bugs—for example, forgotten access checks—that could lead to violation of the invariant. This approach does not lead to a particularly high degree of confidence. It's quite possible, and in many cases likely, that behavior not covered by testing or in-depth code review will harbor bugs. It's telling that well-understood common classes of software vulnerabilities like SQL injection, cross-site scripting (XSS), and buffer overflows have maintained leading positions in "top vulnerability" lists.[2] Absence of evidence is not evidence of absence.

On the other end of the spectrum, you might perform analyses based on provably sound, formal reasoning: the system and the claimed properties are modeled in a formal logic, and you construct a logical proof (typically with the help of an automated proof assistant) that the property holds for the system.[3] This approach is difficult and involves a lot of work. For example, one of the largest software verification projects to date constructed a proof (*https://oreil.ly/qxVk2*) of comprehensive correctness and security properties of a microkernel's implementation at the machine code level; this project took approximately 20 person-years of effort.[4] While formal verification is becoming practically applicable in certain situations, such as microkernels or complex cryptographic library code,[5] it is typically not feasible for large-scale application software development projects.

---

2 Such as those published by SANS (*https://oreil.ly/cYTHM*), MITRE (*https://oreil.ly/-XYhE*), and OWASP (*https://oreil.ly/eChGB*).

3 See Murray, Toby, and Paul van Oorschot. 2018. "BP: Formal Proofs, the Fine Print and Side Effects." *Proceedings of the 2018 IEEE Cybersecurity Development Conference*: 1–10. doi:10.1109/SecDev.2018.00009.

4 See Klein, Gerwin et al. 2014. "Comprehensive Formal Verification of an OS Microkernel." *ACM Transactions on Computer Systems* 32(1): 1–70. doi:10.1145/2560537.

5 See, for example, Erbsen, Andres et al. 2019. "Simple High-Level Code for Cryptographic Arithmetic—With Proofs, Without Compromises." *Proceedings of the 2019 IEEE Symposium on Security and Privacy*: 73–90. doi: 10.1109/SP.2019.00005. For another example, see Chudnov, Andrey et al. 2018. "Continuous Formal Verification of Amazon s2n." *Proceedings of the 30th International Conference on Computer Aided Verification*: 430–446. doi:10.1007/978-3-319-96142-2_26.

This chapter aims to present a practical middle ground. By designing a system with an explicit goal of understandability, you can support principled (but still informal) arguments that the system has certain invariants and gain a fairly high degree of confidence in these assertions with a reasonable amount of effort. At Google, we've found this approach to be practical for large-scale software development, and highly effective in reducing the occurrence of common classes of vulnerabilities. For more discussion on testing and validation, see Chapter 13.

Mental Models

Highly complex systems are difficult for humans to reason about in a holistic way. In practice, engineers and subject matter experts often construct mental models that explain relevant behaviors of a system while leaving out irrelevant details. For a complex system, you may construct multiple mental models that build on each other. In this way, when thinking about the behavior or invariants of a given system or subsystem, you can abstract away the details of its surrounding and underlying components and instead substitute their respective mental models.

Mental models are useful because they simplify reasoning about a complex system. For that same reason, mental models are also limited. If you form a mental model based on experience with a system performing under typical operating conditions, that model may not predict a system's behavior in unusual scenarios. To a large extent, security and reliability engineering is concerned with analyzing systems in exactly those unusual conditions—for example, when a system is actively under attack, or in an overload or component-failure scenario.

Consider a system whose throughput normally increases predictably and gradually with the rate of incoming requests. However, beyond a certain load threshold, the system might reach a state where it responds in a dramatically different fashion. For example, memory pressure might lead to thrashing[6] at the virtual memory or heap/garbage collector level, leaving the system unable to keep up with the additional load. Too much additional load could even lead to *decreased* throughput. When troubleshooting a system in this state, you could be seriously misled by an overly simplified mental model of the system, unless you explicitly recognize that the model no longer applies.

When designing systems, it's valuable to consider the mental models that software, security, and reliability engineers will inevitably construct for themselves. When designing a new component to add to a larger system, ideally, its naturally emerging

---

6 See Denning, Peter J. 1968. "Thrashing: Its Causes and Prevention." *Proceedings of the 1968 Fall Joint Computer Conference*: 915–922. doi:10.1145/1476589.1476705.

mental model should be consistent with the mental models people have formed for similar existing subsystems.

When possible, you should also design systems so that their mental models remain predictive and useful when the system is operating under extreme or unusual conditions. For example, to avoid thrashing, you can configure production servers to run without on-disk virtual memory swap space. If a production service can't allocate memory that it needs to respond to a request, it can quickly return an error in a predictable way. Even if a buggy or misbehaving service can't handle a memory allocation failure and crashes, you can at least clearly attribute the failure to an underlying problem—in this case, memory pressure; that way, the mental models of the people observing the system remain useful.

Designing Understandable Systems

The remainder of this chapter discusses some concrete measures you can take to make a system more understandable, and to maintain a system's understandability as it evolves over time. We'll start by considering the issue of complexity.

Complexity Versus Understandability

The primary enemy of understandability is *unmanaged complexity*.

Some amount of complexity is often inherent and unavoidable because of the scale of modern software systems—especially distributed systems—and the problems they solve. For example, Google employs tens of thousands of engineers, who work in a source repository that contains over a billion lines of code. Those lines of code collectively implement a large number of user-facing services and the backends and data pipelines that support them. Even smaller organizations with a single product offering may implement hundreds of features and user stories in hundreds of thousands of lines of code, which is edited by tens or hundreds of engineers.

Let's take Gmail as an example of a system with significant inherent feature complexity. You could briefly sum up Gmail as a cloud-based email service, but that summary belies its complexity. Among its many features, Gmail offers the following:

- Multiple frontends and UIs (desktop web, mobile web, mobile apps)
- Several APIs (*https://oreil.ly/RaYQx*) that permit third-party developers to develop add-ons
- Inbound and outbound IMAP and POP interfaces
- Attachment handling that's integrated with cloud storage services
- Rendering of attachments in many formats, such as documents and spreadsheets
- An offline-capable web client and underlying synchronization infrastructure

- Spam filtering
- Automatic message categorization
- Systems for extracting structured information about flights, calendar events, etc.
- Spelling correction
- Smart Reply and Smart Compose
- Reminders to reply to messages

A system with such features is inherently more complex than a system without them, but we can't very well tell Gmail's product managers that these features add too much complexity and ask them to remove them for the sake of security and reliability. After all, the features provide value, and are to a large extent what defines Gmail as a product. But if we work diligently to manage this complexity, the system can still be sufficiently secure and reliable.

As mentioned previously, understandability is relevant in the context of specific behaviors and properties of systems and subsystems. Our goal must be to structure a system's design to compartmentalize and contain this inherent complexity in a way that permits a human to reason with high fidelity about these *specific, relevant system properties and behaviors*. In other words, we must specifically manage the aspects of complexity that stand in the way of understandability.

Of course, this is easier said than done. The rest of this section investigates common sources of unmanaged complexity and corresponding decreased understandability, and design patterns that can help keep complexity under control and make systems more understandable.

While our primary concerns are security and reliability, the patterns we discuss largely aren't specific to those two areas—they are very much aligned with general software design techniques aimed at managing complexity and fostering understandability. You might also want to refer to general texts on system and software design, such as John Ousterhout's *A Philosophy of Software Design* (Yaknyam Press, 2018).

Breaking Down Complexity

To understand all the aspects of a complex system's behavior, you need to internalize and maintain a large mental model. Humans simply aren't very good at that.

You can make a system more understandable by composing it from smaller components. You should be able to reason about each component in isolation, and combine them in such a way that you can derive the properties of the whole system from the component properties. This approach allows you to establish whole-system invariants *without* having to think about the entire system in one go.

This approach is not straightforward in practice. Your ability to establish properties of subsystems, and to combine properties of subsystems into system-wide properties, depends on how the whole system is structured into components and the nature of the interfaces and trust relationships between those components. We'll look at these relationships and related considerations in "System Architecture" on page 97.

Centralized Responsibility for Security and Reliability Requirements

As discussed in Chapter 4, security and reliability requirements often apply horizontally across all components of a system. For example, a security requirement might state that for any operation executed in response to a user request, the system must complete some common task (e.g., audit logging and operational metrics collection) or check some condition (e.g., authentication and authorization).

If each individual component is responsible for independently implementing common tasks and checks, it's difficult to determine whether the resulting system actually satisfies the requirement. You can improve upon this design by moving responsibility for common functionalities to a centralized component—often a library or framework. For example, an RPC service framework can ensure that the system implements authentication, authorization, and logging for every RPC method according to a policy that's defined centrally for the entire service. With this design, individual service methods aren't responsible for these security functions, and application developers can't forget to implement them or implement them incorrectly. In addition, a security reviewer can understand a service's authentication and authorization controls without reading each individual service method implementation. Instead, the reviewer just needs to understand the framework and inspect the service-specific configuration.

To provide another example: to prevent cascading failures under load, incoming requests should be subject to time-outs and deadlines. Any logic that retries failures caused by overload should be subject to stringent safety mechanisms. To implement these policies, you might rely on application or service code to configure deadlines for subrequests and appropriately process failures. A mistake or omission in any relevant code in a single application could result in a reliability weakness for the entire system. You can make a system more robust and more understandable with respect to reliability by including mechanisms in the underlying RPC service framework to support automatic deadline propagation and centralized handling of request cancellations.[7]

These examples highlight two benefits of centralizing responsibility for security and reliability requirements:

---

7 For more information, see Chapter 11 in the SRE workbook.

Improved understandability of the system
A reviewer needs to look in only one place in order to understand and validate that a security/reliability requirement is implemented correctly.

Increased likelihood that the resulting system is actually correct
This approach removes the possibility that an ad hoc implementation of the requirement in application code is incorrect or missing.

While there's an up-front cost to building and validating a centralized implementation as part of an application framework or library, this cost is amortized across all applications built based on that framework.

System Architecture

Structuring systems into layers and components is a key tool for managing complexity. Using this approach, you can reason about the system in chunks, rather than having to understand every detail of the whole system all at once.

You also need to think carefully about exactly how you break your system into components and layers. Components that are too tightly coupled are just as hard to understand as a monolithic system. To make a system understandable, you have to pay as much attention to the boundaries and interfaces between components as you do to the components themselves.

Experienced software developers are usually aware that a system must consider inputs from (and sequences of interactions with) its external environment untrustworthy, and that a system can't make assumptions about those inputs. In contrast, it can be tempting to treat callers of internal, lower-layer APIs (such as APIs of in-process service objects, or RPCs exposed by internal backend microservices) as trustworthy, and to rely on those callers to stay within documented constraints on the API's usage.

Suppose that a security property of the system depends on the correct operation of an internal component. Also, suppose that its correct operation in turn depends on preconditions ensured by the component's API's callers, such as correct sequencing of operations, or constraints on values of method parameters. Determining whether the system actually has the desired property requires not only understanding the API's implementation, but understanding every call site of the API across the entire system, and whether every such call site ensures the required precondition.

The fewer assumptions a component makes about its callers, the easier it is to reason about that component in isolation. Ideally, a component makes no assumptions about its callers.

If a component is forced to make assumptions about its callers, it's important to capture these assumptions explicitly in the design of interfaces, or in other constraints on the environment—for example, by restricting the set of principals who can interact with the component.

Understandable Interface Specifications

Structured interfaces, consistent object models, and idempotent operations contribute to a system's understandability. As described in the following sections, these considerations make it easier to predict output behavior and how the interfaces will interact.

Prefer narrow interfaces that offer less room for interpretation

Services can use many different models and frameworks to expose interfaces. To name just a few:

- RESTful HTTP with JSON with OpenAPI
- gRPC
- Thrift
- W3C Web Services (XML/WSDL/SOAP)
- CORBA
- DCOM

Some of these models are very flexible, while others provide more structure. For example, a service that uses gRPC or Thrift defines the name of each RPC method it supports, as well as the types of that method's input and output. By contrast, a free-form RESTful service might accept any HTTP request, while application code validates that the request body is a JSON object with an expected structure.

Frameworks that support user-defined types (such as gRPC, Thrift, and OpenAPI) make it easier to create tooling for features like cross referencing and conformance checks that enhance the discoverability and understandability of an API surface. Such frameworks typically also allow for safer evolution of an API surface over time. For example, OpenAPI has API versioning as a built-in feature. Protocol buffers, used for declaring gRPC interfaces, have well-documented guidelines (*https://oreil.ly/yRUQ3*) on how to update message definitions to retain backward compatibility.

In contrast, an API built on free-form JSON strings can be hard to understand unless you inspect its implementation code and core business logic. This unconstrained approach may lead to security or reliability incidents. For example, if a client and a server are updated independently, they may interpret an RPC payload differently, which could cause one of them to crash.

The lack of an explicit API specification also makes evaluating the security posture of the service difficult. For instance, unless you had access to the API definition, it would be hard to build an automatic security audit system to correlate the policies described in an authorization framework like Istio Authorization Policy (*https://oreil.ly/DjOpK*) with the actual surface area exposed by services.

Prefer interfaces that enforce a common object model

Systems that manage multiple types of resources can benefit from a common object model, such as the model used for Kubernetes (*https://oreil.ly/AtXnp*). Rather than handling each resource type separately, a common object model lets engineers use a single mental model to understand large parts of a system. For example:

- Each object in the system can be guaranteed to satisfy a set of predefined base properties (invariants).
- The system can provide standard ways to scope, annotate, reference, and group objects of all types.
- Operations can have consistent behavior across all types of objects.
- Engineers can create custom object types to support their use cases, and can reason about these object types using the same mental model they use for built-in types.

Google provides general guidelines for designing resource-oriented APIs (*https://oreil.ly/AyMVP*).

Pay attention to idempotent operations

An idempotent operation will yield the same result when applied multiple times. For example, if a person pushes a button for floor two in an elevator, the elevator will go to the second floor every time. Pushing the button again, even multiple times, will not change the outcome.

In distributed systems, idempotency is important because operations may arrive out of order, or a server's response after completing an operation may never reach the client. If an API method is idempotent, a client may retry an operation until it receives a successful result. If a method isn't idempotent, the system may need to use a secondary approach, such as polling the server to see whether a newly created object already exists.

Idempotency also affects engineers' mental models. A mismatch between an API's actual behavior and its expected behavior can lead to unreliable or incorrect results. For example, suppose that a client wants to add a record to a database. Although the request succeeds, the response isn't delivered because of a connection reset. If the client code's authors believe the operation to be idempotent, the client will likely retry the request. But if the operation is not actually idempotent, the system will create a duplicate record.

While nonidempotent operations can be necessary, idempotent operations often lead to a simpler mental model. When an operation is idempotent, engineers (including developers and incident responders) don't need to keep track of when an operation started; they can simply keep trying the operation until they know it succeeds.

Some operations are naturally idempotent, and you can make other operations idempotent by restructuring them. In the preceding example, the database could ask the client to include a unique identifier (e.g., a UUID) with each mutating RPC. If the server receives a second mutation with the same unique identifier, it knows that the operation is a duplicate and can respond accordingly.

Understandable Identities, Authentication, and Access Control

Any system should be able to identify who has access to which resources, especially if the resources are highly sensitive. For example, a payment system auditor needs to understand which insiders have access to customers' personally identifiable information. Typically, systems have authorization and access control policies that limit access of a given entity to a given resource in a given context—in this case, a policy would limit employee access to PII data when credit cards are processed. When this specific access occurs, an auditing framework can log the access. Later, you can automatically analyze the access log, either as part of a routine check or as part of an incident investigation.

Identities

An *identity* is the set of attributes or identifiers that relate to an entity. *Credentials* assert the identity of a given entity. Credentials can take different forms, such as a simple password, an X.509 certificate, or an OAuth2 token. Credentials are typically sent using a defined *authentication protocol*, which access control systems use to identify the entities that access a resource. Identifying entities and choosing a model to identify them can be complex. While it's relatively easy to reason about how the system recognizes human entities (both customers and administrators), large systems need to be able to identify all entities, not just human ones.

Large systems are often composed of a constellation of microservices that call each other, either with or without human involvement. For example, a database service may want to periodically snapshot to a lower-level disk service. This disk service may want to call a quota service to ensure that the database service has sufficient disk quota for the data that needs to be snapshotted. Or, consider a customer authenticating to a food-ordering frontend service. The frontend service calls a backend service, which in turn calls a database to retrieve the customer's food preferences. In general, *active entities* are the set of humans, software components, and hardware components that interact with one another in the system.

Traditional network security practices sometimes use IP addresses as the primary identifier for both access control and logging and auditing (for example, firewall rules). Unfortunately, IP addresses have a number of disadvantages in modern microservices systems. Because they lack stability and security (and are easily spoofable), IP addresses simply don't provide a suitable identifier to identify services and model their level of privilege in the system. For starters, microservices are deployed on pools of hosts, with multiple services hosted on the same host. Ports don't provide a strong identifier, as they can be reused over time or—even worse—arbitrarily chosen by the different services that run on the host. A microservice may also serve different instances running on different hosts, which means you can't use IP addresses as a stable identifier.

Identifier Properties that Benefit Both Security and Reliability

In general, identity and authentication subsystems[8] are responsible for modeling identities and provisioning credentials that represent these identities. In order to be "meaningful," an identity must:

Have understandable identifiers
A human must be able to understand who/what an identifier refers to without having to reference an external source. For example, a number like *24245223* is not very understandable, while a string like *widget-store-frontend-prod* clearly identifies a particular workload. Mistakes in understandable identifiers are also easier to spot—it's much more likely you'll make a mistake when modifying an access control list if the ACL is a string of arbitrary numbers, rather than human-readable names. Malicious intent will be more obvious in human-readable identifiers too, although the administrator controlling the ACL should still be careful to check an identifier when it's added to guard against attackers who use identifiers that look legitimate.

Be robust against spoofing
How you uphold this quality depends on the type of credential (password, token, certificate) and the authentication protocol that backs the identity. For example, a username/password or bearer token used over a clear-text channel is trivially spoofable. It's much harder to spoof a certificate that uses a private key that's backed by a hardware module like a TPM (*https://oreil.ly/2PWij*) and is used in a TLS session.

---

8 There are multiple identity subsystems in the general case. For example, the system may have one identity subsystem for internal microservices and another identity subsystem for human administrators.

Have nonreusable identifiers

> Once an identifier has been used for a given entity, it must not be reused. For example, suppose that a company's access control systems use email addresses as identifiers. If a privileged administrator leaves the company, and a new hire is assigned the administrator's old email address, they could inherit many of the administrator's privileges.

The quality of access control and auditing mechanisms depends on the relevance of the identities used in the system and their trust relationships. Attaching a meaningful identifier to all active entities in a system is a fundamental step for understandability, in terms of both security and reliability. In terms of security, identifiers help you determine who has access to what. In terms of reliability, identifiers help you plan and enforce the use of shared resources like CPU, memory, and network bandwidth.

An organization-wide identity system reinforces a common mental model and means the entire workforce can speak the same language when referring to entities. Having competing identity systems for the same types of entities—for example, coexisting systems of global and local entities—makes comprehension unnecessarily complex for engineers and auditors.

Similar to the external payment processing services in the widget ordering example in Chapter 4, companies can externalize their identity subsystems. OpenID Connect (OIDC) (*https://openid.net/connect*) provides a framework that allows a given provider to assert identities. Rather than implementing its own identity subsystem, the organization is responsible only for configuring which providers it accepts. As with all dependencies, however, there's a tradeoff to consider—in this case, between the simplicity of this model versus the perceived security and reliability robustness of the trusted providers.

Example: Identity model for the Google production system.   Google models identities by using different types of of active entities:

Administrators
> Humans (Google engineers) who can take actions to mutate the state of the system—for example, by pushing a new release or modifying a configuration.

Machines
> Physical machines in a Google datacenter. These machines run the programs that implement our services (like Gmail), along with the services the system itself needs (for example, an internal time service).

Workloads

These are scheduled on machines by the Borg orchestration system, which is similar to Kubernetes.[9] Most of the time, the identity of a workload is different from the identities of the machines it runs on.

Customers

The Google customers who access Google-provided services.

Administrators are at the base of all interactions within the production system. In the case of workload-to-workload interactions, administrators may not actively modify the state of the system, but they initiate the action of starting a workload during the bootstrap phase (which may itself start another workload).

As described in Chapter 5, you can use auditing to trace all actions back to an administrator (or set of administrators), so you can establish accountability and analyze a given employee's level of privilege. Meaningful identities for administrators and the entities they manage make auditing possible.

Administrators are managed by a global directory service integrated with single sign-on. A global group management system can group administrators to represent the concept of teams.

Machines are cataloged in a global inventory service/machine database. On the Google production network, machines are addressable using a DNS name. We also need to tie the machine identity to administrators in order to represent who can modify the software running on the machine. In practice, we usually unite the group that releases the machine's software image with the group that can log on to the machine as root.

Every production machine in Google's datacenters has an identity. The *identity* refers to the typical purpose of the machine. For example, lab machines dedicated to testing have different identities than those running production workloads. Programs like machine management daemons that run core applications on a machine reference this identity.

Workloads are scheduled on machines using an orchestration framework. Each workload has an identity chosen by the requester. The orchestration system is responsible for ensuring that the entity that makes a request has the right to make the request, and specifically that the requestor has the right to schedule a workload running as the requested identity. The orchestration system also enforces constraints on which machines a workload can be scheduled on. Workloads themselves can perform

---

9 For more information on Borg, see Verma, Abhishek et al. 2015. "Large-Scale Cluster Management at Google with Borg." *Proceedings of the European Conference on Computer Systems (EuroSys). https://oreil.ly/zgKsd.*

administrative tasks like group management, but should not have root or admin rights on the underlying machine.

Customer identities also have a specialized identity subsystem. Internally, these identities are used each time a service performs an action on a customer's behalf. *Access control* explains how customer identities work in coordination with workload identities. Externally, Google provides OpenID Connect workflows (*https://oreil.ly/vxJAP*) to allow customers to use their Google identity to authenticate to endpoints not controlled by Google (such as *zoom.us*).

Authentication and transport security

Authentication and transport security are complicated disciplines that require specialized knowledge of areas like cryptography, protocol design, and operating systems. It's not reasonable to expect every engineer to understand all of these topics in depth.

Instead, engineers should be able to understand abstractions and APIs. A system like Google's Application Layer Transport Security (ALTS) (*https://oreil.ly/EsBfd*) provides automatic service-to-service authentication and transport security to applications. That way, application developers don't need to worry about how credentials are provisioned or which specific cryptographic algorithm is used to secure data on the connection.

The mental model for the application developer is simple:

- An application is run as a meaningful identity:
  - A tool on an administrator's workstation to access production typically runs as that administrator's identity.
  - A privileged process on a machine typically runs as that machine's identity.
  - An application deployed as a workload using an orchestration framework typically runs as a workload identity specific to the environment and service provided (such as *myservice-frontend-prod*).
- ALTS provides zero-config transport security on the wire.
- An API for common access control frameworks retrieves authenticated peer information.

ALTS and similar systems—for example, Istio's security model (*https://oreil.ly/17Jm6*)—provide authentication and transport security in an understandable way.

Unless an infrastructure's application-to-application security posture uses a systematic approach, it is difficult or impossible to reason about. For example, suppose that application developers have to make individual choices about the type of credentials to use, and the workload identity these credentials will assert. To verify that the application performs authentication correctly, an auditor would need to manually read all of the application's code. This approach is bad for security—it doesn't scale, and some portion of the code will likely be either unaudited or incorrect.

Access control

Using frameworks to codify and enforce access control policies for incoming service requests is a net benefit for the understandability of the global system. Frameworks reinforce common knowledge and provide a unified way to describe policies, and are thus an important part of an engineer's toolkit.

Frameworks can handle inherently complex interactions, such as the multiple identities involved in transferring data between workloads. For example, Figure 6-1 shows the following:

- A chain of workloads running as three identities: *Ingress*, *Frontend*, and *Backend*
- An authenticated customer making a request

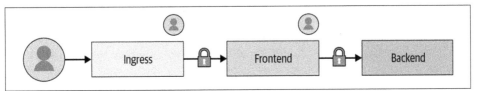

Figure 6-1. Interactions involved in transferring data between workloads

For each link in the chain, the framework must be able to determine whether the workload or the customer is the authority for the request. Policies must also be expressive enough for it to decide which workload identity is allowed to retrieve data on behalf of the customer.

Equipped with one unified way to capture this inherent complexity, the majority of engineers can understand these controls. If each service team had its own ad hoc system for dealing with the same complex use case, understandability would be a challenge.

Frameworks dictate consistency in specifying and applying declarative access control policies. This declarative and unified nature allows engineers to develop tools to evaluate the security exposure of services and user data within the infrastructure. If the access control logic were implemented in an ad hoc fashion at the application code level, developing that tooling would be essentially impossible.

Security Boundaries

The *trusted computing base* (TCB) of a system is "the set of components (hardware, software, human, …) whose correct functioning is sufficient to ensure that the security policy is enforced, or more vividly, whose failure could cause a breach of the security policy."[10] As such, the TCB must uphold the security policy even if any entity *outside* of the TCB misbehaves in arbitrary and possibly malicious ways. Of course, the area outside of the TCB includes your system's external environment (such as malicious actors somewhere across the internet), but this area *also* includes parts of *your own system* that are not within the TCB.

The interface between the TCB and "everything else" is referred to as a *security boundary*. "Everything else"—other parts of the system, the external environment, clients of the system that interact with it via a network, and so on—interacts with the TCB by communicating across this boundary. This communication might be in the form of an interprocess communication channel, network packets, and higher-level protocols built on those foundations (like gRPC). The TCB must treat anything that crosses the security boundary with suspicion—both the data itself and other aspects, like message ordering.

The parts of a system that form a TCB depend upon the security policy you have in mind. It can be useful to think about security policies and the corresponding TCBs necessary to uphold them in layers. For example, the security model of an operating system typically has a notion of "user identity," and provides security policies that stipulate separation between processes running under different users. In Unix-like systems, a process running under user A should not be able to view or modify memory or network traffic associated with a process owned by a different user B.[11] At the software level, the TCB that ensures this property essentially consists of the operating system kernel and all privileged processes and system daemons. In turn, the operating system typically relies on mechanisms provided by the underlying hardware, such as virtual memory. These mechanisms are included in the TCB that pertains to security policies regarding separation between OS-level users.

The software of a network application server (for example, the server exposing a web application or API) is *not* part of the TCB of this OS-level security policy, since it runs under a nonprivileged OS-level role (such as the *httpd* user). However, that application may enforce its own security policy. For example, suppose that a multiuser application has a security policy that makes user data accessible only through explicit document-sharing controls. In that case, the application's code (or portions of it) *is* within the TCB with respect to this application-level security policy.

---

10 Anderson, Ross J. 2008. *Security Engineering: A Guide to Building Dependable Distributed Systems.* Hoboken, NJ: Wiley.

11 This is true unless user A is the root user, as well as under a number of other specific conditions—for example, if shared memory is involved, or if mechanisms such as Linux capabilities confer specific aspects of root's privileges.

To ensure that a system enforces a desired security policy, you have to understand and reason about the entire TCB relevant to that security policy. By definition, a failure or bug in any part of the TCB could result in a breach of the security policy.

Reasoning about a TCB becomes more difficult as the TCB broadens to include more code and complexity. For this reason, it's valuable to keep TCBs as small as possible, and to exclude any components that aren't actually involved in upholding the security policy. In addition to impairing understandability, including these unrelated components in the TCB adds risk: a bug or failure in any of these components could result in a security breach.

Let's revisit our example from Chapter 4: a web application that allows users to buy widgets online. The checkout flow of the application's UI allows users to enter credit card and shipping address information. The system stores some of that information and passes other parts (such as credit card data) to a third-party payment service.

We want to guarantee that only the users themselves can access their own sensitive user data, such as shipping addresses. We'll use $TCB_{AddressData}$ to denote the trusted computing base for this security property.

Using one of the many popular application frameworks, we might end up with an architecture like Figure 6-2.[12]

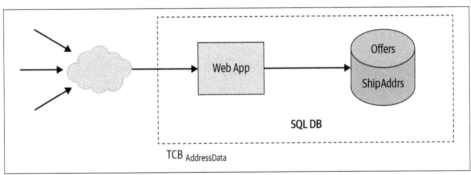

Figure 6-2. Example architecture of an application that sells widgets

In this design, our system consists of a monolithic web application and an associated database. The application might use several modules to implement different features, but they are all part of the same codebase, and the entire application runs as a single server process. Likewise, the application stores all its data in a single database, and all parts of the server have read and write access to the whole database.

---

12 To keep the example simple, Figure 6-2 doesn't show connections to external service providers.

One part of the application handles shopping cart checkout and purchasing, and some parts of the database store information related to purchases. Other parts of the application handle features that are related to purchasing, but that don't themselves depend on purchasing functionality (for example, managing the contents of a shopping cart). Still other parts of the application have nothing to do with purchasing at all (they handle features such as browsing the widget catalog or reading and writing product reviews). Since all of these features are part of a single server, and all of this data is stored in a single database, the entire application and its dependencies—for example, the database server and the OS kernel—are part of the TCB for the security property we want to provide: enforcement of the user data access policy.

Risks include a SQL injection vulnerability in the catalog search code allowing an attacker to obtain sensitive user data, like names or shipping addresses, or a remote code execution vulnerability in the web application server, such as CVE-2010-1870 (*https://oreil.ly/y0xRl*), permitting an attacker to read or modify any part of the application's database.

Small TCBs and strong security boundaries

We can improve the security of our design by splitting the application into microservices. In this architecture, each microservice handles a self-contained part of the application's functionality and stores data in its own separate database. These microservices communicate with each other via RPCs and treat all incoming requests as not necessarily trustworthy, even if the caller is another internal microservice.

Using microservices, we might restructure the application as shown in Figure 6-3.

Instead of a monolithic server, we now have a web application frontend and separate backends for the product catalog and purchasing-related functionality. Each backend has its own separate database.[13] The web frontend never directly queries a database; instead, it sends RPCs to the appropriate backend. For example, the frontend queries the catalog backend to search for items in the catalog or to retrieve the details of a particular item. Likewise, the frontend sends RPCs to the purchasing backend to handle the shopping cart checkout process. As discussed earlier in this chapter, the backend microservice and the database server can rely on workload identity and infrastructure-level authentication protocols like ALTS to authenticate callers and limit requests to authorized workloads.

---

13 In a real-world design, you would likely use a single database with separate groups of tables to which workload identities have been granted appropriate access. This achieves separation of access to data while still allowing the database to ensure data consistency properties across all tables, such as foreign-key constraints between shopping cart contents and catalog items.

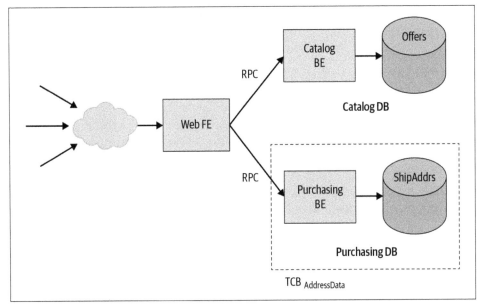

Figure 6-3. Example microservices architecture for widget-selling application

In this new architecture, the trusted computing base for the address data security policy is much smaller: it consists only of the purchasing backend and its database, along with their associated dependencies. An attacker can no longer use a vulnerability in the catalog backend to obtain payment data, since the catalog backend can't access that data in the first place. As a result, this design limits the impact of vulnerabilities in a major system component (a topic discussed further in Chapter 8).

Security boundaries and threat models

A trusted computing base's size and shape will depend on the security property you want to guarantee and the architecture of your system. You can't just draw a dashed line around a component of your system and call it a TCB. You have to think about the component's interface, and the ways in which it might implicitly trust the rest of the system.

Suppose our application allows users to view and update their shipping addresses. Since the purchasing backend handles shipping addresses, that backend needs to expose an RPC method that allows the web frontend to retrieve and update a user's shipping address.

If the purchasing backend allows the frontend to obtain *any* user's shipping address, an attacker who compromises the web frontend can use this RPC method to access or modify sensitive data for any and all users. In other words, if the purchasing backend trusts the web frontend more than it trusts a random third party, then the web frontend is part of the TCB.

Alternatively, the purchasing backend could require the frontend to provide a so-called *end-user context ticket* (EUC) (*https://oreil.ly/0WkhS*) that authenticates a request in the context of a specific external user request. The EUC is an internal short-term ticket that's minted by a central authentication service in exchange for an external-facing credential, such as an authentication cookie or a token (for example, OAuth2) associated with a given request. If the backend provides data only in response to requests with a valid EUC, an attacker who compromises the frontend does *not* have complete access to the purchasing backend, because they can't get EUCs for any arbitrary user. At the worst, they could obtain sensitive data about users who are actively using the application during the attack.

To provide another example that illustrates how TCBs are relative to the threat model under consideration, let's think about how this architecture relates to the security model of the web platform.[14] In this security model, a *web origin* (the fully qualified hostname of the server, plus the protocol and optional port) represents a trust domain: JavaScript running in the context of a given origin can observe or modify any information present in or available to that context. In contrast, browsers restrict access between content and code across different origins based on rules referred to as the *same-origin policy*.

Our web frontend might serve its entire UI from a single web origin, such as *https://widgets.example.com*. This means that, for example, a malicious script injected into our origin via an XSS vulnerability[15] in the catalog display UI can access a user's profile information, and might even be able to "purchase" items in the name of that user. Thus, in a web security threat model, $TCB_{AddressData}$ again includes the entire web frontend.

We can remedy this situation by decomposing the system further and erecting additional security boundaries—in this case, based on web origins. As shown in Figure 6-4, we can operate two separate web frontends: one that implements catalog search and browsing and which serves at *https://widgets.example.com*, and a separate frontend responsible for purchasing profiles and checkout serving at *https://checkout.example.com*.[16] Now, web vulnerabilities such as XSS in the catalog

---

14 Zalewski, Michał. 2012. *The Tangled Web: A Guide to Securing Modern Web Applications*. San Francisco, CA: No Starch Press.

15 See Zalewski, *The Tangled Web*.

16 It's important that we configure our web servers so that the payments frontend is *not* also accessible at, for example, *https://widgets.example.com/checkout*.

UI cannot compromise the payment functionality, because that functionality is segregated into its own web origin.

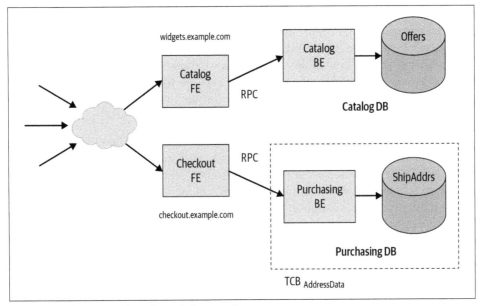

Figure 6-4. Decomposing the web frontend

TCBs and understandability

Aside from their security benefits, TCBs and security boundaries also make systems easier to understand. In order to qualify as a TCB, a component must be isolated from the rest of the system. The component must have a well-defined, clean interface, and you must be able to reason about the correctness of the TCB's implementation in isolation. If the correctness of a component depends on assumptions outside of that component's control, then it's by definition not a TCB.

A TCB is often its own failure domain, which makes understanding how an application might behave in the face of bugs, DoS attacks, or other operational impacts easier. Chapter 8 discusses the benefits of compartmentalizing a system in more depth.

Software Design

Once you've structured a large system into components that are separated by security boundaries, you'll still need to reason about all the code and subcomponents inside a given security boundary, which is often still a rather large and complex piece of software. This section discusses techniques for structuring software to further enable reasoning about invariants at the level of smaller software components, such as modules, libraries, and APIs.

Using Application Frameworks for Service-Wide Requirements

As previously discussed, frameworks can provide pieces of reusable functionality. A given system might have an authentication framework, authorization framework, RPC framework, orchestration framework, monitoring framework, software release framework, and so on. These frameworks can provide a lot of flexibility—often, *too much* flexibility. All the possible combinations of frameworks, and the ways they can be configured, can be overwhelming for the engineers who interact with the service—application and service developers, service owners, SREs, and DevOps engineers alike.

At Google, we've found it useful to create higher-level frameworks to manage this complexity, which we call *application frameworks*. Sometimes these are called *full-stack* or *batteries-included frameworks*. Application frameworks provide a canonical set of subframeworks for individual pieces of functionality, with reasonable default configurations and the assurance that all subframeworks work together. The application framework saves users from having to choose and configure a set of subframeworks.

For example, suppose that an application developer exposes a new service with their favorite RPC framework. They set up authentication using their preferred authentication framework, but forget to configure authorization and/or access control. Functionally, their new service seems to be working fine. But without an authorization policy, their application is dangerously insecure. Any authenticated client (for example, every application in their system) can call this new service at will, violating the principle of least privilege (see Chapter 5). This situation might result in severe security issues—for example, imagine that one method exposed by the service allows the caller to reconfigure all the network switches in a datacenter!

An application framework can avoid this problem by ensuring that every application has a valid authorization policy, and by providing safe defaults by disallowing all clients that aren't explicitly permitted.

In general, application frameworks must provide an opinionated way to enable and configure all the features application developers and service owners need, including (but not limited to) these:

- Request dispatching, request forwarding, and deadline propagation
- User input sanitization and locale detection
- Authentication, authorization, and data access auditing
- Logging and error reporting
- Health management, monitoring, and diagnostics
- Quota enforcement

- Load balancing and traffic management
- Binary and configuration deployments
- Integration, prerelease, and load testing
- Dashboards and alerting
- Capacity planning and provisioning
- Handling of planned infrastructure outages

An application framework addresses reliability-related concerns like monitoring, alerting, load balancing, and capacity planning (see Chapter 12). As such, the application framework allows engineers across multiple departments to speak the same language, thereby increasing understandability and empathy between teams.

Understanding Complex Data Flows

Many security properties rely on assertions about *values* as they flow through a system.

For example, many web services use URLs for various purposes. At first, representing URLs as strings throughout the system seems simple and straightforward. However, an application's code and libraries might make the implicit assumption that URLs are well formed, or that a URL has a specific scheme, such as https. Such code is incorrect (and might harbor security bugs) if it can be invoked with a URL that violates the assumption. In other words, there's an implicit assumption that upstream code that receives inputs from untrustworthy external callers applies correct and appropriate validation.

However, a string-typed value does not carry any explicit assertion as to whether or not it represents a well-formed URL. The "string" type itself confers only that the value is a sequence of characters or code points of a certain length (details depend on the implementation language). Any other assumptions about properties of the value are implicit. Thus, reasoning about the correctness of the downstream code requires understanding of all upstream code, and whether that code actually performs the required validation.

You can make reasoning about properties of data that flows through large, complex systems more tractable by representing the value as a specific data type, whose type contract stipulates the desired property. In a more understandable design, your downstream code consumes the URL not in the form of a basic string type, but rather as a type (implemented, for instance, as a Java class) representing a *well-formed* URL.[17] This type's contract can be enforced by the type's constructors or

---

17 Or more generally, a URL that satisfies specific relevant properties, such as having a particular scheme.

factory functions. For example, a Url.parse(String) factory function would perform runtime validation and either return an instance of Url (representing a well-formed URL) or signal an error or throw an exception for a malformed value.

With this design, understanding code that consumes a URL, and whose correctness relies on its well-formedness, no longer requires understanding all its callers and whether they perform appropriate validation. Instead, you can understand URL handling by understanding two smaller parts. First, you can inspect the Url type's implementation *in isolation*. You can observe that all of the type's constructors ensure well-formedness, and that they guarantee that all instances of the type conform to the type's documented contract. Then, you can *separately* reason about the correctness of the code that consumes the Url-typed value, using the type's contract (i.e., well-formedness) as an assumption in your reasoning.

Using types in this way aids understandability because it can dramatically shrink the amount of code that you have to read and verify. Without types, you have to understand all code that uses URLs, as well as all code that transitively passes URLs to that code in plain string form. By representing URLs as a type, you only have to understand the implementation of data validation inside Url.parse() (and similar constructors and factory functions) and the ultimate uses of Url. You don't need to understand the rest of the application code that merely passes around instances of the type.

In a sense, the type's implementation behaves like a TCB—it's solely responsible for the "all URLs are well-formed" property. However, in commonly used implementation languages, encapsulation mechanisms for interfaces, types, or modules typically do not represent security boundaries. Therefore, you can't treat the internals of a module as a TCB that can stand up to malicious behavior of code outside the module. This is because in most languages, code on the "outside" of a module boundary can nevertheless modify the internal state of the module (for example, by using reflection features or via type casts). Type encapsulation permits you to understand the module's behavior in isolation, but *only under the assumption* that surrounding code was written by nonmalicious developers and that code executes in an environment that hasn't been compromised. This is actually a reasonable assumption in practice; it's normally ensured by organization- and infrastructure-level controls, such as repository access controls, code review processes, server hardening, and the like. But if the assumption doesn't hold true, your security team will need to address the resulting worst-case scenario (see Part IV).

You can use types to reason about more complex properties, too. For example, preventing injection vulnerabilities (such as XSS or SQL injection) depends on appropriately validating or encoding any external and potentially malicious inputs, at some point between when the inputs are received and when they're passed to an injection-prone API.

Asserting that an application is free of injection vulnerabilities requires understanding all code and components involved in passing data from external inputs to so-called *injection sinks* (i.e., APIs that are prone to security vulnerabilities if presented with insufficiently validated or encoded inputs). Such data flows can be very complex in typical applications. It's common to find data flows where values are received by a frontend, passed through one or more layers of microservice backends, persisted in a database, and then later read back and used in the context of an injection sink. A common class of vulnerabilities in such a scenario are so-called *stored XSS* bugs, where untrusted inputs reach an HTML injection sink (such as an HTML template or a browser-side DOM API) via persistent storage, without appropriate validation or escaping. Reviewing and understanding the union of all relevant flows across a large application within a reasonable amount of time is typically well beyond a human's capacity, even if they're equipped with tooling.

One effective way of preventing such injection vulnerabilities to a high degree of confidence is to use types to distinguish values that are known to be safe for use in a specific injection sink context, such as SQL queries or HTML markup:[18]

- Constructors and builder APIs for types such as `SafeSql` or `SafeHtml` are responsible for ensuring that all instances of such types are indeed safe to use in the corresponding sink context (for example, a SQL query API or HTML rendering context). These APIs ensure type contracts through a combination of runtime validation of potentially untrusted values and correct-by-construction API design. Constructors might also rely on more complex libraries, such as fully fledged HTML validators/sanitizers or HTML template systems that apply context-sensitive escaping or validation to data that is interpolated into the template.[19]

- Sinks are modified to accept values of appropriate types. The type contract states that its values are safe to use in the corresponding context, which makes the typed API safe by construction. For example, when using a SQL query API that accepts only values of type `SafeSql` (instead of `String`), you don't have to worry about SQL injection vulnerabilities, since all values of type `SafeSql` are safe to use as a SQL query.

18 See Kern, Christoph. 2014. "Securing the Tangled Web." *Communications of the ACM* 57(9): 38–47. doi: 10.1145/2643134.

19 See Samuel, Mike, Prateek Saxena, and Dawn Song. 2011. "Context-Sensitive Auto-Sanitization in Web Templating Languages Using Type Qualifiers." *Proceedings of the 18th ACM Conference on Computer and Communications Security:* 587–600. doi:10.1145/2046707.2046775.

- Sinks may also accept values of basic types (such as strings), but in this case must not make any assumptions about the value's safety in the sink's injection context. Instead, the sink API is itself responsible for validating or encoding data, as appropriate, to ensure at runtime that the value is safe.

With this design, you can support an assertion that an *entire application* is free of SQL injection or XSS vulnerabilities based *solely* on understanding the implementations of the types and the type-safe sink APIs. You don't need to understand or read any application code that forwards values of these types, since type encapsulation ensures that application code cannot invalidate security-relevant type invariants.[20] You also don't need to understand and review application code that uses the types' safe-by-construction builders to create instances of the types, since those builders were designed to ensure their types' contracts without any assumptions about the behavior of their callers. Chapter 12 discusses this approach in detail.

Considering API Usability

It's a good idea to consider the impact of API adoption and usage on your organization's developers and their productivity. If APIs are cumbersome to use, developers will be slow or reluctant to adopt them. Secure-by-construction APIs have the double benefit of making your code more understandable and allowing developers to focus on the logic of your application, while also automatically building secure approaches into your organization's culture.

Fortunately, it is often possible to design libraries and frameworks such that secure-by-construction APIs are a net benefit for developers, while also promoting a culture of security and reliability (Chapter 21). In return for adopting your secure API, which ideally follows established patterns and idioms that they're already familiar with, your developers gain the benefit of not being responsible for ensuring security invariants related to the API's use.

For example, a contextually autoescaping HTML template system takes full responsibility for correct validation and escaping of all data interpolated into the template. This is a powerful security invariant for the entire application, since it ensures that rendering of any such template cannot result in XSS vulnerabilities, no matter what (potentially malicious) data the template is being fed.

---

20 As noted previously, this assertion holds only under the assumption that the entire codebase of the application is nonmalicious. In other words, the type system is relied upon to uphold invariants in the face of non-malicious mistakes elsewhere in the codebase, but not against actively malicious code that might, for example, use a language's reflection APIs to modify a type's private fields. You can address the latter through additional security mechanisms like code reviews, access controls, and audit trails at the source repository level.

At the same time, from a developer's perspective, using a contextually autoescaping HTML template system is just like using a regular HTML template—you provide data, and the template system interpolates it into placeholders within HTML markup —except you no longer have to worry about adding appropriate escaping or validation directives.

Example: Secure cryptographic APIs and the Tink crypto framework

Cryptographic code is particularly prone to subtle mistakes. Many cryptographic primitives (such as cipher and hash algorithms) have catastrophic failure modes that are difficult for nonexperts to recognize. For example, in certain situations where encryption is combined improperly with authentication (or used without authentication at all), an attacker who can only observe whether a request to a service fails or is accepted can nevertheless use the service as a so-called "decryption oracle" and recover the clear text of encrypted messages.[21] A nonexpert who is not aware of the underlying attack technique has little chance of noticing the flaw: the encrypted data looks perfectly unreadable, and the code is using a standard, recommended, and secure cipher like AES. Nevertheless, because of subtly incorrect usage of the nominally secure cipher, the cryptographic scheme is insecure.

In our experience, code involving cryptographic primitives that was not developed and reviewed by experienced cryptographers commonly has serious flaws. Using crypto correctly is just really, really hard.

Our experience from many security review engagements led Google to develop Tink: a library that enables engineers to use cryptography safely (*https://oreil.ly/7G0mD*) in their applications. Tink was born out of our extensive experience working with Google product teams, fixing vulnerabilities in cryptography implementations, and providing simple APIs that engineers without a cryptographic background can use safely.

Tink reduces the potential for common crypto pitfalls, and provides secure APIs that are easy to use correctly and hard(er) to misuse. The following principles guided Tink's design and development:

Secure by default
    The library provides an API that's hard to misuse. For example, the API does not permit reuse of nonces in Galois Counter Mode—a fairly common but subtle mistake that was specifically called out in RFC 5288 (*https://oreil.ly/3z4CT*), as it allows authentication key recovery that leads to a complete failure of the

---

21 See Rizzo, Juliano, and Thai Duong. 2010. "Practical Padding Oracle Attacks." *Proceedings of the 4th USENIX Conference on Offensive Technologies*: 1–8. *https://oreil.ly/y-OYm*.

AES-GCM mode's authenticity. Thanks to Project Wycheproof (*https://oreil.ly/ 7UhA7*), Tink reuses proven and well-tested libraries.

Usability
The library has a simple and easy-to-use API, so a software engineer can focus on the desired functionality—for example, implementing block and streaming Authenticated Encryption with Associated Data (AEAD) primitives.

Readability and auditability
Functionality is clearly readable in code, and Tink maintains control over employed cryptographic schemes.

Extensibility
It's easy to add new functionality, schemes, and formats—for example, via the registry for key managers.

Agility
Tink has built-in key rotation and supports deprecation of obsolete/broken schemes.

Interoperability
Tink is available in many languages and on many platforms.

Tink also provides a solution for key management, integrating with Cloud Key Management Service (KMS) (*https://oreil.ly/k5A3c*), AWS Key Management Service (*https://oreil.ly/nzkF9*), and Android Keystore (*https://oreil.ly/PUkYz*). Many cryptographic libraries make it easy to store private keys on disk, and make adding private keys to your source code—a practice that's strongly discouraged—even easier. Even if you run "keyhunt" and "password hunt" activities to find and scrub secrets from your codebase and storage systems, it's difficult to eliminate key management–related incidents completely. In contrast, Tink's API does not accept raw key material. Instead, the API encourages use of a key management service.

Google uses Tink to secure the data of many products, and it is now the recommended library for protecting data within Google and when communicating with third parties. By providing abstractions with well-understood properties (such as "authenticated encryption") backed by well-engineered implementations, it allows security engineers to focus on higher-level aspects of cryptographic code without having to be concerned with lower-level attacks on the underlying cryptographic primitives.

It is important to note, however, that Tink cannot prevent higher-level design mistakes in cryptographic code. For example, a software developer without sufficient cryptography background might choose to protect sensitive data by hashing it. This is unsafe if the data in question is from a set that is (in cryptographic terms) relatively modest in size, such as credit card or Social Security numbers. Using a cryptographic hash in such a scenario, instead of authenticated encryption, is a design-level mistake that exhibits itself at a level of granularity above Tink's API. A security reviewer cannot conclude that such mistakes are absent from an application just because the code uses Tink instead of a different crypto library.

Software developers and reviewers must take care to understand what security and reliability properties a library or framework does and does not guarantee. Tink prevents many mistakes that could result in low-level cryptographic vulnerabilities, but does not prevent mistakes based on using the wrong crypto API (or not using crypto at all). Similarly, a secure-by-construction web framework prevents XSS vulnerabilities, but does not prevent security bugs in an application's business logic.

Conclusion

Reliability and security benefit, in a deep and intertwined way, from understandable systems.

Although "reliability" is sometimes treated as synonymous with "availability," this attribute really means upholding all of a system's critical design guarantees—availability, durability, and security invariants, to name a few.

Our primary guidance for building an understandable system is to construct it with components that have clear and constrained purposes. Some of those components may make up its trusted computing base, and therefore concentrate responsibility for addressing security risk.

We also discussed strategies for enforcing desirable properties—such as security invariants, architectural resilience, and data durability—in and between those components. Those strategies include the following:

- Narrow, consistent, typed interfaces
- Consistent and carefully implemented authentication, authorization, and accounting strategies
- Clear assignment of identities to active entities, whether they are software components or human administrators
- Application framework libraries and data types that encapsulate security invariants to ensure that components follow best practices consistently

When your most critical system behaviors are malfunctioning, the understandability of your system can make the difference between a brief incident and a protracted disaster. SREs must be aware of the security invariants of the system in order to do their job. In extreme cases, they may have to take a service offline during a security incident, sacrificing availability for security.

CHAPTER 7

Design for a Changing Landscape

By Maya Kaczorowski, John Lunney, and Deniz Pecel
with Jen Barnason, Peter Duff, and Emily Stark

> Your ability to adapt while fulfilling the service level objectives promised to your users depends on the robustness and flexibility of your service's reliability capabilities. Tools and approaches like frequent builds, releases with automated testing, and containers and microservices will enable you to adapt to short-, medium-, and long-term changes, as well as unexpected complications that arise as you run a service. This chapter also presents multiple examples of how Google has changed and adapted its systems over the years, and the lessons we learned along the way.
>
> While most design decisions—particularly those relating to architecture—are easiest and cheapest to implement in the system design phase, many of the best practices in this chapter can be implemented during later stages of the system lifecycle.

"Change is the only constant" is a maxim[1] that certainly holds true for software: as the number (and variety) of devices we use increases every year, so too does the number of library and application vulnerabilities. Any device or application is potentially susceptible to remote exploit, data leakage, botnet takeover, or other headline-grabbing scenarios.

At the same time, the security and privacy expectations of users and regulators continue to rise, requiring stricter controls like enterprise-specific access restrictions and authentication systems.

---

1 Widely attributed to Heraclitus of Ephesus (*https://oreil.ly/SUdXz*).

To respond to this shifting landscape of vulnerabilities, expectations, and risks, you need to be able to change your infrastructure frequently and quickly, while also maintaining a highly reliable service—not an easy feat. Achieving this balance often boils down to deciding when, and how quickly, to roll out a change.

Types of Security Changes

There are many kinds of changes you might make to improve your security posture or the resilience of your security infrastructure—for example:

- Changes in response to security incidents (see Chapter 18)
- Changes in response to newly discovered vulnerabilities
- Product or feature changes
- Internally motivated changes to improve your security posture
- Externally motivated changes, such as new regulatory requirements

Some types of security-motivated changes require additional considerations. If you're rolling out a feature optionally as a first step toward making it mandatory, you'll need to collect sufficient feedback from early adopters and thoroughly test your initial instrumentation.

If you're considering a change to a dependency—for example, a vendor or third-party code dependency—you'll need to make sure the new solution meets your security requirements.

Designing Your Change

Security changes are subject to the same basic reliability requirements and release engineering principles as any other software changes; for more information, see Chapter 4 in this book and Chapter 8 in the SRE book. The timeline for rolling out security changes may differ (see "Different Changes: Different Speeds, Different Timelines" on page 127), but the overall process should follow the same best practices.

All changes should have the following characteristics:

Incremental
> Make changes that are as small and standalone as possible. Avoid the temptation to tie a change to unrelated improvements, such as refactoring code.

Documented
> Describe both the "how" and the "why" of your change so others can understand the change and the relative urgency of the rollout. Your documentation might include any or all of the following:

- Requirements
- Systems and teams in scope
- Lessons learned from a proof of concept
- Rationale for decisions (in case plans need to be reevaluated)
- Points of contact for all teams involved

Tested

Test your security change with unit tests and—where possible—integration tests (for more information on testing, see Chapter 13). Complete a peer review to gain a measure of confidence that the change will work in production.

Isolated

Use feature flags to isolate changes from one another and avoid release incompatibility; for more information, see Chapter 16 in the SRE workbook. The underlying binary should exhibit no change in behavior when the feature is turned off.

Qualified

Roll out your change with your normal binary release process, proceeding through stages of qualification before receiving production or user traffic.

Staged

Roll out your change gradually, with instrumentation for canarying. You should be able to see differences in behavior before and after your change.

These practices suggest taking a "slow and steady" approach to rollout. In our experience, the conscious tradeoff between speed and safety is worthwhile. You don't want to risk creating a much larger problem like widespread downtime or data loss by rolling out a broken change.

Architecture Decisions to Make Changes Easier

How can you architect your infrastructure and processes to be responsive to the inevitable changes you'll face? Here we discuss some strategies that enable you to flex your system and roll out changes with minimal friction, which also lead to building a culture of security and reliability (discussed in Chapter 21).

Keep Dependencies Up to Date and Rebuild Frequently

Making sure your code points to the latest versions of code dependencies helps make your system less susceptible to new vulnerabilities. Keeping references to dependencies up to date is particularly important for open source projects that change often, like OpenSSL or the Linux kernel. Many large open source projects have well-established security vulnerability response and remediation plans that clarify when a new release contains a critical security patch, and will backport the fix to supported versions. If your dependencies are up to date, it's likely you can apply a critical patch directly instead of needing to merge with a backlog of changes or apply multiple patches.

New releases and their security patches won't make it into your environment until you rebuild. Frequently rebuilding and redeploying your environment means that you'll be ready to roll out a new version when you need to—and that an emergency rollout can pick up the latest changes.

Release Frequently Using Automated Testing

Basic SRE principles recommend cutting and rolling out releases regularly to facilitate emergency changes. By splitting one large release into many smaller ones, you ensure that each release contains fewer changes, which are therefore less likely to require rollback. For a deeper exploration of this topic, see the "virtuous cycle" depicted in Figure 16-1 in the SRE workbook.

When each release contains fewer code changes, it's easier to understand what changed and pinpoint potential issues. When you need to roll out a security change, you can be more confident about the expected outcome.

To take full advantage of frequent releases, automate their testing and validation. This allows good releases to be pushed automatically while preventing deficient releases from reaching production. Automated testing also gives you additional confidence when you need to push out fixes that protect against critical vulnerabilities.

Similarly, by using containers[2] and microservices,[3] you can reduce the surface area you need to patch, establish regular release processes, and simplify your understanding of system vulnerabilities.

Use Containers

Containers decouple the binaries and libraries your application needs from the underlying host OS. Because each application is packaged with its own dependencies and libraries, the host OS does not need to include them, so it can be smaller. As a result, applications are more portable and you can secure them independently. For

---

2 For more information on containers, see the blog post "Exploring Container Security" (*https://oreil.ly/i9DTQ*) by Dan Lorenc and Maya Kaczorowski. See also Burns, Brendan et al. 2016. "Borg, Omega, and Kubernetes: Lessons Learned from Three Container-Management Systems Over a Decade." *ACM Queue* 14(1). *https://oreil.ly/tDKBJ*.

3 For more information on microservices, see "Case Study 4: Running Hundreds of Microservices on a Shared Platform" in Chapter 7 of the SRE book.

example, you can patch a kernel vulnerability in the host operating system without having to change your application container.

Containers are meant to be immutable, meaning they don't change after they're deployed—instead of SSHing into a machine, you rebuild and redeploy the whole image. Because containers are short-lived, they're rebuilt and redeployed quite often.

Rather than patching live containers, you patch the images in your container registry. This means that you can roll out a fully patched container image as one unit, making the patch rollout process the same as your (very frequent) code rollout process— complete with monitoring, canarying, and testing. As a result, you can patch more often.

As these changes roll out to each task, the system seamlessly moves serving traffic to another instance; see "Case Study 4: Running Hundreds of Microservices on a Shared Platform" in Chapter 7 of the SRE book. You can achieve similar results and avoid downtime while patching with blue/green deployments; see Chapter 16 in the SRE workbook.

You can also use containers to detect and patch newly discovered vulnerabilities. Since containers are immutable, they provide content addressability. In other words, you actually know what's running in your environment—for example, which images you've deployed. If you previously deployed a fully patched image that happens to be susceptible to a new vulnerability, you can use your registry to identify the susceptible versions and apply patches, rather than scanning your production clusters directly.

To reduce the need for this kind of ad hoc patching, you should monitor the age of containers running in production and redeploy regularly enough to ensure that old containers aren't running. Similarly, to avoid redeploying older, unpatched images, you should enforce that only recently built containers can be deployed in production.

Use Microservices

An ideal system architecture is easily scalable, provides visibility into system performance, and allows you to manage each potential bottleneck between services in your infrastructure. Using a microservices architecture, you can split workloads into smaller, more manageable units to facilitate maintenance and discovery. As a result, you can independently scale, load balance, and perform rollouts in each microservice, which means you have more flexibility to make infrastructure changes. Since each service handles requests separately, you can use several defenses independently and sequentially, providing defense in depth (see "Defense in Depth" on page 145).

Microservices also naturally facilitate limited or zero trust networking, meaning that your system doesn't inherently trust a service just because it's located in the same network (see Chapter 6). Rather than using a perimeter-based security model with untrusted external versus trusted internal traffic, microservices use a more heterogeneous notion of trust inside the perimeter: internal traffic may have different levels of trust. Current trends are moving toward an increasingly segmented network. As dependence on a single network perimeter, like a firewall, is removed, the network can be further segmented by services. At the extreme end, a network can implement microservice-level segmentation with no inherent trust between services.

A secondary consequence of using microservices is the convergence of security tools, so that some processes, tools, and dependencies can be reused across multiple teams. As your architecture scales, it might make sense to consolidate your efforts to address shared security requirements—for example, by using common cryptographic libraries or common monitoring and alerting infrastructure. That way, you can split critical security services into separate microservices that are updated and managed by a small number of responsible parties. It's important to note that achieving the security advantages of microservices architectures requires restraint to ensure that the services are as simple as possible while still maintaining the desired security properties.

Using a microservices architecture and development process allows teams to address security issues early in the development and deployment lifecycle—when it's less costly to make changes—in a standardized way. As a result, developers can achieve secure outcomes while spending less time on security.

Example: Google's frontend design

Google's frontend design uses microservices to provide resilience and defense in depth.[4] Separating the frontend and backend into different layers has many advantages: Google Front End (GFE) serves as a frontend layer to most Google services, implemented as a microservice, so these services aren't directly exposed to the internet. GFE also terminates traffic for incoming HTTP(S), TCP, and TLS proxies; provides DDoS attack countermeasures; and routes and load balances traffic to Google Cloud services.[5]

GFE allows for independent partitioning of frontend and backend services, which has benefits in terms of scalability, reliability, agility, and security:

- Global load balancing helps move traffic between GFE and backends. For example, we can redirect traffic during a datacenter outage, reducing mitigation time.
- Backend and frontend layers can have several layers within themselves. Because each layer is a microservice, we can load balance each layer. As a result, it's relatively easy to add capacity, make general changes, or apply rapid changes to each microservice.

---

4 See Chapter 2 in the SRE book.

5 See the "Encryption in Transit in Google Cloud" whitepaper (*https://oreil.ly/kZQNh*) for more information.

- If a service becomes overloaded, GFE can serve as a mitigation point by dropping or absorbing connections before the load reaches the backends. This means that not every layer in a microservices architecture needs its own load protection.

- Adoption of new protocols and security requirements is relatively straightforward. GFE can handle IPv6 connections even if some backends aren't yet ready for them. GFE also simplifies certificate management by serving as the termination point for various common services, like SSL.[6] For example, when a vulnerability (*https://oreil.ly/XDPI2*) was discovered in the implementation of SSL renegotiations, GFE's control for limiting these renegotiations protected all the services behind it. Rapid Application Layer Transport Security (*https://oreil.ly/IRkjI*) encryption adoption also illustrates how a microservices architecture facilitates change adoption: Google's security team integrated the ALTS library into its RPC library to handle service credentials, which enabled wide adoption without a significant burden on individual development teams.

In today's cloud world, you can achieve benefits similar to those described here by using a microservices architecture, building layers of security controls, and managing cross-service communications with a service mesh. For example, you might separate request processing from the configuration for managing request processing. The industry refers to this type of deliberate split as *separation of the data plane* (the requests) *and the control plane* (the configuration). In this model, the data plane provides the actual data processing in the system, typically handling load balancing, security, and observability. The control plane provides policy and configuration to the data plane services, thereby providing a manageable and scalable control surface.

Different Changes: Different Speeds, Different Timelines

Not all changes occur on the same timelines or at the same speed. Several factors influence how quickly you might want to make a change:

Severity
> Vulnerabilities are discovered every day, but not all of them are critical, actively being exploited, or applicable to your particular infrastructure. When you *do* hit that trifecta, you likely want to release a patch as soon as possible. Accelerated timelines are disruptive and more likely to break systems. Sometimes speed is necessary, but it's generally safer for a change to happen slowly so you can ensure sufficient product security and reliability. (Ideally, you can apply a critical security patch independently—that way, you can apply the patch quickly without unnecessarily accelerating any other in-flight rollouts.)

---

6 Ibid.

Dependent systems and teams

Some system changes may be dependent on other teams that need to implement new policies or enable a particular feature prior to rollout. Your change may also depend on an external party—for example, if you need to receive a patch from a vendor, or if clients need to be patched before your server.

Sensitivity

The sensitivity of your change may affect when you can deploy it to production. A nonessential change that improves an organization's overall security posture isn't necessarily as urgent as a critical patch. You can roll out that nonessential change more gradually—for example, team by team. Depending on other factors, making the change may not be worth the risk—for example, you may not want to roll out a nonurgent change during critical production windows like a holiday shopping event, where changes are otherwise tightly controlled.

Deadline

Some changes have a finite deadline. For example, a regulatory change might have a specified compliance date, or you may need to apply a patch before a news embargo (see the following sidebar) disclosing a vulnerability drops.

Embargoed Vulnerabilities

Known vulnerabilities that haven't been disclosed via public announcement can be tricky to handle. Information that's *under embargo* can't be released before a certain date, which might be the date that a patch is going to be made available or rolled out, or the date a researcher plans to disclose the issue.

If you are privy to information about a vulnerability under embargo, and rolling out a patch would break the embargo, you must wait for a public announcement before you can patch along with the rest of the industry. If you're involved in incident response prior to the announcement of a vulnerability, work with other parties to agree on an announcement date that suits the rollout processes of most organizations —for example, a Monday.

There is no hard-and-fast rule for determining the speed of a particular change—a change that requires a quick configuration change and rollout in one organization may take months in another organization. While a single team may be able to make a given change according to a specific timeline, there may be a long tail for your organization to fully adopt the change.

In the following sections, we discuss three different time horizons for change and include examples to show what each has looked like at Google:

- A short-term change in reaction to a new security vulnerability
- A medium-term change, where new product adoption could happen gradually
- A long-term change for regulatory reasons, where Google had to build new systems in order to implement the change

Short-Term Change: Zero-Day Vulnerability

Newly discovered vulnerabilities often require short-term action. A *zero-day vulnerability* is one that is known by at least some attackers, but that hasn't been disclosed publicly or discovered by the targeted infrastructure provider. Typically, a patch either isn't available yet or hasn't been widely applied.

There are a variety of ways to find out about new vulnerabilities that might affect your environment, including regular code reviews, internal code scanning (see "Sanitize Your Code" on page 267), fuzzing (see "Fuzz Testing" on page 280), external scans like penetration tests and infrastructure scans, and bug bounty programs.

In the context of short-term changes, we'll focus on vulnerabilities where Google learned about the vulnerability on day zero. Although Google is often involved in embargoed vulnerability responses—for example, when developing patches—a short-term change for a zero-day vulnerability is common behavior for most organizations in the industry.

 Although zero-day vulnerabilities get a lot of attention (both externally and within the organization), they're not necessarily the vulnerabilities that are most exploited by attackers. Before you tackle a same-day zero-day vulnerability response, make sure you're patched for the "top hits" to cover critical vulnerabilities from recent years.

When you discover a new vulnerability, triage it to determine its severity and impact. For example, a vulnerability that allows remote code execution may be considered critical. But the impact to your organization might be very difficult to determine: Which systems use this particular binary? Is the affected version deployed in production? Where possible, you'll also want to establish ongoing monitoring and alerting to determine if the vulnerability is being actively exploited.

To take action, you need to obtain a *patch*—a new version of the affected package or library with a fix applied. Begin by verifying that the patch actually addresses the vulnerability. It can be useful to do this using a working exploit. However, be aware that even if you can't trigger the vulnerability with the exploit, your system might still be vulnerable (recall that the absence of evidence is not evidence of absence). For example, the patch you've applied might address only one possible exploit of a larger class of vulnerabilities.

Once you've verified your patch, roll it out—ideally in a test environment. Even on an accelerated timeline, a patch should be rolled out gradually like any other production change—using the same testing, canarying, and other tools—on the order of hours or days.[7] A gradual rollout allows you to catch potential issues early, as the patch may have an unexpected effect on your applications. For example, an application using an API you were unaware of may impact performance characteristics or cause other errors.

Sometimes you can't directly fix the vulnerability. In this case, the best course of action is to mitigate the risk by limiting or otherwise restricting access to the vulnerable components. This mitigation may be temporary until a patch is available, or permanent if you can't apply the patch to your system—for example, because of performance requirements. If suitable mitigations are already in place to secure your environment, you may not even need to take any further action.

For more details on incident response, see Chapter 17.

Example: Shellshock

On the morning of September 24, 2014, Google Security learned about a publicly disclosed (*https://oreil.ly/mQFJj*), remotely exploitable vulnerability in bash (*https://oreil.ly/qbTqD*) that trivially allowed code execution on affected systems. The vulnerability disclosure was quickly followed by exploits in the wild, starting the same day.

The original report (*https://oreil.ly/4l2W4*) had some muddled technical details and didn't clearly address the status of the embargo on discussing the issue. This report, in addition to the rapid discovery of several similar vulnerabilities, caused confusion about the nature and exploitability of the attack. Google's Incident Response team initiated its Black Swan protocol to address an exceptional vulnerability and coordinated a large-scale response (*https://oreil.ly/v6DeI*) to do the following:[8]

- Identify the systems in scope and the relative risk level for each
- Communicate internally to all teams that were potentially affected
- Patch all vulnerable systems as quickly as possible
- Communicate our actions, including remediation plans, externally to partners and customers

---

7 See the discussion of gradual and staged rollouts in Chapter 27 of the SRE book.

8 See also the YouTube video (*https://oreil.ly/boGtL*) of the panel discussion about this event.

We were not aware of the issue before public disclosure, so we treated it as a zero-day vulnerability that necessitated emergency mitigation. In this case, a patched version of bash was already available.

The team assessed the risk to different systems and acted accordingly:

- We deemed a huge number of Google production servers to be low risk. These servers were easy to patch with an automated rollout. Once servers passed sufficient validation and testing, we patched them much faster than usual, rather than in long phases.
- We deemed a large number of Googler workstations to be higher risk. Fortunately, these workstations were easy to patch quickly.
- A small number of nonstandard servers and inherited infrastructure were deemed high risk and needed manual intervention. We sent notifications to each team detailing the follow-up actions they were required to take, which allowed us to scale the effort to multiple teams and easily track progress.

In parallel, the team developed software to detect vulnerable systems within Google's network perimeter. We used this software to complete the remaining patch work needed, and added this functionality to Google's standard security monitoring.

What we did (and didn't) do well during this response effort offers a number of lessons for other teams and organizations:

- *Standardize software distribution to the greatest extent possible*, so that patching is the easy and simple choice for remediation. This also requires service owners to understand and accept the risk of choosing a nonstandard, nonsupported distribution. A service owner should be responsible for maintaining and patching an alternative option.
- *Use public distribution standards*—ideally, the patch you need to roll out will already be in the right format. That way, your team can start validating and testing the patch quickly, rather than needing to rework the patch to address your specific environment.
- *Ensure that you can accelerate your mechanism to push changes for emergency changes* like zero-day vulnerabilities. This mechanism should allow for faster than usual validation before full rollout to the affected systems. We don't necessarily recommend that you skip validating that your environment still functions —you must balance this step against the need to mitigate the exploit.
- *Make sure that you have monitoring to track the progress of your rollout, that you identify unpatched systems, and that you identify where you're still vulnerable.* If you already have tooling to identify whether a vulnerability is currently being

exploited in your environment, it may help you decide to slow down or speed up based on your current risk.

- *Prepare external communications as early in your response efforts as possible.* You don't want to get bogged down in internal PR approvals when the media is calling for a response.

- *Draft a reusable incident or vulnerability response plan* (see Chapter 17) ahead of time, including language for external communications. If you're not sure what you need, start with the postmortem of a previous event.

- *Know which systems are nonstandard or need special attention.* By keeping track of outliers, you'll know which systems might need proactive notifications and patching assistance. (If you standardize software distribution per our advice in bullet one, outliers should be limited.)

Medium-Term Change: Improvement to Security Posture

Security teams often implement changes to improve an environment's overall security posture and reduce risk. These proactive changes are driven by internal and external requirements and deadlines, and rarely need to be rolled out suddenly.

When planning for changes to your security posture, you need to figure out which teams and systems are affected and determine the best place to start. Following the SRE principles outlined in "Designing Your Change" on page 122, put together an action plan for gradual rollout. Each phase should include success criteria that must be met before moving to the next phase.

Systems or teams affected by security changes can't necessarily be represented as a percentage of a rollout. You can instead phase a rollout according to who is affected and what changes should be made.

In terms of who is affected, roll out your change group by group, where a group might be a development team, system, or set of end users. For example, you might begin by rolling out a change for device policies to users who are frequently on the road, like your sales team. Doing so allows you to quickly test the most common cases and obtain real-world feedback. There are two competing philosophies when it comes to rollout populations:

- Start with the easiest use case, where you'll get the most traction and prove value.
- Start with the hardest use case, where you'll find the most bugs and edge cases.

When you're still seeking buy-in from the organization, it makes sense to start with the easiest use case. If you have leadership support and investment up front, it's more valuable to find implementation bugs and pain points early on. In addition to organizational concerns, you should consider which strategy will lead to the greatest risk reduction, both in the short and the long term. In all cases, a successful proof of concept helps determine how to best move forward. The team making the change should also have to live through it, "eating their own dogfood," so that they understand the user experience.

You might also be able to roll out the change itself incrementally. For example, you may be able to implement progressively more stringent requirements, or the change could initially be opt-in, rather than mandatory. Where possible, you should also consider rolling out a change as a dry run in an alerting or auditing mode before switching to an enforcement mode—that way, users can experience how they'll be affected before the change is mandatory. This allows you to find users or systems that you've improperly identified as in scope, as well as users or systems for whom achieving compliance will be particularly difficult.

Example: Strong second-factor authentication using FIDO security keys

Phishing is a significant security concern at Google. Although we have widely implemented second-factor authentication using one-time passwords (OTPs), OTPs are still susceptible to interception as part of a phishing attack. We assume that even the most sophisticated users are well intentioned and well prepared to deal with phishing, but still susceptible to account takeovers due to confusing user interfaces or user error. To address this risk, starting in 2011, we investigated and tested several stronger two-factor authentication (2FA) methods.[9] We eventually chose universal two-factor (U2F) hardware security tokens because of their security and usability properties. Implementing security keys for Google's large and globally distributed employee population required building custom integrations and coordinating en masse enrollment.

Evaluating potential solutions and our final choice was part of the change process itself. Up front, we defined security, privacy, and usability requirements. We then validated potential solutions with users to understand what was changing, get real-world feedback, and measure the impact of the change on day-to-day workflows.

In addition to security and privacy requirements, the potential solution had to meet usability requirements to facilitate seamless adoption, also critical for building a culture of security and reliability (see Chapter 21). 2FA needed to be easy—fast and "brainless" enough to make using it incorrectly or insecurely difficult. This requirement was particularly critical for SREs—in case of outages, 2FA couldn't slow down response processes. Additionally, internal developers needed to be able to easily integrate the 2FA solution into their websites through simple APIs. In terms of ideal

---

9 See Lang, Juan et al. 2016. "Security Keys: Practical Cryptographic Second Factors for the Modern Web." *Proceedings of the 2016 International Conference on Financial Cryptography and Data Security*: 422–440. *https://oreil.ly/S2ZMU*.

usability requirements, we wanted an efficient solution that scaled for users across multiple accounts and didn't entail additional hardware, and that was physically effortless, easy to learn, and easy to recover if lost.

After evaluating several options, we co-designed FIDO security keys (*https://oreil.ly/UHbVu*). Though these keys did not meet all of our ideal requirements, in initial pilots security keys decreased the total authentication time and had a negligible authentication failure rate.

Once we had a solution, we had to roll out security keys to all users and deprecate OTP support across Google. We began rolling out the security keys in 2013. To ensure wide adoption, enrollment was self-service:

- Initially, many users opted into security keys voluntarily because the keys were simpler to use than the existing OTP tools—they didn't have to type in a code from their phone or use a physical OTP device. Users were given "nano" security keys that could stay in the USB drives of their laptops.

- To obtain a security key, a user could go to any TechStop location in any office.[10] (Distributing the devices to global offices was complicated, requiring legal teams for export compliance and customs import requirements.)

- Users enrolled their security keys via a self-service registration website. Tech-Stops provided assistance for the very first adopters and people who needed additional help. Users needed to use the existing OTP system the first time they authenticated, so keys were trusted on first use (TOFU).

- Users could enroll multiple security keys so they wouldn't need to worry about losing their key. This approach increased the overall cost, but was strongly aligned with our goal of not making the user carry additional hardware.

The team did encounter some issues, like out-of-date firmware, during rollout. When possible, we approached these issues in a self-service manner—for example, by allowing users to update security key firmware themselves.

Making security keys accessible to users was only half the problem, though. Systems using OTPs also needed to convert to using security keys. In 2013, many applications did not natively support this recently developed technology. The team first focused on supporting applications used daily by Googlers, like internal code review tools and dashboards. Where security keys were not supported (for example, in the case of some hardware device certificate management and third-party web applications), Google worked directly with the vendor to request and add support. We then had to deal with the long tail of applications. Since all OTPs were centrally generated, we

---

10 TechStops are Google's IT helpdesks, described in a blog post (*https://oreil.ly/BWn0-*) by Jesus Lugo and Lisa Mauck.

could figure out which application to target next by tracking the clients making OTP requests.

In 2015, the team focused on completing the rollout and deprecating the OTP service. We sent users reminders when they used an OTP instead of a security key, and eventually blocked access via OTP. Though we had dealt with most of the long tail of OTP application needs, there were still a few exceptions, such as mobile device setup. For these cases, we created a web-based OTP generator for exceptional circumstances. Users were required to verify their identity with their security key—a reasonable failure mode with a slightly higher time burden. We successfully completed the company-wide rollout of security keys in 2015.

This experience provided several generally applicable lessons, relevant for building a culture of security and reliability (see Chapter 21):

Make sure the solution you choose works for all users.
It was critical that the 2FA solution was accessible so that visually impaired users weren't excluded.

Make the change easy to learn and as effortless as possible.
This especially applies if the solution is more user-friendly than the initial situation! This is particularly important for an action or change you expect a user to perform frequently, where a little bit of friction can lead to a significant user burden.

Make the change self-service in order to minimize the burden on a central IT team.
For a widespread change that affects all users in everyday activities, it is important that they can easily enroll, unenroll, and troubleshoot issues.

Give the user tangible proof that the solution works and is in their best interest.
Clearly explain the impact of the change in terms of security and risk reduction, and provide an opportunity for them to offer feedback.

Make the feedback loop on policy noncompliance as fast as possible.
This feedback loop can be an authentication failure, a system error, or an email reminder. Letting the user know that their action was not in line with the desired policy within minutes or hours allows them to take action to fix the issue.

Track progress and determine how to address the long tail.
By examining user requests for OTPs by application, we could identify which applications to focus on next. Use dashboards to track progress and identify whether alternative solutions with similar security properties can work for the long tail of use cases.

Long-Term Change: External Demand

In some situations, you either have or need much more time to roll out a change—for example, an internally driven change that requires significant architectural or system changes, or a broader industry-wide regulatory change. These changes may be motivated or restricted by external deadlines or requirements, and might take several years to implement.

When taking on a massive, multiyear effort, you need to clearly define and measure progress against your goal. Documentation is particularly critical, both to ensure you take necessary design considerations into account (see "Designing Your Change" on page 122) and to maintain continuity. Individuals working on the change today might leave the company and need to hand off their work. Keeping documentation up to date with the latest plan and status is important for sustaining ongoing leadership support.

To measure ongoing progress, establish appropriate instrumentation and dashboarding. Ideally, a configuration check or test can measure a change automatically, removing the need to have a human in the loop. Just as you strive for significant test coverage for code in your infrastructure, you should aim for compliance check coverage for systems affected by the change. To scale this coverage effectively, this instrumentation should be self-serve, allowing teams to implement both the change and the instrumentation. Tracking these results transparently helps motivate users and simplifies communications and internal reporting. Rather than duplicating work, you should also use this single source of truth for executive communications.

Conducting any large-scale, long-term change in an organization while maintaining continued leadership support is difficult. To sustain momentum over time, the individuals making these changes need to stay motivated. Establishing finite goals, tracking progress, and demonstrating significant examples of impact can help teams finish the marathon. Implementation will always have a long tail, so figure out a strategy that makes the most sense for your situation. If a change is not required (by regulation, or for other reasons), achieving 80% or 90% adoption can have a measurable impact on reducing security risk, and should therefore be considered a success.

Example: Increasing HTTPS usage

HTTPS adoption on the web has increased dramatically in the last decade, driven by the concerted efforts of the Google Chrome team, Let's Encrypt (*https://letsen crypt.org*), and other organizations. HTTPS provides important confidentiality and integrity guarantees for users and websites, and is critical to the web ecosystem's success—it's now required as part of HTTP/2.

To promote HTTPS use across the web, we conducted extensive research to build a strategy, contacted site owners using a variety of outreach channels, and set up powerful incentives for them to migrate. Long-term, ecosystem-wide change requires a thoughtful strategy and significant planning. We used a data-driven approach to determine the best way to reach each stakeholder group:

- We gathered data about current HTTPS usage worldwide to select target regions.
- We surveyed end users to understand how they perceived the HTTPS UI in browsers.
- We measured site behavior to identify web platform features that could be restricted to HTTPS to protect user privacy.
- We used case studies to understand developer concerns about HTTPS and the types of tooling we could build to help.

This wasn't a one-time effort: we continued to monitor metrics and gather data over a multiyear period, adjusting our strategy when necessary. For example, as we gradually rolled out Chrome warnings for insecure pages over a period of years, we monitored user behavior telemetry to ensure that the UI changes didn't cause unexpected negative effects (for example, a dip in retention or engagement with the web).

Overcommunicating was key to success. Before each change, we used every available outreach channel: blogs, developer mailing lists, press, Chrome help forums, and relationships with partners. This approach maximized our reach so site owners weren't surprised that they were being pushed to move to HTTPS. We also tailored our outreach regionally—for example, devoting special attention to Japan when we realized that HTTPS adoption was lagging there because of slow uptake among top sites.

Ultimately, we focused on creating and emphasizing incentives to provide a business reason to migrate to HTTPS. Even security-minded developers had trouble convincing their organizations unless they could tie the migration to a business case. For example, enabling HTTPS allows websites to use web platform features like Service Worker (*https://oreil.ly/W5t4I*), a background script that enables offline access, push notifications, and periodic background sync. Such features, which are restricted to HTTPS websites, improve performance and availability—and may have a direct impact on a business's bottom line. Organizations were more willing to devote resources to moving to HTTPS when they felt that the move was aligned with their business interests.

As shown in Figure 7-1, Chrome users across platforms now spend over 90% of their time on HTTPS sites, whereas previously this figure was as low as 70% for Chrome users on Windows and 37% for Chrome on Android. Countless people from many organizations—web browser vendors, certificate authorities, and web publishers—contributed to this increase. These organizations coordinated through standards bodies, research conferences, and open communication about the challenges and successes that each faced. Chrome's role in this shift produced important lessons about contributing to ecosystem-wide change:

Understand the ecosystem before committing to a strategy.
> We based our strategy on quantitative and qualitative research, focusing on a broad set of stakeholders including web developers and end users in different countries and on different devices.

Overcommunicate to maximize reach.
> We used a variety of outreach channels to reach the widest range of stakeholders.

Tie security changes to business incentives.
> Organizational leaders were more amenable to HTTPS migration when they could see the business reasons.

Build an industry consensus.
> Multiple browser vendors and organizations supported the web's migration to HTTPS simultaneously; developers saw HTTPS as an industry-wide trend.

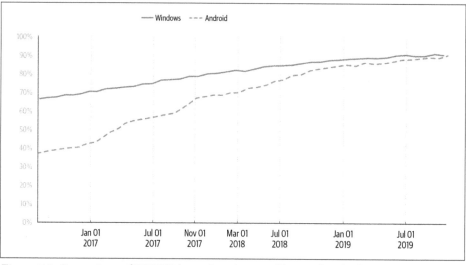

Figure 7-1. Percentage of HTTPS browsing time on Chrome by platform

Complications: When Plans Change

The best-laid plans of security and SRE often go awry. There are many reasons you may either need to accelerate a change or slow it down.

Often, you need to accelerate a change based upon external factors—typically, due to a vulnerability that's actively being exploited. In this case, you might want to speed up your rollout to patch your systems as quickly as possible. Be cautious: speeding up and breaking systems isn't necessarily better for the security and reliability of your systems. Consider whether you can change the order of rollouts to cover certain higher-risk systems sooner, or otherwise remove attackers' access by rate limiting operations or taking a particularly critical system offline.

You may also decide to slow down a change. This approach is usually due to an issue with a patch, such as a higher than expected error rate or other rollout failures. If slowing down a change doesn't address the issue, or you can't roll out fully without negatively impacting your system or users, then rolling back, debugging the issue, and rolling out again is a painful but cautious approach. You may also be able to slow down a change based on updated business requirements—for example, changes to internal deadlines or delays in industry standards. (What do you mean, TLS 1.0 is still in use?!)

In the best-case scenario, your plans change before you start implementing them. In response, you just need to create new plans! Here are some potential reasons to change your plans, and corresponding tactics for doing so:

You might need to delay a change based on external factors.
> If you're not able to start patching as soon as the embargo lifts (see "Different Changes: Different Speeds, Different Timelines" on page 127), work with the vulnerability team to see if any other systems are in your situation, and if it's possible to change the timeline. Either way, make sure you have communications ready to inform affected users of your plan.

You might need to speed up a change based on a public announcement.
> For a vulnerability under embargo, you may have to wait for a public announcement before patching. Your timeline might change if the announcement leaks, if an exploit is made publicly available, or if the vulnerability is exploited in the wild. In this case, you'll want to start patching sooner rather than later. You should have an action plan at every stage for what to do if the embargo is broken.

You might not be severely impacted.
> If a vulnerability or change primarily affects public web-facing services, and your organization has a very limited number of such services, you probably don't need to rush to patch your entire infrastructure. Patch what's affected, and slow down the rate at which you apply patches to other areas of your system.

You might be dependent on external parties.
> Most organizations depend on third parties to distribute patched packages and images for vulnerabilities, or rely on software and hardware delivery as part of an infrastructure change. If a patched OS isn't available or the hardware you need is on backorder, there's likely not much you can do. You'll probably have to start your change later than originally intended.

Example: Growing Scope—Heartbleed

In December 2011, support for SSL/TLS's heartbeat feature was added to OpenSSL, along with an unrecognized bug (*https://xkcd.com/1354*) that allowed a server or client to access 64 KB of another server or client's private memory. In April 2014, the bug was codiscovered by a Googler, Neel Mehta, and an engineer working for Codenomicon (a cybersecurity company); both reported it to the OpenSSL project. The OpenSSL team committed a code change to fix the bug and formulated a plan to publicly disclose it. In a move that surprised many in the security community, Codenomicon made a public announcement and launched the explanatory website *heartbleed.com*. This first use of a clever name and logo caused unexpectedly large media interest.

With early access to the patch, which was under embargo, and ahead of the planned public disclosure, Google infrastructure teams had already quietly patched a small number of key externally facing systems that directly handled TLS traffic. However, no other internal teams knew about the issue.

Once the bug became publicly known, exploits were developed quickly in frameworks such as Metasploit (*https://www.metasploit.com*). Facing an accelerated timeline, many more Google teams now needed to patch their systems in a hurry. Google's security team used automated scanning to uncover additional vulnerable systems, and notified affected teams with instructions to patch and to track their progress. The memory disclosure meant that private keys could be leaked, which meant that a number of services needed key rotation. The security team notified affected teams and tracked their progress in a central spreadsheet.

Heartbleed illustrates a number of important lessons:

Plan for the worst-case scenario of the embargo breaking or being lifted early.
> While responsible disclosure is ideal, accidents (and cute logos that spur media interest) can happen. Do as much pre-work as possible, and move quickly to patch the most vulnerable systems regardless of disclosure agreements (which necessitate internal secrecy about embargoed information). If you can obtain a patch ahead of time, you may be able to deploy it before a public announcement. When that isn't possible, you should still be able to test and validate your patch to ensure a smooth rollout process.

Prepare for rapid deployment at scale.
> Use continuous builds to ensure you can recompile anytime, with a canary strategy to validate without destruction.

Regularly rotate your encryption keys and other secrets.

Key rotation (*https://oreil.ly/TFb4b*) is a best practice to limit the potential blast radius of a key compromise. Practice this operation regularly and confirm that your systems still work as intended; see Chapter 9 in the SRE workbook for details. By doing so, you ensure that swapping out any compromised keys won't be a Herculean effort.

Make sure you have a communication channel to your end users—both internal and external.

When a change fails or causes unexpected behavior, you need to be able to provide updates quickly.

Conclusion

Distinguishing between different kinds of security changes is critically important so that affected teams know what's expected of them and how much support you can offer.

Next time you're tasked with making a security change in your infrastructure, take a deep breath and create a plan. Start small or find volunteers willing to test the change. Have a feedback loop to understand what's not working for users, and make the change self-service. If plans change, don't panic—just don't be surprised, either.

Design strategies such as frequent rollouts, containerization, and microservices make both proactive improvements and emergency mitigation easier, while a layered approach makes for few and well-managed external surface areas. Thoughtful design and ongoing documentation, both with an eye toward change, keep your system healthy, make your team's workload more manageable, and—as you'll see in the next chapter—lead to greater resilience.

CHAPTER 8

Design for Resilience

By Vitaliy Shipitsyn, Mitch Adler,
Zoltan Egyed, and Paul Blankinship
with Jesus Climent, Jessie Yang,
Douglas Colish, and Christoph Kern

Good system design includes planning for *resilience*: the ability to protect against attacks and to withstand unusual circumstances that stress your system and affect its reliability.

Early in the design phase, you should think about how to keep the system completely or partially running when you face multiple simultaneous incidents.

We start this chapter with a story from the ancient world, where defense in depth might have saved an empire. Then we look at modern-day defense-in-depth strategies, with an example from Google App Engine.

The solutions covered in this chapter have different implementation costs and vary in appropriateness for different sizes of organizations. If you're a smaller organization, we suggest focusing on controlled degradation, establishing blast radius controls, and segmenting systems into separate failure domains. As your organization grows, we suggest using continuous validation to confirm and enhance your system's resilience.

As a part of system design, "resilience" describes the system's ability to hold out against a major malfunction or disruption. Resilient systems can recover automatically from failures in parts of the system—or possibly the failure of the entire system—and return to normal operations after the problems are addressed. Services in a resilient system ideally remain running throughout an incident, perhaps in a degraded mode. Designing resilience into every layer of a system's design helps defend that system against unanticipated failures and attack scenarios.

Designing a system for resilience is different from designing for recovery (covered in depth in Chapter 9). Resilience is closely tied to recovery, but while recovery focuses on the ability to fix systems *after* they break, resilience is about designing systems that *delay* or *withstand* breakage. Systems designed with a focus on both resilience and recovery are better able to recover from failures, and require minimal human intervention.

Design Principles for Resilience

A system's resilience properties are built on the design principles discussed earlier in Part II. In order to evaluate a system's resilience, you must have a good understanding of how that system is designed and built. You need to align closely with other design qualities covered in this book—least privilege, understandability, adaptability, and recovery—to strengthen your system's stability and resilience attributes.

The following approaches, each of which this chapter explores in depth, characterize a resilient system:

- Design each layer in the system to be independently resilient. This approach builds defense in depth with each layer.

- Prioritize each feature and calculate its cost, so you understand which features are critical enough to attempt to sustain no matter how much load the system experiences, and which features are less important and can be throttled or disabled when problems arise or resources are constrained. You can then determine where to apply the system's limited resources most effectively, and how to maximize the system's serving capabilities.

- Compartmentalize the system along clearly defined boundaries to promote the independence of the isolated functional parts. This way, it's also easier to build complementary defense behaviors.

- Use compartment redundancy to defend against localized failures. For global failures, have some compartments provide different reliability and security properties.

- Reduce system reaction time by automating as many of your resilience measures as you can safely. Work to discover new failure modes that could benefit either from new automation or improvements to existing automation.

- Maintain the effectiveness of the system by validating its resilience properties—both its automated response and any other resilience attributes of the system.

Defense in Depth

Defense in depth protects systems by establishing multiple layers of defense perimeters. As a result, attackers have limited visibility into the systems, and successful exploits are harder to launch.

The Trojan Horse

The story of the Trojan Horse, as told by Virgil in the *Aeneid*, is a cautionary tale about the dangers of an inadequate defense. After 10 fruitless years besieging the city of Troy, the Greek army constructs a large wooden horse that it presents as a gift to the Trojans. The horse is brought within the walls of Troy, and attackers hiding inside the horse burst forth, exploit the city's defenses from the inside, and then open the city gates to the entire Greek army, which destroys the city.

Imagine this story's ending if the city had planned for defense in depth. First, Troy's defensive forces might have inspected the Trojan Horse more closely and discovered the deception. If the attackers had managed to make it inside the city gates, they could have been confronted with another layer of defense—for example, the horse might have been enclosed in a secure courtyard, with no access to the rest of the city.

What does a 3,000-year-old story tell us about security at scale, or even security itself? First, if you're trying to understand the strategies you need to defend and contain a system, you must first understand the attack itself. If we consider the city of Troy as a system, we can walk through the attackers' steps (stages of the attack) to uncover weaknesses that defense in depth might address.

At a high level, we can divide the Trojan attack into four stages:

1. *Threat modeling and vulnerability discovery*—Assess the target and specifically look for defenses and weaknesses. The attackers couldn't open the city gates from the outside, but could they open them from the inside?

2. *Deployment*—Set up the conditions for the attack. The attackers constructed and delivered an object that Troy eventually brought inside its city walls.

3. *Execution*—Carry out the actual attack, which capitalizes on the previous stages. Soldiers came out of the Trojan Horse and opened the city gates to let in the Greek army.

4. *Compromise*—After successful execution of the attack, the damage occurs and mitigation begins.

The Trojans had opportunities to disrupt the attack at every stage before the compromise, and paid a heavy price for missing them. In the same way, your system's defense in depth can reduce the price you might have to pay if your system is ever compromised.

Threat modeling and vulnerability discovery

Attackers and defenders can both assess a target for weaknesses. Attackers perform reconnaissance against their targets, find weaknesses, and then model attacks. Defenders should do what they can to limit the information exposed to attackers during reconnaissance. But because defenders can't completely prevent this reconnaissance, they must detect it and use it as a signal. In the case of the Trojan Horse, the defenders might have been on the alert because of inquiries from strangers about how the gates were defended. In light of that suspicious activity, they would have then exercised extra caution when they found a large wooden horse at the city gate.

Making note of these strangers' inquiries amounts to gathering intelligence on threats. There are many ways to do this for your own systems, and you can even choose to outsource some of them. For example, you might do the following:

- Monitor your system for port and application scans.
- Keep track of DNS registrations of URLs similar to yours—an attacker might use those registrations for spear phishing attacks.
- Buy threat intelligence data.
- Build a threat intelligence team to study and passively monitor the activities of known and likely threats to your infrastructure. While we don't recommend that small companies invest resources in this approach, it may become cost-effective as your company grows.

As a defender with inside knowledge of your system, your assessment can be more detailed than the attacker's reconnaissance. This is a critical point: if you understand your system's weaknesses, you can defend against them more efficiently. And the more you understand the methods that attackers are currently using or are capable of exploiting, the more you amplify this effect. A word of caution: beware of developing blind spots to attack vectors you consider unlikely or irrelevant.

Deployment of the attack

If you know that attackers are performing reconnaissance against your system, efforts to detect and stop the attack are critical. Imagine that the Trojans had decided not to permit the wooden horse to enter the city gates because it was created by someone they did not trust. Instead, they might have thoroughly inspected the Trojan Horse before allowing it inside, or perhaps they might have just set it on fire.

In modern times, you can detect potential attacks using network traffic inspection, virus detection, software execution control, protected sandboxes,[1] and proper provisioning of privileges for signaling anomalous use.

Execution of the attack

If you can't prevent all deployments from adversaries, you need to limit the blast radius of potential attacks. If the defenders had boxed in the Trojan Horse, thereby limiting their exposure, the attackers would have had a much harder time advancing from their hiding spot unnoticed. Cyberwarfare refers to this tactic (described in more detail in "Runtime layers" on page 149) as *sandboxing*.

Compromise

When the Trojans woke to find their enemies standing over their beds, they knew their city had been compromised. This awareness came well after the actual compromise occurred. Many unfortunate banks faced a similar situation in 2018 after their infrastructure was polluted by EternalBlue (*https://oreil.ly/wNI2u*) and WannaCry (*https://oreil.ly/irovS*).

How you respond from this point forward determines how long your infrastructure remains compromised.

Google App Engine Analysis

Let's consider defense in depth as applied to a more modern case: Google App Engine. Google App Engine allows users to host application code, and to scale as load increases without managing networks, machines, and operating systems. Figure 8-1 shows a simplified architecture diagram of App Engine in its early days. Securing the application code is a developer's responsibility, while securing the Python/Java runtime and the base OS is Google's responsibility.

---

1 Protected sandboxes provide an isolated environment for untrusted code and data.

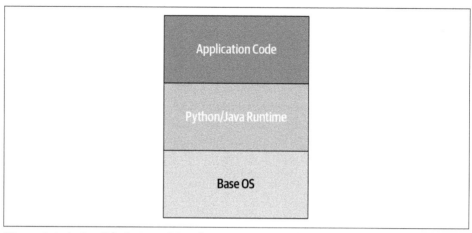

Figure 8-1. A simplified view of Google App Engine architecture

The original implementation of Google App Engine required special process isolation considerations. At that time Google used traditional POSIX user isolation as its default strategy (through distinct user processes), but we decided that running each user's code in an independent virtual machine was too inefficient for the level of planned adoption. We needed to figure out how to run third-party, untrusted code in the same way as any other job within Google's infrastructure.

Risky APIs

Initial threat modeling for App Engine turned up a few worrisome areas:

- Network access was problematic. Up to that point, all applications running within the Google production network were assumed to be trusted and authenticated infrastructure components. Since we were introducing arbitrary, untrusted third-party code into this environment, we needed a strategy to isolate internal APIs and network exposure from App Engine. We also needed to bear in mind that App Engine itself was running on that same infrastructure, and therefore was dependent on access to those same APIs.

- The machines running user code required access to the local filesystem. At least this access was limited to the directories belonging to the given user, which helped protect the execution environment and reduce the risk of user-provided applications interfering with applications of other users on the same machine.

- The Linux kernel meant that App Engine was exposed to a large attack surface, which we wanted to minimize. For example, we wanted to prevent as many classes of local privilege escalation as possible.

To address these challenges, we first examined limiting user access to each API. Our team removed built-in APIs for I/O operations for networking and filesystem interactions at runtime. We replaced the built-in APIs with "safe" versions that made calls to other cloud infrastructure, rather than directly manipulating the runtime environment.

To prevent users from reintroducing the intentionally removed capabilities to the interpreters, we didn't allow user-supplied compiled bytecode or shared libraries. Users had to depend on the methods and libraries we provided, in addition to a variety of permitted runtime-only open source implementations that they might need.

Runtime layers

We also extensively audited the runtime base data object implementations for features that were likely to produce memory corruption bugs. This audit produced a handful of upstream bug fixes in each of the runtime environments we launched.

We assumed that at least some of these defensive measures would fail, as we weren't likely to find and predict every exploitable condition in the chosen runtimes. We decided to specifically adapt the Python runtime to compile down to Native Client (NaCL) bitcode. NaCL allowed us to prevent many classes of memory corruption and control-flow subversion attacks that our in-depth code auditing and hardening missed.

We weren't completely satisfied that NaCL would contain all risky code breakouts and bugs in their entirety, so we added a second layer of ptrace sandboxing to filter and alert on unexpected system calls and parameters. Any violations of these expectations immediately terminated the runtime and dispatched alerts at high priority, along with logs of relevant activity.

Over the next five years, the team caught a few cases of anomalous activity resulting from exploitable conditions in one of the runtimes. In each case, our sandbox layer gave us a significant advantage over attackers (whom we confirmed to be security researchers), and our multiple layers of sandboxing contained their activities within the design parameters.

Functionally, the Python implementation in App Engine featured the sandboxing layers shown in Figure 8-2.

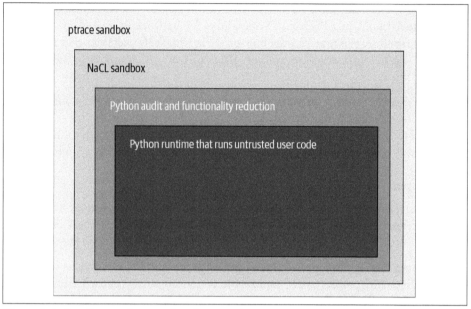

Figure 8-2. Sandboxing layers of Python implementation in App Engine

App Engine's layers are complementary, with each layer anticipating the weak points or likely failures of the previous one. As defense activations move through the layers, signals of a compromise become stronger, allowing us to focus efforts on probable attacks.

Although we took a thorough and layered approach to security for Google App Engine, we still benefited from external help in securing the environment.[2] In addition to our team finding anomalous activity, external researchers discovered several cases of exploitable vectors. We're grateful to the researchers who found and disclosed the gaps.

Controlling Degradation

When designing for defense in depth, we assume that system components or even entire systems can fail. Failures can happen for many reasons, including physical damage, a hardware or network malfunction, a software misconfiguration or bug, or a security compromise. When a component fails, the impact may extend to every system that depends on it. The global pool of similar resources also becomes smaller— for example, disk failures reduce overall storage capacity, network failures reduce bandwidth and increase latency, and software failures reduce the computational

---

2 Google runs bug bounty reward programs (*https://oreil.ly/ZQGNW*).

capacity system-wide. The failures might compound—for example, a storage shortage could lead to software failures.

Resource shortages like these, or a sudden spike in incoming requests like those caused by the Slashdot effect (*https://oreil.ly/Z1UL8*), misconfiguration, or a denial-of-service attack, could lead to system overload. When a system's load exceeds its capacity, its response inevitably begins to degrade, and that can lead to a completely broken system with no availability. Unless you've planned for this scenario in advance, you don't know where the system may break—but this will most likely be where the system is weakest, and not where it's safest.

To control degradation, you must select which system properties to disable or adjust when dire circumstances arise, while doing all you can to protect the system's security. If you *deliberately* design multiple response options for circumstances like these, the system can make use of controlled breakpoints, rather than experiencing a chaotic collapse. Instead of triggering cascading failures and dealing with the mayhem that follows, your system can respond by *degrading gracefully*. Here are some ways you can make that happen:

- Free up resources and decrease the rate of failed operations by disabling infrequently used features, the least critical functions, or high-cost service capabilities. You can then apply the freed resources to preserving important features and functions. For example, most systems that accept TLS connections support both Elliptic Curve (ECC) and RSA cryptosystems. Depending on your system's implementation, one of the two will be cheaper while giving you comparable security. In software, ECC is less resource-intensive for private key operations.[3] Disabling support for RSA when systems are resource-constrained will make room for more connections at the lower cost of ECC.

- Aim for system response measures to take effect quickly and automatically. This is easiest with servers under your direct control, where you can arbitrarily toggle operational parameters of any scope or granularity. User clients are harder to control: they have long rollout cycles because client devices may postpone or be unable to receive updates. Additionally, the diversity of client platforms increases the chance of rollbacks of response measures due to unanticipated incompatibilities.

---

3 See Singh, Soram Ranbir, Ajoy Kumar Khan, and Soram Rakesh Singh. 2016. "Performance Evaluation of RSA and Elliptic Curve Cryptography." *Proceedings of the 2nd International Conference on Contemporary Computing and Informatics*: 302–306. doi:10.1109/IC3I.2016.7917979.

- Understand which systems are critical for your company's mission as well as their relative importance and interdependencies. You might have to preserve the minimal features of these systems in proportion to their relative value. For example, Google's Gmail has a "simple HTML mode" that disables fancy UI styling and search autocompletion but allows users to continue opening mail messages. Network failures limiting bandwidth in a region could deprioritize even this mode if that allowed network security monitoring to continue to defend user data in the region.

If these adjustments meaningfully improve the system's capacity to absorb load or failure, they provide a critical complement to all other resilience mechanisms—and give incident responders more time to respond. It's better to make the essential and difficult choices in advance rather than when under pressure during an incident. Once individual systems develop a clear degradation strategy, it becomes easier to prioritize degradation at a larger scope, across multiple systems or product areas.

Security and Reliability Tradeoff: Controlling Degradation

Remember to consider the role of security when you rank the criticality of your services. You need to determine what degree of increased risk is acceptable. For example, is a 2FA (*https://oreil.ly/aiKg0*) outage during login flow acceptable? When 2FA was a new technology and users were still opting in, letting users log in without 2FA for some services might have been acceptable. On the other hand, a critical service might choose to disable all logins and fail completely if 2FA is unavailable. For example, a bank might prefer to have a service outage rather than allow unauthorized access to customer accounts.

Differentiate Costs of Failures

There is some cost to any failed operation—for example, a failed data upload from a mobile device to an application backend consumes computing resources and network bandwidth to set up an RPC and push some data. If you can refactor your flows to fail early or cheaply, you may be able to reduce or avoid some failure-related waste.

To reason about cost of failures:

Identify the total costs of individual operations.
    For example, you could collect CPU, memory, or bandwidth impact metrics during load testing of a particular API. Focus first on the most impactful operations —either by criticality or frequency—if pressed for time.

Determine at what stage in the operation these costs are incurred.

You could inspect source code or use developer tools to collect introspection data (for example, web browsers offer tracking of request stages). You could even instrument the code with failure simulations at different stages.

Armed with the information you gather about operation costs and failure points, you can look for changes that could defer higher-cost operations until the system progresses further toward success.

Computing resources

The computing resources that a failing operation consumes—from the beginning of the operation until failure—are unavailable to any other operations. This effect multiplies if clients retry aggressively on failure, a scenario that might even lead to a cascading system failure. You can free up computing resources more quickly by checking for error conditions earlier in the execution flows—for example, you can check the validity of data access requests before the system allocates memory or initiates data reads/writes. SYN cookies (*https://oreil.ly/EaL2N*) can let you avoid allocating memory to TCP connection requests originating from spoofed IP addresses. CAPTCHA can help to protect the most expensive operations from automated abuse.

More broadly, if a server can learn that its health is declining (for example, from a monitoring system's signals), you can have the server switch into a lame-duck mode:[4] it continues to serve, but lets its callers know to throttle down or stop sending requests. This approach provides better signals to which the overall environment can adapt, and simultaneously minimizes resources diverted to serving errors.

It's also possible for multiple instances of a server to become unused because of external factors. For example, the services they run could be "drained" or isolated because of a security compromise. If you monitor for such conditions, the server resources could be temporarily released for reuse by other services. Before you reallocate resources, however, you should be certain to secure any data that can be helpful for a forensic investigation.

User experience

The system's interactions with the user should have an acceptable level of behavior in degraded conditions. An ideal system informs users that its services might be malfunctioning, but lets them continue to interact with parts that remain functional. Systems might try different connection, authentication, and authorization protocols or endpoints to preserve the functional state. Any data staleness or security risks due to

---

4 This is described in Chapter 20 of the SRE book.

failures should be clearly communicated to the users. Features that are no longer safe to use should be explicitly disabled.

For example, adding an offline mode to an online collaboration application can preserve core functionality despite temporary loss of online storage, the ability to show updates from others, or integration with chat features. In a chat application with end-to-end encryption, users might occasionally change their encryption key used for protecting communications. Such an application would keep all previous communications accessible, because their authenticity is not affected by this change.

In contrast, an example of a poor design would be a situation where the entire GUI becomes unresponsive because one of its RPCs to a backend has timed out. Imagine a mobile application designed to connect to its backends on startup in order to display only the freshest content. The backends could be unreachable simply because the device's user disabled the connectivity intentionally; still, users would not see even the previously cached data.

A user experience (UX) research and design effort may be required to arrive at a UX solution that delivers usability and productivity in a degraded mode.

Speed of mitigation

The recovery speed of a system after it fails affects the cost of that failure. This response time includes the time between when a human or automation makes a mitigating change and when the last affected instance of the component is updated and recovers. Avoid placing critical points of failure into components like client applications, which are harder to control.

Going back to the earlier example of the mobile application that initiates a freshness update on launch, that design choice turns connectivity to the backends into a critical dependency. In this situation, the initial problems are amplified by the slow and uncontrollable rate of application updates.

Deploy Response Mechanisms

Ideally, a system should actively respond to deteriorating conditions with safe, preprogrammed measures that maximize the effectiveness of the response while minimizing risks to security and reliability. Automated measures can generally perform better than humans—humans are slower to respond, may not have sufficient network or security access to complete a necessary operation, and aren't as good at solving for multiple variables. However, humans should remain in the loop to provide checks and balances, and to make decisions under unforeseen or nontrivial circumstances.

Let's consider in detail managing excessive load—whether due to loss of serving capacity, benign traffic spikes, or even DoS attacks. Humans might not respond fast enough, and traffic could overwhelm servers enough to lead to cascading failures and

an eventual global service crash. Creating a safeguard by permanently overprovisioning servers wastes money and doesn't guarantee a safe response. Instead, servers
should adjust how they respond to load based upon current conditions. You can use
two specific automation strategies here:

- Load shedding is done by returning errors rather than serving requests.
- Throttling of clients is done by delaying responses until closer to the request
  deadline.

Figure 8-3 illustrates a traffic spike that exceeds the capacity. Figure 8-4 illustrates the
effects of load shedding and throttling to manage the load spike. Note the following:

- The curve represents requests per second, and the area under it represents total
  requests.
- Whitespace represents traffic processed without failure.
- The backward-slashed area represents degraded traffic (some requests failed).
- The crosshatched areas represent rejected traffic (all requests failed).
- The forward-slashed area represents traffic subject to prioritization (important
  requests succeeded).

Figure 8-3 shows how the system might actually crash, leading to a greater impact in
terms of both volume (number of requests lost) and time (duration of the outage
extends past the traffic spike). Figure 8-3 also distinguishes the uncontrolled nature
of degraded traffic (the backward-slashed area) prior to system crash. Figure 8-4
shows that the system with load shedding rejects significantly less traffic than in
Figure 8-3 (the crosshatched area), with the rest of the traffic either processed
without failure (whitespace area) or rejected if lower priority (forward-slashed area).

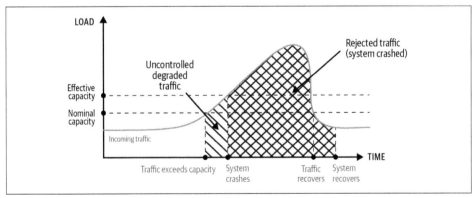

Figure 8-3. Complete outage and a possible cascading failure from a load spike

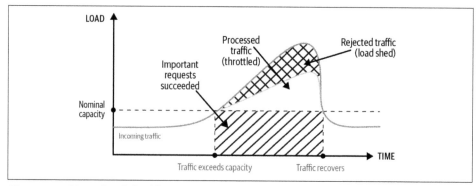

Figure 8-4. Using load shedding and throttling to manage a load spike

Load shedding

The primary resilience objective of load shedding (described in Chapter 22 of the SRE book) is to stabilize components at maximum load, which can be especially beneficial for preserving security-critical functions. When the load on a component starts to exceed its capacity, you want the component to serve errors for all excessive requests rather than crashing. Crashing makes *all* of the component's capacity unavailable—not just the capacity for the excess requests. When this capacity is gone, the load just shifts elsewhere, possibly causing a cascading failure.

Load shedding allows you to free server resources even before a server's load reaches capacity, and to make those resources available for more valuable work. To select which requests to shed, the server needs to have notions of request priority and request cost. You can define a policy that determines how many of each request type to shed based upon request priority, request cost, and current server utilization. Assign request priorities based on the business criticality of the request or its dependents (security-critical functions should get high priority). You can either measure or empirically estimate request costs.[5] Either way, these measurements should be comparable to server utilization measurements, such as CPU and (possibly) memory usage. Computing request costs should of course be economical.

Throttling

Throttling (described in Chapter 21 of the SRE book) indirectly modifies the client's behavior by delaying the present operation in order to postpone future operations. After the server receives a request, it may wait before processing the request or, once it has finished processing the request, wait before sending the response to the client. This approach reduces the rate of requests the server receives from clients (if clients

---

5 See Chapter 21 of the SRE book.

send requests sequentially), which means that you can redirect the resources saved during wait times.

Similar to load shedding, you could define policies to apply throttling to specific offending clients, or more generally to all clients. Request priority and cost play a role in selecting which requests to throttle.

Automated response

Server utilization statistics can help determine when to consider applying controls like load shedding and throttling. The more heavily a server is loaded, the less traffic or load it can handle. If controls take too long to activate, higher-priority requests may end up being dropped or throttled.

To effectively manage these degradation controls at scale, you may need a central internal service. You can translate business considerations about mission-critical features and the costs of failure into policies and signals for this service. This internal service can also aggregate heuristics about clients and services in order to distribute updated policies to all servers in near real time. Servers can then apply these policies according to rules based on server utilization.

Some possibilities for automated response include the following:

- Implementing load-balancing systems that can respond to throttling signals and attempt to shift traffic to servers with lower loads
- Providing DoS protections that can assist in response to malicious clients if throttling is ineffective or damaging
- Using reports of heavy load shedding for critical services to trigger preparation for failover to alternative components (a strategy that we discuss later in this chapter)

You can also use automation for self-reliant failure detection: a server that determines that it can't serve some or all classes of requests can degrade itself to a full load-shedding mode. Self-contained or self-hosted detection is desirable because you don't want to rely on external signals (possibly simulated by an attacker) to force an entire fleet of servers into an outage.

As you implement graceful degradation, it's important to determine and record levels of system degradation, regardless of what triggered the problem. This information is useful for diagnosing and debugging. Reporting the actual load shedding or throttling (whether self-imposed or directed) can help you evaluate global health and capacity and detect bugs or attacks. You also need this information in order to evaluate the current remaining system capacity and user impact. In other words, you want to know how degraded the individual components and the entire system are, and what manual actions you might need to take. After the event, you'll want to evaluate the effectiveness of your degradation mechanisms.

Automate Responsibly

Exercise caution when creating automated response mechanisms so that they do not degrade system security and reliability to an unintended degree.

Failing safe versus failing secure

When designing a system to handle failure, you must balance between optimizing for reliability by failing open (safe) and optimizing for security by failing closed (secure):[6]

- To maximize *reliability*, a system should resist failures and serve as much as possible in the face of uncertainty. Even if the system's integrity is not intact, as long as its configuration is viable, a system optimized for availability will serve what it can. If ACLs failed to load, the assumed default ACL is "allow all."

- To maximize *security*, a system should lock down fully in the face of uncertainty. If the system cannot verify its integrity—regardless of whether a failed disk took away a part of its configs or an attacker changed the configs for an exploit—it can't be trusted to operate and should protect itself as much as possible. If ACLs failed to load, the assumed default ACL is "deny all."

These principles of reliability and security are clearly at odds. To resolve this tension, each organization must first determine its minimal nonnegotiable security posture, and then find ways to provide the required reliability of critical features of security services. For example, a network configured to drop low-QoS (quality of service) packets might require that security-oriented RPC traffic be tagged for special QoS to prevent packet drops. Security-oriented RPC servers might need special tagging to avoid CPU starvation by workload schedulers.

---

6 The concepts of "failing open" and "fail closed" refer to the service *remaining operational* (being reliable) or *shutting down* (being secure), respectively. The terms "fail open" and "fail closed" are often used interchangeably with "fail safe" and "fail secure," as described in Chapter 1.

Security and Reliability Tradeoff: Response Mechanisms

Security-critical operations should not fail open. Failing open could permit an attacker to degrade the security of a system by using DoS attacks alone, for example. However, this doesn't mean that security-critical operations don't qualify for controlled degradation at all. A lower-cost alternative component (see "Component Types" on page 169) could replace failing regular security controls. If that component applies *stronger* security controls, it becomes counterproductive for an attacker to attempt breaking regular security controls. This effectively enhances the system's resilience.

A foothold for humans

Sometimes humans must get involved in service degradation decisions. For example, the ability of rule-based systems to make a judgment call is inherently limited by predefined rules. Automation doesn't act when faced with unforeseen circumstances that don't map to any of the system's predefined responses. An automated response might also produce unforeseen circumstances due to a programming error. Allowing appropriate human intervention to deal with these and similar situations requires some forethought in system design.

First, you should prevent automation from disabling the services that employees use to recover your infrastructure (see "Emergency Access" on page 210). It's important to design protections for these systems so that even DoS attacks cannot completely prevent access. For example, a SYN attack must not stop a responder from opening a TCP connection for an SSH session. Be sure to implement low-dependency alternatives, and continuously validate the capabilities of those alternatives.

In addition, don't allow automation to make unsupervised policy changes of either large magnitude (for example, a single server shedding *all* RPCs) or substantial scope (*all* servers shedding some RPC). Consider implementing a change budget instead. When automation exhausts that budget, no automatic refresh occurs. Instead, a human must increase the budget or make a different judgment call. Note that despite this human intervention, automation is still in place.

Controlling the Blast Radius

You can add another layer to your defense-in-depth strategy by limiting the scope of each part of your system. For example, consider network segmentation. In the past, it was common for an organization to have a single network that contained all of its resources (machines, printers, storage, databases, and so on). These resources were visible to any user or service on that network, and access was controlled by the resource itself.

Today, a common way to improve security is to *segment* your network and grant access to each segment to specific classes of users and services. You can do this by using virtual LANs (VLANs) with network ACLs, which is an easy-to-configure, industry-standard solution. You can control traffic into each segment, and control which segments are allowed to communicate. You can also limit each segment's access to "need to know" information.

Network segmentation is a good example of the general idea of compartmentalization, which we discussed in Chapter 6. *Compartmentalization* involves deliberately creating small individual operational units (compartments) and limiting access to and from each one. It's a good idea to compartmentalize most aspects of your systems—servers, applications, storage, and so on. When you use a single-network setup, an attacker who compromises a user's credentials can potentially access every device on the network. When you use compartmentalization, however, a security breach or traffic overload in one compartment does not jeopardize all of the compartments.

Controlling the blast radius means compartmentalizing the impact of an event, similar to the way compartments on a ship grant resilience against the whole ship sinking. Designing for resilience, you should create compartmental barriers that constrain both attackers *and* accidental failures. These barriers allow you to better tailor and automate your responses. You can also use these boundaries to create failure domains that deliver component redundancy and failure isolation, as discussed in "Failure Domains and Redundancies" on page 166.

Compartments also aid in quarantine efforts, reducing the need for responders to actively balance defending and preserving evidence. Some compartments can be isolated and frozen for analysis while other compartments are recovered. Additionally, compartments create natural boundaries for replacement and repair during incident response—a compartment may be jettisoned to save the remainder of the system.

To control the blast radius of an incursion, you must have a way to establish boundaries and to be sure those boundaries are secure. Consider a job running in production as one compartment.[7] This job must permit some access (you want the compartment to be useful), but not unrestricted access (you want to protect the compartment). Restricting who can access the job relies on your ability to recognize endpoints in production and confirm their identity.

You can do this by using authenticated remote procedure calls, which identify both parties within one connection. To protect the parties' identities from spoofing and to conceal their contents from the network, these RPCs use mutually authenticated connections, which can certify the identities of both parties connected to the service. To

---

7 See Chapter 2 of the SRE book for a description of the production environment at Google.

permit endpoints to make more informed decisions about other compartments, you may add additional information that endpoints publish along with their identity. For example, you can add location information to the certificate so that you can reject nonlocal requests.

Once mechanisms to establish compartments are in place, you face a difficult trade-off: you need to constrain your operations with enough separation to deliver useful-sized compartments, but without creating *too much* separation. For example, one balanced approach to compartmentalization would be to consider every RPC method as a separate compartment. This aligns compartments along logical application boundaries, and the count of compartments is linear to the number of system features.

Compartment separation that controls the acceptable parameter values of RPC methods would warrant more careful consideration. While this would create tighter security controls, the number of possible violations per RPC method is proportional to the number of RPC clients. This complexity would compound across all of the system's features, and require coordination of changes in client code and server policy. On the other hand, compartments that wrap an entire server (regardless of its RPC services or their methods) are much easier to manage, but provide comparatively much less value. When balancing this tradeoff, it's necessary to consult with the incident management and operations teams to consider your choices of compartment types and to validate the utility of your choices.

Imperfect compartments that don't perfectly cover all edge cases can also provide value. For example, the process of finding the edge cases may cause an attacker to make a mistake that alerts you to their presence. Any time that it takes such an adversary to escape a compartment is additional time that your incident response team has to react.

Incident management teams must plan and practice tactics for sealing compartments to contain an incursion or a bad actor. Turning off part of your production environment is a dramatic step. Well-designed compartments give incident management teams the option to perform actions that are proportional to the incidents, so they don't necessarily have to take an entire system offline.

When you implement compartmentalization, you face a tradeoff between having all customers share a single instance of a given service,[8] or running separate service instances that support individual customers or subsets of customers.

For example, running two virtual machines (VMs)—each controlled by different mutually distrustful entities—on the same hardware comes with a certain risk:

---

8 Typically, this instance of the service would still be served by many replicas of the underlying server, but it would function as a single logical compartment.

exposure to zero-day vulnerabilities in the virtualization layer perhaps, or subtle cross-VM information leaks. Some customers may choose to eliminate these risks by compartmentalizing their deployments based on physical hardware. To facilitate this approach, many cloud providers offer deployment on per-customer dedicated hardware.[9] In this case, the cost of reduced resource utilization is reflected in a pricing premium.

Compartment separation adds resilience to a system as long as the system has mechanisms to maintain the separation. The difficult task is tracking those mechanisms and ensuring they remain in place. To prevent regressions, it's valuable to validate that operations prohibited across separation boundaries indeed fail (see "Continuous Validation" on page 174). Conveniently, because operational redundancy relies on compartmentalization (covered in "Failure Domains and Redundancies" on page 166), your validation mechanisms can cover both prohibited and expected operations.

Google compartmentalizes by role, location, and time. When an attacker tries to compromise a compartmentalized system, the potential scope of any single attack is greatly reduced. If the system is compromised, the incident management teams have options to disable only parts of it to purge the effects of the compromise while leaving other parts operational. The following sections explore the different types of compartmentalization in detail.

Role Separation

Most modern microservices architecture systems allow users to run jobs as particular *roles*, sometimes referred to as *service accounts*. The jobs are then provided with credentials that allow them to authenticate to other microservices on the network in their specific roles. If an adversary compromises a single job, they will be able to impersonate the job's corresponding role across the network. Because this allows the adversary to access all data that the other jobs running as that role could access, this effectively means that adversary has compromised the other jobs as well.

To limit the blast radius of such a compromise, different jobs should typically be run as different roles. For example, if you have two microservices that need access to two different classes of data (say, photos and text chats), running these two microservices as different roles can increase the resilience of your system even if the two microservices are developed and run by the same team.

Location Separation

Location separation helps to limit an attacker's impact along an additional dimension: the location where the microservice is running. For example, you might want to

---

9 For example, Google Cloud Platform offers so-called sole-tenant nodes (*https://oreil.ly/anLXq*).

prevent an adversary who has physically compromised a single datacenter from being able to read data in all your other datacenters. Similarly, you might want your most powerful administrative users to have their access permissions limited to only specific regions to mitigate insider risk.

The most obvious way to achieve location separation is to run the same microservices as different roles in different locations (like datacenters or cloud regions, which also typically correspond to different physical locations). You can then use your normal access control mechanisms to protect instances of the same service in different locations from each other, just as you would protect different services running as different roles from each other.

Location separation helps you resist an attack that moves from one location to another. Location-based cryptographic compartments let you limit access to applications and their stored data to specific locations, containing the blast radius of local attacks.

Physical location is a natural compartmentalization border, since many adverse events are connected to physical locations. For example, natural disasters are confined to a region, as are other localized mishaps such as fiber cuts, power outages, or fires. Malicious attacks that require the physical presence of the attacker are also confined to locations the attacker can actually get to, and all but the most capable (state-level attackers, for example) likely don't have the capability to send attackers to many locations all at once.

Similarly, the degree of risk exposure can depend on the nature of the physical location. For example, the risk of specific kinds of natural disasters varies with geographical region. Also, the risk of an attacker tailgating into a building and finding an open network port to plug into is higher in an office location with heavy employee and visitor traffic, as opposed to a datacenter with tightly controlled physical access.

With this in mind, you'll want to take location into account when designing your systems, to ensure that localized impacts stay confined to systems in that region, while letting your multiregional infrastructure continue to operate. For example, it's important to ensure that a service provided by servers in several regions does not have a critical dependency on a backend that is single-homed in one datacenter. Similarly, you'll want to ensure that physical compromise of one location does not allow an attacker to easily compromise other locations: tailgating into an office and plugging into an open port in a conference room should not give an intruder network access to production servers in your datacenter.

Aligning physical and logical architecture

When compartmentalizing an architecture into logical failure and security domains, it's valuable to align relevant physical boundaries with logical boundaries. For example, it's useful to segment your network on both network-level risks (such as networks exposed to malicious internet traffic versus trusted internal networks) and risks of physical attacks. Ideally, you'd have network segregation between corporate and production environments housed in physically separate buildings. Beyond that, you might further subdivide your corporate network to segregate areas with high visitor traffic, such as conference and meeting areas.

In many cases, a physical attack, such as stealing or backdooring a server, can give an attacker access to important secrets, encryption keys, or credentials that then might permit them to further penetrate your systems. With this in mind, it's a good idea to logically compartmentalize distribution of secrets, keys, and credentials to physical servers to minimize the risk of a physical compromise.

For example, if you operate web servers in several physical datacenter locations, it can be advantageous to deploy a separate certificate to each server, or share a certificate only across servers in one location, instead of sharing a single certificate across *all* your servers. This can make your response to the physical compromise of one datacenter more agile: you can drain its traffic, revoke just the cert(s) deployed to that datacenter, and take the datacenter offline for incident response and recovery, all the while serving traffic from your remaining datacenters. If you had a single certificate deployed to all servers, you'd instead have to very quickly replace the cert on all of them—even the ones that were not actually compromised.

Isolation of trust

While services may need to communicate across location boundaries to operate properly, a service might also want to reject requests from locations it doesn't expect to communicate with. To do this, you can restrict communications by default, and allow only the expected communications across location boundaries. It's also unlikely that all APIs on any service will use the same set of location restrictions. User-facing APIs are typically open globally, while control plane APIs are usually constrained. This makes fine-grained (per API call) control of permitted locations necessary. Creating tools that make it easy for any given service to measure, define, and enforce location limits on individual APIs enables teams to use their per-service knowledge to implement location isolation.

To restrict communications based on location, each identity needs to include location metadata. Google's job control system certifies and runs jobs in production. When the system certifies a job to run in a given compartment, it annotates the job's certificate with that compartment's location metadata. Each location has its own copy of the job control system that certifies jobs to run in that location, and machines in that location only accept jobs from that system. This is designed to prevent an attacker from piercing the compartment boundary and affecting other locations. Contrast this approach to a single centralized authority—if there were only one job control system for all of Google, its location would be quite valuable to an attacker.

Once trust isolation is in place, we can extend ACLs on stored data to include location restrictions. This way, we can separate locations for storage (where we put the data) from locations for access (who can retrieve or modify the data). This also opens up the possibility of trusting physical security versus trusting access by API—sometimes the additional requirement of a physical operator is worthwhile, as it removes the possibility of remote attacks.

To help control compartment violations, Google has a root of trust in each location and distributes the list of trusted roots and the locations they represent to all machines in the fleet. This way, each machine can detect spoofing across locations. We can also revoke a location's identity by distributing an updated list to all machines declaring the location untrustworthy.

Limitations of location-based trust. At Google, we have chosen to design our corporate network infrastructure so that location does not imply any trust. Instead, under the the zero trust networking paradigm of our BeyondCorp infrastructure (see Chapter 5), a workstation is trusted based on a certificate issued to the individual machine, and assertions about its configuration (such as up-to-date software). Plugging an untrusted machine into an office-floor network port will assign it to an untrusted guest VLAN. Only authorized workstations (authenticated via the 802.1x protocol) are assigned to the appropriate workstation VLAN.

We have also chosen to not even rely on physical location to establish trust for servers in datacenters. One motivating experience came out of a Red Team assessment of a datacenter environment. In this exercise, the Red Team placed a wireless device on top of a rack and quickly plugged it into an open port, to allow further penetration of the datacenter's internal network from outside the building. When they returned to clean up after the exercise, they found that an attentive datacenter technician had neatly zip-tied the access point's cabling—apparently offended by the untidy install job and on the assumption that the device must be legitimate. This story illustrates the difficulty of ascribing trust based on physical location, even within a physically secure area.

In Google's production environment, similarly to the BeyondCorp design, authentication between production services is rooted in machine-to-machine trust based on per-machine credentials. A malicious implant on an unauthorized device would not be trusted by Google's production environment.

Isolation of confidentiality

Once we have a system to isolate trust, we need to isolate our encryption keys to ensure that data secured through a root of encryption in one location is not compromised by exfiltration of encryption keys in another location. For example, if one branch of a company is compromised, attackers should not be able to read data from the company's other branches.

Google has base encryption keys that protect key trees. These keys eventually protect data at rest through key wrapping and key derivation.

To isolate encryption and key wrapping to a location, we need to ensure that the root keys for a location are only available to the correct location. This requires a distribution system that only places root keys in the correct locations. A key access system should leverage trust isolation to ensure that these keys cannot be accessed by entities that aren't in the appropriate location.

Using these principles, a given location allows the use of ACLs on local keys to prevent remote attackers from decrypting data. Decryption is prevented even if attackers have access to the encrypted data (through internal compromise or exfiltration).

Transitioning from a global key tree to a local key tree should be gradual. While any part of the tree may move from global to local independently, isolation isn't complete for a given leaf or branch of the tree until all keys above it have transitioned to local keys.

Time Separation

Finally, it's useful to limit the abilities of an adversary over time. The most common scenario to consider here is an adversary who has compromised a system and stolen a key or credential. If you rotate your keys and credentials over time and expire the old ones, the adversary must maintain their presence to reacquire the new secrets, which gives you more opportunities to detect the theft. Even if you never do detect the theft, rotation is still critical because you might close the avenue the adversary used to gain access to the key or credential during normal security hygiene work (e.g., by patching the vulnerability).

As we discuss in Chapter 9, doing key and credential rotation and expiration reliably requires careful tradeoffs. For example, using wall clock–based expiration for credentials can be problematic if there's a failure that prevents rotation to new credentials before the time the old credentials expire. Providing useful time separation requires balancing the frequency of rotation against the risk of downtime or loss of data if the rotation mechanism fails.

 # Failure Domains and Redundancies

So far we've covered how to design systems that adjust their behavior in response to attacks and contain attack fallout by using compartmentalization. To address complete failures of system components, system design must incorporate redundancies and distinct failure domains. These tactics can hopefully limit the impact of failures and avert complete collapse. It's particularly important to mitigate failures of critical components, since any system that depends on failed critical components is also at risk of complete failure.

Rather than aiming to prevent all failures at all times, you can create a balanced solution for your organization by combining the following approaches:

- Break up systems into independent failure domains.
- Aim to reduce the probability of a single root cause affecting elements in multiple failure domains.
- Create redundant resources, components, or procedures that can replace the failed ones.

Failure Domains

A *failure domain* is a type of blast radius control. Instead of structurally separating by role, location, or time, failure domains achieve functional isolation by partitioning a system into multiple equivalent but completely independent copies.

Functional isolation

A failure domain looks like a single system to its clients. If necessary, any of the individual partitions can take over for the entire system during an outage. Because a partition has only a fraction of the system's resources, it can support only a fraction of the system's capacity. Unlike managing role, location, and time separations, operating failure domains and maintaining their isolation requires ongoing effort. In exchange, failure domains increase system resilience in ways other blast radius controls can't.

Failure domains help protect systems from global impact because a single event doesn't typically affect all failure domains at once. However, in extreme cases, a significant event can disrupt multiple, or even all, failure domains. For example, you can think of a storage array's underlying devices (HDDs or SSDs) as failure domains. Although any one device may fail, the entire storage system remains functional because it creates a new data replica elsewhere. If a large number of storage devices fail and there aren't sufficient spare devices to maintain data replicas, further failures might result in data loss in the storage system.

Data isolation

You need to prepare for the possibility of having bad data at the data source or within individual failure domains. Therefore, each failure domain instance needs its own data copy in order to be functionally independent of the other failure domains. We recommend a twofold approach to achieve data isolation.

First, you can restrict how data updates can enter a failure domain. A system accepts new data only after it passes all validation checks for typical and safe changes. Some exceptions are escalated for justification, and a breakglass mechanism[10] may allow new data to enter the failure domain. As a result, you are more likely to prevent attackers or software bugs from making disruptive changes.

For example, consider ACL changes. A human mistake or a bug in ACL-generating software could produce an empty ACL, which might result in denying access to everyone.[11] Such an ACL change could cause system malfunction. Similarly, an attacker might try to expand their reach by adding a "permit all" clause to an ACL.

At Google, individual services generally have an RPC endpoint for intake of new data and for signaling. Programming frameworks, such as those presented in Chapter 12, include APIs for versioning data snapshots and evaluating their validity. Client applications can take advantage of the programming framework's logic for qualifying new data as safe. Centralized data push services implement quality controls for data updates. The data push services check where to get the data from, how to package it, and when to push the packaged data. To prevent automation from causing a widespread outage, Google rate limits global changes using per-application quotas. We prohibit actions that change multiple applications at once or that change the application capacity too quickly within a time period.

Second, enabling systems to write the last known good configuration to disk makes the systems resilient to losing access to configuration APIs: they can use the saved config. Many of Google's systems preserve old data for a limited duration of time in case the most recent data becomes corrupted for any reason. This is another example of defense in depth, helping provide long-term resilience.

Practical aspects

Even splitting a system into only two failure domains brings substantial benefits:

- Having two failure domains provides A/B regression capabilities and limits the blast radius of system changes to a single failure domain. To achieve this functionality, use one failure domain as a canary, and have a policy that doesn't allow updates to both failure domains at the same time.

- Geographically separated failure domains can provide isolation for natural disasters.

- You can use different software versions in different failure domains, thereby reducing the chances of a single bug breaking all servers or corrupting all data.

---

10 A breakglass mechanism is one that can bypass policies to allow engineers to quickly resolve outages. See "Breakglass" on page 67.

11 Systems using ACLs must fail closed (secure), with access explicitly granted by ACL entries.

Combining data and functional isolation enhances overall resilience and incident management. This approach limits the risk of data changes that are accepted without justification. When issues do arise, isolation delays their propagation to the individual functional units. This gives other defense mechanisms more time to detect and react, which is especially beneficial during hectic and time-sensitive incident response. By pushing multiple candidate fixes to distinct failure domains in parallel, you can independently evaluate which fixes have the intended effect. That way, you can avoid accidentally pushing a rushed update with a mistaken "fix" globally, further degrading your entire system.

Failure domains incur operational costs. Even a simple service with a few failure domains requires you to maintain multiple copies of service configurations, keyed by failure domain identifiers. Doing so requires the following:

- Ensuring configuration consistency
- Protecting all configurations from simultaneous corruption
- Hiding the separation into failure domains from client systems to prevent accidental coupling to a particular failure domain
- Potentially partitioning all dependencies, because one shared dependency change might accidentally propagate to all failure domains

It's worth noting that a failure domain may suffer complete failure if even one of its critical components fails. After all, you partitioned the original system into failure domains in the first place so that the system can stay up even when a failure domain's copies fail completely. However, failure domains simply shift the problem one level down. The following section discusses how you can use alternative components to mitigate the risk of complete failure of all failure domains.

Component Types

The resilient quality of a failure domain is expressed as the combined reliability of both its components and their dependencies. Resilience of the entire system increases with the number of failure domains. However, this increased resilience is offset by the operational overhead of maintaining more and more failure domains.

You can achieve further improvements in resilience by slowing down or stopping new feature development, gaining more stability in exchange. If you avoid adding a new dependency, you also avoid its potential failure modes. If you stop updating code, the rate of new bugs decreases. However, even if you halt all new feature development, you still need to react to occasional changes in state, like security vulnerabilities and increases in user demand.

Obviously, halting all new feature development isn't a viable strategy for most organizations. In the following sections, we present a hierarchy of alternative approaches to balancing reliability and value. In general, there are three broad classes of reliability for services: high capacity, high availability, and low dependency.

High-capacity components

The components that you build and run in the normal course of business make up your *high-capacity* service. That's because these components make up the main fleet serving your users. This is where your service absorbs spikes in user requests or resource consumption due to new features. High-capacity components also absorb DoS traffic, until DoS mitigation takes effect or graceful degradation kicks in.

Because these components are the most critically important to your service, you should focus your efforts here first—for example, by following best practices for capacity planning, software and configuration rollouts, and more, as covered in Part III of the SRE book and Part II of the SRE workbook.

High-availability components

If your system has components whose failures impact all users, or otherwise have significant wide-reaching consequences—the high-capacity components discussed in the preceding section—you may mitigate these risks by deploying copies of those components. These copies of components are *high availability* if they offer a provably lower probability of outages.

To achieve lower probability of outages, the copies should be configured with fewer dependencies and a limited rate of changes. This approach reduces the chances of infrastructure failures or operational errors breaking the components. For example, you might do the following:

- Use data cached on local storage to avoid depending on a remote database.
- Use older code and configs to avoid recent bugs in newer versions.

Running high-availability components has little operational overhead, but it requires additional resources whose costs scale proportionally to the size of the fleet. Determining whether the high-availability components should sustain your entire user base or only a portion of that base is a cost/benefit decision. Configure graceful degradation capabilities the same way between each high-capacity and high-availability component. This allows you to trade fewer resources for more aggressive degradation.

Low-dependency components

If failures in the high-availability components are unacceptable, a *low-dependency* service is the next level of resilience. Low dependency requires an alternative implementation with minimal dependencies. Those minimal dependencies are also low dependency. The total set of services, processes, or jobs that may fail is as small as the business needs and costs can bear. High-capacity and high-availability services can serve large user bases and offer rich features because of layers of cooperating platforms (virtualization, containerization, scheduling, application frameworks). While these layers help scaling by permitting services to add or move nodes rapidly, they also incur higher rates of outages as error budgets across the cooperating platforms add up.[12] In contrast, low-dependency services have to simplify their serving stack until they can accept the stack's aggregate error budget. In turn, simplifying the serving stack may lead to having to remove features.

Low-dependency components require you to determine if it's possible to build an alternative for a critical component, where the critical and alternative components do not share any failure domains. After all, the success of redundancy is inversely proportional to the probability of the same root cause affecting both components.

Consider storage space as a fundamental building block of a distributed system—you might want to store local data copies as a fallback when the RPC backends for data storage are unavailable. However, a general approach of storing local data copies isn't always practical. Operational costs increase to support the redundant components, while the benefit the extra components provide is typically zero.

In practice, you end up with a small set of low-dependency components with limited users, features, and costs, but that are confidently available for temporary loads or recovery. While most useful features usually rely on multiple dependencies, a severely degraded service is better than an unavailable one.

As a small-scale example, imagine a device for which write-only or read-only operations are presumed to be available over the network. In a home security system, such operations include recording event logs (write-only) and looking up emergency phone numbers (read-only). An intruder's break-in plan includes disabling the home's internet connectivity, thus disrupting the security system. To counter this type of failure, you configure the security system to also use a local server that implements the same APIs as the remote service. The local server writes event logs to local storage, updates the remote service, and retries failed attempts. The local server also responds to emergency phone number lookup requests. The phone number list is periodically refreshed from the remote service. From the home security console's perspective, the system is working as expected, writing logs and accessing emergency numbers. Additionally, a low-dependency, hidden landline may provide dialing capabilities as backup to a disabled wireless connection.

As a business-scale example, a global network failure is one of the scariest types of outages, because it impacts both service functionality and the ability of responders to

---

12 See Chapter 3 in the SRE book.

fix the outage. Large networks are managed dynamically and are more at risk for global outages. Building an alternative network that fully avoids reusing the same network elements as in the main network—links, switches, routers, routing domains, or SDN (*https://oreil.ly/Row8c*) software—requires careful design. This design must target a specific and narrow subset of use cases and operating parameters, allowing you to focus on simplicity and understandability. Aiming for minimal capital expenditures for this infrequently used network also naturally leads to limiting the available features and bandwidth. Despite the limitations, the results are sufficient. The goal is to support only the most critical features, and only for a fraction of the usual bandwidth.

Controlling Redundancies

Redundant systems are configured to have more than a single option for each of their dependencies. Managing the choice between these options is not always straightforward, and attackers can potentially exploit the differences between the redundant systems—for example, by pushing the system toward the less secure option. Remember that a resilient design achieves security *and* reliability without sacrificing one for the other. If anything, when low-dependency alternatives have stronger security, this can serve as a disincentive to attackers who are considering wearing down your system.

Failover strategies

Supplying a set of backends, usually through load-balancing technologies, adds resilience in the face of a backend failure. For example, it is impractical to rely on a single RPC backend. Whenever that backend needs to restart, the system will hang. For simplicity, the system usually treats redundant backends as *interchangeable*, as long as all backends provide the same feature behaviors.

A system that needs different *reliability* behaviors (for the same set of feature behaviors) should rely on a distinct set of interchangeable backends that provide the desired reliability behaviors. The system itself must implement logic to determine which set of behaviors to use and when to use them—for example, through flags. This gives you full control over the system's reliability, especially during recovery. Contrast this approach to requesting low-dependency behavior from the same high-availability backend. Using an RPC parameter, you might prevent the backend from attempting to contact its unavailable runtime dependency. If the runtime dependency is also a startup dependency, your system is still one process restart from disaster.

When to fail over to a component with better stability is situation-specific. If automatic failover is a goal, you should address the differences in available capacity by using the means covered in "Controlling Degradation" on page 150. After failover, such a system switches to using throttling and load-shedding policies tuned for the alternative component. If you want the system to fail back after the failed component recovers, provide a way to disable that failback—you may need to stabilize fluctuations or precisely control failover in some cases.

Common pitfalls

We've observed some common pitfalls with operating alternative components, regardless of whether they're high availability or low dependency.

For instance, over time you can grow to rely on alternative components for normal operation. Any dependent system that begins to treat the alternative systems as backup likely overloads them during an outage, making the alternative system an unexpected cause for denial of service. The opposite problem occurs when the alternative components are not routinely used, resulting in rot and surprise failures whenever they are needed.

Another pitfall is unchecked growth of dependence on other services or amounts of required compute resources. Systems tend to evolve as user demands change and developers add features. Over time, dependencies and dependents grow, and systems may use resources less efficiently. High-availability copies may fall behind high-capacity fleets, or low-dependency services may lose consistency and reproducibility when their intended operating constraints are not continuously monitored and validated.

It is crucial that failover to alternative components does not compromise the system's integrity or security. Consider the following scenarios in which the right choice depends on your organization's circumstances:

- You have a high-availability service that runs six-week-old code for security reasons (to defend against recent bugs). However, this same service requires an urgent security fix. Which risk would you choose: not applying the fix, or potentially breaking the code with the fix?

- A remote key service's startup dependency for fetching private keys that decrypt data may be made low dependency by storing private keys on local storage. Does this approach create an unacceptable risk to those keys, or can an increase in key rotation frequency sufficiently counteract that risk?

- You determine that you can free up resources by reducing the frequency of updates to data that changes infrequently (for example, ACLs, certificate revocation lists, or user metadata). Is it worthwhile to free up these resources, even if doing so potentially gives an attacker more time to make changes to that data or enables those changes to persist undetected for longer?

Finally, you need to make certain to prevent your system from autorecovering at the wrong time. If resilience measures automatically throttled the system's performance, it's OK for those same measures to automatically unthrottle it. However, if you applied a manual failover, don't permit automation to override the failover—the drained system might be quarantined because of a security vulnerability, or your team might be mitigating a cascading failure.

Continuous Validation

From both a reliability and a security perspective, we want to be sure that our systems behave as anticipated under both normal and unexpected circumstances. We also want to be sure that new features or bug fixes don't gradually erode a system's layered resilience mechanisms. There is no substitute for actually exercising the system and validating that it works as intended.

Validation focuses on observing the system under *realistic* but *controlled* circumstances, targeting workflows within a single system or across multiple systems.[13] Unlike chaos engineering (*https://oreil.ly/Fvx4L*), which is exploratory in nature, validation confirms specific system properties and behaviors covered in this chapter and Chapters 5, 6, and 9. When you validate regularly, you ensure that the outcomes remain as expected and that the validation practices themselves remain functional.

There's some art to making validation *meaningful*. To start with, you can use some of the concepts and practices covered in Chapter 15—for example, how to choose what to validate, and how to measure effective system attributes. Then you can gradually evolve your validation coverage by creating, updating, or removing checks. You can also extract useful details from actual incidents—these details are the ultimate truths of your system's behaviors, and often highlight needed design changes or gaps in your validation coverage. Finally, it's important to remember that as business factors change, individual services tend to evolve and change as well, potentially resulting in incompatible APIs or unanticipated dependencies.

A general validation maintenance strategy includes the following:

1. Discovering new failures
2. Implementing validators for each failure
3. Executing all validators repeatedly
4. Phasing out validators when the relevant features or behaviors no longer exist

To discover relevant failures, rely on the following sources:

- Regular bug reports from users and employees
- Fuzzing and fuzzing-like approaches (described in Chapter 13)

---

13 This differs from unit tests, integration tests, and load tests, which are covered in Chapter 13.

- Failure-injection approaches (akin to the Chaos Monkey tool (*https://oreil.ly/ fvSKQ*))
- Analytical judgment of subject matter experts who operate your systems

Building an automation framework can help you schedule incompatible checks to run at different times so that they don't conflict with each other. You should also monitor and establish periodic audits of automation to catch broken or compromised behaviors.

Validation Focus Areas

It's beneficial to validate whole systems and the end-to-end cooperation among their services. But because validating the failure response of whole systems that serve real users is expensive and risky, you have to compromise. Validating smaller system replicas is usually more affordable, and still provides insights that are impossible to obtain by validating individual system components in isolation. For example, you can do the following:

- Tell how callers react to an RPC backend that is responding slowly or becoming unreachable.
- See what happens when resource shortages occur, and whether it's feasible to obtain an emergency resource quota when resource consumption spikes.

Another practical solution is to rely upon logs to analyze interactions between systems and/or their components. If your system implements compartmentalization, operations that attempt to cross boundaries of role, location, or time separation should fail. If your logs record unexpected successes instead, these successes should be flagged. Log analysis should be active at all times, letting you observe actual system behaviors during validation.

You should validate the attributes of your security design principles: least privilege, understandability, adaptability, and recovery. Validating recovery is especially critical, because recovery efforts necessarily involve human actions. Humans are unpredictable, and unit tests cannot check human skills and habits. When validating recovery design, you should review both the readability of recovery instructions and the efficacy and interoperability of different recovery workflows.

Validating security attributes means going beyond ensuring correct system responses. You should also check that the code or configuration doesn't have any known vulnerabilities. Active penetration testing of a deployed system gives a black-box view of the system's resilience, often highlighting attack vectors the developers did not consider.

Interactions with low-dependency components deserve special attention. By definition, these components are deployed in the most critical circumstances. There is no fallback beyond these components. Fortunately, a well-designed system should have a limited number of low-dependency components, which makes the goal of defining validators for all critical functions and interactions feasible. You realize the return on investment in these low-dependency components *only* if they work when needed. Your recovery plans should often rely on the low-dependency components, and you should validate their use by humans for the possible situation where the system degrades to that level.

Validation in Practice

This section presents a few validation scenarios that have been used at Google to demonstrate the wide spectrum of approaches to continuous validation.

Inject anticipated changes of behavior

You can validate system response to load shedding and throttling by injecting a change of behavior into the server, and then observing whether all affected clients and backends respond appropriately.

For example, Google implements server libraries and control APIs that permit us to add arbitrary delays or failures to any RPC server. We use this functionality in periodic disaster readiness exercises, and teams may easily run experiments at any time. Using this approach, we study isolated RPC methods, whole components, or larger systems, and specifically look for signs of cascading failures. Starting with a small increase in latency, we build a step function toward simulating a full outage. Monitoring graphs clearly reflect changes in response latencies just as they would for real problems, at the step points. Correlating these timelines with monitoring signals from clients and backend servers, we can observe the propagation of effect. If error rates spike disproportionately to the patterns we observed at the earlier steps, we know to step back, pause, and investigate whether the behavior is unexpected.

It's important to have a reliable mechanism for canceling the injected behaviors quickly and safely. If there's a failure, even if the cause doesn't seem related to the validation, the right decision is to abort experiments first, and then evaluate when it is safe to try again.

Exercise emergency components as part of normal workflows

We can be certain that a low-dependency or high-availability system is functioning correctly and ready to roll out to production when we observe the system performing its intended functions. To test readiness, we push either a small fraction of real traffic or a small fraction of real users to the system we are validating.

High-availability systems (and sometimes low-dependency systems) are validated by mirroring requests: clients send two identical requests, one to the high-capacity component and one to the high-availability component. By modifying the client code or injecting a server that can duplicate one input traffic stream into two equivalent output streams,[14] you can compare the responses and report the differences. Monitoring services send alerts when the response discrepancies exceed anticipated levels. Some discrepancies are expected; for example, if the fallback system has older data or features. For that reason, a client should use the response from the high-capacity system, unless an error occurs or the client was explicitly configured to ignore that system—both of which might happen in emergencies. Mirroring the requests requires not only code changes at the client, but also the ability to customize the mirroring behavior. Because of that, this strategy is easier to deploy on frontend or backend servers rather than on end-user devices.

Low-dependency systems (and occasionally high-availability systems) are better suited for validation by real users than by request mirroring. This is because low-dependency systems differ substantially from their higher-unreliability counterparts in terms of features, protocols, and system capacity. At Google, on-call engineers use low-dependency systems as an integral part of their on-call duties. We use this strategy for a few reasons:

- Many engineers participate in on-call rotations, but only a small fraction of engineers are on call at once. This naturally restricts the set of people involved in validating.

- When engineers are on call, they might need to rely on emergency paths. Well-practiced use of low-dependency systems reduces the time it takes an on-call engineer to switch to using these systems in a true emergency, and avoids the risk of unexpected misconfiguration.

Transitioning on-call engineers to using only low-dependency systems can be implemented gradually and by different means, depending on the business criticality of each system.

Split when you cannot mirror traffic

As an alternative to request mirroring, you can split requests between disjoint sets of servers. This is appropriate if request mirroring is not feasible—for example, when you have no control over client code, but load balancing at the level of request routing is feasible. Consequently, splitting requests works only when alternative

---

14 This is similar to what the Unix command tee does for stdin.

components use the same protocols, as is often the case with high-capacity and high-availability versions of a component.

Another application of this strategy is to distribute traffic across a set of failure domains. If your load balancing targets a single failure domain, you can run focused experiments against that domain. Because a failure domain has lower capacity, attacking it and eliciting resilient responses requires less load. You can quantify the impact of your experiment by comparing the monitoring signals from other failure domains. By adding load shedding and throttling, you further increase the quality of output from the experiment.

Oversubscribe but prevent complacency

Quota assigned to customers but not consumed is a waste of resources. Therefore, in the interest of maximizing resource utilization, many services oversubscribe resources by some sane margin. A margin call on resources may happen at any time. A resilient system tracks priorities so it can release lower-priority resources to fulfill demand for higher-priority resources. However, you should validate whether the system can actually release those resources reliably, and in an acceptable amount of time.

Google once had a service that needed a lot of disk space for batch processing. User services take priority over batch processing and allocate significant disk reserves for usage spikes. We permitted the batch processing service to utilize disks unused by the user services, under a specific condition: any disks in a particular cluster must be fully released within X hours. The validation strategy we developed consisted of periodically moving the batch processing service out of a cluster, measuring how long the move took, and fixing any new issues uncovered at each attempt. This was not a simulation. Our validation ensured that the engineers who promised the SLO of X hours had both real evidence and real experience.

These validations are expensive, but most of the costs are absorbed by automation. Load balancing limits the costs to managing the resource provisioning at the source and target locations. If resource provisioning is mostly automated—for example, as is the case with cloud services—it becomes a matter of running scripts or playbooks to execute a series of requests to the automation.

For smaller services or companies, the strategy of periodically executing a rebalancing applies similarly. The resulting confidence in responding predictably to shifts in application load is part of the foundation for software architecture that can serve a global user base.

Measure key rotation cycles

Key rotation is simple in theory, but in practice it may bring unpleasant surprises, including full service outages. When validating that key rotation works, you should look for at least two distinct outcomes:

Key rotation latency
    The time it takes to complete a single rotation cycle

Verified loss of access
    Certainty that the old key is fully useless after rotation

We recommend periodically rotating keys so they remain ready for nonnegotiable emergency key rotations prompted by a security compromise. This means rotating keys even if you don't have to. If the rotation process is expensive, look for ways to lower its costs.

At Google, we've experienced that measuring key rotation latency helps with multiple objectives:

- You learn whether every service that uses the key is actually able to update its configuration. Perhaps a service was not designed for key rotation, or was designed for it but was never tested, or a change broke what previously worked.
- You learn how long each service takes to rotate your key. Key rotation might be as trivial as a file change and server restart, or as involved as a gradual rollout across all world regions.
- You discover how other system dynamics delay the key rotation process.

Measuring key rotation latency has helped us form a realistic expectation of the entire cycle, both in normal and emergency circumstances. Account for possible rollbacks (caused by key rotation or other events), change freezes for services out of error budget, and serialized rollouts due to failure domains.

How to verify loss of access via an old key is likely case-specific. It's not easy to prove that all instances of the old key were destroyed, so ideally you can demonstrate that attempting to use the old key fails, after which point you can destroy the old key. When this approach isn't practical, you can rely on key deny-list mechanisms (for example, CRLs). If you have a central certificate authority and good monitoring, you may be able to create alerts if any ACLs list the old key's fingerprint or serial number.

Practical Advice: Where to Begin

Designing resilient systems isn't a trivial task. It takes time and energy, and diverts efforts from other valuable work. You need to consider the tradeoffs carefully, according to the degree of resilience you want, and then pick from the wide spectrum of options we describe—the few or many solutions that fit your needs.

In order of costs:

1. Failure domains and blast radius controls have the lowest costs because of their relatively static nature, yet offer significant improvements.

2. High-availability services are the next most cost-effective solution.

Consider these options next:

3. Consider deploying load-shedding and throttling capabilities if your organization's scale or risk aversion justifies investing in active automation for resilience.

4. Evaluate the effectiveness of your defenses against DoS attacks (see Chapter 10).

5. If you build a low-dependency solution, introduce a process or a mechanism to ensure that it stays low dependency over time.

It can be hard to overcome a resistance to invest in resilience improvements, because the benefits manifest as an absence of problems. These arguments might help:

- Deploying failure domains and blast radius controls will have a lasting effect on future systems. The isolation techniques can encourage or enforce good separation of operational failure domains. Once in place, they will inevitably make it harder to design and deploy unnecessarily coupled or fragile systems.

- Regular key change and rotation techniques and exercises not only ensure preparation for security incidents, but also give you general cryptographic agility—for example, knowing you can upgrade encryption primitives.

- The relatively low additional cost of deploying high-availability instances of a service provides for a cheap way to examine how much you might be able to improve the service's availability. It's also cheap to abandon.

- Load-shedding and throttling capabilities, along with the other approaches covered in "Controlling Degradation" on page 150, reduce the cost of the resources the company needs to maintain. The resulting user-visible improvements often apply to the most valued product features.

- Controlling degradation critically contributes to the speed and effectiveness of first reaction when defending against DoS attacks.

- Low-dependency solutions are relatively expensive yet rarely used in practice. To determine whether they are worth their cost, it can help to know how much time it would take to bring up all the dependencies of the business-critical services.

You can then compare the costs and conclude whether it's better to invest your time elsewhere.

Whatever resilience solutions you put together, look for affordable ways to keep them continuously validated, and avoid cost cutting that risks their effectiveness. The benefit from investing in validation is in locking in, for the long term, the compounding value of all other resilience investments. If you automate these techniques, the engineering and support teams can focus on delivering new value. The cost of automating and monitoring will ideally be amortized across other efforts and products your company is pursuing.

You will probably periodically run out of money or time you can invest into resilience. The next time you have the opportunity to spend more of these limited resources, consider streamlining the costs of your already deployed resilience mechanisms first. Once you are confident in their quality and efficiency, venture into more resilience options.

Conclusion

In this chapter, we discussed various ways to build resilience into the security and reliability of a system, starting from the design phase. In order to provide resilience, humans need to make choices. We can optimize some choices with automation, but for others we still need humans.

Resilience of reliability properties helps preserve a system's most important functionality, so the system doesn't fully succumb under conditions of excessive load or extensive failures. If the system does break, this functionality extends the time available for responders to organize, prevent more damage, or, if necessary, engage in manual recovery. Resilience helps systems withstand attacks and defends against attempts to gain long-term access. If an attacker breaks into the system, design features like blast radius controls limit the damage.

Ground your design strategies in defense in depth. Examine a system's security the same way you view uptime and reliability. At its core, defense in depth is like N+1 redundancy for your defenses. You don't trust all of your network capacity to a single router or switch, so why trust a single firewall or other defense measure? In designing for defense in depth, always assume and check for failures in different layers of security: failures in outer perimeter security, the compromise of an endpoint, an insider attack, and so on. Plan for lateral moves with the intent of stopping them.

Even when you design your systems to be resilient, it's possible that resilience will fall short at some point and your system will break. The next chapter discusses what happens *after* that happens: how do you recover broken systems, and how can you minimize the damage caused by breakages?

CHAPTER 9

Design for Recovery

By Aaron Joyner, Jon McCune, and Vitaliy Shipitsyn
with Constantinos Neophytou, Jessie Yang, and Kristina Bennett

All complex systems experience reliability issues, and attackers explicitly try to make systems fail or otherwise deviate from their intended function. During the early stages of product development, you should anticipate such failures and plan for the inevitable recovery process that follows.

In this chapter, we discuss strategies like the use of rate limiting and version numbering. We take a deep dive into tradeoffs like rollbacks and revocation mechanisms that can bring a system back to a healthy state, but that can also reintroduce security vulnerabilities. No matter which recovery approach you choose, it's critical that you know the state that your system needs to return to, and what to do when you can't access that known good state through existing methods.

Modern distributed systems are subject to many types of failures—failures that result from both unintentional errors and deliberately malicious actions. When exposed to accumulating errors, rare failure modes, or malicious actions by attackers, humans must intervene to recover even the most secure and resilient systems.

The act of recovering a failed or compromised system into a stable and secure state can be complex in unanticipated ways. For example, rolling back an unstable release may reintroduce security vulnerabilities. Rolling out a new release to patch a security vulnerability may introduce reliability issues. Risky mitigations like these are full of more subtle tradeoffs. For example, when deciding how quickly to deploy changes, a quick rollout is more likely to win the race against attackers, but also limits the amount of testing you're able to do on it. You might end up widely deploying new code with critical stability bugs.

It's far from ideal to begin considering these subtleties—and your system's lack of preparedness to handle them—during a stressful security or reliability incident. Only conscious design decisions can prepare your system to have the reliability and the flexibility it needs to natively support varying recovery needs. This chapter covers some design principles that we've found effective in preparing our systems to facilitate recovery efforts. Many of these principles apply across a range of scales, from planet-scale systems to firmware environments within individual machines.

What Are We Recovering From?

Before we dive into design strategies to facilitate recovery, we'll cover some scenarios that lead a system to require recovery. These scenarios fall into several basic categories: random errors, accidental errors, malicious actions, and software errors.

Random Errors

All distributed systems are built from physical hardware, and all physical hardware fails. The unreliable nature of physical devices and the unpredictable physical environment in which they operate lead to random errors. As the amount of physical hardware supporting the system grows, the likelihood that a distributed system will experience random errors increases. Aging hardware also leads to more errors.

Some random errors are easier to recover from than others. Total failure or isolation of some part of the system, such as a power supply or a critical network router, is one of the simplest failures to handle.[1] It's more complicated to address short-lived corruption caused by unexpected bit flips,[2] or long-lived corruption caused by a failing instruction on one core in a multicore CPU. These errors are especially insidious when they occur silently.

Fundamentally unpredictable events outside a system can also introduce random errors into modern digital systems. A tornado or earthquake may cause you to suddenly and permanently lose a particular part of the system. A power station or substation failure or an anomaly in a UPS or battery may compromise the delivery of electrical power to one or many machines. This can introduce a voltage sag or swell that can lead to memory corruption or other transient errors.

---

1 The CAP theorem (*https://oreil.ly/WP_FI*) describes some tradeoffs involved in scaling distributed systems and their consequences.

2 Unexpected bit flips can be caused by failing hardware, noise from other systems, or even cosmic rays. Chapter 15 discusses failing hardware in more detail.

Accidental Errors

All distributed systems are operated by humans, either directly or indirectly, and all humans make mistakes. We define *accidental errors* as errors caused by humans with good intent. The human error rate varies according to the type of task. Roughly speaking, as the complexity of a task increases, the error rate increases.[3] An internal analysis of Google outages from 2015 through 2018 indicated that a meaningful fraction of outages (though not most outages) were caused by a unilateral human action that wasn't subject to an engineering or procedural safety check.

Humans can make errors in relation to any portion of your system, so you need to consider how human error can occur throughout the entire stack of tools, systems, and job processes in the system lifecycle. Accidental errors may also impact your system in a random way that's external to the system—for example, if a backhoe used for unrelated construction cuts through a fiber-optic cable.

Software Errors

You can address the error types we've discussed so far with design changes and/or software. To paraphrase a classic quote[4] and its corollary,[5] all errors can be solved with software...except bugs in software. Software errors are really just a special, delayed case of accidental errors: errors made during software development. Your code will have bugs, and you'll need to fix these bugs. Some basic and well-discussed design principles—for example, modular software design, testing, code review, and validating the inputs and outputs of dependent APIs—help you address bugs. Chapters 6 and 12 cover these topics in more depth.

In some cases, software bugs mimic other types of errors. For example, automation lacking a safety check may make sudden and dramatic changes to production, mimicking a malicious actor. Software errors also magnify other types of errors—for example, sensor errors that return unexpected values that the software can't handle properly, or unexpected behavior that looks like a malicious attack when users circumvent a faulty mechanism during the normal course of their work.

Malicious Actions

Humans can also work against your systems deliberately. These people may be privileged and highly knowledgeable insiders with the intent to do harm. Malicious actors

---

3 An entire area of research known as Human Reliability Analysis (HRA) catalogs the likelihood of human errors at a given task. For more information, see the US Nuclear Regulatory Commission's Probabilistic Risk Assessment (*https://oreil.ly/fGTHa*).

4 "All problems in computer science can be solved by another level of indirection." —David Wheeler

5 "... except too many levels of indirection." —Unknown

refer to an entire category of humans actively working to subvert the security controls and reliability of your system(s), or possibly working to imitate random, accidental, or other kinds of errors. Automation can reduce, but not eliminate, the need for human involvement. As the size and complexity of your distributed system scales, the size of the organization maintaining it has to scale alongside the system (ideally, in a sublinear way). At the same time, the likelihood of one of the humans in that organization violating the trust you place in them also grows.

These violations of trust may come from an insider who abuses their legitimate authority over the system by reading user data not pertinent to their job, leaking or exposing company secrets, or even actively working to cause a prolonged outage. The person may have a brief lapse of good decision making, have a genuine desire to cause harm, fall victim to a social engineering attack, or even be coerced by an external actor (*https://xkcd.com/538*).

A third-party compromise of a system can also introduce malicious errors. Chapter 2 covers the range of malicious actors in depth. When it comes to system design, mitigation strategies are the same regardless of whether the malicious actor is an insider or a third-party attacker who compromises system credentials.

Design Principles for Recovery

The following sections provide some design principles for recovery based upon our years of experience with distributed systems. This list isn't meant to be exhaustive—we'll provide recommendations for further reading. These principles also apply across a range of organizations, not just to Google-scale organizations. Overall, when designing for recovery, it's important to be open-minded about the breadth and variety of problems that might arise. In other words, don't spend time worrying about how to classify nuanced edge cases of errors; focus on being ready to recover from them.

Design to Go as Quickly as Possible (Guarded by Policy)

During a compromise or a system outage, there's a lot of pressure to recover your system to its intended working state as soon as possible. However, the mechanisms you use to make rapid changes to systems can themselves risk making the wrong changes too quickly, exacerbating the issue. Likewise, if your systems are maliciously compromised, premature recovery or cleanup actions can cause other problems—for example, your actions might tip off an adversary that they've been discovered.[6] We've

---

6 For a detailed discussion of how to respond when you've been compromised, and the meta problem of determining whether your recovery systems are themselves compromised, see Chapter 18. Chapter 7 also has additional design patterns and examples describing how to choose an appropriate rate.

found a few approaches effective in balancing the tradeoffs involved in designing systems to support variable rates of recovery.

To recover your system from any of our four classes of errors—or better yet, to avoid the need for recovery—you must be able to change the state of the system. When building an update mechanism (for example, a software/firmware rollout process, configuration change management procedure, or batch scheduling service), we recommend designing the update system to operate as fast as you can imagine it might ever need to operate (or faster, to the limits of practicality). Then, add controls to constrain the rate of change to match your current policy for risk and disruption. There are several advantages to decoupling your ability to perform rollouts from your rate and frequency policies for rollouts.

The rollout needs and policies of any organization change over time. For example, in its early days, a company might perform rollouts monthly, and never on nights or weekends. If the rollout system is designed around policy changes, a change in policy might entail difficult refactoring and intrusive code changes. If the design of a rollout system instead clearly separates the timing and rate of change from the action and content of that change, it's much easier to adjust to inevitable policy changes that govern timing and rates of change.

Sometimes, new information you receive halfway through a rollout affects how you respond. Imagine that in response to an internally discovered security vulnerability, you're deploying an internally developed patch. Typically, you wouldn't need to deploy this change rapidly enough to risk destabilizing your service. However, your risk calculation may change in response to a landscape change (see Chapter 7): if you discover halfway through the rollout that the vulnerability is now public knowledge and being actively exploited in the wild, you may want to accelerate the procedure.

Inevitably, there will come a time when a sudden or unexpected event changes the risk you're willing to accept. As a result, you want to push out a change very, very quickly. Examples can range from security bugs (ShellShock,[7] Heartbleed,[8] etc.) to discovering an active compromise. *We recommend designing your emergency push system to simply be your regular push system turned up to maximum.* This also means that your normal rollout system and emergency rollback system are one and the same. We often say that untested emergency practices won't work when you need them. Enabling your regular system to handle emergencies means that you don't have

---

7 See CVE-2014-6271 (*https://oreil.ly/mRhGN*), CVE-2014-6277 (*https://oreil.ly/yyf6K*), CVE-2014-6278 (*https://oreil.ly/7ii2u*), and CVE-2014-7169 (*https://oreil.ly/0ZD04*).

8 See CVE-2014-0160 (*https://oreil.ly/cJTQ8*).

to maintain two separate push systems, and that you exercise your emergency release system often.[9]

If responding to a stressful situation only requires you to modify rate limits in order to quickly push a change, you'll have much more confidence that your rollout tooling works as expected. You can then focus your energy on other unavoidable risks, such as potential bugs in quickly deployed changes, or making sure you close the vulnerabilities attackers may have used to access your systems.

Isolate Your Rate-Limiting Mechanism to Increase Reliability

If your system *can* deploy changes extremely quickly, how can you protect against unwanted rapid execution? One strategy is to build the rate-limiting mechanism as an independent, standalone, single-purpose microservice that constrains the rate of change to a particular system or systems. Make this microservice as simple as possible and amenable to rigorous testing. For example, a rate-limiting microservice might provide a short-lived cryptographic token that asserts that the microservice reviewed and approved a particular change at a certain time.

The rate-limiting service is also an excellent point at which to collect change logs for auditing purposes. While the additional service dependency adds one more moving part to the full rollout system, we find the tradeoff worthwhile: the separation explicitly communicates that change actuation should be decoupled from change rate (for safety). It also discourages engineers from circumventing the rate-limiting service, because other rate-limiting code that offers redundant functionality is likely to be a clear sign of unsafe design.

We learned these lessons as the rollout of our internal Linux distribution evolved. Until recently, Google installed all the machines in our datacenters with a "base" or "golden" image, which contained a known set of static files. There were a few specific customizations, such as hostname, network configuration, and credentials, per machine. Our policy was to roll out a new "base" image across the fleet every month. Over several years, we built a set of tools and a software update system around that policy and workflow: bundle all of the files into a compressed archive, have the set of changes reviewed by a senior SRE, and then gradually update the fleet of machines to the new image.

We built our rollout tooling around this policy, and designed the tooling to map a particular base image to a collection of machines. We designed the configuration language to express how to change that mapping over the course of several weeks, and

---

9 A corollary to this principle: if you have a methodology that works in an emergency (often because it's low dependency), make that your standard methodology.

then used a few mechanisms to layer exceptions on top of the base image. One exception included security patches for a growing number of individual software packages: as the list of exceptions grew more complicated, it made less sense for our tooling to follow a monthly pattern.

In response, we decided to abandon the assumption of a monthly update to the base image. We designed more granular release units that corresponded to each software package. We also built a clean new API that specified the exact set of packages to install, one machine at a time, on top of the existing rollout mechanism. As shown in Figure 9-1, this API decoupled the software that defined a few different aspects:

- The rollout and the rate at which each package was supposed to change
- The configuration store that defined the current config of all machines
- The rollout actuator that manages applying updates to each machine

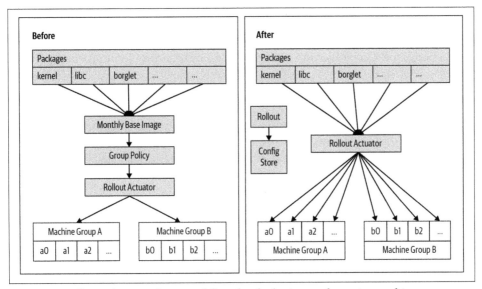

Figure 9-1. The evolution of our workflow for deploying packages to machines

As a result, we could develop each aspect independently. We then repurposed an existing config store to specify the configuration of all the packages applied to each machine, and built a rollout system to track and update the independent rollouts of each package.

By decoupling the image build from the monthly rollout policy, we could enable a much wider range of release velocities for different packages. At the same time, while still preserving a stable and consistent rollout to most machines in the fleet, some test machines could follow the latest builds of all the software. Better still, decoupling the policy unlocked new uses of the whole system. We now use it to distribute a subset of carefully vetted files to the whole fleet regularly. We can also use our normal tooling for emergency releases simply by adjusting some rate limits and approving the release of one type of package to proceed faster than normal. The end result was simpler, more useful, and safer.

Limit Your Dependencies on External Notions of Time

Time—that is, ordinary time of day as reported by devices like wristwatches and wall clocks—is a form of state. Because you're generally unable to alter how your system experiences the passage of time, any location where your system incorporates wall-clock time can potentially threaten your ability to complete a recovery. Mismatches between the time when you undertake your recovery effort and the time when the system was last operating normally can lead to unexpected system behaviors. For example, a recovery that involves replaying digitally signed transactions may fail if some transactions are signed by expired certificates, unless you design the recovery process to consider the original transaction date when validating certificates.

Your system's time dependence may be even more likely to introduce security or reliability issues if it depends on an external notion of time that you don't control. This pattern arises in the form of multiple types of errors—for example, software errors like Y2K (*https://oreil.ly/zV9E0*), the Unix epoch rollover (*https://oreil.ly/heY_0*), or accidental errors where developers choose certificate expiration times so far in the future that it's "not their problem anymore." Clear-text or unauthenticated NTP (*https://oreil.ly/9IG8s*) connections also introduce risk if an attacker is able to control the network. A fixed date or time offset in code exhibits a code smell (*https://oreil.ly/zxfz2*) indicating that you may be creating a time bomb.

Tying events to wall-clock time is often an anti-pattern. Instead of wall-clock time, we recommend using one of the following:

- Rates
- Manually advanced notions of forward progress like epoch numbers or version numbers
- Validity lists

As mentioned in Chapter 8, Google's ALTS transport security system does not use expiration time in its digital certificates, and instead relies on a revocation system. The active revocation list is made up of vectors that define valid versus revoked ranges of certificate serial numbers, and works without depending on wall-clock time. You can achieve isolation goals through healthy, periodic pushes of updated revocation lists to create time compartments. You can perform an emergency push of a new revocation list to revoke certificates if you suspect an adversary may have gained access to underlying keys, and you can stop the periodic pushes during unusual circumstances to enable debugging or forensics. See "Use an Explicit Revocation Mechanism" on page 200 for more discussion of that particular topic.

Design choices that depend on wall-clock time may also lead to security weaknesses. Because of reliability constraints, you may be tempted to disable certificate validity checking in order to perform a recovery. However, in this case, the cure is worse than the disease—it would be better to omit the certificate expiration (from the SSH key pair that allows login access to a cluster of servers) than to skip validity checking. To provide one notable exception, wall-clock time *is* useful for deliberately time-bounded access. For example, you might want to require that most employees reauthenticate daily. In cases like this, it's important to have a path for repairing the system that doesn't rely on wall-clock time.

Relying on absolute time can also lead to problems when you attempt to recover from crashes, or when databases that expect monotonically increasing time attempt to recover from corruption. Recovery may require an exhaustive transaction replay (which rapidly becomes infeasible as data sets grow) or an attempt to roll back time in a coordinated way across multiple systems. To provide a simpler example: correlating logs across systems that have inaccurate notions of time burdens your engineers with an unnecessary layer of indirection, which makes accidental errors more common.

You can also eliminate wall-clock time dependencies by using epoch or version advancement, which requires all parts of a system to coordinate around an integer value that represents a forward progression of "valid" versus "expired." An epoch might be an integer stored in a distributed systems component like a lock service, or machine-local state that is ratcheted forward (allowed to move in only a forward direction) according to policy. To enable your systems to perform releases as quickly as possible, you might design them to allow rapid epoch advancement. A single service may be responsible for announcing the current epoch or initiating an epoch advancement. In the face of trouble, you can halt epoch advancement until you understand and remediate the issue. To return to our earlier public-key example: although certificates may age, you won't be tempted to entirely disable certificate verification because you can stop epoch advancement. Epochs have some similarities with the MASVN scheme discussed in "Minimum Acceptable Security Version Numbers" on page 195.

 Aggressively incremented epoch values could roll over or overflow. Be wary of how fast your system deploys changes, and how many intermediate epoch or version values you can tolerably skip.

An adversary with temporary control of your system might inflict lasting damage to the system by dramatically accelerating epoch advancement or causing an epoch roll-over. A common solution to this problem is to choose an epoch value with a sufficiently large range and build in an underlying backstop rate limit—for example, a 64-bit integer rate limited to increment no more than once per second. Hardcoding a backstop rate limit is an exception to our earlier design recommendation to roll out changes as quickly as possible and to add policy to designate the rate of change. However, in this case, it's difficult to imagine a reason to change the system state more than once per second, since you're going to be dealing with billions of years. This strategy is also reasonable because a 64-bit integer is generally inexpensive on modern hardware.

Even in scenarios where waiting for elapsed wall-clock time is desirable, consider simply measuring elapsed time without requiring the actual time of day. A backstop rate limit will work even when the system isn't aware of wall-clock time.

Rollbacks Represent a Tradeoff Between Security and Reliability

The first step to recovery during incident response is to mitigate the incident, typically by safely rolling back any suspect changes. A large fraction of production issues that require human attention are self-inflicted (see "Accidental Errors" and "Software Errors" on page 185), meaning that an intended change to the system contains a bug or other misconfiguration that causes an incident. When this happens, basic tenets of reliability call for a system rollback to the last known good state as quickly and safely as possible.

In other cases, you need to *prevent* rollbacks. When patching security vulnerabilities, you are often racing against attackers, trying to deploy a patch before an attacker exploits the vulnerability. Once the patch is successfully deployed and shown to be stable, you need to prevent attackers from applying a rollback that reintroduces the vulnerability, while still leaving yourself the option to voluntarily roll back—because security patches themselves are code changes, they may contain their own bugs or vulnerabilities.

In light of these considerations, determining the appropriate conditions for a rollback can be complicated. Application-layer software is a more straightforward case. System software, like an operating system or privileged package management daemon, can easily kill and restart tasks or processes. You can collect the names of undesirable versions (usually unique label strings, numbers, or hashes[10]) into a deny list, which you can then incorporate into your deployment system's release policies.

---

10 For example, a cryptographic hash (such as SHA256) of the complete program or firmware image.

Alternatively, you can manage an allow list and build your automation to include deployed application software on that list.

Privileged or low-level system components that are responsible for processing their own updates are more challenging. We call these components *self-updating*. Examples include a package management daemon that updates itself by overwriting its own executable file and then reexecuting itself, or a firmware image such as a BIOS that reflashes a replacement image on top of itself and then forces a reboot. These components may actively prevent themselves from being updated if they are maliciously modified. Hardware-specific implementation requirements add to the challenge. You need rollback control mechanisms that work even for these components, but the intended behavior itself may be challenging to define. Let's consider two example policies and their flaws to better appreciate the problem:

Allow arbitrary rollbacks
: This solution is not secure, because any factor that prompts you to perform a rollback may reintroduce a known security vulnerability. The older or more visible the vulnerability, the more likely it is that stable, weaponized exploitations of that vulnerability are readily available.

Never allow rollbacks
: This solution eliminates the path to return to a known stable state, and only allows you to move forward to newer states. It's unreliable because if an update introduces a bug, you can no longer roll back to the last known good version. This approach implicitly requires the build system to generate new versions to which you can roll forward, adding time and avoidable dependencies to the build and release engineering infrastructure.

Many alternatives to these two extreme approaches offer practical tradeoffs. These include the following:

- Using deny lists
- Using Security Version Numbers (SVNs) and Minimum Acceptable Security Version Numbers (MASVNs)
- Rotating signing keys

In the following discussion, we assume in all cases that updates are cryptographically signed and that the signature covers the component image and its version metadata.

A combination of all three techniques discussed here may best manage the security/reliability tradeoffs for self-updating components. However, the complexity of this combination, and its reliance on `ComponentState`, makes this approach a huge undertaking. We recommend introducing one functionality at a time, and allowing sufficient time to identify any bugs or corner cases for each component you introduce. Ultimately, all healthy organizations should use key rotation, but deny list and MASVN capabilities are useful for high-velocity responses.

Deny lists

As you discover bugs or vulnerabilities in release versions, you may want to build a deny list to prevent known bad versions from being (re)activated, perhaps by hard-coding the deny list in the component itself. In the following example, we write this as Release[DenyList]. After the component is updated to a newly released version, it refuses an update to a deny-listed version:

```
def IsUpdateAllowed(self, Release) -> bool:
    return Release[Version] not in self[DenyList]
```

Unfortunately, this solution addresses only accidental errors, because hardcoded deny lists present an unresolvable security/reliability tradeoff. If the deny list always leaves room for rollback to at least one older, known good image, the scheme is vulnerable to *unzipping*—an attacker can incrementally roll back versions until they arrive at an older version that contains a known vulnerability that they can exploit. This scenario essentially collapses to the "allow arbitrary rollbacks" extreme described earlier, with intermediate hops along the way. Alternatively, configuring the deny list to altogether prevent rollbacks for critical security updates leads to the "never allow rollbacks" extreme, with its accompanying reliability pitfalls.

If you're recovering from a security or reliability incident when multiple updates may be in progress across your fleet, hardcoded deny lists are a good choice for setting up your system to avoid accidental errors. It's quick and relatively easy to append a single version to a list, since doing so has little or no impact on the validity of any other versions. However, you need a more robust strategy to resist malicious attacks.

A better deny-listing solution encodes the deny list outside of the self-updating component itself. In the following example, we write this as ComponentState[DenyList]. This deny list survives across component upgrades and downgrades because it's independent of any single release—but the component still needs logic in order to maintain the deny list. Each release may reasonably encode the most comprehensive deny list known at the time of its release: Release[DenyList]. The maintenance logic then unites these lists and stores them locally (note that we write self[DenyList] instead of Release[DenyList] to indicate that "self" is installed and actively running):

```
ComponentState[DenyList] = ComponentState[DenyList].union(self[DenyList])
```

Check tentative updates for validity against the list, and refuse deny-listed updates (don't explicitly reference "self" because its contribution to the deny list is already reflected in ComponentState, where it remains even after future versions are installed):

```
def IsUpdateAllowed(self, Release, ComponentState) -> bool:
    return Release[Version] not in ComponentState[DenyList]
```

Now you can make the security/reliability tradeoff deliberately as a matter of policy. When you're deciding what to include in Release[DenyList], you can weigh the risk of unzipping attacks against the risk of an unstable release.

This approach also has drawbacks, even when you encode deny lists in a Component State data structure that's maintained outside of the self-updating component itself:

- Even though the deny list exists outside the configured intent of your centralized deployment system, you still have to monitor and consider it.
- If an entry is ever accidentally added to the deny list, you may want to remove that entry from the list. However, introducing a removal capability may open the door to unzipping attacks.
- The deny list may grow without bound, eventually hitting the size limits of storage. How do you manage garbage collection (*https://oreil.ly/_TsjS*) of a deny list?

Minimum Acceptable Security Version Numbers

Over time, deny lists become large and unwieldy as entries are appended. You can use a separate Security Version Number, written as Release[SVN], to drop older entries from the deny list, while still preventing them from being installed. As a result, you reduce the cognitive load on the humans responsible for the system.

Keeping Release[SVN] independent of other version notions allows a compact and mathematically comparable way to logically follow large numbers of releases without requiring the overhead space a deny list needs. Whenever you apply a critical security fix and demonstrate its stability, you increment Release[SVN], marking a security milestone that you use to regulate rollback decisions. Because you have a straightforward indicator of each version's security status, you have the flexibility to conduct ordinary release testing and qualification, and the confidence that you can quickly and safely make rollback decisions when you discover bugs or stability issues.

Remember that you also want to prevent malicious actors from somehow rolling your systems back to known bad or vulnerable versions.[11] To prevent these actors from getting a foothold in your infrastructure and using that foothold to prevent recovery, you can use a MASVN to define a low-water mark below which your

---

11 "Known bad" versions may result from successful but irreversible changes, such as a major schema change, or from bugs and vulnerabilities.

systems should never operate.[12] This must be an ordered value (not a cryptographic hash), preferably a simple integer. You can manage the MASVN similarly to how you manage the deny list:

- Each release version includes a MASVN value that reflects the acceptable versions at its time of release.

- You maintain a global value outside of the deployment system, written as `ComponentState[MASVN]`.

As a precondition for applying the update, all releases include logic verifying that a tentative update's `Release[SVN]` is at least as high as the `ComponentState[MASVN]`. It is expressed as pseudocode as follows:

```
def IsUpdateAllowed(self, Release, ComponentState) -> bool:
    return Release[SVN] >= ComponentState[MASVN]
```

The maintenance operation for the global `ComponentState[MASVN]` is not part of the deployment process. Instead, maintenance takes place as the new release initializes for the first time. You hardcode a target MASVN into each release—the MASVN that you want to enforce for that component at the time when that release is created, written as `Release[MASVN]`.

When a new release is deployed and executed for the first time, it compares its `Release[MASVN]` (written as `self[MASVN]`, to reference the release that is installed and running) with `ComponentState[MASVN]`. If `Release[MASVN]` is higher than the existing `ComponentState[MASVN]`, then `ComponentState[MASVN]` updates to the new larger value. In fact, this logic runs every time the component initializes, but `ComponentState[MASVN]` only changes following a successful update with a higher `Release[MASVN]`. It is expressed as pseudocode as follows:

```
ComponentState[MASVN] = max(self[MASVN], ComponentState[MASVN])
```

This scheme can emulate either of the extreme policies mentioned earlier:

- Allowing arbitrary rollback, by never modifying `Release[MASVN]`

- Never allowing rollback, by modifying `Release[MASVN]` in lockstep with `Release[SVN]`

In practice, `Release[MASVN]` is often raised in release $i+1$, following a release that mitigates a security issue. This ensures that $i-1$ or older versions are never executed again. Since `ComponentState[MASVN]` is external to the release itself, version i no

---

12 Another widely deployed example of carefully managed Security Version Numbers exists in Intel's microcode SVN, used for example to mitigate security issue CVE-2018-3615 (*https://oreil.ly/fN9f3*).

---

longer allows downgrade to $i-1$ after $i+1$ has been installed, even though it did allow such downgrades when it was initially deployed. Figure 9-2 illustrates sample values for a sequence of three releases and their impact on ComponentState[MASVN].

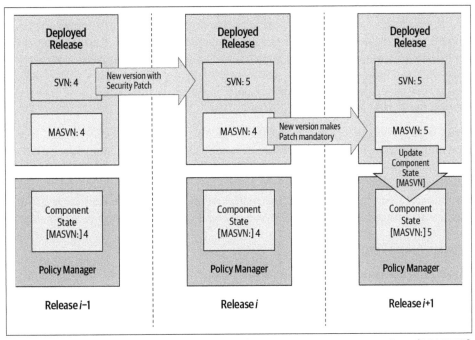

Figure 9-2. A sequence of three releases and their impact on ComponentState[MASVN]

To mitigate a security vulnerability in release $i-1$, release i includes the security patch and an incremented Release[SVN]. Release[MASVN] doesn't change in release i, because even security patches can have bugs. Once release i is proven to be stable in production, the next release, $i+1$, increments the MASVN. This indicates that the security patch is now mandatory, and releases without it are disallowed.

In keeping with the "go as quickly as possible" design tenet, the MASVN scheme separates the policy for reasonable rollback targets from the infrastructure that performs the rollbacks. It's technically feasible to introduce a specific API in the self-updating component and receive a command from the centralized deployment management system to increment ComponentState[MASVN]. With that command, you might raise ComponentState[MASVN] on components that receive an update late in the deployment pipeline, after qualifying the release on enough devices that you have high confidence that it will work as planned. An API like this may be useful when you're responding to an active compromise or a particularly severe vulnerability, where velocity is critical and risk tolerance is higher than normal for availability issues.

So far, this example has avoided introducing a dedicated API to mutate Component State. ComponentState is a delicate collection of values that impacts your ability to recover systems through updates or rollbacks. It is component-local, and external to the configured intent that a centralized piece of automation directly controls. The actual sequence of software/firmware versions experienced by each individual component may vary across a fleet of similar or identical devices, in the face of concurrent development, testing, canary analysis, and rollout. Some components or devices may walk the full set of releases, while others may experience many rollbacks. Still others may experience minimal change, and hop directly from a buggy or vulnerable version to the next stable, qualified release.

Using MASVNs is therefore a useful technique to combine with deny listing for self-updating components. In this scenario, you may perform deny listing very rapidly—potentially under incident response conditions. You then perform MASVN maintenance under calmer circumstances, to garbage-collect the deny list and permanently exclude (on a per-component-instance basis) any releases that are vulnerable or sufficiently old, and are never intended to execute again on a given component instance.

Rotating signing keys

Many self-updating components include support to cryptographically authenticate tentative updates—in other words, part of the release cycle for a component includes cryptographically signing that release. These components often include a hardcoded list of known public keys, or support for an independent key database, as part of Com ponentState. For example:

```
def IsUpdateAllowed(self, Release, KeyDatabase) -> bool:
    return VerifySignature(Release, KeyDatabase)
```

You can prevent rollback by modifying the set of public keys trusted by a component, typically to remove an old or compromised key or to introduce a new key for signing future releases. Older releases are invalidated because newer releases no longer trust the public signature verification key needed to verify the signatures on the older releases. You must manage key rotation carefully, however, because a sudden change from one signing key to another can leave systems perilously exposed to reliability issues.

Alternatively, you can rotate keys more gradually by introducing a new update signature verification key, $k+1$, alongside an older verification key, k, and allowing updates that authenticate with either key to proceed. Once stability is demonstrated, you drop trust in key k. This scheme requires support for multiple signatures over a release artifact, and for multiple verification keys when authenticating candidate updates. It also has the advantage that signing key rotation—a best practice for cryptographic key management—is exercised regularly and therefore likely to work when needed in the wake of an incident.

Key rotation can help you recover from a very serious compromise whereby an attacker manages to temporarily control release management and sign and deploy a release with Release[MASVN] set to the maximum value. In this type of attack, by setting ComponentState[MASVN] to its maximum value, the attacker forces you to set Release[SVN] to its maximum in order for future releases to be viable, thereby rendering the whole MASVN scheme useless. In response, you can revoke the compromised public key in new releases signed by a new key, and add dedicated logic to recognize the unusually high ComponentState[MASVN] and reset it. Since this logic is itself subtle and potentially dangerous, you should use it with care, and aggressively revoke any releases that include it as soon as they've served their purpose.

This chapter does not cover the full complexity of incident response for a serious and targeted compromise. See Chapter 18 for more information.

Rolling back firmware and other hardware-centric constraints

Hardware devices with their own corresponding firmware—such as a machine and its BIOS, or a network interface card (NIC) and its firmware—are common manifestations of self-updating components. These devices present additional challenges for robust MASVN or key rotation schemes, which we touch on briefly here. These details play an important role in recovery because they help to enable scalable or automated recovery from potentially malicious actions.

Sometimes, one-time-programmable (OTP) devices like fuses are used by ROM or firmware to implement a forward-only MASVN scheme by storing Component State[MASVN]. These schemes have significant reliability risks because rollback is infeasible. Additional software layers help address the constraints of physical hardware. For example, the OTP-backed ComponentState[MASVN] covers a small, single-purpose bootloader that contains its own MASVN logic and has exclusive access to a separate mutable MASVN storage region. This bootloader then exposes the more robust MASVN semantics to the higher-level software stack.

For authenticating signed updates, hardware devices sometimes use OTP memory to store public keys (or their hashes) and revocation information related to those keys. The number of key rotations or revocations supported is typically heavily limited. In these cases, a common pattern is again to use the OTP-encoded public key and revocation information to validate a small bootloader. This bootloader then contains its own layer of verification and key management logic, analogous to the MASVN example.

When dealing with a large fleet of hardware devices that actively leverage these mechanisms, managing spare parts can be a challenge. Spare parts that sit in inventory for years before they're deployed will necessarily have very old firmware when they're put to use. This old firmware must be updated. If older keys are completely disused, and newer releases are signed only by newer keys that didn't exist when the spare part was originally manufactured, then the new update won't verify.

One solution is to walk devices through a sequence of upgrades, making sure that they make a stop at all releases that trust both an old and a new key during a key rotation event. Another solution is to support multiple signatures per release. Even though newer images (and devices that have been updated to run these newer images) don't trust an older verification key, these newer images can still carry a signature by that older key. Only older firmware versions can validate that signature—a desired action that allows them to recover after being starved of updates.

Consider how many keys are likely to be used across the lifetime of a device, and make sure that the device has sufficient space for keys and signatures. For example, some FPGA products support multiple keys for authenticating or encrypting their bitstreams.[13]

Use an Explicit Revocation Mechanism

A revocation system's primary role is to stop some kind of access or function. In the face of an active compromise, a revocation system can be a lifesaver, allowing you to quickly revoke attacker-controlled credentials and recover control of your systems. However, once a revocation system is in place, accidental or malicious behavior may lead to reliability and security consequences. If possible, consider these issues during the design phase. Ideally, the revocation system should serve its purpose at all times without introducing too many security and reliability risks of its own.

To illustrate general concepts about revocation, we'll consider the following unfortunate but common scenario: you discover that an attacker has somehow gained control of valid credentials (such as a client SSH key pair that allows login access to a cluster of servers), and you want to revoke these credentials.[14]

---

13 One example is the hardware root of trust support in Xilinx Zynq Ultrascale+ devices (*https://oreil.ly/hfydr*).

14 Revoking the credentials immediately may not always be the best choice. For a discussion on responding to a compromise, see Chapter 17.

Revocation is a complex topic that touches on many aspects of resilience, security, and recovery. This section discusses only some aspects of revocation that are relevant for recovery. Additional topics to explore include when to use an allow list versus a deny list, how to hygienically rotate certificates in a crash-resilient manner, and how to safely canary new changes during rollout. Other chapters in this book offer guidance on many of these topics, but bear in mind that no single book is an adequate reference in and of itself.

A centralized service to revoke certificates

You might choose to use a centralized service to revoke certificates. This mechanism prioritizes security by requiring your systems to communicate with a centralized certificate validity database that stores certificate validity information. You must carefully monitor and maintain this database in the interest of keeping your systems secure, as it becomes the authoritative store of record for which certificates are valid. This approach is similar to building a separate rate-limiting service independent from the service designed to enact changes, as discussed earlier in the chapter. Requiring communication with a certificate validity database does have a shortcoming, however: if the database is ever down, all the other dependent systems also go down. There's a strong temptation to fail open if the certificate validity database is unavailable, so that other systems won't also become unavailable. Proceed with great caution!

Failing open

Failing open avoids lockout and simplifies recovery, but also poses a dangerous tradeoff: this strategy circumvents an important access protection against misuse or attack. Even partial fail-open scenarios may cause problems. For example, imagine that a system the certificate validity database depends on goes down. Let's suppose the database depends on a time or epoch service, but accepts all properly signed credentials. If the certificate validity database cannot reach the time/epoch service, then an attacker who performs a relatively simple denial-of-service attack—such as overwhelming network links to the time/epoch service—may be able to reuse even extremely old revoked credentials. This attack works because revoked certificates are once again valid while the DoS attack persists. An attacker may breach your network or find new ways to propagate through the network while you're trying to recover.

Instead of failing open, you may want to distribute known good data from the revocation service to individual servers in the form of a revocation list, which nodes can cache locally. Nodes then proceed with their best understanding of the state of the world until they obtain better data. This choice is far more secure than a time-out-and-fail-open policy.

Handling emergencies directly

In order to revoke keys and certificates quickly, you may want to design infrastructure to handle emergencies directly by deploying changes to a server's *authorized_users* or Key Revocation List (KRL) files.[15] This solution is troublesome for recovery in several ways.

 It's especially tempting to manage *authorized_keys* or *known_hosts* files directly when dealing with small numbers of nodes, but doing so scales poorly and smears ground truth across your entire fleet. It is very difficult to ensure that a given set of keys has been removed from the files on all servers, particularly if those files are the sole source of truth.

Instead of managing *authorized_keys* or *known_hosts* files directly, you can ensure update processes are consistent by centrally managing keys and certificates, and distributing state to servers through a revocation list. In fact, deploying explicit revocation lists is an opportunity to minimize uncertainty during risky situations when you're moving at maximum speed: you can use your usual mechanisms for updating and monitoring files—including your rate-limiting mechanisms—on individual nodes.

Removing dependency on accurate notions of time

Using explicit revocation has another advantage: for certificate validation, this approach removes the dependency on accurate notions of time. Whether it's caused by accident or malice, incorrect time wreaks havoc on certificate validation. For example, old certificates may suddenly become valid again, letting in attackers, and correct certificates may suddenly fail validation, causing a service outage. These are complications you don't want to experience during a stressful compromise or service outage.

It's better for your system's certificate validation to depend on aspects you directly control, such as pushing out files containing root authority public keys or files containing revocation lists. The systems that push the files, the files themselves, and the central source of truth are likely to be much better secured, maintained, and monitored than the distribution of time. Recovery then becomes a matter of simply pushing out files, and monitoring only needs to check whether these are the intended files —standard processes that your systems already use.

---

15 A KRL file is a compact binary representation of which keys issued by a certificate authority (CA) have been revoked. See the ssh-keygen(1) manpage (*https://oreil.ly/rRqkZ*) for details.

Revoking credentials at scale

When using explicit revocation, it's important to consider the implications of scalability. Scalable revocation requires care, because an attacker who has partially compromised your systems can use this partial compromise as a powerful tool to deny further service—maybe even revoking every valid credential in your entire infrastructure. Continuing the SSH example mentioned earlier, an attacker may try to revoke all SSH host certificates, but your machines need to support operations like updating a KRL file in order to apply new revocation information. How do you safeguard those operations against abuse?

When updating a KRL file, blindly replacing the old file with a new one is a recipe for trouble[16]—a single push can revoke every valid credential in your entire infrastructure. One safeguard is to have the target server evaluate the new KRL before applying it, and refuse any update that revokes its own credentials. A KRL that revokes the credentials of all hosts is ignored by all hosts. Because an attacker's best strategy is to revoke half your machines, you have a worst-case guarantee that at the very least, half of your machines will still function after each KRL push. It's much easier to recover and restore half of your infrastructure than all of it.[17]

Avoiding risky exceptions

Because of their size, large distributed systems may encounter issues distributing revocation lists. These issues may limit how quickly you can deploy a new revocation list, and slow your response time when removing compromised credentials.

To address this shortcoming, you might be tempted to build a dedicated "emergency" revocation list. However, this solution may be less than ideal. Since you will rarely use that emergency list, the mechanism is less likely to work when you need it the most. A better solution is to shard your revocation list so that you update it incrementally. That way, revoking credentials during an emergency requires updating only a subset of the data. Consistently using sharding means that your system always uses a multi-part revocation list, and you use the same mechanisms under both normal and emergency circumstances.

Similarly, beware of adding "special" accounts (such as accounts offering direct access to senior employees) that circumvent revocation mechanisms. These accounts

---

16 While this chapter is focused on *recovery*, it is critical to also consider the *resilience* of operations like this. When replacing a critical configuration file on a POSIX system such as Linux, ensuring robust behavior in the face of crashes or other failures requires care. Consider using the `renameat2` system call with the `RENAME_EXCHANGE` flag.

17 Successive malicious KRL pushes may broaden the negative impact, but the speed and breadth constraints still materially expand the response window.

are very attractive targets for attackers—a successful attack on such an account might render all of your revocation mechanisms ineffective.

Know Your Intended State, Down to the Bytes

Recovery from any category of errors—whether they're random, accidental, malicious, or software errors—requires returning the system to a known good state. Doing so is much easier if you actually know the intended state of the system and have a means to read the deployed state. This point may seem obvious, but not knowing the intended state is a common source of problems. The more thoroughly you encode the intended state and reduce the mutable state at every layer—per service, per host, per device, and so on—the easier it is to recognize when you return to a good working state. Ultimately, thoroughly encoding the intended state is the foundation of excellent automation, security, intrusion detection, and recovery to a known state.

What Is State?

The *state* of a system includes all the necessary information the system needs to perform its desired function. Even systems described as "stateless" (e.g., a simple REST web service that tells you if an integer is odd or even) have state—for example, the version of the code, the port on which the service is listening, and whether the service starts automatically at host/VM/container startup. For the purposes of this chapter, *state* describes not only the operation of the system in response to a sequence of requests, but also the configuration and environmental setup of the service itself.

Host management

Let's say you manage an individual host, such as a physical machine, a virtual machine, or even a simple Docker container. You've set up the infrastructure to perform automated recovery, and this brings a lot of value because it efficiently handles many of the issues that may occur, such as those discussed in detail in Chapter 7 of the SRE book. In order to enable automation, you need to encode the state of that individual machine, including the workloads running on it. You encode enough of this information to let automation safely return the machine to a good state. At Google, we apply this paradigm at every layer of abstraction, up and down the hardware and software stack.

Google's system that distributes our host's software packages to the fleet of machines, as described in "Design to Go as Quickly as Possible (Guarded by Policy)" on page 186, continually monitors the entire state of the system in an unconventional way. Each machine continually watches its local filesystem, maintaining a map that includes the name and a cryptographic checksum of each file in the filesystem. We gather those maps with a central service and compare them with the assigned set of packages—that is, the intended state—for each machine. When we find a deviation between the intended state and the current state, we append that information to a list of deviations.

Because it unifies various means of recovery into one process, the strategy of capturing the state of the machine gives powerful advantages for recovery. If a cosmic ray randomly corrupts a bit on disk, we discover the checksum mismatch and repair the deviation. If the intended state of the machine changes because a software rollout for one component inadvertently changes a file for a different component, altering the contents of that file, we repair the deviation. If someone attempts to modify the local configuration of a machine outside of the normal management tooling and review process (either accidentally or maliciously), we repair that deviation too. You might instead choose to repair deviations by reimaging the entire system—an approach that's less sophisticated and easier to implement, but more disruptive at scale.

In addition to capturing the state of files on disk, many applications also have a corresponding in-memory state. An automated recovery must repair both states. For example, when an SSH daemon starts, it reads its configuration from disk and does not reload the configuration unless instructed to do so. To ensure that in-memory state is updated as needed, each package is required to have an idempotent post_install command,[18] which runs whenever a deviation in its files is being repaired. The OpenSSH package's post_install restarts the SSH daemon. A similar pre_rm command cleans up any in-memory state before the files are removed. These simple mechanisms can maintain all of the in-memory state of the machine, and report and repair deviations.

Encoding this state lets automation inspect every deviation for any malicious discrepancies. The rich information on the state of your machines is also extremely valuable during the forensic analysis that follows a security incident, helping you better understand the attacker's actions and intent. For example, perhaps the attacker found a way to deposit malicious shellcode on some of your machines, but wasn't able to reverse-engineer the monitoring and repair system, which reverted the unexpected changes on one or more machines. It will be much harder for the attacker to cover their tracks

---

18 The post_install and pre_rm concepts are borrowed from Debian's (*https://oreil.ly/H9q9p*) familiar pre inst, postinst, prerm, and postrm. Google's package management system takes a more heavy-handed approach: it does not allow separate configuration and installation of packages, or half-successful installs. Any package change is guaranteed to succeed, or the machine is rolled back completely to the previous state. If the rollback fails, the machine is sent through our repairs process for reinstallation and potential hardware replacement. This approach allows us to eliminate much of the complexity of the package states.

because the central service will have noticed and logged the deviations reported by the host.[19]

In summary, all state changes are equal at this level of abstraction. You can automate, secure, and validate all state changes in a similar way, treating both a rollback of a binary that failed canary analysis and an emergency rollout of an updated bash binary as routine changes. Using the same infrastructure enables you to make consistent policy decisions about how quickly to apply each change. Rate limits at this level protect against unintended collisions between the types of changes and establish a maximum acceptable rate of change.

Device firmware

For firmware updates, you may also capture state further down the stack. The individual pieces of hardware in a modern computer have their own software and configuration parameters. In the interest of safety and reliability, you should at least track the version of each device's firmware. Ideally, you should capture all the settings available to that firmware, and ensure they're set to their expected values.

When managing the firmware and its configuration on Google's machines, we leverage the same systems and processes that we use to manage updates to our host software and for deviation analysis (see "Host management" on page 204). Automation securely distributes the intended state for all the firmware as a package, reports back any deviations, and repairs the deviations according to our rate-limiting policies and other policies on handling disruption.

The intended state is often not directly exposed to the local daemon monitoring the filesystem, which has no special knowledge of device firmware. We decouple the complexity of interacting with the hardware from this daemon by allowing each package to reference an activation check—a script or binary in the package that runs periodically to determine if the package is correctly installed. The script or binary does whatever is necessary to talk to the hardware and compare the firmware version and configuration parameters, and then reports any unexpected deviations. This functionality is especially useful for recovery, because it empowers subject matter experts (i.e., subsystem owners) to take appropriate steps to remedy problems in their area of expertise. For example, automation keeps track of target state, current state, and deviations. If a machine is targeted to run BIOS version 3 but is currently running BIOS version 1, the automation has no opinion about BIOS version 2. The package management scripts determine if they can upgrade the BIOS to version 3, or if unique constraints require walking a subsystem through multiple installed versions.

---

19 For further discussion about responding to a compromise, see Chapter 17.

A few specific examples illustrate why managing the intended state is critical for both security and reliability. Google uses special vendor-supplied hardware to interface with external time sources (for example, GNSS/GPS systems and atomic clocks) to facilitate accurate timekeeping in production—a precondition for Spanner.[20] Our hardware stores two different firmware versions, on two different chips on the device. In order to correctly operate these time sources, we need to carefully configure these firmware versions. As an added complication, some versions of the firmware have known bugs that affect how they handle leap seconds and other edge cases. If we don't carefully maintain the firmware and settings on these devices, we can't provide accurate time in production. It's important that state management also covers fallback, secondary, or otherwise inactive code or configuration that may suddenly become live during recovery—recovery is a bad time to start figuring out what bugs reside in an inactive image. In this case, if the machines boot but the clock hardware doesn't provide an accurate enough time to run our services, then our system hasn't sufficiently recovered.

To provide another example, a modern BIOS has numerous parameters critical to the security of a booting (and a booted) system. For instance, you may want the boot order to prefer SATA over USB boot devices in order to prevent a malicious actor in a datacenter from easily booting the system from a USB drive. More advanced deployments track and maintain the database of keys allowed to sign BIOS updates, both to manage rotations and to guard against tampering. If your primary boot device experiences a hardware failure during recovery, you don't want to discover that your BIOS is stuck waiting for keyboard input because you forgot to monitor and specify the settings for the secondary boot device.

Global services

The highest layer of abstraction in your service, and the most persistent parts of your infrastructure—for example, storage, naming, and identity—may be the hardest areas for your system to recover. The paradigm of capturing state also applies to these high levels of the stack. When building or deploying new global singleton systems like Spanner or Hadoop (*https://hadoop.apache.org*), make sure you support multiple instances—even if you never plan to use more than one instance, and even for the very first deployment. Beyond backups and restores, you might need to rebuild a new instance of the entire system to restore the data on that system.

Instead of setting up your services by hand, you might set them up by writing imperative turnup automation or using a declarative high-level configuration language (e.g., a container orchestration configuration tool like Terraform). In these scenarios,

---

20 Spanner (*https://oreil.ly/YGCjO*) is Google's globally distributed database that supports externally consistent distributed transactions. It requires very tight time synchronization between datacenters.

you should capture the state of how the service is created. Doing so is analogous to the way test-driven development captures the intended behavior of your code, which then guides your implementation and helps clarify the public API. Both practices lead to more maintainable systems.

The popularity of containers, which are often hermetically built and deployed from source, means that the state of many building blocks of global services is captured by default. While automatically capturing "most" of a service's state is great, don't be lulled into a false sense of security. Restoring your infrastructure from scratch requires exercising a complex chain of dependencies. This may lead you to uncover unexpected capacity problems or circular dependencies. If you run on physical infrastructure, ask yourself: do you have enough spare machines, disk space, and network capacity to bring up a second copy of your infrastructure? If you run on a large cloud platform like GCP or AWS, you may be able to purchase as many physical resources as you need, but do you have enough quota to use these resources on short notice? Have your systems organically grown any interdependencies that prevent a clean startup from scratch? It can be useful to conduct disaster testing under controlled circumstances to make sure you're prepared for the unexpected.[21]

Persistent data

No one cares about backups; they only care about restores.[22]

So far, we've focused on securely restoring the infrastructure necessary to run your service. This is sufficient for some stateless services, but many services also store persistent data, which adds a special set of challenges. There's a lot of excellent information out there on the challenges of backing up and restoring persistent data.[23] Here, we discuss some key aspects in relation to security and reliability.

To defend against the types of errors mentioned earlier—especially malicious errors—your backups need the same level of integrity protection as your primary storage. A malicious insider may change the contents of your backups, and then force a restore from a corrupted backup. Even if you have strong cryptographic signatures that cover your backups, those signatures are useless if your restore tooling doesn't validate them as part of the restore process, or if your internal access controls don't properly restrict the set of humans who can manually make signatures.

---

21 See Krishnan, Kripa. 2012. "Weathering the Unexpected." *ACM Queue* 10(9). *https://oreil.ly/vJ66c*.

22 Many variations of this excellent advice have been attributed to many highly respected engineers. The oldest version we could find in print, which happened to be in a book on one of the authors' bookshelves, is from W. Curtis Preston's *Unix Backup & Recovery* (O'Reilly). He attributes the quote to Ron Rodriguez as "No one cares if you can back up—only if you can restore."

23 For a primer, see Kristina Bennett's SREcon18 talk "Tradeoffs in Resiliency: Managing the Burden of Data Recoverability" (*https://oreil.ly/V-FEC*).

It's important to compartmentalize the security protection of persistent data where possible. If you detect corruption in your serving copy of the data, you should isolate the corruption to the smallest subset of data that's practical. Restoring 0.01% of your persistent data is much faster if you can identify that subset of the backup data and validate its integrity without reading and validating the other 99.99% of the data. This ability becomes especially important as the size of the persistent data grows, although if you're following best practices for large distributed system design, compartmentalization generally occurs naturally. Calculating the chunk size for compartmentalization often requires a tradeoff between storage and compute overhead, but you should also consider the effect of chunk size on MTTR.

You should account for how frequently your system requires partial restores, too. Consider how much common infrastructure is shared between your systems that are involved in restores and data migrations: a data migration is usually very similar to a low-priority partial restore. If every data migration—whether to another machine, rack, cluster, or datacenter—exercises and builds confidence in the critical parts of your recovery system, you'll know that the infrastructure involved is more likely to work and be understood when you need it the most.

Data restores may also introduce their own security and privacy issues. Deleting data is a necessary and often legally required function for many systems.[24] Make sure that your data recovery systems don't inadvertently allow you to restore data that's assumed to be destroyed. Be conscious of the distinction between deleting encryption keys and deleting encrypted data. It may be efficient to render data inaccessible by destroying the relevant encryption keys, but this approach requires compartmentalizing the keys used for various types of data in a way that's compatible with the requirements of granular data deletion.

Design for Testing and Continuous Validation

As discussed in Chapter 8, continuous validation can help maintain a robust system. To be prepared for recovery, your testing strategy needs to include tests of recovery processes. By their nature, recovery processes perform unusual tasks under unfamiliar conditions, and without testing they will encounter unforeseen challenges. For example, if you are automating the creation of a clean system instance, a good test design may uncover an assumption that a particular service will have only one global instance, and so help identify situations where it's difficult to create a second instance for the restoration of that service. Consider testing conceivable recovery scenarios so that you strike the right balance between test efficiency and production realism.

---

24 For example, see Google's data retention policies (*https://oreil.ly/abNZP*).

You may also consider testing niche situations where recovery is especially difficult. For example, at Google we implement a cryptographic key management protocol in a diverse set of environments: Arm and x86 CPUs, UEFI and bare-metal firmware, Microsoft Visual C++ (MSVC), Clang, GCC compilers, and so on. We knew that exercising all the failure modes for this logic would be challenging—even with substantial investment in end-to-end testing, it's difficult to realistically emulate hardware failures or interrupted communication. Instead, we opted to implement the core logic once, in a portable, compiler-neutral, bit width–neutral way. We unit tested the logic extensively, and paid attention to the interface design for abstract external components. For example, in order to fake individual components and exercise their failure behavior, we created interfaces for reading and writing bytes from flash, for cryptographic key storage, and for performance-monitoring primitives. This method of testing environmental conditions has withstood the test of time, since it explicitly captures the classes of failure from which we want to recover.

Finally, look for ways to build confidence in your recovery methods via continuous validation. Recovery involves actions taken by humans, and humans are unreliable and unpredictable. Unit tests alone, or even continuous integration/delivery/deployment, cannot catch mistakes resulting from human skills or habits. For example, in addition to validating the effectiveness and interoperability of recovery workflows, you must validate that recovery instructions are readable and easy to comprehend.

Emergency Access

The recovery methods described in this chapter rely on a responder's ability to interact with the system, and we've advocated for recovery processes that exercise the same primary services as normal operations. However, you may need to design a special-purpose solution to deploy when normal access methods are *completely* broken.

Emergency Access Is Critical for Reliability and Security

Emergency access is an extreme example where we can't overstate the importance of both reliability and security—there are no more layers to absorb failure. Emergency access should include the absolute minimum of all technologies responders use to reach your company's core administrative interfaces (e.g., root-level access to network devices, machine OSs, or application admin consoles) and to communicate with other responders during the most severe outages, while still preserving access controls as much as possible. Relevant assets include the networks over which responders can connect, any access control systems along the way, and any recovery tools you might need.

Organizations usually have unique needs and options for emergency access. The key is to have a plan and build mechanisms that maintain and protect that access. In addition, you need to be aware of system layers outside your control—any failures in those layers are not actionable, even though they impact you. In these cases, you may need to stand by while someone else fixes the services your company depends on. To minimize the impact of third-party outages on your service, look for any potential cost-effective redundancies you can deploy at any level of your infrastructure. Of course, there may not be any cost-effective alternatives, or you may already have reached the top SLA your service provider guarantees. In that case, remember that you're only as available as the sum of your dependencies.[25]

Google's remote access strategy centers around deploying self-contained critical services to geographically distributed racks. To anchor recovery efforts, we aim to provide remote access control, efficient local communications, alternative networking, and critical fortified points in the infrastructure. During a global outage, since each rack remains available to at least some portion of responders, responders can start to fix the services on the racks they can access, then radially expand the recovery progress. In other words, when global collaboration is practically impossible, arbitrary smaller regions can to try to fix the issues themselves. Despite the fact that responders may lack the context to discover where they're needed the most, and the risk of regions diverging, this approach may meaningfully accelerate recovery.

Access Controls

It's critical that the organization's access control services don't become single points of failure for all remote access. Ideally, you'll be able to implement alternative components that avoid the same dependencies, but the reliability of these alternative components may require different security solutions. While their access policies must be equally strong, they may be less convenient and/or have a degraded feature set, for technical or pragmatic reasons.

Because they rely on dependencies that may be unavailable, remote access credentials cannot depend on typical credential services. Therefore, you can't derive access credentials from the dynamic components of access infrastructure, like single sign-on (SSO) or federated identity providers, unless you can replace those components with low-dependency implementations. In addition, choosing the lifetime of those credentials poses a difficult risk management tradeoff: the good practice of enforcing short-term access credentials for users or devices becomes a time bomb if the outage outlasts them, so you're forced to expand the lifetime of the credentials to exceed the length of any anticipated outages, despite the additional security risk (see "Time Separation" on page 166). Furthermore, if you are issuing remote access credentials

---

25 See Treynor, Ben et al. 2017. "The Calculus of Service Availability." *ACM Queue* 15(2). *https://oreil.ly/It4-h.*

proactively on a fixed schedule rather than activating them on demand at the start of an outage, an outage may begin just as they are about to expire.

If the network access employs user or device authorization, any reliance on dynamic components has risks similar to the risks the credentials service faces. As increasingly more networks use dynamic protocols,[26] you may need to provide alternatives that are more static. Your list of available network providers may limit your options. If dedicated network connections with static network access controls are feasible, make sure their periodic updates don't break either routing or authorization. It may be especially important to implement sufficient monitoring to detect where inside the network access breaks, or to help distinguish network access issues from the issues in the layers above the network.

Google's Fallback for Access Control

Google's corporate network achieves its zero trust properties via automated trust assessments of every employee device, short-term credentials from an SSO service with two-factor authorization, and multi-party authorization for some administrative operations. Each of these functions is implemented in software with nontrivial dependencies. A failure of any of these dependencies could prevent all employee access, including for incident responders. To address this eventuality, we provisioned alternate credentials to be available offline and deployed alternate authentication and authorization algorithms. These provisions delivered a matching degree of security, while dramatically reducing the total set of dependencies. To limit the new attack surface, operating costs, and impact of relatively worse usability, these provisions are restricted to the people who need access immediately, while the rest of the company waits for those people to fix the normal access control services.

Communications

Emergency communication channels are the next critical factor in emergency response. What should on-callers do when their usual chat service is down or unreachable? What if that chat service is compromised or being eavesdropped on by the attacker?

Pick a communications technology (e.g., Google Chat, Skype, or Slack) that has as few dependencies as possible and is useful enough for the size of your responder teams. If that technology is outsourced, is the system reachable by the responders, even if the system layers outside your control are broken? Phone bridges, though inefficient, also exist as an old-school option, though they're increasingly deployed

---

26 For example, software-defined networking (SDN).

using IP telephony that depends on the internet. Internet Relay Chat (IRC) infrastructure is reliable and self-contained if your company wants to deploy its own solution, but it lacks some security aspects. Additionally, you still have to make sure your IRC servers remain somewhat accessible during network outages. When your communication channels are hosted outside your own infrastructure, you may also want to consider whether the providers guarantee enough authentication and confidentiality for your company's needs.

Responder Habits

The uniqueness of emergency access technologies often results in practices distinct from normal day-to-day operations. If you don't prioritize the end-to-end usability of these technologies, responders may not know how to use them in an emergency, and you'll lose the benefits of those technologies. It may be difficult to integrate low-dependency alternatives, but that's only part of the problem—once you mix in human confusion under stress with rarely used processes and tools, the resulting complexity may obstruct all access. In other words, humans, rather than technology, may render breakglass tools ineffective.[27]

The more you can minimize the distinction between normal and emergency processes, the more responders are able to draw on habit. This frees up more of their cognitive capacity to focus on what *does* differ. As a result, organizational resilience to outages may improve. For example, at Google, we centralized on Chrome, its extensions, and any controls and tools associated with it as the single platform sufficient for remote access. Introducing an emergency mode into Chrome extensions allowed us to achieve the minimum possible increase in cognitive load up front, while retaining the option to integrate it into more extensions later.

To ensure that your responders exercise emergency access practices regularly, introduce policies that integrate emergency access into the daily habits of on-call staff, and continuously validate the usability of the relevant systems. For example, define and enforce a minimum period between required exercises. The team lead can send email notifications when a team member needs to complete required credential-refresh or training tasks, or may choose to waive the exercise if they determine that the individual regularly engages in equivalent activities. This increases confidence that when an incident occurs, the rest of the team *does* have the relevant credentials and has recently completed the necessary training. Otherwise, make practicing breakglass operations and any related processes mandatory for your staff.

---

27 Breakglass tools are mechanisms that can bypass policies to allow engineers to quickly resolve outages. See "Breakglass" on page 67.

Finally, make sure that relevant documentation, such as policies, standards, and how-to guides, is available. People tend to forget details that are rarely used, and such documentation also relieves stress and doubt under pressure. Architecture overviews and diagrams are also helpful for incident responders, and bring people who are unfamiliar with the subject up to speed without too much dependence on subject matter experts.

Unexpected Benefits

The design principles described in this chapter, built on top of principles of resilient design, improve your system's ability to recover. Unexpected benefits beyond reliability and security might help you convince your organization to adopt these practices. Consider a server engineered for firmware update authentication, rollback, locking, and attestation mechanisms. With these primitives, you may confidently recover a machine from a detected compromise. Now consider using this machine in a "bare metal" cloud hosting service, where the provider wants to clean and resell machines using automation. The machines engineered with recovery in mind already have a secure and automated solution in place.

The benefits compound even further with respect to supply chain security. When machines are assembled from many different components, you need to pay less attention to supply chain security for components whose integrity is recovered in an automated way. Your first-touch operations simply require running a recovery procedure. As an extra bonus, repurposing the recovery procedure means that you exercise your critical recovery capabilities regularly, so your staff is ready to act when an incident occurs.

Designing systems for recovery is considered an advanced topic, whose business value is proven only when a system is out of its intended state. But, given that we recommend operating systems use an error budget to maximize cost efficiency,[28] we expect such systems to be in an error state regularly. We hope your teams will slowly start investing in rate-limiting or rollback mechanisms as early in the development process as possible. For more insights about how to influence your organization, see Chapter 21.

Conclusion

This chapter explored various aspects of designing systems for recovery. We explained why systems should be flexible in terms of the rate at which they deploy changes: this flexibility allows you to roll out changes slowly when possible and avoid

---

[28] For more information on error budgets, see Chapter 3 in the SRE book.

coordinated failures, but also to roll out changes quickly and confidently when you have to accept more risk to meet security objectives. The ability to roll back changes is essential for building reliable systems, but sometimes you may need to prevent rollback to versions that are insecure or sufficiently old. Understanding, monitoring, and reproducing the state of your system to the greatest extent possible—through software versions, memory, wall-clock time, and so on—is key to reliably recovering the system to any previously working state, and ensuring that its current state matches your security requirements. As a last resort, emergency access permits responders to remain connected, assess a system, and mitigate the situation. Thoughtfully managing policy versus procedure, the central source of truth versus local functions, and the expected state versus the system's actual state paves the way to recoverable systems, while also promoting resilience and robust everyday operations.

CHAPTER 10

Mitigating Denial-of-Service Attacks

By Damian Menscher
with Vitaliy Shipitsyn and Betsy Beyer

> Security and reliability intersect when an active adversary can trigger an outage by conducting a denial-of-service (DoS) attack. In addition to an action by an adversary, denial of service can be caused by unexpected circumstances—from a backhoe slicing through a fiber-optic cable to a malformed request crashing a server—and target any layer of the stack. Most commonly, it manifests as a sudden surge in usage. While you can apply some mitigations on top of existing systems, minimizing the effects of a DoS attack often requires careful system design. This chapter discusses some strategies for defending against DoS attacks.

Security practitioners often think about the systems they protect in terms of *attack* and *defense*. But in a typical denial-of-service attack, economics offers more helpful terms: the adversary attempts to cause the *demand* for a particular service to exceed the *supply* of that service's capacity.[1] The end result is that the service is left with insufficient capacity to serve its legitimate users. The organization must then decide whether to incur even greater expenses by attempting to absorb the attack, or to suffer downtime (and corresponding financial losses) until the attack stops.

While some industries are more frequently targeted by DoS attacks than others, any service may be attacked in this way. *DoS extortion*, a financial attack in which

---

1 For the sake of discussion, we'll focus on the common case, where the attacker doesn't have physical access and a backhoe or knowledge of a crashing bug.

the adversary threatens to disrupt a service unless paid, strikes relatively indiscriminately.[2]

Strategies for Attack and Defense

Attackers and defenders have limited resources, which they must use efficiently to achieve their goals. When formulating a defensive strategy, it's helpful to start by understanding your adversary's strategy so you can find weaknesses in your defenses before they do. With this understanding, you can construct defenses for known attacks and can design systems with the flexibility to quickly mitigate novel attacks.

Attacker's Strategy

An attacker must focus on efficiently using their limited resources to exceed the capacity of their target. A clever adversary may be able to disrupt the services of a more powerful opponent.

A typical service has several dependencies. Consider the flow of a typical user request:

1. A DNS query provides the IP address of the server that should receive the user's traffic.

2. The network carries the request to the service frontends.

3. The service frontends interpret the user request.

4. Service backends provide database functionality for custom responses.

An attack that can successfully disrupt any of those steps will disrupt the service. Most novice attackers will attempt to send a flood of application requests or network traffic. A more sophisticated attacker may generate requests that are more costly to answer—for example, by abusing the search functionality present on many websites.

Because a single machine is rarely sufficient to disrupt a large service (which is often backed by multiple machines), a determined adversary will develop tools for harnessing the power of many machines in what's called a *distributed denial-of-service* (DDoS) attack. To carry out a DDoS attack, the attacker can either compromise vulnerable machines and join them together into a *botnet*, or launch an *amplification attack*.

---

2 Some extortionists will launch a small "demonstration attack" to motivate their target to pay. In nearly all cases, these attackers have no ability to generate a larger attack, and will not make further threats if their demands are ignored.

Amplification Attacks

In all types of communications, a request typically generates a response. Imagine that a farm supply store that sells fertilizer receives an order for a truckload of manure. The business will likely dump a pile of cow dung at the address listed. But what if the requestor's identity was faked? The response will go to the wrong place, and the recipient will likely not be pleased by the surprise delivery.

An *amplification attack* works on the same principle, but rather than making a single request, the adversary spoofs repeated requests from a single address to thousands of servers. The response traffic causes a distributed, reflected DoS attack toward the spoofed IP address.

While network providers should prevent their customers from spoofing the source IP (which is similar to a return address) in outbound packets, not all providers enforce this constraint, and not all providers are consistent in their enforcement. Malicious attackers can take advantage of gaps in enforcement to reflect small requests off of open servers, which then return a larger response to the victim. There are several protocols that allow for an amplification effect, such as DNS, NTP, and memcache.[3]

The good news is, it's easy to identify most amplification attacks because the amplified traffic comes from a well-known source port. You can efficiently defend your systems by using network ACLs that throttle UDP traffic from abusable protocols.[4]

Defender's Strategy

A well-resourced defender can absorb attacks simply by overprovisioning their entire stack, but only at great cost. Datacenters full of power-hungry machines are expensive, and provisioning always-on capacity to absorb the largest attacks is infeasible. While automatic scaling may be an option for services built on a cloud platform with ample capacity, defenders typically need to utilize other cost-effective approaches to protect their services.

When figuring out your best DoS defense strategy, you need to take engineering time into account—you should prioritize strategies that have the greatest impact. While it's tempting to focus on addressing yesterday's outage, recency bias can result in rapidly changing priorities. Instead, we recommend using a threat model approach to

---

3 See Rossow, Christian. 2014. "Amplification Hell: Revisiting Network Protocols for DDoS Abuse." *Proceedings of the 21st Annual Network and Distributed System Security Symposium.* doi:10.14722/ndss.2014.23233.

4 TCP-based protocols can also be exploited for this type of attack. For a discussion, see Kührer, Mark et al. 2014. "Hell of a Handshake: Abusing TCP for Reflective Amplification DDoS Attacks." *Proceedings of the 8th USENIX Workshop on Offensive Technologies. https://oreil.ly/0JCPP.*

concentrate your efforts on the weakest link in the dependency chain. You can compare threats according to the number of machines an attacker would need to control in order to cause user-visible disruption.

 We use the term *DDoS* to refer to DoS attacks that are effective only because of their distributed nature, and that use either a large botnet or an amplification attack. We use the term *DoS* to refer to attacks that could be sourced from a single host. The distinction is relevant when designing defenses, as you can often deploy DoS defenses at the application layer, while DDoS defenses frequently utilize filtering within the infrastructure.

Designing for Defense

An ideal attack focuses all its power on a single constrained resource, such as network bandwidth, application server CPU or memory, or a backend service like a database. Your goal should be to protect each of these resources in the most efficient way possible.

As attack traffic makes its way deeper into the system, it becomes both more focused and more expensive to mitigate. Therefore, layered defenses, whereby each layer protects the layer behind it, are an essential design feature. Here we examine the design choices that lead to defendable systems in two major layers: shared infrastructure and the individual service.

Defendable Architecture

Most services share some common infrastructure, such as peering capacity, network load balancers, and application load balancers.

The shared infrastructure is a natural place to provide shared defenses. Edge routers can throttle high-bandwidth attacks, protecting the backbone network. Network load balancers can throttle packet-flooding attacks to protect the application load balancers. Application load balancers can throttle application-specific attacks before the traffic reaches service frontends.

Layering defenses tends to be cost-effective, since you only need to capacity-plan inner layers for styles of DoS attacks that can breach the defenses of outer layers. Eliminating attack traffic as early as possible conserves both bandwidth and processing power. For example, by deploying ACLs at the network edge, you can drop suspicious traffic before it has a chance to consume the bandwidth of the internal network. Deploying caching proxies near the network edge can similarly provide significant cost savings, while also reducing latency for legitimate users.

Stateful firewall rules are often not an appropriate first line of defense for production systems that receive inbound connections.[5] An adversary can conduct a *state exhaustion attack*, in which a large number of unused connections fill the memory of a firewall with connection tracking enabled. Instead, use router ACLs to restrict traffic to the necessary ports without introducing a stateful system to the data path.

Implementing defenses in shared infrastructure also provides a valuable economy of scale. While it may not be cost-effective to provision significant defense capabilities for any individual service, shared defenses allow you to cover a broad range of services while provisioning only once. For example, Figure 10-1 shows how an attack targeting one site produced an amount of traffic that was much higher than normal for that site, but was still manageable when compared to the amount of traffic received by all of the sites protected by Project Shield (*https://projectshield.withgoogle.com*). Commercial DoS mitigation services use a similar bundling approach to provide a cost-effective solution.

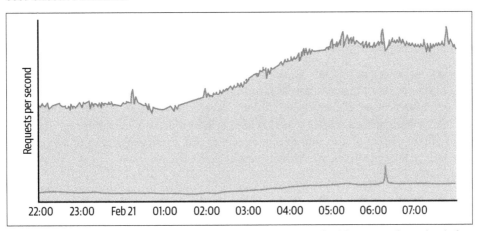

Figure 10-1. A DDoS attack on a site protected by Project Shield, as seen from (top) the perspective of the individual site, and (bottom) the perspective of the Project Shield load balancers

A particularly large DDoS attack could overwhelm the capacity of a datacenter, much as a magnifying glass can harness the power of the sun to ignite a fire. Any defense strategy must ensure that the power achieved by a distributed attack cannot be focused onto any single component. You can use network and application load

---

5 Stateful firewalls, which perform connection tracking, are best used to protect servers that originate outbound traffic.

balancers to continually monitor incoming traffic and spread the traffic to the nearest datacenter that has available capacity, preventing this type of overload.[6]

You can defend shared infrastructure without relying on a reactive system by using *anycast* (*https://oreil.ly/m0HRU*), a technique in which an IP address is announced from multiple locations. Using this technique, each location attracts traffic from nearby users. As a result, a distributed attack will be dispersed across locations all over the world, and therefore can't focus its power on any single datacenter.

Defendable Services

Website or application design can have a significant impact on the defense posture of a service. Although ensuring that the service degrades gracefully in overload conditions provides the best defense, several simple changes can be made to improve resilience to attack and allow for significant cost savings in normal operation:

Utilize caching proxies
Using the `Cache-Control` and related headers can permit repeated requests for content to be served by proxies, without the need for every request to hit the application backend. This applies to most static images, and may even apply to the home page.

Avoid unnecessary application requests
Every request consumes server resources, so it's best to minimize the number of requests needed. If a web page contains several small icons, it is more efficient to serve them all in a single (larger) image, a technique known as *spriting*.[7] As a side benefit, reducing the number of requests real users make to the service will reduce false positives when identifying malicious bots.

Minimize egress bandwidth
While traditional attacks attempt to saturate ingress bandwidth, it's possible for an attack to saturate your bandwidth by requesting a large resource. Resizing images to be only as large as necessary will conserve egress bandwidth and reduce page load times for users. Rate limiting or deprioritizing unavoidably large responses is another option.

---

6 They may also drop traffic if the service is in global overload.

7 One of our service designs used rounded corners for all UI elements. In its initial form, the browser fetched images for each of the four corners. By changing the site to download a circle and then splitting the image client-side, we saved 10 million requests/day.

Mitigating Attacks

While a defendable architecture provides the ability to withstand many DoS attacks, you may also need active defenses to mitigate large or sophisticated attacks.

Monitoring and Alerting

Outage resolution time is dominated by two factors: mean time to detection (MTTD) and mean time to repair (MTTR). A DoS attack may cause server CPU utilization to spike, or the application to run out of memory while queueing requests. To rapidly diagnose the root cause, you need to monitor the request rate in addition to CPU and memory usage.

Alerting on unusually high request rates can give the incident response team a clear indication of an attack. However, make sure that your pager alerts are actionable. If the attack is not causing user-facing harm, it is often best to simply absorb it. We recommend alerting only when demand exceeds service capacity and automated DoS defenses have engaged.

The principle of alerting only when human action may be required applies equally to network-layer attacks. Many synflood attacks can be absorbed, but may warrant an alert if syncookies are triggered.[8] Similarly, high-bandwidth attacks are only page-worthy if a link becomes saturated.

Graceful Degradation

If absorbing an attack isn't feasible, you should reduce the user-facing impact to the extent possible.

During a large attack you can use network ACLs to throttle suspicious traffic, providing an effective switch to immediately limit attack traffic. It's important to not block suspicious traffic all the time, so you can retain visibility into your system and minimize the risk of impacting legitimate traffic that matches the attack signature. Because a clever adversary may simulate legitimate traffic, throttles may not be sufficient. In addition, you can use quality-of-service (QoS) controls to prioritize critical traffic. Using a lower QoS for less-important traffic like batch copies can release bandwidth to higher QoS queues if needed.

---

8 In a synflood attack, TCP connection requests are sent at a high rate, but without completing the handshake. If the receiving server doesn't implement a defense mechanism, it will run out of memory to track all the inbound connections. A common defense is to use syncookies, which provide a stateless mechanism to validate new connections.

In case of overload, applications can also revert to a degraded mode. For example, Google deals with overload in the following ways:

- Blogger serves in read-only mode, disabling comments.
- Web Search continues serving with a reduced feature set.
- DNS servers answer as many requests as they can, but are designed to not crash under any amount of load.

For more ideas on handling overload, see Chapter 8.

A DoS Mitigation System

Automated defenses, such as throttling the top IP addresses or serving a JavaScript or CAPTCHA challenge, can quickly and consistently mitigate an attack. This gives the incident response team time to understand the problem and determine if a custom mitigation is warranted.

An automated DoS mitigation system can be divided into two components:

Detection
> The system must have visibility into the incoming traffic, with as much detail as possible. This may require statistical sampling at all endpoints, with aggregation up to a central control system. The control system identifies anomalies that may indicate attacks, while working in conjunction with load balancers that understand service capacity to determine if a response is warranted.

Response
> The system must have the ability to implement a defense mechanism—for example, by providing a set of IP addresses to block.

In any large-scale system, false positives (and false negatives) are unavoidable. This is especially true when blocking by IP address, as it is common for multiple devices to share a single network address (e.g., when network address translation is used). To minimize the collateral damage to other users behind the same IP address, you can utilize a CAPTCHA to allow real users to bypass application-level blocks.

 CAPTCHA Implementation

A CAPTCHA bypass needs to give the user a long-term exemption so they're not repeatedly challenged for subsequent requests. You can implement a CAPTCHA without introducing additional server state by issuing a browser cookie, but need to carefully construct the exemption cookie to guard against abuse. Google's exemption cookies contain the following information:

- A pseudo-anonymous identifier, so we can detect abuse and revoke the exemption
- The type of challenge that was solved, allowing us to require harder challenges for more suspicious behaviors
- The timestamp when the challenge was solved, so we can expire older cookies
- The IP address that solved the challenge, preventing a botnet from sharing a single exemption
- A signature to ensure the cookie cannot be forged

You must also consider the failure modes of your DoS mitigation system—problems might be triggered by an attack, a configuration change, an unrelated infrastructure outage, or some other cause.

The DoS mitigation system must itself be resilient to attack. Accordingly, it should avoid dependencies on production infrastructure that may be impacted by DoS attacks. This advice extends beyond the service itself, to the incident response team's tools and communications procedures. For example, since Gmail or Google Docs might be impacted by DoS attacks, Google has backup communication methods and playbook storage.

Attacks often result in immediate outages. While graceful degradation reduces the impact of an overloaded service, it's best if the DoS mitigation system can respond in seconds rather than minutes. This characteristic creates a natural tension with the best practice of deploying changes slowly to guard against outages. As a tradeoff, we canary all changes (including automated responses) on a subset of our production infrastructure before deploying them everywhere. That canary can be quite brief—in some cases as little as 1 second!

If the central controller fails, we don't want to either fail closed (as that would block all traffic, leading to an outage) or fail open (as that would let an ongoing attack through). Instead, we fail static, meaning the policy does not change. This allows the control system to fail during an attack (which has actually happened at Google!) without resulting in an outage. Because we fail static, the DoS engine doesn't have to be as highly available as the frontend infrastructure, thus lowering the costs.

Strategic Response

When responding to an outage, it's tempting to be purely reactive and attempt to filter the current attack traffic. While fast, this approach may not be optimal. Attackers may give up after their first attempt fails, but what if they don't? An adversary has unlimited opportunities to probe defenses and construct bypasses. A strategic response avoids informing the adversary's analysis of your systems. As an example, we once received an attack that was trivially identified by its User-Agent: I AM BOT NET. If we simply dropped all traffic with that string, we'd be teaching our adversary to use a more plausible User-Agent, like Chrome. Instead, we enumerated the IPs sending that traffic, and intercepted *all* of their requests with CAPTCHAs for a period of time. This approach made it harder for the adversary to use A/B testing (*https://oreil.ly/xuQrD*) to learn how we isolated the attack traffic. It also proactively blocked their botnet, even if they modified it to send a different User-Agent.

An understanding of your adversary's capabilities and goals can guide your defenses. A small amplification attack suggests that your adversary may be limited to a single server from which they can send spoofed packets, while an HTTP DDoS attack fetching the same page repeatedly indicates they likely have access to a botnet. But sometimes the "attack" is unintentional—your adversary may simply be trying to scrape your website at an unsustainable rate. In that case, your best solution may be to ensure that the website is not easily scraped.

Finally, remember that you are not alone—others are facing similar threats. Consider working with other organizations to improve your defenses and response capabilities: DoS mitigation providers can scrub some types of traffic, network providers can perform upstream filtering, and the network operator community can identify and filter attack sources.

Dealing with Self-Inflicted Attacks

During the adrenaline rush of a major outage, the natural response is to focus on the goal of defeating your adversary. But what if there is no adversary to defeat? There are some other common causes for a sudden increase in traffic.

User Behavior

Most of the time, users make independent decisions and their behavior averages out into a smooth demand curve. However, external events can synchronize their behavior. For example, if a nighttime earthquake wakes up everyone in a population center, they may suddenly turn to their devices to search for safety information, post to social media, or check in with friends. These concurrent actions can cause services to receive a sudden increase in usage, like the traffic spike shown in Figure 10-2.

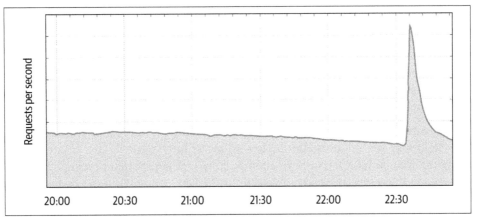

Figure 10-2. Web traffic, measured in HTTP requests per second, reaching Google infrastructure serving users in the San Francisco Bay Area when a magnitude 4.5 earthquake hit the region on October 14, 2019

Bot or Not?

In 2009, Google Web Search received a significant burst of traffic that lasted about a minute. Despite the weekend timing, several SREs started to investigate. Our investigation turned up very odd results: the requests were all for German words, and all began with the same letters. We speculated this was a botnet conducting a dictionary-based attack.

The attack repeated about 10 minutes later (but with a different set of characters prefixing each word), and then a third time. Deeper analysis led us to question our initial suspicion of this being an attack, for a couple of reasons:

- The requests originated from machines in Germany.
- The requests came from the expected distribution of browsers.

Could this traffic be coming from real users, we wondered? What would cause them to behave in this anomalous way?

We later discovered the explanation: a televised game show. Contestants were provided the prefix of a word, and challenged to complete the prefix with the word that would return the most search results on Google. Viewers were playing along at home.

We addressed this "attack" with a design change: we launched a feature that suggests word completions as you type.

Client Retry Behavior

Some "attacks" are unintentional, and are simply caused by misbehaving software. If a client expects to fetch a resource from your server, and the server returns an error, what happens? The developer may think a retry is appropriate, leading to a loop if the server is still serving errors. If many clients are caught in this loop, the resulting demand makes recovering from the outage difficult.[9]

Client software should be carefully designed to avoid tight retry loops. If a server fails, the client may retry, but should implement exponential backoff—for example, doubling the wait period each time an attempt fails. This approach limits the number of requests to the server, but on its own is not sufficient—an outage can synchronize all clients, causing repeated bursts of high traffic. To avoid synchronous retries, each client should wait for a random duration, called *jitter*. At Google, we implement exponential backoff with jitter in most of our client software.

What can you do if you don't control the client? This is a common concern for people operating authoritative DNS servers. If they suffer an outage, the resulting retry rate from legitimate recursive DNS servers can cause a significant increase in traffic—often around 30x normal usage. This demand can make it difficult to recover from the outage and often thwarts attempts to find its root cause: operators may think a DDoS attack is the cause rather than a symptom. In this scenario, the best option is to simply answer as many requests as you can, while keeping the server healthy via upstream request throttling. Each successful response will allow a client to escape its retry loop, and the problem will soon be resolved.

Conclusion

Every online service should prepare for DoS attacks, even if they don't consider themselves a likely target. Each organization has a limit of traffic it can absorb, and the defender's task is to mitigate attacks that exceed deployed capacity in the most efficient way possible.

It's important to remember the economic constraints of your DoS defenses. Simply absorbing an attack is rarely the most inexpensive approach. Instead, utilize cost-effective mitigation techniques, starting in the design phase. When under attack, consider all of your options, including blocking a problematic hosting provider (which may include a small number of real users) or suffering a short-term outage and explaining the situation to your users. Also remember that the "attack" may be unintentional.

---

9 See Chapter 22 in the SRE book.

Implementing defenses at each layer of the serving stack requires collaboration with several teams. For some teams, DoS defense may not be a top priority. To gain their support, focus on the cost savings and organizational simplifications a DoS mitigation system can provide. Capacity planning can focus on real user demand, rather than needing to absorb the largest attacks at every layer of the stack. Filtering known malicious requests using a web application firewall (WAF) allows the security team to focus on novel threats. If you discover application-level vulnerabilities, the same system can block exploitation attempts, allowing the developers team time to prepare a patch.

Through careful preparation, you can determine the functionality and failure modes of your service on your own terms—not those of an adversary.

Implementing Systems

Once you've analyzed and designed your systems, it's time to implement your plans. In some cases, implementation might mean buying an off-the-shelf solution. Chapter 11 provides one example of Google's thought process in deciding to build a custom software solution.

Part III of this book focuses on integrating security and reliability during the implementation phase of the software development lifecycle. Chapter 12 reiterates the idea that frameworks will simplify your systems. Adding static analysis and fuzzing during testing, as described in Chapter 13, will harden the code. Chapter 14 discusses why you should also invest in verifiable builds and further controls—safeguards around coding, building, and testing have limited effect if adversaries can bypass them by reaching your production environment.

Even if your entire software supply chain is resilient to security and reliability failures, you'll inevitably need to analyze your systems when problems arise. Chapter 15 discusses the careful balance you must strike between granting appropriate debugging access and the security requirements of storing and accessing logs.

CHAPTER 11

Case Study: Designing, Implementing, and Maintaining a Publicly Trusted CA

By Andy Warner, James Kasten, Rob Smits,
Piotr Kucharski, and Sergey Simakov

SREs, developers, and administrators sometimes need to interact with certificate authorities (CAs) to obtain certificates for encryption and authentication, or to handle functionality like VPNs and code signing. This case study focuses on Google's journey of designing, implementing, and maintaining a publicly trusted CA using the best practices discussed in this book. This journey was informed by internal scalability needs, compliance requirements, and security and reliability requirements.

Background on Publicly Trusted Certificate Authorities

Publicly trusted certificate authorities act as trust anchors for the transport layer of the internet by issuing certificates for Transport Layer Security (TLS),[1] S/MIME,[2] and other common distributed trust scenarios. They are the set of CAs that browsers, operating systems, and devices trust by default. As such, writing and maintaining a publicly trusted CA raises a number of security and reliability considerations.

To become publicly trusted and maintain that status, a CA must pass a number of criteria that span different platforms and use cases. At minimum, publicly trusted CAs must undergo audits against standards such as WebTrust (*https://oreil.ly/ubToZ*) and those set by organizations like the European Telecommunications

---

[1] The latest version of TLS is described in RFC 8446 (*https://oreil.ly/dB0au*).

[2] Secure/Multipurpose Internet Mail Extensions is a common method to encrypt email content.

Standards Institute (ETSI) (*https://www.etsi.org*). Publicly trusted CAs must also meet the objectives of the CA/Browser Forum Baseline Requirements (*https://oreil.ly/gfdBF*). These evaluations assess logical and physical security controls, procedures, and practices, and a typical publicly trusted CA spends at least one quarter of each year on these audit(s). Additionally, most browsers and operating systems have their own unique requirements that a CA must meet before it's trusted by default. As requirements change, CAs need to be adaptable and amenable to making process or infrastructure changes.

Chances are, your organization will never need to build a publicly trusted CA[3]—most organizations rely on third parties for acquiring public TLS certificates, code signing certificates, and other types of certificates that require broad trust by users. With that in mind, the goal of this case study is not to show you how to build a publicly trusted CA, but to highlight some of our findings that might resonate with projects in your environment. Key takeaways included the following:

- Our choice of programming language and decision to use segmentation or containers when handling data generated by third parties made the overall environment more secure.

- Rigorously testing and hardening code—both code we generated ourselves and third-party code—was critical for addressing fundamental reliability and security issues.

- Our infrastructure became safer and more reliable when we reduced complexity in the design and replaced manual steps with automation.

- Understanding our threat model enabled us to build validation and recovery mechanisms that allow us to better prepare for a disaster ahead of time.

Why Did We Need a Publicly Trusted CA?

Our business needs for a publicly trusted CA changed over time. In Google's early days, we purchased all of our public certificates from a third-party CA. This approach had three inherent problems we wanted to solve:

Reliance on third parties
    Business requirements that necessitate a high level of trust—for example, offering cloud services to customers—meant we needed strong validation and control over how certificates were issued and handled. Even if we performed mandatory audits in the CA ecosystem, we were unsure of whether third parties could meet

---

3 We recognize that many organizations do build and operate private CAs, using common solutions such as Microsoft's AD Certificate Services. These are typically for internal use only.

a high standard of safety. Notable lapses in security at publicly trusted CAs solidified our views about safety.[4]

Need for automation
Google has thousands of company-owned domains that serve users globally. As part of our ubiquitous TLS efforts (see "Example: Increasing HTTPS usage" on page 136), we wanted to protect every domain we own and rotate certificates frequently. We also wanted to provide an easy way for customers to get TLS certificates. Automating the acquisition of new certificates was difficult because third-party publicly trusted CAs often did not have extensible APIs, or provided SLAs below our needs. As a result, much of the request process for these certificates involved error-prone manual methods.

Cost
Given the millions of TLS certificates Google wanted to use for its own web properties and on behalf of customers, cost analysis showed it would be more cost-effective to design, implement, and maintain our own CA rather than continuing to obtain certificates from third-party root CAs.

The Build or Buy Decision

Once Google decided it wanted to operate a publicly trusted CA, we had to decide whether to buy commercial software to operate the CA or to write our own software. Ultimately, we decided to develop the core of the CA ourselves, with the option to integrate open source and commercial solutions where necessary. Among a number of deciding factors, there were a few primary motivators behind this decision:

Transparency and validation
Commercial solutions for CAs often didn't come with the level of auditability for code or the supply chain that we needed for such critical infrastructure. Even though it was integrated with open source libraries and used some third-party proprietary code, writing and testing our own CA software gave us increased confidence in the system we were building.

Integration capabilities
We wanted to simplify implementation and maintenance of the CA by integrating with Google's secure critical infrastructure. For example, we could set up regular backups in Spanner (*https://oreil.ly/ZnhV-*) with one line in a configuration file.

---

4 DigiNotar went out of business (*https://oreil.ly/nwNnG*) after attackers compromised and misused its CA.

Flexibility

The wider internet community was developing new initiatives that would provide increased security for the ecosystem. Certificate Transparency (*https://www.certificate-transparency.org*)—a way to monitor and audit certificates—and domain validation using DNS, HTTP, and other methods[5] are two canonical examples. We wanted to be early adopters of these kinds of initiatives, and a custom CA was our best option for being able to add this flexibility quickly.

Design, Implementation, and Maintenance Considerations

To secure our CA, we created a three-layer tiered architecture, where each layer is responsible for a different part of the issuance process: certificate request parsing, Registration Authority functions (routing and logic), and certificate signing. Each layer is composed of microservices with well-defined responsibilities. We also devised a dual trust zone architecture, where untrusted input is handled in a different environment than critical operations. This segmentation creates carefully defined boundaries that promote understandability and ease of review. The architecture also makes mounting an attack more difficult: since components are limited in functionality, an attacker who gains access to a given component will be similarly limited in the functionality they can affect. To gain additional access, the attacker would have to bypass additional audit points.

Each microservice is designed and implemented with simplicity as a key principle. Over the lifetime of the CA, we continually refactor each component with simplicity in mind. We subject code (both internally developed and third-party) and data to rigorous testing and validation. We also containerize code when doing so will improve safety. This section describes our approach to addressing security and reliability through good design and implementation choices in more detail.

---

5 A good reference for domain validation guidelines is the CA/Browser Forum Baseline Requirements (*https://oreil.ly/OkYRq*).

Programming Language Choice

The choice of programming language for parts of the system that accept arbitrary untrusted input was an important aspect of the design. Ultimately, we decided to write the CA in a mix of Go and C++, and chose which language to use for each sub-component based upon its purpose. Both Go and C++ have interoperability with well-tested cryptographic libraries, exhibit excellent performance, and have a strong ecosystem of frameworks and tools to implement common tasks.

Since Go is memory-safe, it has some additional upsides for security where the CA handles arbitrary input. For example, Certificate Signing Requests (CSRs) (*https://oreil.ly/8YkPI*) represent untrusted input into the CA. CSRs could come from one of our internal systems, which may be relatively safe, or from an internet user (perhaps even a malicious actor). There is a long history of memory-related vulnerabilities in code that parses DER (Distinguished Encoding Rules, the encoding format used for certificates),[6] so we wanted to use a memory-safe language that provided extra security. Go (*https://oreil.ly/WM_zw*) fit the bill.

C++ is not memory-safe, but has good interoperability for critical subcomponents of the system—especially for certain components of Google's core infrastructure. To secure this code, we run it in a secure zone and validate all data before it reaches that zone. For example, for CSR handling, we parse the request in Go before relaying it to the C++ subsystem for the same operation, and then compare the results. If there is a discrepancy, processing does not proceed.

Additionally, we enforce good security practices and readability (*https://oreil.ly/m8dug*) at pre-submit time for all C++ code, and Google's centralized toolchain enables various compile-time and runtime mitigations. These include the following:

---

6 The Mitre CVE database (*https://cve.mitre.org*) contains hundreds of vulnerabilities discovered in various DER handlers.

W^X (https://oreil.ly/9gNIa)
> Breaks the common exploitation trick of `mmap`ing with `PROT_EXEC` by copying shellcode and jumping into that memory. This mitigation does not incur a CPU or memory performance hit.

Scudo Allocator (https://oreil.ly/xpo5t)
> A user-mode secure heap allocator.

SafeStack (https://oreil.ly/EPwod)
> A security mitigation technique that protects against attacks based on stack buffer overflows.

Complexity Versus Understandability

As a defensive measure, we explicitly chose to implement our CA with limited functionality compared to the full range of options available in the standards (see "Designing Understandable Systems" on page 94). Our primary use case was to issue certificates for standard web services with commonly used attributes and extensions. Our evaluation of commercial and open source CA software options showed that their attempts to accommodate esoteric attributes and extensions that we didn't need led to complexity in the system, making the software difficult to validate and more error-prone. Therefore, we opted to write a CA with limited functionality and better understandability, where we could more easily audit expected inputs and outputs.

We continuously work on simplifying the architecture of the CA to make it more understandable and maintainable. In one case, we realized that our architecture had created too many different microservices, resulting in increased maintenance costs. While we wanted the benefits of a modular service with well-defined boundaries, we found that it was simpler to consolidate some parts of the system. In another case, we realized that our ACL checks for RPC calls were implemented manually in each instance, creating opportunities for developer and reviewer error. We refactored the codebase to centralize ACL checks and eliminate the possibility of new RPCs being added without ACLs.

Securing Third-Party and Open Source Components

Our custom CA relies on third-party code, in the form of open source libraries and commercial modules. We needed to validate, harden, and containerize this code. As a first step, we focused on the several well-known and widely used open source packages the CA uses. Even open source packages that are widely used in security contexts, and that originate from individuals or organizations with strong security backgrounds, are susceptible to vulnerabilities. We conducted an in-depth security review of each, and submitted patches to address issues we found. Where possible, we also subjected all third-party and open source components to the testing regime detailed in the next section.

Our use of two secure zones—one for handling untrusted data and one for handling sensitive operations—also gives us some layered protection against bugs or malicious insertions into code. The previously mentioned CSR parser relies on open source X.509 libraries and runs as a microservice in the untrusted zone in a Borg container.[7] This provides an extra layer of protection against issues in this code.

We also had to secure proprietary third-party closed-source code. Running a publicly trusted CA requires using a hardware security module (HSM)—a dedicated cryptographic processor—provided by a commercial vendor to act as a vault protecting the CA's keys. We wanted to provide an extra layer of validation for the vendor-provided code that interacts with the HSM. As with many vendor-supplied solutions, the kinds of testing we could perform were limited. To protect the system from problems like memory leaks, we took these steps:

- We built parts of the CA that had to interact with the HSM libraries defensively, as we knew that the inputs or outputs might be risky.
- We ran the third-party code in *nsjail* (*https://oreil.ly/QaE4s*), a lightweight process isolation mechanism.
- We reported issues we found to the vendor.

Testing

To maintain project hygiene, we write unit and integration tests (see Chapter 13) to cover a wide range of scenarios. Team members are expected to write these tests as part of the development process, and peer reviews ensure this practice is adhered to. In addition to testing for expected behavior, we test for negative conditions. Every few minutes, we generate test certificate issuance conditions that meet good criteria, and others that contain egregious errors. For example, we explicitly test that accurate error messages trigger alarms when an unauthorized person makes an issuance. Having a repository of both positive and negative test conditions enables us to perform high-confidence end-to-end testing on all new CA software deployments very quickly.

---

7 Borg containers are described in Verma, Abhishek et al. 2015. "Large-Scale Cluster Management at Google with Borg." *Proceedings of the 10th European Conference on Computer Systems*: 1–17. doi: 10.1145/2741948.2741964.

By using Google's centralized software development toolchains, we also gain the benefits of integrated automated code testing on both pre-submit and post-build artifacts. As discussed in "Integration of Static Analysis in the Developer Workflow" on page 296, all code changes at Google are inspected by Tricorder, our static analysis platform. We also subject the CA's code to a variety of sanitizers, such as AddressSanitizer (ASAN) and ThreadSanitizer, to identify common errors (see "Dynamic Program Analysis" on page 277). Additionally, we perform targeted fuzzing of the CA code (see "Fuzz Testing" on page 280).

Using Fixits to Harden the CA

As part of our ongoing hardening efforts, we participate in engineering-wide *fixit* exercises. Fixits are a Google engineering tradition where we set aside all of our normal work tasks for a defined period of time and pull together to achieve a common goal. One such fixit focused on fuzzing, where we subjected parts of the CA to intensive testing. In doing so, we found an issue in the Go X.509 parser that could potentially lead to an application crash. We learned a valuable lesson: the relatively new Go library for X.509 parsing may not have received the same degree of scrutiny its older counterparts (such as OpenSSL and BoringSSL) had over the years. This experience also showed how dedicated fixits (in this case, a *Fuzzit*) can shine a spotlight on libraries that need further testing.

Resiliency for the CA Key Material

The most severe risk to a CA is theft or misuse of CA key material. Most of the mandated security controls for a publicly trusted CA address common problems that can lead to such abuse, and include standard advice such as using HSMs and strict access controls.

We keep the CA's root key material offline and secure it with multiple layers of physical protection that require two-party authorization for each access layer. For day-to-day certificate issuance, we use intermediary keys that are available online, which is standard practice across the industry. Since the process of getting a publicly trusted CA included broadly in the ecosystem (that is, in browsers, televisions, and cellphones) can take years, rotating keys as part of a recovery effort after compromise (see "Rotating signing keys" on page 198) is not a straightforward or timely process. Therefore, loss or theft of key material can cause significant disruption. As a defense against this scenario, we mature other root key material in the ecosystem (by distributing the material to browsers and other clients that make use of encrypted connections) so we can swap in alternate material if necessary.

Data Validation

Aside from loss of key material, issuance errors are the most serious mistakes a CA can make. We sought to design our systems to ensure that human discretion cannot influence validation or issuance, which means we can focus our attention on the correctness and robustness of the CA code and infrastructure.

Continuous validation (see "Continuous Validation" on page 174) ensures a system is behaving as anticipated. To implement this concept in Google's publicly trusted CA, we automatically run certificates through linters at multiple stages of the issuance process.[8] The linters check for error patterns—for example, ensuring that certificates have a valid lifetime or that subject:commonName has a valid length. Once the certificate is validated, we enter it into Certificate Transparency logs, which allows for ongoing validation by the public. As a final defense against malicious issuance, we also use multiple independent logging systems, which we can reconcile by comparing the two systems entry by entry to ensure consistency. These logs are signed before they reach the log repository for further safety and later validation, if needed.

Conclusion

Certificate authorities are an example of infrastructure that has strong requirements for security and reliability. Using the best practices outlined in this book for the implementation of infrastructure can lead to long-term positive outcomes for security and reliability. These principles should be part of a design early on, but you should also use them to improve systems as they mature.

---

8 For example, ZLint (*https://github.com/zmap/zlint*) is a linter written in Go that verifies that the contents of a certificate are consistent with RFC 5280 and the CA/Browser Forum requirements.

CHAPTER 12

Writing Code

By Michał Czapiński and Julian Bangert
with Thomas Maufer and Kavita Guliani

Code will inevitably include bugs. However, you can avoid common security vulnerabilities and reliability issues by using hardened frameworks and libraries designed to be resilient against these problem classes.

This chapter presents software development patterns that should be applied during the implementation of a project. We start by looking at an RPC backend example and exploring how frameworks help us automatically enforce desired security properties and mitigate typical reliability anti-patterns. We also focus on code simplicity, which is achieved by controlling the accumulation of technical debt and refactoring the codebase when needed. We conclude with tips on how to select the right tools and make the most of your chosen development languages.

Security and reliability cannot easily be retrofitted into software, so it's important to account for them in software design from the earliest phases. Tacking on these features after a launch is painful and less effective, and may require you to change other fundamental assumptions about the codebase (see Chapter 4 for a deeper discussion on this topic).

The first and most important step in reducing security and reliability issues is to educate developers. However, even the best-trained engineers make mistakes—security experts can write insecure code and SREs can miss reliability issues. It's difficult to keep the many considerations and tradeoffs involved in building secure and reliable systems in mind simultaneously, especially if you're also responsible for producing software.

Instead of relying solely on developers to vet code for security and reliability, you can task SREs and security experts with reviewing code and software designs. This approach is also imperfect—manual code reviews won't find every issue, and no reviewer will catch *every* security problem that an attacker could potentially exploit. Reviewers can also be biased by their own experience or interests. For example, they may naturally gravitate toward seeking out new classes of attacks, high-level design issues, or interesting flaws in cryptographic protocols; in contrast, reviewing hundreds of HTML templates for cross-site scripting (XSS) flaws or checking the error-handling logic for each RPC in an application may be seen as less thrilling.

While code reviews may not find every vulnerability, they do have other benefits. A strong review culture encourages developers to structure their code in a way that makes the security and reliability properties easy to review. This chapter discusses strategies for making these properties obvious to reviewers and for integrating automation into the development process. These strategies can free up a team's bandwidth to focus on other issues and lead to building a culture of security and reliability (see Chapter 21).

Frameworks to Enforce Security and Reliability

As discussed in Chapter 6, the security and reliability of an application rely on domain-specific invariants. For example, an application is secure against SQL injection attacks if all of its database queries consist only of developer-controlled code, with external inputs supplied via query parameter bindings. A web application can prevent XSS attacks if all user input that's inserted into HTML forms is properly escaped or sanitized to remove any executable code.

Common Security and Reliability Invariants

Almost any multiuser application has application-specific security invariants that govern which users can perform which actions on data; every action should consistently maintain these invariants. To prevent cascading failures in a distributed system, each application must also follow sensible policies, such as backing off retries on failing RPCs. Similarly, in order to avoid memory corruption crashes and security issues, C++ programs should access only valid memory locations.

In theory, you can create secure and reliable software by carefully writing application code that maintains these invariants. However, as the number of desired properties and the size of the codebase grows, this approach becomes almost impossible. It's unreasonable to expect any developer to be an expert in all these subjects, or to constantly maintain vigilance when writing or reviewing code.

If humans need to manually review every change, those humans will have a hard time maintaining global invariants because reviewers can't always keep track of global context. If a reviewer needs to know which function parameters are passed user input by callers and which arguments only contain developer-controlled, trustworthy values, they must also be familiar with all transitive callers of a function. Reviewers are unlikely to be able to keep this state over the long run.

A better approach is to handle security and reliability in common frameworks, languages, and libraries. Ideally, libraries only expose an interface that makes writing code with common classes of security vulnerabilities impossible. Multiple applications can use each library or framework. When domain experts fix an issue, they remove it from all the applications the framework supports, allowing this engineering approach to scale better. Compared to manual review, using a centralized hardened framework also reduces the chances of future vulnerabilities creeping in. Of course, no framework can protect against all security vulnerabilities, and it is still possible for attackers to discover an unforeseen class of attacks or find mistakes in the implementation of the framework. But if you discover a new vulnerability, you can address it in one place (or a few) instead of throughout the codebase.

To provide one concrete example: SQL injection (SQLI) holds the top spot on both the OWASP (*https://oreil.ly/TnBaK*) and SANS (*https://oreil.ly/RWvPF*) lists of common security vulnerabilities. In our experience, when you use a hardened data library such as `TrustedSqlString` (see "SQL Injection Vulnerabilities: TrustedSqlString" on page 252), these types of vulnerabilities become a nonissue. Types make these assumptions explicit, and are automatically enforced by the compiler.

Benefits of Using Frameworks

Most applications have similar building blocks for security (authentication and authorization, logging, data encryption) and reliability (rate limiting, load balancing, retry logic). Developing and maintaining such building blocks from scratch for every service is expensive, and leads to a patchwork of different bugs in each service.

Frameworks enable code reuse: rather than accounting for all of the security and reliability aspects affecting a given functionality or feature, developers only need to customize a specific building block. For example, a developer can specify which information from the incoming request credentials is important for authorization without worrying about the credibility of that information—that credibility is verified by the framework. Equally, a developer can specify which data needs to be logged without worrying about storage or replication. Frameworks also make propagating updates easier, as you need to apply an update in only one location.

Using frameworks leads to increased productivity for all developers in an organization, a benefit for building a culture of security and reliability (see Chapter 21). It's much more efficient for a team of domain experts to design and develop the framework building blocks than for each individual team to implement security and reliability features itself. For example, if the security team handles cryptography, all other teams benefit from their knowledge. None of the developers using the frameworks need to worry about their internal details, and they can instead focus on an application's business logic.

Frameworks further increase productivity by providing tools that are easy to integrate with. For example, frameworks can provide tools that automatically export basic operational metrics, like the total number of requests, the number of failed requests broken down by error type, or the latency of each processing stage. You can use that data to generate automated monitoring dashboards and alerting for a service. Frameworks also make integrating with load-balancing infrastructure easier, so a service can automatically redirect traffic away from overloaded instances, or spin up new service instances under heavy load. As a result, services built on top of frameworks exhibit significantly higher reliability.

Using frameworks also makes reasoning about the code easy by clearly separating business logic from common functions. This enables developers to make assertions about the security or reliability of a service with more confidence. In general, frameworks lead to reduced complexity—when code across multiple services is more uniform, it's easier to follow common good practices.

It doesn't always make sense to develop your own frameworks. In many cases, the best strategy is to reuse existing solutions. For example, almost any security professional will advise you against designing and implementing your own cryptographic framework—instead, you might use a well-established and widely used framework such as Tink (discussed in "Example: Secure cryptographic APIs and the Tink crypto framework" on page 117).

Before deciding to adopt any specific framework, it's important to evaluate its security posture. We also suggest using actively maintained frameworks and continuously updating your code dependencies to incorporate the latest security fixes for any code on which your code depends.

The following case study is a practical example demonstrating the benefits of frameworks: in this case, a framework for creating RPC backends.

Example: Framework for RPC Backends

Most RPC backends follow a similar structure. They handle request-specific logic and typically also perform the following:

- Logging
- Authentication
- Authorization
- Throttling (rate limiting)

Instead of reimplementing this functionality for every single RPC backend, we recommend using a framework that can hide the implementation details of these building blocks. Then developers just need to customize each step to accommodate their service's needs.

Figure 12-1 presents a possible framework architecture based on predefined *interceptors* that are responsible for each of the previously mentioned steps. You can potentially also use interceptors for custom steps. Each interceptor defines an action to be performed *before* and *after* the actual RPC logic executes. Each stage can report an error condition, which prevents further interceptors from executing. However, when this occurs, the *after* steps of each interceptor that has already been called are executed in the reverse order. The framework between the interceptors can transparently perform additional actions—for example, exporting error rates or performance metrics. This architecture leads to a clear separation of the logic performed at every stage, resulting in increased simplicity and reliability.

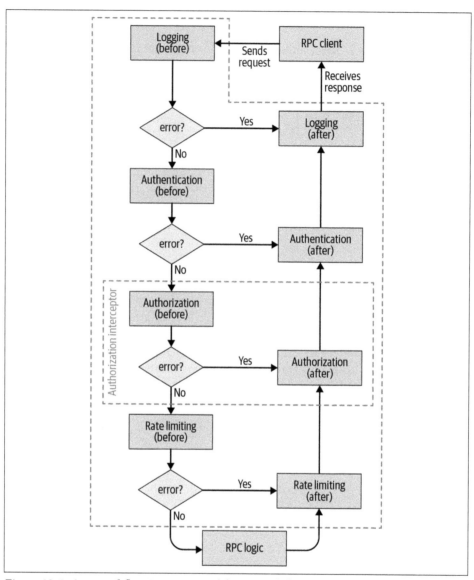

Figure 12-1. A control flow in a potential framework for RPC backends: the typical steps are encapsulated in predefined interceptors and authorization is highlighted as an example

In this example, the *before* stage of the logging interceptor could log the call, and the *after* stage could log the status of the operation. Now, if the request is unauthorized, the RPC logic doesn't execute, but the "permission denied" error is properly logged. Afterward, the system calls the authentication and logging interceptors' *after* stages (even if they are empty), and only then does it send the error to the client.

Interceptors share state through a *context object* that they pass to each other. For example, the authentication interceptor's *before* stage can handle all the cryptographic operations associated with certificate handling (note the increased security from reusing a specialized crypto library rather than reimplementing one yourself). The system then wraps the extracted and validated information about the caller in a convenience object, which it adds to the context. Subsequent interceptors can easily access this object.

The framework can then use the context object to track request execution time. If at any stage it becomes obvious that the request won't complete before the deadline, the system can automatically cancel the request. You can increase service reliability by notifying the client quickly, which also conserves resources.

A good framework should also enable you to work with dependencies of the RPC backend—for example, another backend that's responsible for storing logs. You might register these as either soft or hard dependencies, and the framework can constantly monitor their availability. When it detects the unavailability of a hard dependency, the framework can stop the service, report itself as unavailable, and automatically redirect traffic to other instances.

Sooner or later, overload, network issues, or some other issue will result in a dependency being unavailable. In many cases, it would be reasonable to retry the request, but implement retries carefully in order to avoid a *cascading failure* (akin to falling dominoes).[1] The most common solution is to retry with an *exponential backoff*.[2] A good framework should provide support for such logic, rather than requiring the developer to implement the logic for every RPC call.

A framework that gracefully handles unavailable dependencies and redirects traffic to avoid overloading the service or its dependencies naturally improves the reliability of both the service itself and the entire ecosystem. These improvements require minimal involvement from developers.

Example code snippets

Examples 12-1 through 12-3 demonstrate the RPC backend developer's perspective of working with a security- or reliability-focused framework. The examples are in Go and use Google Protocol Buffers (*https://oreil.ly/yzES2*).

---

1 See Chapter 22 of the SRE book for more on cascading failures.

2 Also described in Chapter 22 of the SRE book.

Example 12-1. Initial type definitions (the before stage of an interceptor can modify the context; for example, the authentication interceptor can add verified information about the caller)

```
type Request struct {
  Payload proto.Message
}

type Response struct {
  Err error
  Payload proto.Message
}

type Interceptor interface {
  Before(context.Context, *Request) (context.Context, error)
  After(context.Context, *Response) error
}

type CallInfo struct {
  User string
  Host string

  ...
}
```

Example 12-2. Example authorization interceptor that allows only requests from whitelisted users

```
type authzInterceptor struct {
  allowedRoles map[string]bool
}

func (ai *authzInterceptor) Before(ctx context.Context, req *Request) (context.Con-
text, error) {
  // callInfo was populated by the framework.
  callInfo, err := FromContext(ctx)
  if err != nil { return ctx, err }

  if ai.allowedRoles[callInfo.User] { return ctx, nil }
  return ctx, fmt.Errorf("Unauthorized request from %q", callInfo.User)
}

func (*authzInterceptor) After(ctx context.Context, resp *Response) error {
  return nil  // Nothing left to do here after the RPC is handled.
}
```

Example 12-3. Example logging interceptor that logs every incoming request (before stage) and then logs all the failed requests with their status (after stage); WithAttemptCount is a framework-provided RPC call option that implements exponential backoff

```go
type logInterceptor struct {
  logger *LoggingBackendStub
}

func (*logInterceptor) Before(ctx context.Context,
                             req *Request) (context.Context, error) {
  // callInfo was populated by the framework.
  callInfo, err := FromContext(ctx)
  if err != nil { return ctx, err }
  logReq := &pb.LogRequest{
    timestamp: time.Now().Unix(),
    user: callInfo.User,
    request: req.Payload,
  }
  resp, err := logger.Log(ctx, logReq, WithAttemptCount(3))
  return ctx, err
}

func (*logInterceptor) After(ctx context.Context, resp *Response) error {
  if resp.Err == nil { return nil }

  logErrorReq := &pb.LogErrorRequest{
    timestamp: time.Now().Unix(),
    error: resp.Err.Error(),
  }
  resp, err := logger.LogError(ctx, logErrorReq, WithAttemptCount(3))
  return err
}
```

Common Security Vulnerabilities

In large codebases, a handful of classes account for the majority of security vulnerabilities, despite ongoing efforts to educate developers and introduce code review. OWASP and SANS publish lists of common vulnerability classes. Table 12-1 lists the 10 most common vulnerability risks according to OWASP (*https://oreil.ly/bUZq8*), along with some potential approaches to mitigate each at a framework level.

Table 12-1. Top 10 most common vulnerability risks according to OWASP

OWASP top 10 vulnerability	Framework hardening measures
[SQL] Injection	`TrustedSQLString` (see the following section).
Broken authentication	Require authentication using a well-tested mechanism like OAuth before routing a request to the application. (See "Example: Framework for RPC Backends" on page 247.)
Sensitive data exposure	Use distinct types (instead of strings) to store and handle sensitive data like credit card numbers. This approach can restrict serialization to prevent leaks and enforce appropriate encryption. Frameworks can additionally enforce transparent in-transit protection, like HTTPS with LetsEncrypt. Cryptographic APIs such as Tink (*https://oreil.ly/38Vpd*) can encourage appropriate secret storage, such as loading keys from a cloud key management system instead of a configuration file.
XML external entities (XXE)	Use an XML parser without XXE enabled; ensure this risky feature is disabled in libraries that support it.[a]
Broken access control	This is a tricky problem, because it's often application-specific. Use a framework that requires every request handler or RPC to have well-defined access control restrictions. If possible, pass end-user credentials to the backend, and enforce an access control policy in the backend.
Security misconfiguration	Use a technology stack that provides secure configurations by default and restricts or doesn't allow risky configuration options. For example, use a web framework that does not print error information in production. Use a single flag to enable all debug features, and set up your deployment and monitoring infrastructure to ensure this flag is not enabled for public users. The `environment` flag in Rails is one example of this approach.
Cross-site scripting (XSS)	Use an XSS-hardened template system (see "Preventing XSS: SafeHtml" on page 254).
Insecure deserialization	Use deserialization libraries that are built for handling untrusted inputs, such as Protocol Buffers (*https://oreil.ly/hlezU*).
Using components with known vulnerabilities	Choose libraries that are popular and actively maintained. Do not pick components that have a history of unfixed or slowly fixed security issues. Also see "Lessons for Evaluating and Building Frameworks" on page 256.
Insufficient logging & monitoring	Instead of relying on ad hoc logging, log and monitor requests and other events as appropriate in a low-level library. See the logging interceptor described in the previous section for an example.

[a] See the XXE Prevention Cheat Sheet (*https://oreil.ly/AOYev*) for more information.

SQL Injection Vulnerabilities: TrustedSqlString

SQL injection (*https://xkcd.com/327*) is a common class of security vulnerability. When untrustworthy string fragments are inserted into a SQL query, attackers can potentially inject database commands. The following is a simple password reset web form:

```
db.query("UPDATE users SET pw_hash = '" + request["pw_hash"]
       + "' WHERE reset_token = '" + request.params["reset_token"] + "'")
```

In this case, the user's request is directed to a backend with an unguessable reset_token specific to their account. However, because of the string concatenation, a malicious user could craft a custom reset_token with extra SQL commands (such as ' or username='admin) and *inject* this token into the backend. The result could reset the password hash of a different user—in this case, the admin account.

SQL injection vulnerabilities can be harder to spot in more complicated codebases. The database engine can help you prevent SQL injection vulnerabilities by providing bound parameters and prepared statements:

```
Query q = db.createQuery(
    "UPDATE users SET pw_hash = @hash WHERE token = @token");
q.setParameter("hash", request.params["hash"]);
q.setParameter("token", request.params["token"]);
db.query(q);
```

However, merely establishing a guideline to use prepared statements does not result in a scalable security process. You would need to educate every developer about this rule, and security reviewers would have to review all application code to ensure consistent use of prepared statements. Instead, you can design the database API so that mixing user input and SQL becomes impossible by design. For example, you can create a separate type called TrustedSqlString and enforce by construction that all SQL query strings are created from developer-controlled input. In Go, you could implement the type as follows:

```
struct Query {
    sql strings.Builder;
}
type stringLiteral string;
// Only call this function with string literal parameters.
func (q *Query) AppendLiteral(literal stringLiteral) {
    q.sql.writeString(literal);
}
// q.AppendLiteral("foo") will work, q.AppendLiteral(foo) will not
```

This implementation guarantees by construction that the contents of q.sql are entirely concatenated from string literals present in your source code, and the user cannot provide string literals. To enforce this contract at scale, you can use a language-specific mechanism to make sure AppendLiteral is called only with string literals. For example:

In Go
> Use a package-private type alias (stringLiteral). Code outside the package cannot refer to this alias; however, string literals are implicitly converted to this type.

In Java
> Use the Error Prone (*https://errorprone.info*) code checker, which provides a @CompileTimeConstant annotation for parameters.

In C++

Use a template constructor that depends on each character value in the string.

You can find similar mechanisms for other languages.

You can't build some features—like a data analytics application that by design runs arbitrary SQL queries provided by the user who owns the data—using just compile-time constants. To handle complicated use cases, at Google we allow a way to bypass the type restrictions with approval from a security engineer. For example, our database API has a separate package, `unsafequery`, that exports a distinct `unsafequery.String` type, which can be constructed from arbitrary strings and appended to SQL queries. Only a small fraction of our queries use the unchecked APIs. The burden of reviewing new uses of SQL queries that are not inherently safe and other restricted API patterns is handled by one (rotating) engineer on a part-time basis, for hundreds to thousands of active developers. See "Lessons for Evaluating and Building Frameworks" on page 256 for other benefits of reviewed exemptions.

Preventing XSS: SafeHtml

The type-based safety approach we described in the previous section is not specific to SQL injection. Google uses a more complex version of the same design to reduce cross-site scripting vulnerabilities in web applications.[3]

At their core, XSS vulnerabilities occur when a web application renders untrustworthy input without appropriate sanitization. For example, an application might interpolate an attacker-controlled `$address` value into an HTML snippet such as `<div>$address</div>`, which is shown to another user. An attacker can then set `$address` to `<script>exfiltrate_user_data();</script>` and execute arbitrary code in the context of another user's page.

HTML does not have the equivalent of binding query parameters. Instead, untrustworthy values must be appropriately sanitized or escaped before they are inserted into an HTML page. Furthermore, different HTML attributes and elements have different semantics, so application developers have to treat values differently depending on the context in which they appear. For example, an attacker-controlled URL can cause code execution with the `javascript:` scheme.

A type system can capture these requirements by introducing different types for values meant for different contexts—for example, `SafeHtml` to represent the contents of an HTML element, and `SafeUrl` for URLs that are safe to navigate to. Each of the types is a (immutable) wrapper around a string; the contracts are upheld by the

---

3 This system is described in more detail in Kern, Christoph. 2014. "Securing the Tangled Web." *Communications of the ACM* 57(9): 38–47. *https://oreil.ly/drZss*.

constructors available for each type. The constructors make up the trusted codebase that's responsible for ensuring the security properties of the application.

Google has created different builder libraries for different use cases. Individual HTML elements can be constructed with builder methods that require the correct type for each attribute value, and SafeHtml for the element contents. The template system with strict contextual escaping guarantees the SafeHtml contract for more complicated HTML. That system does the following:

1. Parses the partial HTML in the template

2. Determines the context for each substitution point

3. Either requires the program to pass in a value of the correct type, or correctly escapes or sanitizes untrusted string values

For example, if you have the following Closure Template:

```
{template .foo kind="html"}<script src="{$url}"></script>{/template}
```

trying to use a string value for $url will fail:

```
templateRendered.setMapData(ImmutableMap.of("url", some_variable));
```

Instead, the developer has to provide a TrustedResourceUrl value, e.g.:

```
templateRenderer.setMapData(
    ImmutableMap.of("x", TrustedResourceUrl.fromConstant("/script.js"))
).render();
```

If HTML originates from an untrusted source, you won't want to embed it into your application's web UI, since doing so would result in an easily exploitable XSS vulnerability. Instead, you can use an HTML sanitizer that parses the HTML and performs runtime checks to determine that each value meets its contract. The sanitizer removes elements that do not meet their contract, or elements for which it is impossible to check the contract at runtime. You can also use a sanitizer to interoperate with other systems that don't use safe types, because many HTML fragments are unchanged by sanitization.

Different HTML construction libraries target different developer productivity and code readability tradeoffs. However, they all enforce the same contract and should be equally trustworthy (apart from any bugs in their trusted implementations). In fact, to reduce the maintenance burden at Google, we code-generate the builder functions in various languages from a declarative configuration file. This file lists HTML elements and the required contracts for the values of each attribute. Some of our HTML sanitizers and template systems use the same configuration file.

A mature open source implementation of safe types for HTML is available in Closure Templates (*https://oreil.ly/6x6Yb*), and there is an effort underway to introduce type-based security (*https://oreil.ly/VrN4w*) as a web standard.

Lessons for Evaluating and Building Frameworks

The previous sections discussed how to structure libraries to establish security and reliability properties. However, you can't elegantly express all such properties with API design, and in some cases you can't even change the API easily—for example, when interacting with the standardized DOM API exposed by a web browser.

Instead, you can introduce compile-time checks to prevent developers from using risky APIs. Plug-ins for popular compilers, such as Error Prone (*https://error prone.info*) for Java and Tsetse (*https://tsetse.info*) for TypeScript, can prohibit risky code patterns.

Our experience has shown that compiler errors provide immediate and actionable feedback. Tools running on an opt-in basis (like linters) or at code review time provide feedback much later. By the time code is sent for review, developers usually have a finished, working unit of code. Learning that you need to perform some rearchitecting in order to use a strictly typed API that late in the development process can be frustrating.

It's much easier to equip developers with compiler errors or faster feedback mechanisms like IDE plug-ins that underline problematic code. Typically, developers iterate through compilation issues quickly, and already have to fix other compiler diagnostics like trivial misspellings and syntactic errors. Because the developers are already working on the specific lines of code affected, they have full context, so making changes is easier—for example, changing the type of a string to SafeHtml.

You can improve the developer experience even further by suggesting automatic fixes that work as a starting point for a safe solution. For example, when you detect a call to a SQL query function, you can automatically insert a call to TrustedSql Builder.fromConstant with the query parameter. Even if the resulting code does not quite compile (perhaps because the query is a string variable and not a constant), developers know what to do, and don't need to bother with the mechanical details of the API by finding the right function, adding the correct import declarations, and so on.

In our experience, as long as the feedback cycle is quick, and fixing each pattern is relatively easy, developers embrace inherently safe APIs much more readily—even when we can't prove that their code was insecure, or when they do a good job of writing secure code using the unsafe APIs. Our experience contrasts with existing research literature, which focuses on reducing the false-positive and false-negative rates.[4]

---

4 See Bessey, Al et al. 2010. "A Few Billion Lines of Code Later: Using Static Analysis to Find Bugs in the Real World." *Communications of the ACM* 53(2): 66–75. doi:10.1145/1646353.1646374.

We've found that focusing on those rates often results in complicated checkers that take much longer to produce findings. For example, a check might have to analyze whole-program data flows across a complicated application. It's often difficult to explain how to remove the issue that the static analysis detects to developers, as the workings of the checker are much harder to explain than a simple syntactic property. Understanding a finding takes as much work as tracking down a bug in GDB (the GNU Debugger). On the other hand, fixing a type safety error at compile time while writing new code is usually not much harder than fixing a trivial type error.

Simple, Safe, Reliable Libraries for Common Tasks

Building a safe library that covers all possible use cases and handles each reliably can be very challenging. For example, an application developer working on an HTML templating system might write the following template:

```
<a onclick="showUserProfile('{{username}}');">Show profile</a>">
```

To be XSS-proof, if `username` is attacker-controlled, the template system must nest three different layers of context: a single-quoted string, inside JavaScript, inside an attribute in an HTML element. Creating a template system that can handle all possible combinations of corner cases is complicated, and using that system won't be straightforward. In other domains, this issue can grow even more complex. For example, business needs might dictate complex rules about who can perform an action and who cannot. Unless your authorization library is as expressive (and as hard to analyze) as a general-purpose programming language, you might not be able to meet all developer needs.

Instead, you can start with a simple, small library that covers only common use cases but is easier to use correctly. Simple libraries are easier to explain, document, and use. These qualities reduce developer friction and may help you convince other developers to adopt the secure-by-design library. In some cases, it might make sense to offer different libraries optimized for different use cases. For example, you might have both HTML templating systems for complicated pages and builder libraries for short snippets.

You can accommodate other use cases with expert-reviewed access to an unconstrained, risky library that bypasses safety guarantees. If you see repeated similar requests for a use case, you can support that feature in the inherently safe library. As we observed in "SQL Injection Vulnerabilities: TrustedSqlString" on page 252, the review load is usually manageable.

Because the volume of review requests is relatively small, security reviewers can look at the code in depth and suggest extensive improvements—and the reviews tend to be unique use cases, which keeps reviewers motivated and prevents mistakes due to repetition and fatigue. Exemptions also act as a feedback mechanism: If developers repeatedly need exemptions for a use case, library authors should consider building a library for that use case.

Rollout Strategy

Our experience has shown that using types for security properties is very useful for new code. In fact, applications created in one widely used Google-internal web framework, which was developed from the outset with safe types for HTML, have had far fewer reported XSS vulnerabilities (by two orders of magnitude) than applications written without safe types, despite careful code review. The few reported vulnerabilities were caused by components of the application that did not use safe types.

It is more challenging to adapt existing code to use safe types. Even if you are starting with a brand new codebase, you need a strategy for migrating legacy code—you might discover new classes of security and reliability issues you want to protect against, or you might need to refine existing contracts.

We have experimented with several strategies for refactoring existing code; we discuss our two most successful approaches in the following subsections. These strategies require that you are able to access and modify the entire source code of your application. Most of Google's source code is stored in a single repository[5] with centralized processes for making, building, testing, and submitting changes. Code reviewers also enforce common readability and code organization standards, which reduces the complexity of changing an unfamiliar codebase. In other environments, large-scale refactorings can be more challenging. It helps to get broad agreement so every code owner is willing to accept changes to their source code, which contributes to the goal of building a culture of security and reliability.

 Google's company-wide style guide incorporates the concept of language *readability*: a certification that an engineer understands Google's best practices and coding style for a given language. Readability ensures a baseline for code quality. An engineer must either have readability in the language they're working with, or get a code review from someone with readability. For particularly complex or critically important code, in-person code reviews can be the most productive and effective way to improve your codebase's quality.

Incremental rollout

Fixing the entire codebase at once is often not feasible. Different components might be in different repositories, and authoring, reviewing, testing, and submitting a single

---

5 Potvin, Rachel, and Josh Levenberg. 2016. "Why Google Stores Billions of Lines of Code in a Single Repository." *Communications of the ACM* 59(7): 78–87. doi:10.1145/2854146.

change that touches multiple applications is often brittle and error-prone. Instead, at Google, we initially exempt legacy code from enforcement, and address existing unsafe API users one by one.

For example, if you already have a database API with a `doQuery(String sql)` function, you could introduce an overload, `doQuery(TrustedSqlString sql)`, and restrict the unsafe version to existing callers. Using the Error Prone framework, you can add a `@RestrictedApi(whitelistAnnotation={LegacyUnsafeStringQueryAllowed.class})` annotation and add the `@LegacyUnsafeStringQueryAllowed` annotation to all existing callers.

Then, by introducing *Git hooks* that analyze every commit, you can prevent new code from using the string-based overload. Alternatively, you can restrict the visibility of the unsafe API—for example, Bazel visibility whitelists (*https://oreil.ly/ajmrr*) would allow a user to call the API only if a security team member approves the pull request (PR). If your codebase is under active development, it will organically move toward the safe API. After you reach the point at which only a small fraction of callers use the deprecated string-based API, you can manually clean up the remainder. At that point, your code will be immune to SQL injection by design.

Legacy conversions

It is also often worthwhile to consolidate all of your exemption mechanisms into a single function that is obvious in the source code being read. For example, you can create a function that takes an arbitrary string and returns a safe type. You can use this function to replace all calls to string-typed APIs with more precisely typed calls. Typically, there will be a lot fewer types than functions consuming them. Instead of restricting and monitoring the removal of many legacy APIs (for example, every DOM API that consumes a URL), you have to remove only a single legacy conversion function per type.

Simplicity Leads to Secure and Reliable Code

Whenever practical, try to keep your code clean and simple. There are a number of publications on this topic,[6] so here we focus on two lightweight stories that were published in the Google Testing Blog (*https://testing.googleblog.com*). Both stories highlight strategies for avoiding quickly increasing codebase complexity.

---

6 See, e.g., Ousterhout, John. 2018. *A Philosophy of Software Design*. Palo Alto, CA: Yaknyam Press.

Avoid Multilevel Nesting

Multilevel nesting is a common anti-pattern that can lead to simple mistakes. If the error is in the most common code path, it will likely be captured by the unit tests. However, unit tests don't always check error handling paths in multilevel nested code. The error might result in decreased reliability (for example, if the service crashes when it mishandles an error) or a security vulnerability (like a mishandled authorization check error).

Can you spot a bug in the code in Figure 12-2? The two versions are equivalent.[7]

```
response = stub.Call(rpc, request)              response = stub.Call(request, rpc)

if rpc.status.ok():                             if !rpc.status.ok():
  if response.GetAuthorizedUser():                raise RpcError(rpc.ErrorText())
    if response.GetEnc() == 'utf-8':
      if response.GetRows():                    if not response.GetAuthorizedUser():
        vals = [ParseRow(r) for r in              raise ValueError('wrong encoding')
                response.GetRows()]
        avg = sum(vals) / len(vals)             if response.GetEnc() != 'utf-8':
        return avg, vals                          raise AuthError('unauthorized')
      else:
        raise ValueError('no rows')             if not response.GetRows():
    else:                                         raise ValueError('no rows')
      raise AuthError('unauthorized')
  else:                                         vals = [ParseRow(r) for r in
    raise ValueError('wrong encoding')                  response.GetRows()]
else:                                           avg = sum(vals) / len(vals)
  raise RpcError(rpc.ErrorText())               return avg, vals
```

Figure 12-2. Errors are often harder to spot in code with multiple levels of nesting

The "wrong encoding" and "unauthorized" errors are swapped. This bug is easier to see in the refactored version because the checks occur as soon as the errors are handled.

Eliminate YAGNI Smells

Sometimes developers overengineer solutions by adding functionality that may be useful in the future, "just in case." This goes against the YAGNI (You Aren't Gonna Need It) principle (*https://oreil.ly/K4Oan*), which recommends implementing only the code that you need. YAGNI code adds unnecessary complexity because it needs to be documented, tested, and maintained. Consider the following example:[8]

```
class Mammal { ...
  virtual Status Sleep(bool hibernate) = 0;
```

---

7 Source: Karpilovsky, Elliott. 2017. "Code Health: Reduce Nesting, Reduce Complexity." *https://oreil.ly/PO1QR*.

8 Source: Eaddy, Marc. 2017. "Code Health: Eliminate YAGNI Smells." *https://oreil.ly/NYr7y*.

```
  };
  class Human : public Mammal { ...
    virtual Status Sleep(bool hibernate) {
      age += hibernate ? kSevenMonths : kSevenHours;
      return OK;
    }
  };
```

The Human::Sleep code must handle the case when hibernate is true, even though all callers should always pass false. In addition, callers must handle the returned status, even though that status should always be OK. Instead, until you need classes other than Human, this code can be simplified to the following:

```
  class Human { ...
    void Sleep() { age += kSevenHours; }
  };
```

If the developer's assumptions about possible requirements for future functionality are actually true, they can easily add that functionality later by following the principle of *incremental development and design*. In our example, it will be easier to create a Mammal interface with a better common API when we generalize based on several existing classes.

To summarize, avoiding YAGNI code leads to improved reliability, and simpler code leads to fewer security bugs, fewer opportunities to make mistakes, and less developer time spent maintaining unused code.

Repay Technical Debt

It is a common practice for developers to mark places that require further attention with TODO or FIXME annotations. In the short term, this habit can accelerate the delivery velocity for the most critical functionality, and allow a team to meet early deadlines—but it also incurs *technical debt*. Still, it's not necessarily a bad practice, as long as you have a clear process (and allocate time) for repaying such debt.

Technical debt can include the erroneous handling of exceptional situations and the introduction of unnecessarily complex logic into the code (often written to work around other areas of technical debt). Either behavior can introduce security vulnerabilities and reliability issues that are rarely detected during testing (because of insufficient coverage of rare cases), and which consequently become part of the production environment.

You can deal with technical debt in many ways. For example:

- Keeping dashboards with code health metrics. These can range from simple dashboards that show test coverage or the number and average age of TODOs, to more sophisticated dashboards including metrics like *cyclomatic complexity* (*https://oreil.ly/pXJBL*) or *maintainability index* (*https://oreil.ly/_N25V*).

- Using analysis tools like linters to detect common code defects such as dead code, unnecessary dependencies, or language-specific gotchas. Often, such tools can also automatically fix your code.

- Creating notifications when code health metrics drop below predefined thresholds or when the number of automatically detected issues is too high.

In addition, it's important to maintain a team culture that embraces and focuses on good code health. Leadership can support this culture in many ways. For example, you can schedule regular *fixit* weeks during which developers focus on improving code health and fixing outstanding bugs rather than adding new functionality. You can also support continuous contributions to code health within the team with bonuses or other forms of recognition.

Refactoring

Refactoring is the most effective way to keep a codebase clean and simple. Even a healthy codebase occasionally needs to be refactored when you extend the existing feature set, change the backend, and so on.

Refactoring is particularly useful when working with old, inherited codebases. The first step of refactoring is measuring code coverage and increasing that coverage to a sufficient level.[9] In general, the higher the coverage, the higher your confidence in the safety of refactoring. Unfortunately, even 100% test coverage can't guarantee success, because the tests may not be meaningful. You can address this issue with other kinds of testing, such as *fuzzing,* which is covered in Chapter 13.

 Regardless of the reasons behind refactoring, you should always follow one golden rule: *never mix refactoring and functional changes in a single commit to the code repository.* Refactoring changes are typically significant and can be difficult to understand. If a commit also includes functional changes, there's a higher risk that an author or reviewer might overlook bugs.

A complete overview of refactoring techniques is beyond the scope of this book. For more on this topic, see Martin Fowler's excellent book[10] and the discussions of

---

9 A wide selection of code coverage tools are available. For an overview, see the list on Stackify (*https://oreil.ly/-w6DM*).

10 Fowler, Martin. 2019. *Refactoring: Improving the Design of Existing Code.* Boston, MA: Addison-Wesley.

tooling for automated, large-scale refactorings provided by Wright et al. (2013),[11] Wasserman (2013),[12] and Potvin and Levenberg (2016).

Security and Reliability by Default

In addition to using frameworks with strong guarantees, you can use several other techniques to automatically improve the security and reliability posture of your application, as well as that of your team culture, which you'll read more about in Chapter 21.

Choose the Right Tools

Choosing a language, framework, and libraries is a complicated task that's often influenced by a combination of factors, such as these:

- Integration with the existing codebase
- Availability of libraries
- Skills or preferences of the developer team

Be aware of the enormous impact that language choice can have on the security and reliability of the project.

Use memory-safe languages

At BlueHat Israel in February 2019, Microsoft's Matt Miller claimed that around 70% of all security vulnerabilities are due to memory safety issues.[13] This statistic has remained consistent over at least the last 12 years.

In a 2016 presentation, Nick Kralevich from Google reported that 85% of all bugs in Android (including bugs in the kernel and other components) were caused by memory management errors (slide 54).[14] Kralevich concluded that "we need to move towards memory safe languages." By using any language with higher-level memory management (such as Java or Go) rather than a language with more memory allocation difficulties (like C/C++), you can avoid this entire class of security (and reliabil-

---

11 Wright, Hyrum et al. 2013. "Large-Scale Automated Refactoring Using Clang." *Proceedings of the 29th International Conference on Software Maintenance*: 548–551. doi:10.1109/ICSM.2013.93.

12 Wasserman, Louis. 2013. "Scalable, Example-Based Refactorings with Refaster." *Proceedings of the 2013 ACM Workshop on Refactoring Tools*: 25–28 doi:10.1145/2541348.2541355.

13 Miller, Matt. 2019. "Trends, Challenges, and Strategic Shifts in the Software Vulnerability Mitigation Landscape." BlueHat IL. *https://goo.gl/vKM7uQ*.

14 Kralevich, Nick. 2016. "The Art of Defense: How Vulnerabilities Help Shape Security Features and Mitigations in Android." BlackHat. *https://oreil.ly/16rCq*.

ity) vulnerabilities by default. Alternatively, you can use code sanitizers that detect most memory management pitfalls (see "Sanitize Your Code" on page 267).

Use strong typing and static type checking

In a *strongly typed* language, "whenever an object is passed from a calling function to a called function, its type must be compatible with the type declared in the called function."[15] A language without that requirement is referred to as *weakly* or *loosely typed*. You can enforce type checking either during compilation (*static type checking*) or at runtime (*dynamic type checking*).

The benefits of strong typing and static type checking are especially noticeable when working on large codebases with multiple developers, as you can enforce invariants and eliminate a wide range of errors at compilation time rather than at runtime. This leads to more reliable systems, fewer security issues, and better-performing code in a production environment.

In contrast, when using dynamic type checking (for example, in Python), you can infer almost nothing about the code unless it has 100% test coverage—which is great in principle, but rarely observed in practice. Reasoning about the code becomes even harder in weakly typed languages, often leading to surprising behavior. For example, in JavaScript, every literal is by default treated as a string: `[9, 8, 10].sort() -> [10, 8, 9]`.[16] In both of these cases, because invariants aren't enforced at compilation time, you can only capture mistakes during testing. In consequence, you more often detect reliability and security issues, especially in less frequently exercised code paths, in the production environment rather than during development.

If you want to use languages that have dynamic type checking or weak typing by default, we recommend using extensions like the following to improve the reliability of your code. These extensions offer support for stricter type checking, and you can incrementally add them to existing codebases:

- Pytype for Python (*https://oreil.ly/_AAvo*)
- TypeScript for JavaScript (*https://www.typescriptlang.org*)

---

15 Liskov, Barbara, and Stephen Zilles. 1974. "Programming with Abstract Data Types." *Proceedings of the ACM SIGPLAN Symposium on Very High Level Languages*: 50–59. doi:10.1145/800233.807045

16 For many more surprises in JavaScript and Ruby, see Gary Bernhardt's lightning talk from CodeMash 2012 (*https://oreil.ly/M69rg*).

Use Strong Types

Using untyped primitives (such as strings or integers) can lead to the following issues:

- Passing conceptually invalid parameters to a function
- Unwanted implicit type conversions
- Difficult-to-understand type hierarchy[17]
- Confusing measurement units

The first situation—passing conceptually invalid parameters to a function—occurs if the primitive type of a function parameter does not have enough context, and therefore becomes confusing when it's called. For example:

- For the function `AddUserToGroup(string, string)`, it's unclear whether the group name is provided as the first or the second argument.
- What is the order of height and width in the `Rectangle (3.14, 5.67)` constructor call?
- Does `Circle(double)` expect a radius or diameter?

Documentation can correct for ambiguity, but developers are still bound to make mistakes. Unit tests can catch most of these errors if we've done our due diligence, but some errors may surface only at runtime.

When using strong types, you can catch these mistakes at compilation time. To return to our earlier example, the required calls would look like the following:

- `Add(User("alice"), Group("root-users"))`
- `Rectangle(Width(3.14), Height(5.67))`
- `Circle(Radius(1.23))`

where `User`, `Group`, `Width`, `Height`, and `Radius` are strong type wrappers around string or double primitives. This approach is less error-prone and makes the code more self-documenting—in this context, in the first example it's sufficient to call the function `Add`.

---

17 See Eaddy, Mark. 2017. "Code Health: Obsessed with Primitives?" *https://oreil.ly/0DvJI.*

In the second situation, implicit type conversions may lead to the following:

- Truncation when converting from larger to smaller integer types
- Precision loss when converting from larger to smaller floating-point types
- Unexpected object creation

In some cases, a compiler will report the first two issues (for example, when using the {} direct initialization syntax in C++), but many instances will likely be overlooked. Using strong types protects your code from errors of this type that a compiler doesn't capture.

Now let's consider the case of the difficult-to-understand type hierarchy:

```
class Bar {
 public:
  Bar(bool is_safe) {...}
};

void Foo(const Bar& bar) {...}

Foo(false);  // Likely OK, but is the developer aware a Bar object was created?
Foo(5);      // Will create Bar(is_safe := true), but likely by accident.
Foo(NULL);   // Will create Bar(is_safe := false), again likely by accident.
```

The three calls here will compile and execute, but will the outcome of the operation match developers' expectations? By default, a C++ compiler attempts to implicitly cast (*coerce*) parameters to match function argument types. In this case, the compiler will attempt to match the type Bar, which conveniently has a single-value constructor taking a parameter of type bool. Most C++ types implicitly cast to bool.

Implicit casting in constructors is sometimes intended (for example, when converting floating-point values to the std::complex class), but can be dangerous in most situations. To prevent dangerous outcomes, at a minimum, make single-value constructors *explicit*—for example, explicit Bar(bool is_safe). Note that the last call will result in a compilation error when using nullptr rather than NULL because there is no implicit conversion to bool.

Finally, unit confusion is an endless source of mistakes. These mistakes might be characterized as follows:

Harmless
> For example, code that sets a timer for 30 seconds instead of 30 minutes because the programmer didn't know what units Timer(30) uses.

Dangerous

For example, AirCanada's "Gimli Glider" airplane (*https://oreil.ly/5r61w*) had to make an emergency landing after ground crew calculated the necessary fuel in pounds instead of kilograms, leaving it with only half the required fuel.

Expensive

For example, scientists lost the $125 million Mars Climate Orbiter (*https://oreil.ly/ZMbIO*) because two separate engineering teams used different units of measurement (imperial versus metric).

As before, strong types are a solution to this issue: they can encapsulate the unit, and represent only abstract concepts such as timestamp, duration, or weight. Such types typically implement the following:

Sensible operations

For example, adding two timestamps is not normally a useful operation, but subtracting them returns a duration that can be useful for many use cases. Adding two durations or weights is similarly useful.

Unit conversions

For example, `Timestamp::ToUnix`, `Duration::ToHours`, `Weight::ToKilograms`.

Some languages provide such abstractions natively: examples include the `time` package (*https://golang.org/pkg/time*) in Go and the `chrono` library (*http://www.wg21.link/p0355*) in the upcoming C++20 standard. Other languages might require a dedicated implementation.

The Fluent C++ blog (*https://oreil.ly/Urmzl*) has more discussion on applications of strong types and example implementations in C++.

Sanitize Your Code

It's very useful to automatically validate that your code is not experiencing any typical memory management or concurrency pitfalls. You can run these checks as a presubmit action for each change list or as part of a continuous build and test automation harness. The list of pitfalls to check is language-dependent. This section presents some solutions for C++ and Go.

C++: Valgrind or Google Sanitizers

C++ allows for low-level memory management. As we mentioned earlier, memory management errors are a leading cause of security issues, and can result in the following failure scenarios:

- Reading unallocated memory (before `new` or after `delete`)

- Reading outside of the allocated memory (buffer overflow attack scenario)
- Reading uninitialized memory
- Memory leaks when a system loses the address of allocated memory or doesn't deallocate unused memory early

Valgrind (*http://www.valgrind.org*) is a popular framework that allows developers to catch those sorts of errors, even if unit tests don't catch them. Valgrind has the benefit of providing a virtual machine that interprets a user's binary, so users don't need to recompile their code to use it. The Valgrind tool Helgrind (*https://oreil.ly/mBSSw*) can additionally detect common synchronization errors such as these:

- Misuses of the POSIX pthreads API (e.g., unlocking a not-locked mutex, or a mutex held by another thread)
- Potential deadlocks arising from lock ordering problems
- Data races caused by accessing memory without adequate locking or synchronization

Alternatively, the Google Sanitizers suite (*https://oreil.ly/qqdMy*) offers various components that can detect all the same issues that Valgrind's Callgrind (a cache and branch prediction profiler) can detect:

- AddressSanitizer (ASan) detects memory errors (buffer overflows, use after free, incorrect initialization order).
- LeakSanitizer (LSan) detects memory leaks.
- MemorySanitizer (MSan) detects when a system is reading uninitialized memory.
- ThreadSanitizer (TSan) detects data races and deadlocks.
- UndefinedBehaviorSanitizer (UBSan) detects situations that have undefined behavior (using misaligned pointers; signed integer overflow; converting to, from, or between floating-point types that will overflow the destination).

The main advantage of the Google Sanitizers suite is speed: it's up to 10 times faster (*https://oreil.ly/iyxQ1*) than Valgrind. Popular IDEs like CLion (*https://oreil.ly/yGhh-*) also provide first-class integration with Google Sanitizers. The next chapter provides more details on sanitizers and other dynamic program analysis tools.

Go: Race Detector

While Go is designed to disallow memory corruption issues typical to C++, it may still suffer from data race conditions. Go Race Detector (*https://oreil.ly/RU46m*) can detect these conditions.

Conclusion

This chapter presented several principles that guide developers toward designing and implementing more secure and reliable code. In particular, we recommend using frameworks as a powerful strategy, as they reuse proven building blocks for sensitive areas of code prone to reliability and security issues: authentication, authorization, logging, rate limiting, and communication in distributed systems. Frameworks also tend to improve developer productivity—both for the people writing the framework and the people using the framework—and make reasoning about the code much easier. Additional strategies for writing secure and reliable code include aiming for simplicity, choosing the right tools, using strong rather than primitive types, and continuously sanitizing the codebase.

Investing extra effort in improving security and reliability while writing software pays off in the long run, and reduces the effort you have to spend reviewing your application or fixing issues after your application is deployed.

CHAPTER 13

Testing Code

By Phil Ames and Franjo Ivančić
with Vera Haas and Jen Barnason

> A reliable system is resilient to failures and meets its documented service level objectives, which may also include security guarantees. Robust software testing and analysis are useful aids in mitigating failure risks, and should be a particular focus during the project implementation phase.
>
> In this chapter, we discuss several approaches to testing, including unit and integration testing. We also cover additional security deep-dive topics like static and dynamic program analysis and fuzz testing, which can help strengthen your software's resilience against the inputs it encounters.

No matter how careful the engineers developing your software are, some mistakes and overlooked edge cases are inevitable. Unexpected input combinations may trigger data corruption or result in availability issues like the "Query of Death" example in Chapter 22 of the SRE book. Coding errors can cause security problems like buffer overflows and cross-site scripting vulnerabilities. Put simply, there are many ways software is prone to failure in the real world.

The techniques discussed in this chapter, used in different stages and contexts of software development, have a variety of cost–benefit profiles.[1] For example, *fuzzing—* sending random requests to a system—can help you harden that system in terms of both security and reliability. This technique can potentially help you catch

---

[1] We recommend checking out Chapter 17 of the SRE book for a reliability-focused perspective.

information leaks and reduce serving errors by exposing the service to a multitude of edge cases. To identify potential bugs in systems that you can't patch easily and quickly, you'll likely need to perform thorough up-front testing.

Unit Testing

Unit testing can increase system security and reliability by pinpointing a wide range of bugs in individual software components before a release. This technique involves breaking software components into smaller, self-contained "units" that have no external dependencies, and then testing each unit. Unit tests consist of code that exercises a given unit with different inputs selected by the engineer writing the test. Popular unit test frameworks are available for many languages; systems based on the xUnit (*https://oreil.ly/jZgl5*) architecture are very common.

Frameworks following the xUnit paradigm allow common setup and teardown code to execute with each individual test method. These frameworks also define roles and responsibilities for individual testing framework components that help standardize the test result format. That way, other systems have detailed information about what exactly went wrong. Popular examples include JUnit for Java, GoogleTest for C++, go2xunit for Golang, and the built-in `unittest` module in Python.

Example 13-1 is a simple unit test (*https://oreil.ly/4Dkod*) written using the GoogleTest framework.

Example 13-1. Unit test for a function that checks whether the provided argument is a prime number, written using the GoogleTest framework

```
TEST(IsPrimeTest, Trivial) {
  EXPECT_FALSE(IsPrime(0));
  EXPECT_FALSE(IsPrime(1));
  EXPECT_TRUE(IsPrime(2));
  EXPECT_TRUE(IsPrime(3));
}
```

Unit tests typically run locally as part of engineering workflows to provide fast feedback to developers before they submit changes to the codebase. In continuous integration/continuous delivery (CI/CD) pipelines, unit tests often run before a commit is merged into a repository's mainline branch. This practice attempts to prevent code changes that break behavior that other teams rely on.

Writing Effective Unit Tests

The quality and comprehensiveness of unit tests can significantly impact the robustness of your software. Unit tests should be fast and reliable to give engineers immediate feedback on whether a change has broken expected behavior. By writing and maintaining unit tests, you can ensure that as engineers add new features and code, they do not break existing behavior covered by the relevant tests. As discussed in Chapter 9, your tests should also be hermetic—if a test can't repeatedly produce the same results in an isolated environment, you can't necessarily rely on the test results.

Consider a system that manages the amount of storage bytes a team can use in a given datacenter or region. Suppose that the system allows teams to request additional quota if the datacenter has available unallocated bytes. A simple unit test might involve validating requests for quota in a set of imaginary clusters partially occupied by imaginary teams, rejecting requests that would exceed the available storage capacity. Security-focused unit tests might check how requests involving negative amounts of bytes are handled, or how the code handles capacity overflows for large transfers that result in quota values near the limit of the variable types used to represent them. Another unit test might check whether the system returns an appropriate error message when sent malicious or malformed input.

It's often useful to test the same code with different parameters or environmental data, such as the initial starting quota usages in our example. To minimize the amount of duplicated code, unit test frameworks or languages often provide a way to invoke the same test with different parameters. This approach helps reduce duplicate boilerplate code, which can make refactoring efforts less tedious.

When to Write Unit Tests

A common strategy is to write tests shortly after writing the code, using the tests to verify that the code performs as expected. These tests typically accompany the new code in the same commit, and often encompass the cases that the engineer writing the code checked manually. For instance, our example storage management application might require that "Only billing administrators for the group that owns the service can request more quota." You can translate this type of requirement into several unit tests.

In organizations that practice code review, a peer reviewer can double-check the tests to ensure they're sufficiently robust to maintain the quality of the codebase. For example, a reviewer may notice that although new tests accompany a change, the tests may pass even if the new code is removed or inactive. If a reviewer can replace a statement like if (condition_1 || condition_2) with if (false) or if (true) in the new code, and none of the new tests fail, then the test may have overlooked important test cases. For more information about Google's experience with automating this kind of *mutation testing*, see Petrović and Ivanković (2018).[2]

---

2 Petrović, Goran, and Marko Ivanković. 2018. "State of Mutation Testing at Google." *Proceedings of the 40th International Conference on Software Engineering*: 163–171. doi:10.1145/3183519.3183521.

Instead of writing tests *after* writing code, test-driven development (TDD) methodologies encourage engineers to write unit tests based on established requirements and expected behaviors *before* writing code. When testing new features or bug fixes, the tests will fail until the behavior is completely implemented. Once a feature is implemented and the tests pass, engineers progress to the next feature, where the process repeats.

For existing projects that weren't built using TDD models, it is common to slowly integrate and improve test coverage in response to bug reports or proactive efforts to increase confidence in a system. But even once you achieve full coverage, your project isn't necessarily bug-free. Unknown edge cases or sparsely implemented error handling can still cause incorrect behavior.

You can also write unit tests in response to internal manual testing or code review efforts. You might write these tests during standard development and review practices, or during milestones like a security review before a launch. New unit tests can verify that a proposed bug fix works as expected, and that later refactoring won't reintroduce the same bug. This type of testing is particularly important if the code is hard to reason about and potential bugs impact security—for example, when writing access control checks in a system with a complicated permission model.

 In the interest of covering as many scenarios as possible, you'll often spend more time writing tests than writing the code being tested—especially when dealing with nontrivial systems. This extra time pays off in the long run, since early testing yields a higher-quality codebase with fewer edge cases to debug.

How Unit Testing Affects Code

To improve the comprehensiveness of your tests, you may need to design new code to include testing provisions, or refactor older code to make it more testable. Typically, refactoring involves providing a way to intercept calls to external systems. Using that introspection ability, you can test code in a variety of ways—for example, to verify that the code invokes the interceptor the correct number of times, or with the correct arguments.

Consider how you might test a piece of code that opens tickets in a remote issue tracker when certain conditions are met. Creating a real ticket every time the unit test runs would generate unnecessary noise. Even worse, this testing strategy may fail randomly if the issue tracker system is unavailable, violating the goal of quick, reliable test results.

To refactor this code, you could remove direct calls to the issue tracker service and replace those calls with an abstraction—for example, an interface for an `IssueTrack erService` object. The implementation for testing could record data when it receives calls such as "Create an issue," and the test could inspect that metadata to make a pass or fail conclusion. By contrast, the production implementation would connect to remote systems and call the exposed API methods.

This refactor dramatically reduces the "flakiness" of a test that depends on real-world systems. Because they rely on behavior that isn't guaranteed—like an external dependency, or the order of elements when retrieving items from some container types—flaky tests are often more of a nuisance than a help. Try to fix flaky tests as they arise; otherwise, developers may get in the habit of ignoring test results when checking in changes.

 These abstractions and their corresponding implementations are called *mocks*, *stubs*, or *fakes*. Engineers sometimes use these words interchangeably, despite the fact that the concepts vary in implementation complexity and features, so it's important to ensure everyone at your organization uses consistent vocabulary. If you practice code review or use style guides, you can help reduce confusion by providing definitions that teams can align around.

It's easy to fall into the trap of overabstraction, where tests assert mechanical facts about the order of function calls or their arguments. Overly abstracted tests often don't provide much value, as they tend to "test" the language's control flow implementation rather than the behavior of the systems you care about.

If you have to completely rewrite your tests every time a method changes, you may need to rethink the tests—or even the architecture of the system itself. To help avoid constant test rewrites, you might consider asking engineers familiar with the service to provide suitable fake implementations for any nontrivial testing needs. This solution is advantageous to both the team responsible for the system and the engineers testing the code: the team that owns the abstraction can ensure it tracks the feature set of the service as it evolves, and the team using the abstraction now has a more realistic component to use in its tests.[3]

Correctness Validation

Carefully designed test suites can evaluate the correctness of different pieces of software that perform the same task. This functionality can be very useful in specialized domains. For example, compilers often have test suites that focus on esoteric corner cases of programming languages. One such example is the GNU C Compiler's "torture test" suite (*https://oreil.ly/nn6u0*).

---

3 For more discussion of common unit testing pitfalls encountered at Google, see Wright, Hyrum, and Titus Winters. 2015. "All Your Tests Are Terrible: Tales from the Trenches." CppCon 2015. *https://oreil.ly/idleN*.

Another example is the Wycheproof (*https://oreil.ly/ecCr9*) set of test vectors, which is designed to validate the correctness of cryptographic algorithm implementations against certain known attacks. Wycheproof takes advantage of Java's standardized interface—the Java Cryptography Architecture (JCA)—to access cryptography functions. Authors of cryptography software write implementations against JCA, and JCA's cryptography providers handle calls to cryptography functions. The provided test vectors can also be used with other programming languages.

There are also test suites that aim to exercise every rule in an RFC for parsing a particular media format. Engineers attempting to design drop-in replacement parsers can rely on such tests to ensure that the old and new implementations are compatible and produce equivalent observable outputs.

Integration Testing

Integration testing moves beyond individual units and abstractions, replacing fake or stubbed-out implementations of abstractions like databases or network services with real implementations. As a result, integration tests exercise more complete code paths. Because you must initialize and configure these other dependencies, integration testing may be slower and flakier than unit testing—to execute the test, this approach incorporates real-world variables like network latency as services communicate end-to-end. As you move from testing individual low-level units of code to testing how they interact when composed together, the net result is a higher degree of confidence that the system is behaving as expected.

Integration testing takes different shapes, which are determined by the complexity of the dependencies they address. When the dependencies that integration testing needs are relatively simple, an integration test may look like a base class that sets up a few shared dependencies (for example, a database in a preconfigured state) from which other tests extend. As services grow in complexity, integration tests can become far more complex, requiring supervising systems to orchestrate the initialization or setup of dependencies to support the test. Google has teams focused exclusively on infrastructure that enables standardized integration test setup for common infrastructure services. For organizations using a continuous build and delivery system like Jenkins (*https://jenkins.io*), integration tests may run either alongside or separately from unit tests, depending on the size of the codebase and the number of available tests in a project.

As you build integration tests, keep the principles discussed in Chapter 5 in mind: make sure the data and systems access requirements of the tests don't introduce security risks. It can be tempting to mirror actual databases into test environments since the databases provide a rich set of real-world data, but you should avoid this anti-pattern because they may contain sensitive data that will be available to anyone running tests that use those databases. Such an implementation is inconsistent with the principle of least privilege and may pose a security risk. Instead, you can seed these systems with nonsensitive test data. This approach also makes it easy to wipe test environments to a known clean state, reducing the likelihood of integration test flakiness.

Writing Effective Integration Tests

Like unit tests, integration tests may be influenced by design choices in your code. To continue with our earlier example of an issue tracker that files tickets, a unit test mock may simply assert that the method was invoked to file a ticket with the remote service. An integration test would more likely use a real client library. Rather than creating spurious bugs in production, the integration test would communicate with a QA endpoint. Test cases would exercise the application logic with inputs that trigger calls to the QA instance. Supervising logic could then query the QA instance to verify that externally visible actions took place successfully from an end-to-end perspective.

Understanding why integration tests fail when all unit tests pass can require a lot of time and energy. Good logging at key logical junctures of your integration tests can help you debug and understand where breakdowns occur. Bear in mind too that because integration tests go beyond individual units by examining interactions between components, they can tell you only a limited amount about how well those units will conform to your expectations in other scenarios. This is one of the many reasons using each type of testing in your development lifecycle adds value—one form of testing is often not a substitute for another.

Dynamic Program Analysis

Program analysis allows users to carry out a number of useful actions—for example, performance profiling, checking for security-related correctness, code coverage reporting, and dead code elimination. As discussed later in this chapter, you can perform program analysis *statically* to investigate software without executing it. Here, we focus on *dynamic* approaches. Dynamic program analysis analyzes software by running programs, potentially in virtualized or emulated environments, for purposes beyond just testing.

Performance profilers (which are used to find performance issues in programs) and code coverage report generators are the best-known types of dynamic analysis. The previous chapter introduced the dynamic program analysis tool Valgrind (*http://www.valgrind.org*), which provides a virtual machine and various tools to interpret a binary and check whether an execution exhibits various common bugs. This section focuses on dynamic analysis approaches that rely on compiler support (often called *instrumentation*) to detect memory-related errors.

Compilers and dynamic program analysis tools let you configure instrumentation to collect runtime statistics on the binaries that the compilers produce, such as performance profiling information, code coverage information, and profile-based optimizations. The compiler inserts additional instructions and callbacks to a backend runtime library that surfaces and collects the relevant information when the binary is executed. Here, we focus on security-relevant memory misuse bugs for C/C++ programs.

The Google Sanitizers suite provides compilation-based dynamic analysis tools. They were initially developed as part of the LLVM (*https://llvm.org*) compiler infrastructure to capture common programming mistakes, and are now supported by GCC and other compilers, as well. For example, AddressSanitizer (ASan) (*https://oreil.ly/NkxYL*) finds a number of common memory-related bugs, such as out-of-bounds memory accesses, in C/C++ programs. Other popular sanitizers include the following:

UndefinedBehaviorSanitizer (https://oreil.ly/fRXLV)
    Performs runtime flagging of undefined behavior

ThreadSanitizer (https://oreil.ly/b6-wy)
    Detects race conditions

MemorySanitizer (https://oreil.ly/u9Jfh)
    Detects reading of uninitialized memory

LeakSanitizer (https://oreil.ly/Z9O5m)
    Detects memory leaks and other types of leaks

As new hardware features allow tagging of memory addresses, there are proposals (*https://oreil.ly/8BXt4*) to use those new features to further improve the performance of ASan.

ASan provides fast performance by building a custom, instrumented binary of the program under analysis. During compilation, ASan adds certain instructions to make callbacks into the provided sanitizer runtime. The runtime maintains metadata about the program execution—for example, which memory addresses are valid to access. ASan uses a shadow memory to record whether a given byte is safe for the program to access, and uses compiler-inserted instructions to check the shadow memory when the program tries to read or write that byte. It also provides custom memory allocation and deallocation (`malloc` and `free`) implementations. For example, the `malloc` function allocates additional memory immediately before and after the returned requested memory region. This creates a buffer memory region that allows ASan to easily report buffer overflows and underflows with precise information about what went wrong and where. To do so, ASan marks these regions (also called *red zones*) as *poisoned*. Similarly, ASan marks memory that was freed as poisoned, allowing you to catch use-after-free bugs easily.

The following example illustrates a simple run of ASan, using the Clang compiler. The shell commands instrument and run a particular input file with a use-after-free bug, which occurs when a memory address belonging to a previously deallocated memory region is read. A security exploit can use this type of access as a building block. The option -fsanitize=address turns on the ASan instrumentation:

```
$ cat -n use-after-free.c
 1  #include <stdlib.h>
 2  int main() {
 3      char *x = (char*)calloc(10, sizeof(char));
 4      free(x);
 5      return x[5];
 6  }

$ clang -fsanitize=address -O1 -fno-omit-frame-pointer -g use-after-free.c
```

After the compilation finishes, we can see the error report ASan produces when executing the generated binary. (For the sake of brevity, we've omitted the full ASan error message.) Note that ASan allows error reports to indicate the source file information, such as line numbers, by using the LLVM symbolizer, as described in the "Symbolizing the Reports" section (*https://oreil.ly/0VfIH*) of the Clang documentation. As you can see in the output report, ASan finds a 1-byte use-after-free read access (emphasis added). The error message includes information for the original allocation, the deallocation, and the subsequent illegal use:

```
% ./a.out
=================================================================
==142161==ERROR: AddressSanitizer: heap-use-after-free on address
0x602000000015
at pc 0x00000050b550 bp 0x7ffc5a603f70 sp 0x7ffc5a603f68
READ of size 1 at 0x602000000015 thread T0
    #0 0x50b54f in main use-after-free.c:5:10
    #1 0x7f89ddd6452a in __libc_start_main
    #2 0x41c049 in _start

0x602000000015 is located 5 bytes inside of 10-byte region
[0x602000000010,0x60200000001a)
freed by thread T0 here:
    #0 0x4d14e8 in free
    #1 0x50b51f in main use-after-free.c:4:3
    #2 0x7f89ddd6452a in __libc_start_main
```

```
previously allocated by thread T0 here:
    #0 0x4d18a8 in calloc
    #1 0x50b514 in main use-after-free.c:3:20
    #2 0x7f89ddd6452a in __libc_start_main

SUMMARY: AddressSanitizer: heap-use-after-free use-after-free.c:5:10 in main
[...]
==142161==ABORTING
```

Performance Tradeoffs in Dynamic Program Analysis

Dynamic program analysis tools like sanitizers provide developers with useful feedback about correctness and other dimensions, such as performance and code coverage. This feedback comes at a performance cost: the compiler-instrumented binaries can be orders of magnitude slower than the native binaries. As a result, many projects are adding sanitizer-enhanced pipelines to their existing CI/CD systems, but running those pipelines less frequently—for example, nightly. This practice may catch otherwise hard-to-identify bugs caused by memory corruption issues. Other program analysis–based CI/CD-enabled pipelines collect additional developer signals, such as nightly code coverage metrics. Over time, you can use these signals to gauge various code health metrics.

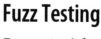 # Fuzz Testing

Fuzz testing (often referred to as *fuzzing*) is a technique that complements the previously mentioned testing strategies. Fuzzing involves using a *fuzz engine* (or *fuzzer*) to generate large numbers of candidate inputs that are then passed through a *fuzz driver* to the *fuzz target* (the code that processes the inputs). The fuzzer then analyzes how the system handles the input. Complex inputs handled by all kinds of software are popular targets for fuzzing—for example, file parsers, compression algorithm implementations, network protocol implementations, and audio codecs.

Security and Reliability Benefits of Fuzzing

One motivation for fuzzing is to find bugs like memory corruption that have security implications. Fuzzing can also identify inputs that trigger runtime exceptions that may cause a cascading denial of service in languages like Java and Go.

Fuzzing can be useful for testing service resilience. Google performs regular manual and automated disaster recovery testing exercises. The automated exercises are valuable for finding regressions in a controlled manner. If a system crashes when given malformed input, or if the system returns an error when using a special character, the

---

results can have serious effects on the error budget[4] and can result in customer dissatisfaction. Practices referred to as *chaos engineering* (*https://oreil.ly/SfYxy*) help automatically identify such weaknesses by injecting different kinds of faults like latency and service failure into a system. Netflix's Simian Army (*https://oreil.ly/GZmUW*) is an early example of a suite of tools that can perform this testing. Some of its components are now integrated into other release engineering tools, like Spinnaker (*https://oreil.ly/HpYx2*).

You can also use fuzzing to evaluate different implementations of the same functionality. For example, if you are considering moving from library A to library B, a fuzzer can generate inputs, pass them to each library for processing, and compare the results. The fuzzer can report any nonmatching result as a "crash," which can help engineers determine what subtle behavior changes may result. This crash-on-different-outputs action is typically implemented as part of the fuzz driver, as seen in OpenSSL's BigNum fuzzer (*https://oreil.ly/jWQsI*).[5]

Since fuzzing can execute indefinitely, it's not feasible to block every commit on the results of an extended test. This means that when the fuzzer finds a bug, that bug may already be checked in. Ideally, other testing or analysis strategies will have prevented the bug in the first place, so fuzzing acts as a complement by generating test cases that engineers may not have considered. As an added benefit, another unit test can use the generated input samples that identify bugs in the fuzz target to ensure that later changes don't regress the fix.

How Fuzz Engines Work

Fuzz engines can vary in complexity and sophistication. At the low end of the spectrum, a technique often referred to as *dumb fuzzing* simply reads bytes from a random number generator and passes them to the fuzz target in an attempt to find bugs. Fuzz engines have grown increasingly smart through integration with compiler toolchains. They can now generate more interesting and meaningful samples by taking advantage of the compiler instrumentation features discussed earlier. It is considered a good industry practice to use as many fuzz engines as you can integrate into your build toolchain, and to monitor metrics like the percentage of code covered. If code coverage plateaus at some point, it's usually worth investigating why the fuzzer can't reach other areas.

---

4 See Chapter 2 of the SRE workbook.

5 The fuzz target compares the results of two modular exponentiation implementations inside OpenSSL, and will fail if the results ever differ.

Some fuzz engines accept dictionaries of interesting keywords from the specifications or grammars of well-specified protocols, languages, and formats (like HTTP, SQL, and JSON). The fuzz engine can then generate input that's likely to be accepted by the program under test, since the input may simply be rejected by generated parser code if it contains illegal keywords. Providing a dictionary increases the likelihood of reaching the code you actually want to test through fuzzing. Otherwise, you may end up exercising code that rejects input based on invalid tokens and never finds any interesting bugs.

Fuzz engines like Peach Fuzzer (*https://oreil.ly/_n1KP*) allow a fuzz driver author to programmatically define the format of the input and the expected relationships between fields, so the fuzz engine can generate test cases that violate those relationships. Fuzz engines also commonly accept a set of sample input files, referred to as a *seed corpus*, that are representative of what the code being fuzzed expects. The fuzz engine then mutates these seed inputs, in addition to carrying out any other supported input generation strategies. Some software packages come with sample files (such as MP3s for audio libraries or JPEGs for image processing) as part of their existing test suites—these sample files are great candidates for a seed corpus. Otherwise, you can curate a seed corpus from real-world or hand-generated files. Security researchers also publish seed corpora for popular file formats, such as those provided by the following:

- OSS-Fuzz (*https://oreil.ly/K39Q2*)
- The Fuzzing Project (*https://oreil.ly/ywq1N*)
- American Fuzzy Lop (AFL) (*https://oreil.ly/mJBh1*)

In recent years, improvements to compiler toolchains have resulted in significant advancements toward making smarter fuzz engines. For C/C++, compilers such as LLVM Clang can instrument the code (as discussed earlier) to allow the fuzz engine to observe what code is executed while processing a specific sample input. When the fuzz engine finds a new code path, it preserves the samples that triggered the code path and uses them to generate future samples. Other languages or fuzz engines may require a specific compiler—such as afl-gcc for AFL (*https://github.com/google/AFL*) or go-fuzz-build for the go-fuzz engine (*https://github.com/dvyukov/go-fuzz*)—to properly trace the execution paths to increase code coverage.

When a fuzz engine generates an input that triggers a crash in a sanitizer-instrumented code path, it records the input along with metadata extracted from the program in the crashed state. This metadata can include information such as a stack trace indicating what line of code triggered the crash, or the process's memory layout at the time. This information provides engineers with details about the cause of the crash, which can help them understand its nature, prepare fixes, or prioritize bugs. For example, when an organization is considering how to prioritize fixes for different types of issues, a memory read access violation may be considered less critical than a write access violation. Such prioritization contributes to a culture of security and reliability (see Chapter 21).

The way your program reacts when the fuzz engine triggers a potential bug depends on a wide variety of circumstances. A fuzz engine is most effective at detecting bugs if encountering them triggers consistent and well-defined events—for example, receiving a signal or executing a specific function when memory corruption or undefined behavior occurs. These functions can explicitly signal the fuzz engine when the system reaches a particular error state. Many of the sanitizers mentioned earlier work this way.

Some fuzz engines also allow you to set an upper time bound for processing a particular generated input. If, for example, a deadlock or infinite loop causes an input to exceed the time limit, the fuzzer categorizes the sample as "crashing." It also saves that sample for further investigation so development teams can prevent DoS issues that might render the service unavailable.

"Known Safe" Functions

In some cases, benign bugs may impede fuzzing. This can happen with code that triggers undefined behavior semantics, notably in C/C++ programs. For example, C++ does not define what happens in the case of signed integer overflow (*https://oreil.ly/ LmLCV*). Suppose a function has an easily reachable signed integer that triggers an UndefinedBehaviorSanitizer crash. If the value is discarded or unused in contexts like determining allocation sizes or indexing, an overflow doesn't have any security or reliability consequences. However, this "shallow crash" may prevent fuzzing from reaching more interesting code. If it's not feasible to patch the code by moving to unsigned types or clamping the bounds, you can manually annotate functions as "known safe" to disable specific sanitizers—for example, __attribute__((no_sani tize("undefined"))) in order to uncover deeper bugs. Because this approach can lead to false negatives, add manual annotations only after careful review and consideration.

The Heartbleed bug (CVE-2014-0160) that caused web servers to leak memory (including memory containing TLS certificates or cookies) can be identified relatively quickly by fuzzing with the right fuzz driver and sanitizer. Google's fuzzer-test-suite GitHub repository (*https://oreil.ly/f1J7X*) contains an example Dockerfile that demonstrates successful identification of the bug. Here is an excerpt of the ASan report for the Heartbleed bug, triggered by the __asan_memcpy function call that the sanitizer compiler plug-in inserted (emphasis added):

```
==19==ERROR: AddressSanitizer: heap-buffer-overflow on address 0x629000009748 at pc
0x0000004e59c9 bp 0x7ffe3a541360 sp 0x7ffe3a540b10
READ of size 65535 at 0x629000009748 thread T0
    #0 0x4e59c8 in __asan_memcpy /tmp/final/llvm.src/projects/compiler-rt/lib/asan/asan_intercep-
tors_memintrinsics.cc:23:3
    #1 0x522e88 in tls1_process_heartbeat /root/heartbleed/BUILD/ssl/t1_lib.c:2586:3
    #2 0x58f94d in ssl3_read_bytes /root/heartbleed/BUILD/ssl/s3_pkt.c:1092:4
    #3 0x59418a in ssl3_get_message /root/heartbleed/BUILD/ssl/s3_both.c:457:7
    #4 0x55f3c7 in ssl3_get_client_hello /root/heartbleed/BUILD/ssl/s3_srvr.c:941:4
    #5 0x55b429 in ssl3_accept /root/heartbleed/BUILD/ssl/s3_srvr.c:357:9
    #6 0x51664d in LLVMFuzzerTestOneInput /root/FTS/openssl-1.0.1f/target.cc:34:3
    [...]

0x629000009748 is located 0 bytes to the right of 17736-byte region [0x629000005200,
0x629000009748)
allocated by thread T0 here:
    #0 0x4e68e3 in __interceptor_malloc /tmp/final/llvm.src/projects/compiler-rt/lib/asan/
asan_malloc_linux.cc:88:3
    #1 0x5c42cb in CRYPTO_malloc /root/heartbleed/BUILD/crypto/mem.c:308:8
    #2 0x5956c9 in freelist_extract /root/heartbleed/BUILD/ssl/s3_both.c:708:12
    #3 0x5956c9 in ssl3_setup_read_buffer /root/heartbleed/BUILD/ssl/s3_both.c:770
    #4 0x595cac in ssl3_setup_buffers /root/heartbleed/BUILD/ssl/s3_both.c:827:7
    #5 0x55bff4 in ssl3_accept /root/heartbleed/BUILD/ssl/s3_srvr.c:292:9
    #6 0x51664d in LLVMFuzzerTestOneInput /root/FTS/openssl-1.0.1f/target.cc:34:3
    [...]
```

The first portion of the output describes the type of issue (in this case, heap-buffer-overflow—specifically, a read access violation) and an easy-to-read symbolized stack trace pointing to the exact line of code that reads beyond the allocated buffer size. The second portion contains metadata about a nearby memory region and how it was allocated to help an engineer analyze the issue and understand how the process reached the invalid state.

The compiler and sanitizer instrumentation make this analysis possible. However, this instrumentation has limits: fuzzing with sanitizers doesn't work as well when some portions of the software are handwritten assembly for performance reasons. The compiler can't instrument the assembly code because the sanitizer plug-ins operate at a higher layer. As such, the handwritten assembly code that does not get instrumented may be responsible for false positives or undetected bugs.

Fuzzing entirely without sanitizers is possible, but it diminishes your ability to detect invalid program states and the metadata available to analyze a crash. For example, in order for fuzzing to produce any useful information if you're not using a sanitizer, the program must encounter an "undefined behavior" scenario, and then signal this error state to the external fuzz engine (typically by crashing or exiting). Otherwise, the undefined behavior carries on undetected. Likewise, if you're not using ASan or similar instrumentation, your fuzzer may not identify states where memory has been corrupted but is not used in a way that causes the operating system to terminate the process.

If you are working with libraries that are only available in binary form, compiler instrumentation is not an option. Some fuzz engines, like American Fuzzy Lop, also integrate with processor emulators like QEMU to instrument interesting instructions at the CPU level. This type of integration may be an appealing option for binary-only libraries you need to fuzz, at the expense of speed. This approach allows the fuzz engine to understand which code paths a generated input might trigger when compared to another generated input, but does not provide as much bug detection assistance as source code builds with compiler-added sanitizer instructions.

Many modern fuzz engines, like libFuzzer (*https://oreil.ly/uRzhZ*), AFL (*https://oreil.ly/gJ64J*), and Honggfuzz (*https://oreil.ly/b418b*), use some combination of the previously described techniques, or variations of these techniques. It's possible to build a single fuzz driver that works with multiple fuzz engines. When working with multiple fuzz engines, it's a good idea to make sure that you periodically move interesting input samples generated by each one back into the seed corpus that the other fuzz engines are configured to use. One engine might be successful at taking an input generated by another engine, mutating it, and triggering a crash.

Writing Effective Fuzz Drivers

To make these fuzzing concepts more concrete, we'll go into more detail about a fuzz driver using the framework provided by LLVM's libFuzzer engine, which is included with the Clang compiler. This particular framework is convenient because other fuzz engines (like Honggfuzz and AFL) also work with the libFuzzer entry point. As a fuzzer author, using this framework means you only have to write a single driver that implements the function prototype:

```
int LLVMFuzzerTestOneInput(const uint8_t *data, size_t size);
```

The respective fuzz engines will then generate byte sequences and invoke your driver, which can pass the input to the code you want to test.

The goal of the fuzz engines is to execute the fuzz target via the driver as quickly as possible with as many unique and interesting inputs as they can generate. To enable reproducible crashes and quick fuzzing, try to avoid the following in your fuzz drivers:

- Nondeterministic behavior, such as relying on random number generators or specific multithreading behavior.
- Slow operations, like console logging or disk I/O. Instead, consider creating "fuzzer-friendly" builds that disable these slow operations, or using a memory-based filesystem.
- Crashing intentionally. The idea behind fuzzing is to find crashes you didn't intend to have. The fuzz engine can't disambiguate intentional crashes.

These properties can also be desirable for the other types of testing described in this chapter.

You should also avoid any specialized integrity checks (like CRC32 or message digests) that an adversary can "fix up" in a generated input sample. The fuzz engine is unlikely to ever produce a valid checksum and pass the integrity check without specialized logic. A common convention is to use compiler preprocessor flags like -DFUZZING_BUILD_MODE_UNSAFE_FOR_PRODUCTION to enable this fuzzer-friendly behavior and to help reproduce crashes identified through fuzzing.

An Example Fuzzer

This section follows the steps of writing a fuzzer for a simple open source C++ library called Knusperli (*https://oreil.ly/1zV0T*). Knusperli is a JPEG decoder that might see a wide range of input if it's encoding user uploads or processing images (including potentially malicious images) from the web.

Knusperli also provides a convenient interface for us to fuzz: a function that accepts a sequence of bytes (the JPEG) and size parameter, as well as a parameter that controls which sections of the image to parse. For software that does not expose such a straightforward interface, you can use helper libraries like FuzzedDataProvider (*https://oreil.ly/HnrdZ*) to help transform the byte sequence into useful values for the target interface. Our example fuzz driver targets this function (*https://oreil.ly/zTtl-*):

```
bool ReadJpeg(const uint8_t* data, const size_t len, JpegReadMode mode,
              JPEGData* jpg);
```

Knusperli builds with the Bazel build system (*https://bazel.build*). By modifying your *.bazelrc* file, you can create a convenient shorthand way to build targets using the various sanitizers, and build libFuzzer-based fuzzers directly. Here's an example for ASan:

```
$ cat ~/.bazelrc
build:asan --copt -fsanitize=address --copt -O1 --copt -g -c dbg
build:asan --linkopt -fsanitize=address --copt -O1 --copt -g -c dbg
build:asan --copt -fno-omit-frame-pointer --copt -O1 --copt -g -c dbg
```

At this point, you should be able to build a version of the tool with ASan enabled:

```
$ CC=clang-6.0 CXX=clang++-6.0 bazel build --config=asan :knusperli
```

You can also add a rule to the *BUILD* file for the fuzzer we're about to write:

```
cc_binary(
    name = "fuzzer",
    srcs = [
        "jpeg_decoder_fuzzer.cc",
    ],
    deps = [
        ":jpeg_data_decoder",
        ":jpeg_data_reader",
    ],
```

```
        linkopts = ["-fsanitize=address,fuzzer"],
    )
```

Example 13-2 shows what a simple attempt at the fuzz driver might look like.

Example 13-2. jpeg_decoder_fuzzer.cc

```
1   #include <cstddef>
2   #include <cstdint>
3   #include "jpeg_data_decoder.h"
4   #include "jpeg_data_reader.h"
5
6   extern "C" int LLVMFuzzerTestOneInput(const uint8_t *data, size_t sz) {
7     knusperli::JPEGData jpg;
8     knusperli::ReadJpeg(data, sz, knusperli::JPEG_READ_HEADER, &jpg);
9       return 0;
10  }
```

We can build and run the fuzz driver with these commands:

```
$ CC=clang-6.0 CXX=clang++-6.0 bazel build --config=asan :fuzzer
$ mkdir synthetic_corpus
$ ASAN_SYMBOLIZER_PATH=/usr/lib/llvm-6.0/bin/llvm-symbolizer bazel-bin/fuzzer \
  -max_total_time 300 -print_final_stats synthetic_corpus/
```

The preceding command runs the fuzzer for five minutes using an empty input corpus. LibFuzzer places interesting generated samples in the *synthetic_corpus/* directory
to use in future fuzzing sessions. You receive the following results:

```
[...]
INFO:       0 files found in synthetic_corpus/
INFO: -max_len is not provided; libFuzzer will not generate inputs larger than
4096 bytes
INFO: A corpus is not provided, starting from an empty corpus
#2      INITED cov: 110 ft: 111 corp: 1/1b exec/s: 0 rss: 36Mb
[...]
#3138182        DONE   cov: 151 ft: 418 corp: 30/4340b exec/s: 10425 rss: 463Mb
[...]
Done 3138182 runs in 301 second(s)
stat::number_of_executed_units: 3138182
stat::average_exec_per_sec:    10425
stat::new_units_added:         608
stat::slowest_unit_time_sec:   0
stat::peak_rss_mb:             463
```

Adding a JPEG file—for example, the color bar pattern seen on broadcast TV—to the
seed corpus also results in improvements. That single seed input brings >10%
improvement in the code blocks executed (the cov metric):

```
#2      INITED cov: 169 ft: 170 corp: 1/8632b exec/s: 0 rss: 37Mb
```

To reach even more code, we can use different values for the `JpegReadMode` parameter. The valid values (*https://oreil.ly/h4ok1*) are as follows:

```
enum JpegReadMode {
    JPEG_READ_HEADER,   // only basic headers
    JPEG_READ_TABLES,   // headers and tables (quant, Huffman, ...)
    JPEG_READ_ALL,      // everything
};
```

Rather than writing three different fuzzers, we can hash a subset of the input and use that result to exercise different combinations of library features in a single fuzzer. Be careful to use enough input to create a varied hash output. If the file format mandates that the first *N* bytes of an input all look the same, use at least one more than *N* when deciding what bytes will influence which options to set.

Other approaches include using the previously mentioned `FuzzedDataProvider` to split the input, or dedicating the first few bytes of input to setting the library parameters. The remaining bytes are then passed as the input to the fuzz target. Whereas hashing the input may result in wildly different configuration if a single input bit changes, the alternative approaches to splitting the input allow the fuzz engine to better track the relationship between the selected options and the way the code behaves. Be mindful of how these different approaches can affect the usability of potential existing seed inputs. In this case, imagine that you create a new pseudoformat by deciding to rely on the first few input bytes to set the options to the library. As a result, you can no longer easily use all the existing JPEG files in the world as possible seed inputs, unless you first preprocess the files to add initial parameters.

To explore the idea of configuring the library as a function of the generated input sample, we'll use the number of bits set in the first 64 bytes of input to select a `JpegReadMode`, as illustrated in Example 13-3.

Example 13-3. Fuzzing by splitting the input

```
#include <cstddef>
#include <cstdint>
#include "jpeg_data_decoder.h"
#include "jpeg_data_reader.h"

const unsigned int kInspectBytes = 64;
const unsigned int kInspectBlocks = kInspectBytes / sizeof(unsigned int);

extern "C" int LLVMFuzzerTestOneInput(const uint8_t *data, size_t sz) {
  knusperli::JPEGData jpg;
  knusperli::JpegReadMode rm;
  unsigned int bits = 0;

  if (sz <= kInspectBytes) {  // Bail on too-small inputs.
    return 0;
```

```
  }

  for (unsigned int block = 0; block < kInspectBlocks; block++) {
    bits +=
      __builtin_popcount(reinterpret_cast<const unsigned int *>(data)[block]);
  }

  rm = static_cast<knusperli::JpegReadMode>(bits %
                               (knusperli::JPEG_READ_ALL + 1));

  knusperli::ReadJpeg(data, sz, rm, &jpg);

  return 0;
}
```

When using the color bar as the only input corpus for five minutes, this fuzzer gives the following results:

```
#851071 DONE   cov: 196 ft: 559 corp: 51/29Kb exec/s: 2827 rss: 812Mb
[...]
Done 851071 runs in 301 second(s)
stat::number_of_executed_units: 851071
stat::average_exec_per_sec:     2827
stat::new_units_added:          1120
stat::slowest_unit_time_sec:    0
stat::peak_rss_mb:              812
```

Executions per second have dropped because the changes enable more features of the library, causing this fuzz driver to reach much more code (indicated by the rising cov metric). If you run the fuzzer without any time-out limits, it will continue to generate inputs indefinitely until the code triggers a sanitizer error condition. At that point, you will see a report like the one shown earlier for the Heartbleed bug. You can then make code changes, rebuild, and run the fuzzer binary that you built with the saved artifact as a way to reproduce the crash or to verify that the code change will fix the issue.

Continuous Fuzzing

Once you have written some fuzzers, running them regularly over a codebase as it's developed can provide a valuable feedback loop to engineers. A continuous build pipeline can generate daily builds of fuzzers in your codebase to be consumed by a system that runs the fuzzers, collects crash information, and files bugs in an issue tracker. Engineering teams can use the results to focus on identifying vulnerabilities or eliminating root causes that make the service miss its SLO.

Example: ClusterFuzz and OSSFuzz

ClusterFuzz (*https://oreil.ly/10wuR*) is an open source implementation of a scalable fuzzing infrastructure released by Google. It manages pools of virtual machines that run fuzzing tasks and provides a web interface to view information about the fuzzers. ClusterFuzz does not build fuzzers, but instead expects a continuous build/integration pipeline to push fuzzers to a Google Cloud Storage bucket. It also provides services like corpus management, crash deduplication, and lifecycle management for the crashes that it identifies. The heuristics ClusterFuzz uses for crash deduplication are based on the state of the program at the time of the crash. By preserving the samples that cause a crash, ClusterFuzz can also periodically retest these issues to determine whether they still reproduce, and automatically close the issue when the latest version of the fuzzer no longer crashes on the offending sample.

The ClusterFuzz web interface shows metrics you can use to understand how well a given fuzzer is performing. The metrics available depend on what's exported by the fuzz engines integrated into your build pipeline (as of early 2020, ClusterFuzz supports libFuzzer and AFL). The ClusterFuzz documentation provides instructions for extracting code coverage information from fuzzers built with Clang code coverage support, then converting that information into a format you can store in a Google Cloud Storage bucket and display in the frontend. Using this functionality to explore the code covered by the fuzzer written in the previous section would be a good next step for determining additional improvements to the input corpus or fuzz driver.

OSS-Fuzz (*https://oreil.ly/tWlyz*) combines modern fuzzing techniques (*https://oreil.ly/yIaKz*) with a scalable distributed execution of ClusterFuzz that's hosted on the Google Cloud Platform. It uncovers security vulnerabilities and stability issues, and reports them directly to developers—within five months of its launch in December 2016, OSS-Fuzz had discovered over a thousand bugs (*https://oreil.ly/r-jx6*), and since then it has found tens of thousands more.

Once a project is integrated (*https://oreil.ly/AReAc*) with OSS-Fuzz, the tool uses continuous and automated testing to find issues only hours after modified code is introduced into the upstream repository, before any users are affected. At Google, by unifying and automating our fuzzing tools, we've consolidated our processes into a single workflow based on OSS-Fuzz. These integrated OSS projects also benefit from being reviewed (*https://oreil.ly/_TiJc*) by both Google's internal tools and external fuzzing tools. Our integrated approach increases code coverage and discovers bugs faster, improving the security posture of Google projects and the open source ecosystem.

Static Program Analysis

Static analysis is a means of analyzing and understanding computer programs by inspecting their source code without executing or running them. Static analyzers parse the source code and build an internal representation of the program that's suitable for automated analysis. This approach can discover potential bugs in source code, preferably before the code is checked in or deployed in production. Numerous tools (*https://oreil.ly/p3yP1*) are available for various languages, as well as tools for cross-language analyses.

Static analysis tools make different tradeoffs between depth of analysis versus cost of analyzing the source code. For example, the shallowest analyzers perform simple textual or abstract syntax tree (AST)–based pattern matches. Other techniques rely on reasoning about a program's state-based semantic constructs, and basing that reasoning on the program's control flow and data flow.

Tools also target different analysis tradeoffs between false positives (incorrect warnings) and false negatives (missed warnings). Tradeoffs are unavoidable, partially because of the fundamental limit to static analysis: statically verifying any program is an *undecidable problem* (*https://oreil.ly/4CPo_*)—that is, it is not possible to develop an algorithm that can determine whether any given program will execute without violating any given property.

Given that constraint, tool providers focus on generating useful signals for developers at various stages of development. Depending on the integration point for static analysis engines, different tradeoffs with respect to analysis speed and expected analysis feedback are acceptable. For example, a static analysis tool that's integrated within a code review system will likely target only newly developed source code, and will issue precise warnings that focus on very probable issues. On the other hand, source code undergoing a final predeployment release analysis for a safety-critical program (e.g., for domains like avionics software or medical device software with potential governmental certification requirements) may require more formal and stricter analysis.[6]

The following sections present static analysis techniques adapted for various needs during different stages of the development process. We highlight automated code inspection tools, abstract interpretation–based tools (this process is sometimes referred to as *deep static analysis*), and more resource-intensive approaches, such as formal methods. We also discuss how to integrate static analyzers into developer workflows.

Automated Code Inspection Tools

Automated code inspection tools perform a syntactic analysis of source code with respect to language features and usage rules. These tools, commonly referred to as *linters*, generally don't model complex program behaviors like interprocedural data flow. Because they perform relatively shallow analysis, the tools scale easily to arbitrary code sizes—they can often complete their source code analysis in about the

---

6 For an example, see Bozzano, Marco et al. 2017. "Formal Methods for Aerospace Systems." In *Cyber-Physical System Design from an Architecture Analysis Viewpoint*, edited by Shin Nakajima, Jean-Pierre Talpin, Masumi Toyoshima, and Huafeng Yu. Singapore: Springer.

same amount of time it takes to compile the code. Code inspection tools are also easily extensible—you can simply add new rules that cover many types of bugs, especially bugs related to language features.

Over the past few years, code inspection tools have focused on stylistic and readability changes, because such code improvement suggestions have a high acceptance rate by developers. Many organizations enforce style and format checks by default in order to maintain a cohesive codebase that's easier to manage across large developer teams. These organizations also routinely run checks that reveal potential code smells (*https://oreil.ly/ONE8f*) and highly likely bugs.

The following example focuses on tools that perform one particular type of analysis—AST pattern matching. An *AST* is a tree representation of a program's source code based on the syntactic structure of the programming language. Compilers commonly parse a given source code input file into such a representation, and then manipulate that representation during the compilation process. For example, an AST may contain a node representing an `if-then-else` construct, which has three child nodes: one node for the condition of the `if` statement, one node representing the subtree for the `then` branch, and another node representing the subtree of the `else` branch.

Error Prone (*https://errorprone.info*) for Java and Clang-Tidy (*https://oreil.ly/qFh_k*) for C/C++ are widely used across projects at Google. Both of these analyzers allow engineers to add custom checks. For example, as of early 2018 (*https://oreil.ly/gKJDy*), 162 authors had submitted 733 checks to Error Prone. For certain types of bugs, both Error Prone and Clang-Tidy can produce suggested fixes. Some compilers (like Clang and MSVC) also support the community-developed C++ core guidelines (*https://oreil.ly/y2Eqd*). With help from the Guideline Support Library (GSL), these guidelines prevent many common mistakes in C++ programs.

AST pattern-matching tools allow users to add new checks by writing rules on the parsed AST. For example, consider the `absl-string-find-startsWith` (*https://oreil.ly/3w5sM*) Clang-Tidy warning. The tool attempts to improve the readability and performance of code that checks for string prefix matches using the C++ `string::find` API (*https://oreil.ly/tg1HX*): Clang-Tidy recommends using the `StartsWith` API provided by ABSL (*https://oreil.ly/lmrox*) instead. To perform its analysis, the tool creates an AST subtree pattern that compares the output of the C++ `string::find` API with the integer value 0. The Clang-Tidy infrastructure provides the tooling to find AST subtree patterns in the AST representation of the program being analyzed.

Consider the following code snippet:

```
std::string s = "...";
if (s.find("Hello World") == 0) { /* do something */ }
```

The `absl-string-find-startsWith` Clang-Tidy warning flags this code snippet and suggests that the code be changed in the following way:

```
std::string s = "...";
if (absl::StartsWith(s, "Hello World")) { /* do something */ }
```

In order to suggest a fix, Clang-Tidy (conceptually speaking) provides the capability to transform an AST subtree, given a pattern. The left side of Figure 13-1 shows an AST pattern match. (The AST subtree is simplified for the sake of clarity.) If the tool finds a matching AST subtree in the parse AST tree of the source code, it notifies the developer. AST nodes also contain line and column information, which allows the AST pattern-matcher to report a specific warning to the developer.

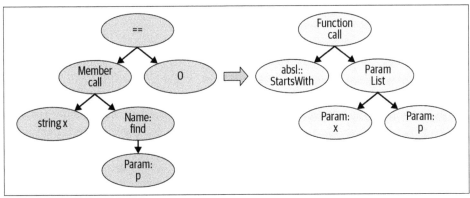

Figure 13-1. AST pattern-match and replacement suggestion

In addition to performance and readability checks, Clang-Tidy also provides many common bug pattern checks. Consider running Clang-Tidy on the following input files:[7]

```
$ cat -n sizeof.c
1  #include <string.h>
2  const char* kMessage = "Hello World!";
3  int main() {
4    char buf[128];
5    memcpy(buf, kMessage, sizeof(kMessage));
6    return 0;
7  }

$ clang-tidy sizeof.c
[...]
Running without flags.
1 warning generated.
sizeof.c:5:32: warning: 'memcpy' call operates on objects of type 'const char'
```

---

7 You can install Clang-Tidy using standard package managers. It is generally called clang-tidy.

```
while the size is based on a different type 'const char *'
[clang-diagnostic-sizeof-pointer-memaccess]
  memcpy(buf, kMessage, sizeof(kMessage));
                                ^
sizeof.c:5:32: note: did you mean to provide an explicit length?
  memcpy(buf, kMessage, sizeof(kMessage));

$ cat -n sizeof2.c
 1  #include <string.h>
 2  const char kMessage[] = "Hello World!";
 3  int main() {
 4    char buf[128];
 5    memcpy(buf, kMessage, sizeof(kMessage));
 6    return 0;
 7  }


$ clang-tidy sizeof2.c
[...]
Running without flags.
```

The two input files differ only in the type declaration of kMessage. When kMessage is defined as a pointer to initialized memory, sizeof(kMessage) returns the size of a pointer type. Therefore, Clang-Tidy produces the clang-diagnostic-sizeof-pointer-memaccess (*https://oreil.ly/Q3teN*) warning. On the other hand, when kMessage is of type const char[], the sizeof(kMessage) operation returns the appropriate, expected length, and Clang-Tidy doesn't produce a warning.

For some pattern checks, in addition to reporting a warning, Clang-Tidy can suggest code fixes. The absl-string-find-startsWith Clang-Tidy warning suggestion presented earlier is one such instance. The righthand side of Figure 13-1 shows the appropriate AST-level replacement. When such suggestions are available, you can tell Clang-Tidy to automatically apply them to the input file, using the --fix command-line option.

You can also use automatically applied suggestions to update a codebase using the Clang-Tidy modernize fixes. Consider the following sequence of commands, which showcases the modernize-use-nullptr (*https://oreil.ly/9K8vD*) pattern. The sequence finds instances of zero-constants used for pointer assignments or comparisons, and changes them to use nullptr instead. In order to run all modernize checks, we use Clang-Tidy with the option --checks=modernize-*; then --fix applies the suggestions to the input file. At the end of the sequence of commands, we highlight the four changes by printing the transformed file (emphasis added):

```
$ cat -n nullptr.cc
 1  #define NULL 0x0
 2
 3  int *ret_ptr() {
 4    return 0;
 5  }
```

```
 6
 7  int main() {
 8    char *a = NULL;
 9    char *b = 0;
10    char c = 0;
11    int *d = ret_ptr();
12    return d == NULL ? 0 : 1;
13  }
```

`$ clang-tidy nullptr.cc -checks=modernize-* --fix`
```
[...]
Running without flags.
4 warnings generated.
nullptr.cc:4:10: warning: use nullptr [modernize-use-nullptr]
  return 0;
         ^
         nullptr
nullptr.cc:4:10: note: FIX-IT applied suggested code changes
  return 0;
         ^
nullptr.cc:8:13: warning: use nullptr [modernize-use-nullptr]
  char *a = NULL;
            ^
            nullptr
nullptr.cc:8:13: note: FIX-IT applied suggested code changes
  char *a = NULL;
            ^
nullptr.cc:9:13: warning: use nullptr [modernize-use-nullptr]
  char *b = 0;
            ^
            nullptr
nullptr.cc:9:13: note: FIX-IT applied suggested code changes
  char *b = 0;
            ^
nullptr.cc:12:15: warning: use nullptr [modernize-use-nullptr]
  return d == NULL ? 0 : 1;
              ^
              nullptr
nullptr.cc:12:15: note: FIX-IT applied suggested code changes
  return d == NULL ? 0 : 1;
              ^
clang-tidy applied 4 of 4 suggested fixes.
```

`$ cat -n nullptr.cc`
```
 1  #define NULL 0x0
 2
 3  int *ret_ptr() {
 4    return nullptr;
 5  }
 6
 7  int main() {
 8    char *a = nullptr;
```

```
 9    char *b = nullptr;
10    char c = 0;
11    int *d = ret_ptr();
12    return d == nullptr ? 0 : 1;
13  }
```

Other languages have similar automated code inspection tools. For example, GoVet (*https://oreil.ly/m815w*) analyzes Go source code for common suspicious constructs, Pylint (*https://www.pylint.org*) analyzes Python code, and Error Prone provides analysis and auto-fix capabilities for Java programs. The following example briefly demonstrates running Error Prone via Bazel build rule (emphasis added). In Java, the subtraction operation i-1 on the variable i of type Short returns a value of type int. Therefore, it is infeasible for the remove operation to succeed:

```
$ cat -n ShortSet.java
 1  import java.util.Set;
 2  import java.util.HashSet;
 3
 4  public class ShortSet {
 5    public static void main (String[] args) {
 6      Set<Short> s = new HashSet<>();
 7      for (short i = 0; i < 100; i++) {
 8        s.add(i);
 9        s.remove(i - 1);
10      }
11      System.out.println(s.size());
12    }
13  }
```

```
$ bazel build :hello
ERROR: example/myproject/BUILD:29:1: Java compilation in rule '//example/mypro-
ject:hello'
ShortSet.java:9: error: [CollectionIncompatibleType] Argument 'i - 1' should
not be
passed to this method;
its type int is not compatible with its collection's type argument Short
      s.remove(i - 1);
              ^
    (see http://errorprone.info/bugpattern/CollectionIncompatibleType)
1 error
```

Integration of Static Analysis in the Developer Workflow

It's considered good industry practice to run relatively fast static analysis tools as early as possible in the development cycle. Finding bugs early is important because the cost of fixing them increases substantially if they're pushed into the source code repository or deployed to users.

There's a low barrier to integrating static analysis tools into your CI/CD pipeline, with a potentially high positive impact on the productivity of your engineers. For example, a developer can get an error and a suggestion about how to fix null pointer dereferencing. And if they can't push their code, they can't forget to fix the issue and accidentally cause the system to crash or expose information, which contributes to a culture of security and reliability (see Chapter 21).

To this end, Google developed the Tricorder program analysis platform[8] and an open-source version of Tricorder called Shipshape (*https://github.com/google/ship shape*). Tricorder performs static analysis of approximately 50,000 code review changes per day. The platform runs many types of program analysis tools and surfaces warnings to developers during code review, when they are accustomed to evaluating suggestions. The tools aim to provide code findings that are easy to understand and easy to fix, with a low user-perceived false-positive rate (10%, at most).

Tricorder is designed to allow users to run many different program analysis tools. As of early 2018, the platform included 146 analyzers covering over 30 source languages. Most of these analyzers were contributed by Google developers. Generally speaking, commonly available static analysis tools are not very complex. Most checkers run by Tricorder are automated code inspection tools. These tools target a variety of languages, check for conformance to coding style guidelines, and find bugs. As previously mentioned, Error Prone and Clang-Tidy can produce suggested fixes in certain scenarios. The code author can then apply the fixes with the click of a button.

Figure 13-2 shows a screenshot of Tricorder analysis results for a given Java input file, as presented to a code reviewer. The results show two warnings, one from the Java linter and one from Error Prone. Tricorder measures the user-perceived false-positive rate by allowing code reviewers to provide feedback on surfaced warnings via a "Not useful" link. The Tricorder team uses these signals to disable individual checks. The code reviewer can also send a request to the code author to "Please fix" an individual warning.

---

8 See Sadowski, Caitlin et al. 2018. "Lessons from Building Static Analysis Tools at Google." *Communications of the ACM* 61(4): 58–66. doi:10.1145/3188720.

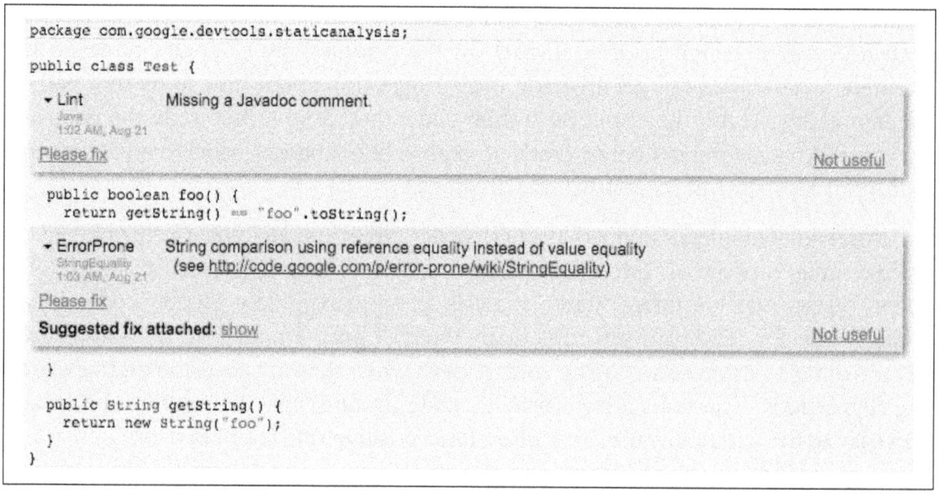

```
package com.google.devtools.staticanalysis;

public class Test {

    ▾ Lint          Missing a Javadoc comment.
      Java
      1:02 AM, Aug 21
    Please fix                                                                    Not useful

    public boolean foo() {
        return getString() == "foo".toString();

    ▾ ErrorProne    String comparison using reference equality instead of value equality
      StringEquality    (see http://code.google.com/p/error-prone/wiki/StringEquality)
      1:03 AM, Aug 21
    Please fix
    Suggested fix attached: show                                                  Not useful

    }

    public String getString() {
        return new String("foo");
    }
}
```

Figure 13-2. Screenshot of static analysis results during code review provided via Tricorder

Figure 13-3 shows the automatically applied code changes suggested by Error Prone during code review.

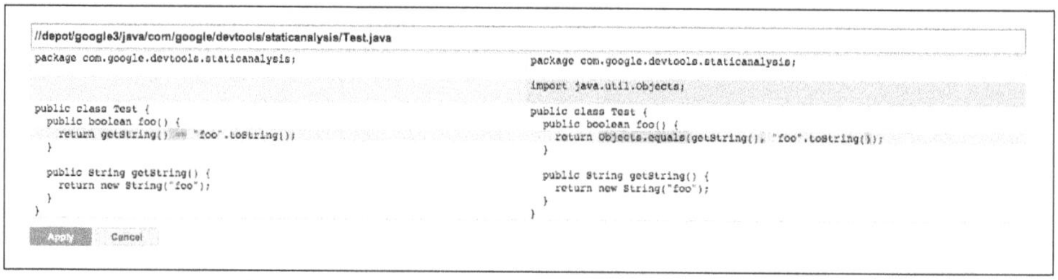

```
//depot/google3/java/com/google/devtools/staticanalysis/Test.java
package com.google.devtools.staticanalysis;          package com.google.devtools.staticanalysis;

                                                     import java.util.Objects;

public class Test {                                  public class Test {
    public boolean foo() {                               public boolean foo() {
    return getString() == "foo".toString();              return Objects.equals(getString(), "foo".toString());
}                                                    }

    public String getString() {                          public String getString() {
    return new String("foo");                            return new String("foo");
}                                                    }
}                                                    }

  Apply    Cancel
```

Figure 13-3. Screenshot of the preview fix view for the Error Prone warning from Figure 13-2

Reverse Engineering and Test Input Generation

Program analysis techniques, both static and dynamic, have been used for purposes beyond testing and ensuring code correctness—for example, to reverse engineer software. Reverse engineering can be useful when trying to understand the behavior of binaries where source code is not available. A common use case for reverse engineering occurs when a security engineer is trying to understand a potentially malicious binary. This analysis often involves using so-called *decompilers* or *disassemblers*: a disassembler translates machine language into assembly code, while a decompiler translates from machine language to source code. These tools do not guarantee that they can re-create the original source code itself. However, the generated code can help a security engineer who is trying to understand the program and its behavior. One popular tool for reverse engineering is Ghidra (*https://ghidra-sre.org*).

Some engineers also use program analysis techniques to help with test input generation. One technique that has recently become popular, *concolic testing,* combines a regular execution (called a *concrete* execution since it utilizes concrete values) with symbolic analysis techniques (hence the name concolic—*conc*rete + symb*olic*). Users can then automatically generate test inputs that are guaranteed to cover some other execution paths in the target program. Concolic tests can make this guarantee by executing a given program given a concrete input (e.g., the integer value 123), while shadowing each execution step with a formula that corresponds to the observed statements and branches. For example, you might substitute the concrete input value 123 with the symbol α. As the execution proceeds, at every branch point, such as an if statement, concolic execution asks a constraint solver whether it is possible to find a different value for α that would lead down the alternative branch. With each collected input value, you can start new concolic executions that increase branch coverage. KLEE (*https://klee.github.io*) is one popular concolic testing tool.

Abstract Interpretation

Abstract interpretation–based tools statically perform a semantic analysis of program behaviors.[9] This technique has been used successfully to verify safety-critical software, such as flight control software.[10] Consider the simple example of a program that generates the 10 smallest positive even integers. During its regular execution, the program generates the integer values 2, 4, 6, 8, 10, 12, 14, 16, 18, and 20. In order to allow efficient static analysis of such a program, we want to summarize all the possible values using a compact representation that covers all the observed values. Using the so-called interval or range domain, we can represent all observed values using the abstract interval value [2, 20] instead. The interval domain allows the static analyzer to reason efficiently about all program executions by simply remembering the lowest and highest possible values.

In order to ensure that we're capturing all possible program behaviors, it's important to cover all observed values with the abstract representation. However, this approach also introduces an approximation that may lead to *imprecision,* or false warnings. For example, if we wanted to guarantee that the actual program never produces the value 11, an analysis using an integer domain would lead to a false positive.

---

9 See Cousot, Patrick, and Radhia Cousot. 1976. "Static Determination of Dynamic Properties of Programs." *Proceedings of the 2nd International Symposium on Programming*: 106–130. https://oreil.ly/4xLgB.

10 Souyris, Jean et al. 2009. "Formal Verification of Avionics Software Products." *Proceedings of the 2nd World Conference on Formal Methods*: 532–546. doi:10.1007/978-3-642-05089-3_34.

Static analyzers utilizing abstract interpretation generally compute an abstract value for every program point. To do so, they rely on a *control-flow graph* (CFG) representation of a program. CFGs are commonly used during compiler optimizations, and to statically analyze programs. Each node in a CFG represents a basic block in the program, which corresponds to a sequence of program statements that are always executed in order. That is, there are no jumps from within this sequence of statements, and no jump targets in the middle of the sequence. Edges in a CFG represent control flow in the program, where a jump occurs either through intraprocedural control flow—for example, due to `if` statements or loop constructs—or interprocedural control flow due to function calls. Note that the CFG representation is also used by coverage-guided fuzzers (discussed previously). For instance, libFuzzer keeps track of which basic blocks and edges are covered during fuzzing. The fuzzer uses this information to decide whether to consider an input for future mutations.

Abstract interpretation–based tools perform a semantic analysis that reasons about data flow and control flow in programs, often across function calls. For that reason, they take much longer to run than the previously discussed automated code inspection tools. While you can integrate automated code inspection tools into interactive development environments such as code editors, abstract interpretation is generally not similarly integrated. Instead, developers might run abstract interpretation–based tools on committed code occasionally (nightly, for example), or during code review in differential settings, analyzing only the changed code while reusing analysis facts for unchanged code.

A number of tools rely on abstract interpretation for a variety of languages and properties. For example, the Frama-C tool (*https://frama-c.com*) allows you to find common runtime errors and assertion violations including buffer overflows, segmentation faults due to dangling or null pointers, and division by zero in programs written in C. As previously discussed, these types of bugs—especially memory-related bugs—can have security implications. The Infer tool (*https://fbinfer.com*) reasons about memory and pointer changes performed by programs and can find bugs like dangling pointers in Java, C, and other languages. The AbsInt tool (*https://www.absint.com*) can perform worst-case execution time analysis of tasks in real-time systems. The App Security Improvement (ASI) program (*https://oreil.ly/60tlV*) performs a sophisticated interprocedural analysis on every Android app that's uploaded to the Google Play Store, for safety and security. If it finds a vulnerability, ASI flags the vulnerability and presents suggestions for addressing the issue. Figure 13-4 shows a sample security alert. As of early 2019, this program had led to over one million app fixes (*https://oreil.ly/my8fa*) in the Play Store by over 300,000 app developers.

Figure 13-4. An App Security Improvement alert

Formal Methods

Formal methods allow users to specify properties of interest for software or hardware systems. Most of these are so-called *safety properties* that specify that a certain bad behavior should never be observable. For example, "bad behavior" can include assertions in programs. Others include *liveness properties,* which allow users to specify a desired outcome—for example, that a submitted print job is eventually processed by a printer. Users of formal methods can verify these properties for particular systems or models, and even develop such systems using *correct-by-construction*–based approaches. As highlighted in "Analyzing Invariants" on page 92, formal methods–based approaches often have a relatively high up-front cost. This is partially because these approaches require an a priori description of system requirements and properties of interest. These requirements must be specified in a mathematically rigorous and formal way.

Formal methods–based techniques have been successfully integrated into hardware design and verification tools.[11] In hardware design, it is now standard practice to use formal or semiformal tools provided by electronic design automation (EDA) vendors. These techniques have also been successfully applied to software in specialized domains, such as safety-critical systems or cryptographic protocol analysis. For example, a formal methods–based approach continuously analyzes the cryptographic protocols used in TLS within computer network communications.[12]

---

11 See, e.g., Kern, Christoph, and Mark R. Greenstreet. 1999. "Formal Verification in Hardware Design: A Survey." *ACM Transactions on Design Automation of Electronic Systems* 4(2): 123–193. doi: 10.1145/307988.307989. See also Hunt Jr. et al. 2017. "Industrial Hardware and Software Verification with ACL2." *Philosophical Transactions of The Royal Society A Mathematical Physical and Engineering Sciences* 375(2104): 20150399. doi: 10.1098/rsta.2015.0399.

12 See Chudnov, Andrey et al. 2018. "Continuous Formal Verification of Amazon s2n." *Proceedings of the 30th International Conference on Computer Aided Verification:* 430–446. doi:10.1007/978-3-319-96142-2_26.

Conclusion

Testing software for security and reliability is a vast topic, of which we've just scratched the surface. The testing strategies presented in this chapter, combined with practices around writing secure code to eliminate entire bug classes (see Chapter 12), have been key in helping Google teams scale reliably, minimizing outages and security problems. It's important to build software with testability in mind from the earliest stages of development, and to engage in comprehensive testing throughout the development lifecycle.

At this point, we want to emphasize the value of fully integrating all of these testing and analysis methods into your engineering workflows and CI/CD pipelines. By combining and regularly using these techniques consistently throughout your codebase, you can identify bugs more quickly. You'll also raise confidence in your ability to detect or prevent bugs when you deploy your applications—a topic covered in the next chapter.

CHAPTER 14

Deploying Code

By Jeremiah Spradlin and Mark Lodato
with Sergey Simakov and Roxana Loza

Is the code running in your production environment the code you assume it is? Your system needs controls to prevent or detect unsafe deployments: the deployment itself introduces changes to your system, and any of those changes might become a reliability or security issue. To keep from deploying unsafe code, you need to implement controls early in the software development lifecycle. This chapter begins by defining a software supply chain threat model and sharing some best practices to protect against those threats. We then deep dive into advanced mitigation strategies such as verifiable builds and provenance-based deployment policies, and conclude with some practical advice about how to deploy such changes.

Previous chapters addressed how to consider security and reliability when writing and testing your code. However, that code has no real impact until it's built and deployed. Therefore, it's important to carefully consider security and reliability for all elements of the build and deployment process. It can be difficult to determine if a deployed artifact is safe purely by inspecting the artifact itself. Controls on various stages of the software supply chain can increase your confidence in the safety of a software artifact. For example, code reviews can reduce the chance of mistakes and deter adversaries from making malicious changes, and automated tests can increase your confidence that the code operates correctly.

Controls built around the source, build, and test infrastructure have limited effect if adversaries can bypass them by deploying directly to your system. Therefore, systems should reject deployments that don't originate from the proper software supply chain. To meet this requirement, each step in the supply chain must be able to offer proof that it has executed properly.

Concepts and Terminology

We use the term *software supply chain* to describe the process of writing, building, testing, and deploying a software system. These steps include the typical responsibilities of a version control system (VCS), a continuous integration (CI) pipeline, and a continuous delivery (CD) pipeline.

While implementation details vary across companies and teams, most organizations have a process that looks something like Figure 14-1:

1. Code must be checked into a version control system.
2. Code is then built from a checked-in version.
3. Once built, the binary must be tested.
4. Code is then deployed to some environment where it is configured and executed.

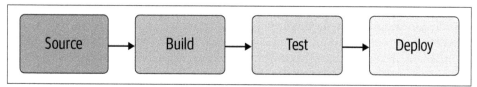

Figure 14-1. A high-level view of a typical software supply chain

Even if your supply chain is more complicated than this model, you can usually break it into these basic building blocks. Figure 14-2 shows a concrete example of how a typical deployment pipeline executes these steps.

You should design the software supply chain to mitigate threats to your system. This chapter focuses on mitigating threats presented by insiders (or malicious attackers impersonating insiders), as defined in Chapter 2, without regard to whether the insider is acting with malicious intent. For example, a well-meaning engineer might unintentionally build from code that includes unreviewed and unsubmitted changes, or an external attacker might attempt to deploy a backdoored binary using the privileges of a compromised engineer's account. We consider both scenarios equally.

In this chapter, we define the steps of the software supply chain rather broadly.

A *build* is any transformation of input artifacts to output artifacts, where an *artifact* is any piece of data—for example, a file, a package, a Git commit, or a virtual machine (VM) image. A *test* is a special case of a build, where the output artifact is some logical result—usually "pass" or "fail"—rather than a file or executable.

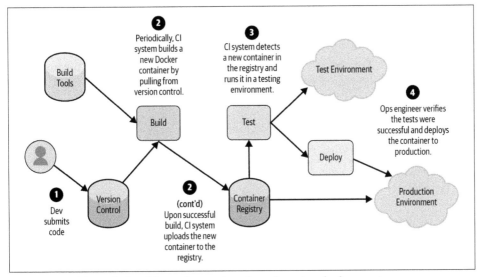

Figure 14-2. Typical cloud-hosted container-based service deployment

Builds can be chained together, and an artifact can be subject to multiple tests. For example, a release process might first "build" binaries from source code, then "build" a Docker image from the binaries, and then "test" the Docker image by running it in a development environment.

A *deployment* is any assignment of some artifact to some environment. You can consider each of the following to be a deployment:

- Pushing code:
  - Issuing a command to cause a server to download and run a new binary
  - Updating a Kubernetes Deployment object to pick up a new Docker image
  - Booting a VM or physical machine, which loads initial software or firmware
- Updating configuration:
  - Running a SQL command to change a database schema
  - Updating a Kubernetes Deployment object to change a command-line flag
- Publishing a package or other data, which will be consumed by other users:
  - Uploading a deb package to an apt repository
  - Uploading a Docker image to a container registry
  - Uploading an APK to the Google Play Store

Post-deployment changes are out of scope for this chapter.

Threat Model

Before hardening your software supply chain to mitigate threats, you have to identify your adversaries. For the purpose of this discussion, we'll consider the following three types of adversaries. Depending on your system and organization, your list of adversaries may differ:

- Benign insiders who may make mistakes
- Malicious insiders who try to gain more access than their role allows
- External attackers who compromise the machine or account of one or more insiders

Chapter 2 describes attacker profiles and provides guidance on how to model against insider risk.

Next, you must think like an attacker and try to identify all the ways an adversary can subvert the software supply chain to compromise your system. The following are some examples of common threats; you should tailor this list to reflect the specific threats to your organization. For the sake of simplicity, we use the term *engineer* to refer to benign insiders, and *malicious adversary* to refer to both malicious insiders and external attackers:

- An engineer submits a change that accidentally introduces a vulnerability to the system.
- A malicious adversary submits a change that enables a backdoor or introduces some other intentional vulnerability to the system.
- An engineer accidentally builds from a locally modified version of the code that contains unreviewed changes.
- An engineer deploys a binary with a harmful configuration. For example, the change enables debug features in production that were intended only for testing.
- A malicious adversary deploys a modified binary to production that begins exfiltrating customer credentials.
- A malicious adversary modifies the ACLs of a cloud bucket, allowing them to exfiltrate data.
- A malicious adversary steals the integrity key used to sign the software.
- An engineer deploys an old version of the code with a known vulnerability.
- The CI system is misconfigured to allow requests to build from arbitrary source repositories. As a result, a malicious adversary can build from a source repository containing malicious code.

- A malicious adversary uploads a custom build script to the CI system that exfiltrates the signing key. The adversary then uses that key to sign and deploy a malicious binary.
- A malicious adversary tricks the CD system to use a backdoored compiler or build tool that produces a malicious binary.

Once you've compiled a comprehensive list of potential adversaries and threats, you can map the threats you identified to the mitigations you already have in place. You should also document any limitations of your current mitigation strategies. This exercise will provide a thorough picture of the potential risks in your system. Threats that don't have corresponding mitigations, or threats for which existing mitigations have significant limitations, are areas for improvement.

Best Practices

The following best practices can help you mitigate threats, fill any security gaps you identified in your threat model, and continuously improve the security of your software supply chain.

Require Code Reviews

Code review is the practice of having a second person (or several people) review changes to the source code before those changes are checked in or deployed.[1] In addition to improving code security, code reviews provide multiple benefits for a software project: they promote knowledge sharing and education, instill coding norms, improve code readability, and reduce mistakes,[2] all of which helps to build a culture of security and reliability (for more on this idea, see Chapter 21).

From a security perspective, code review is a form of multi-party authorization,[3] meaning that no individual has the privilege to submit changes on their own. As described in Chapter 5, multi-party authorization provides many security benefits.

To be implemented successfully, code reviews must be mandatory. An adversary will not be deterred if they can simply opt out of the review! Reviews must also be comprehensive enough to catch problems. The reviewer must understand the details of

---

1 Code reviews also apply to changes to configuration files; see "Treat Configuration as Code" on page 310.

2 Sadowski, Caitlin et al. 2018. "Modern Code Review: A Case Study at Google." *Proceedings of the 40th International Conference on Software Engineering:* 181–190. doi:10.1145/3183519.3183525.

3 When combined with configuration-as-code and the deployment policies described in this chapter, code reviews form the basis of a multi-party authorization system for arbitrary systems.

any change and its implications for the system, or ask the author for clarifications—otherwise, the process can devolve into rubber-stamping.[4]

Many publicly available tools allow you to implement mandatory code reviews. For example, you can configure GitHub, GitLab, or BitBucket to require a certain number of approvals for every pull/merge request. Alternatively, you can use standalone review systems like Gerrit or Phabricator in combination with a source repository configured to accept only pushes from that review system.

Code reviews have limitations with respect to security, as described in the introduction to Chapter 12. Therefore, they are best implemented as one "defense in depth" security measure, alongside automated testing (described in Chapter 13) and the recommendations in Chapter 12.

Rely on Automation

Ideally, automated systems should perform most of the steps in the software supply chain.[5] Automation provides a number of advantages. It can provide a consistent, repeatable process for building, testing, and deploying software. Removing humans from the loop helps prevent mistakes and reduces toil. When you run the software supply chain automation on a locked-down system, you harden the system from subversion by malicious adversaries.

Consider a hypothetical scenario in which engineers manually build "production" binaries on their workstations as needed. This scenario creates many opportunities to introduce errors. Engineers can accidentally build from the wrong version of the code or include unreviewed or untested code changes. Meanwhile, malicious adversaries—including external attackers who have compromised an engineer's machine—might intentionally overwrite the locally built binaries with malicious versions. Automation can prevent both of these outcomes.

Adding automation in a secure manner can be tricky, as an automated system itself might introduce other security holes. To avoid the most common classes of vulnerabilities, we recommend, at minimum, the following:

Move all build, test, and deployment steps to automated systems.
At a minimum, you should script all steps. This allows both humans and automation to execute the same steps for consistency. You can use CI/CD systems (such as Jenkins (*https://jenkins.io*)) for this purpose. Consider establishing a

---

4 For more on the responsibilities of the code reviewer, see "Culture of Review" on page 474.

5 The *chain* of steps need not be fully automatic. For example, it is usually acceptable for a human to be able to initiate a build or deployment step. However, the human should not be able to influence the behavior of that step in any meaningful way.

---

policy that requires automation for all new projects, since retrofitting automation into existing systems can often be challenging.

Require peer review for all configuration changes to the software supply chain.
Often, treating configuration as code (as discussed shortly) is the best way to accomplish this. By requiring review, you greatly decrease your chances of making errors and mistakes, and increase the cost of malicious attacks.

Lock down the automated system to prevent tampering by administrators or users.
This is the most challenging step, and implementation details are beyond the scope of this chapter. In short, consider all of the paths where an administrator could make a change without review—for example, making a change by configuring the CI/CD pipeline directly or using SSH to run commands on the machine. For each path, consider a mitigation to prevent such access without peer review.

For further recommendations on locking down your automated build system, see "Verifiable Builds" on page 319.

Automation is a win-win, reducing toil while simultaneously increasing reliability and security. Rely on automation whenever possible!

Verify Artifacts, Not Just People

The controls around the source, build, and test infrastructure have limited effect if adversaries can bypass them by deploying directly to production. It is not sufficient to verify *who* initiated a deployment, because that actor may make a mistake or may be intentionally deploying a malicious change.[6] Instead, deployment environments should verify *what* is being deployed.

Deployment environments should require proof that each automated step of the deployment process occurred. Humans must not be able to bypass the automation unless some other mitigating control checks that action. For example, if you run on Google Kubernetes Engine (GKE), you can use Binary Authorization (*https://oreil.ly/0jsVi*) to by default accept only images signed by your CI/CD system, and monitor the Kubernetes cluster audit log for notifications when someone uses the breakglass feature to deploy a noncompliant image.[7]

One limitation of this approach is that it assumes that all components of your setup are secure: that the CI/CD system accepts build requests only for sources that are allowed in production, that the signing keys (if used) are accessible only by the

---

6 That said, such authorization checks are still necessary for the principle of least privilege (see Chapter 5).

7 A breakglass mechanism can bypass policies to allow engineers to quickly resolve outages. See "Breakglass" on page 67.

CI/CD system, and so on. "Advanced Mitigation Strategies" on page 314 describes a more robust approach of directly verifying the desired properties with fewer implicit assumptions.

Treat Configuration as Code

A service's configuration is just as critical to security and reliability as the service's code. Therefore, all the best practices regarding code versioning and change review apply to configuration as well. Treat configuration as code by requiring that configuration changes be checked in, reviewed, and tested prior to deployment, just like any other change.[8]

To provide an example: suppose your frontend server has a configuration option to specify the backend. If someone were to point your production frontend to a testing version of the backend, you'd have a major security and reliability problem.

Or, as a more practical example, consider a system that uses Kubernetes and stores the configuration in a YAML (*https://yaml.org*) file under version control.[9] The deployment process calls the kubectl binary and passes in the YAML file, which deploys the approved configuration. Restricting the deployment process to use only "approved" YAML—YAML from version control with required peer review—makes it much more difficult to misconfigure your service.

You can reuse all of the controls and best practices this chapter recommends to protect your service's configuration. Reusing these approaches is usually much easier than other methods of securing post-deployment configuration changes, which often require a completely separate multi-party authorization system.

The practice of versioning and reviewing configuration is not nearly as widespread as code versioning and review. Even organizations that implement configuration-as-code usually don't apply code-level rigor to configuration. For example, engineers generally know that they shouldn't build a production version of a binary from a locally modified copy of the source code. Those same engineers might not think twice before deploying a configuration change without first saving the change to version control and soliciting review.

Implementing configuration-as-code requires changes to your culture, tooling, and processes. Culturally, you need to place importance on the review process. Technically, you need tools that allow you to easily compare proposed changes (i.e.,

---

8 This concept is discussed in more detail in Chapter 8 of the SRE book and Chapters 14 and 15 of the SRE workbook. The recommendations in all of those chapters apply here.

9 YAML is the configuration language (*https://oreil.ly/UKo2t*) used by Kubernetes.

`diff`, `grep`) and that provide the ability to manually override changes in case of emergency.[10]

Don't Check In Secrets!

Passwords, cryptographic keys, and authorization tokens are often necessary for a service to operate. The security of your system depends on maintaining the confidentiality of these secrets. Fully protecting secrets is outside the scope of this chapter, but we'd like to highlight several important tips:

- Never check secrets into version control or embed secrets into source code. It may be feasible to embed *encrypted* secrets into source code or environment variables—for example, to be decrypted and injected by a build system. While this approach is convenient, it may make centralized secret management more difficult.

- Whenever possible, store secrets in a proper secret management system, or encrypt secrets with a key management system such as Cloud KMS (*https:// cloud.google.com/kms*).

- Strictly limit access to the secrets. Only grant services access to secrets, and only when needed. Never grant humans direct access. If a human needs access to a secret, it's probably a password, not an application secret. Where this is a valid use, create separate credentials for humans and services.

Securing Against the Threat Model

Now that we've defined some best practices, we can map those processes to the threats we identified earlier. When evaluating these processes with respect to your specific threat model, ask yourself: Are all of the best practices necessary? Do they sufficiently mitigate all the threats? Table 14-1 lists example threats, along with their corresponding mitigations and potential limitations of those mitigations.

---

10 You must log and audit these manual overrides, lest an adversary use manual overrides as an attack vector.

Table 14-1. Example threats, mitigations, and potential limitations of mitigations

Threat	Mitigation	Limitations
An engineer submits a change that accidentally introduces a vulnerability to the system.	Code review plus automated testing (see Chapter 13). This approach significantly reduces the chance of mistakes.	
A malicious adversary submits a change that enables a backdoor or introduces some other intentional vulnerability to the system.	Code review. This practice increases the cost for attacks and the chance of detection—the adversary has to carefully craft the change to get it past code review.	Does not protect against collusion or external attackers who are able to compromise multiple insider accounts.
An engineer accidentally builds from a locally modified version of the code that contains unreviewed changes.	An automated CI/CD system that always pulls from the correct source repository performs builds.	
An engineer deploys a harmful configuration. For example, the change enables debug features in production that were intended only for testing.	Treat configuration the same as source code, and require the same level of peer review.	Not all configuration can be treated "as code."
A malicious adversary deploys a modified binary to production that begins exfiltrating customer credentials.	The production environment requires proof that the CI/CD system built the binary. The CI/CD system is configured to pull sources from only the correct source repository.	An adversary may figure out how to bypass this requirement by using emergency deployment breakglass procedures (see "Practical Advice" on page 328). Sufficient logging and auditing can mitigate this possibility.
A malicious adversary modifies the ACLs of a cloud bucket, allowing them to exfiltrate data.	Consider resource ACLs as configuration. The cloud bucket only allows configuration changes by the deployment process, so humans can't make changes.	Does not protect against collusion or external attackers who are able to compromise multiple insider accounts.
A malicious adversary steals the integrity key used to sign the software.	Store the integrity key in a key management system that is configured to allow only the CI/CD system to access the key, and that supports key rotation. For more information, see Chapter 9. For build-specific suggestions, see the recommendations in "Advanced Mitigation Strategies" on page 314.	

Figure 14-3 shows an updated software supply chain that includes the threats and mitigations listed in the preceding table.

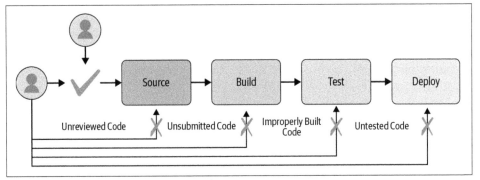

Figure 14-3. A typical software supply chain—adversaries should not be able to bypass the process

We have yet to match several threats with mitigations from best practices:

- An engineer deploys an old version of the code with a known vulnerability.
- The CI system is misconfigured to allow requests to build from arbitrary source repositories. As a result, a malicious adversary can build from a source repository containing malicious code.
- A malicious adversary uploads a custom build script to the CI system that exfiltrates the signing key. The adversary then uses that key to sign and deploy a malicious binary.
- A malicious adversary tricks the CD system to use a backdoored compiler or build tool that produces a malicious binary.

To address these threats, you need to implement more controls, which we cover in the following section. Only you can decide whether these threats are worth addressing for your particular organization.

Trusting Third-Party Code

Modern software development commonly makes use of third-party and open source code. If your organization relies upon these types of dependencies, you need to figure out how to mitigate the risks they pose.

If you fully trust the people who maintain the project, the code review process, the version control system, and the tamper-proof import/export process, then importing third-party code into your build is straightforward: pull in the code as though it originated from any of your first-party version control systems.

However, if you have less than full trust in the people who maintain the project or the version control system, or if the project doesn't guarantee code reviews, then you'll want to perform some level of code review prior to build. You may even keep an internal copy of the third-party code and review all patches pulled from upstream.

The level of review will depend on your level of trust in the vendor. It's important to understand the third-party code you use and to apply the same level of rigor to third-party code as you apply to first-party code.

Regardless of your trust in the vendor, you should always monitor your dependencies for vulnerability reports and quickly apply security patches.

 # Advanced Mitigation Strategies

You may need complex mitigations to address some of the more advanced threats to your software supply chain. Because the recommendations in this section are not yet standard across the industry, you may need to build some custom infrastructure to adopt them. These recommendations are best suited for large and/or particularly security-sensitive organizations, and may not make sense for small organizations with low exposure to insider risk.

Binary Provenance

Every build should produce *binary provenance* describing exactly how a given binary artifact was built: the inputs, the transformation, and the entity that performed the build.

To explain why, consider the following motivating example. Suppose you are investigating a security incident and see that a deployment occurred within a particular time window. You'd like to determine if the deployment was related to the incident. Reverse engineering the binary would be prohibitively expensive. It would be much easier to inspect the source code, preferably by looking at changes in version control. But how do you know what source code the binary came from?

Even if you don't anticipate that you'll need these types of security investigations, you'll also need binary provenance for provenance-based deployment policies, as discussed later in this section.

What to put in binary provenance

The exact information you should include in the provenance depends on the assumptions built into your system and the information that consumers of the provenance will eventually need. To enable rich deployment policies and allow for ad hoc analysis, we recommend the following provenance fields:

Authenticity (required)

Connotes implicit information about the build, such as which system produced it and why you can trust the provenance. This is usually accomplished using a cryptographic signature protecting the rest of the fields of the binary provenance.[11]

Outputs (required)

The output artifacts to which this binary provenance applies. Usually, each output is identified by a cryptographic hash of the content of the artifact.

Inputs

What went into the build. This field allows the verifier to link properties of the source code to properties of the artifact. It should include the following:

Sources

The "main" input artifacts to the build, such as the source code tree where the top-level build command ran. For example: "Git commit `270f...ce6d` from `https://github.com/mysql/mysql-server`"[12] or "file `foo.tar.gz` with SHA-256 content `78c5...6649`."

Dependencies

All other artifacts you need for the build—such as libraries, build tools, and compilers—that are not fully specified in the sources. Each of these inputs can affect the integrity of the build.

Command

The command used to initiate the build. For example: "`bazel build //main:hello-world`". Ideally, this field is structured to allow for automated analysis, so our example might become "`{"bazel": {"command": "build", "target": "//main:hello_world"}}`".

Environment

Any other information you need to reproduce the build, such as architecture details or environment variables.

Input metadata

In some cases, the builder may read metadata about the inputs that downstream systems will find useful. For example, a builder might include the timestamp of the source commit, which a policy evaluation system then uses at deployment time.

---

11 Note that authenticity implies integrity.

12 Git commit IDs are cryptographic hashes that provide integrity of the entire source tree.

Debug info

Any extra information that isn't necessary for security but may be useful for debugging, such as the machine on which the build ran.

Versioning

A build timestamp and provenance format version number are often useful to allow for future changes—for example, so you can invalidate old builds or change the format without being susceptible to rollback attacks.

You can omit fields that are implicit or covered by the source itself. For example, Debian's provenance format omits the build command because that command is always `dpkg-buildpackage`.

Input artifacts should generally list both an *identifier*, such as a URI, and a *version*, such as a cryptographic hash. You typically use the identifier to verify the authenticity of the build—for example, to verify that code came from the proper source repository. The version is useful for various purposes, such as ad hoc analysis, ensuring reproducible builds, and verification of chained build steps where the output of step i is the input to step $i+1$.

Be aware of the attack surface. You need to verify anything not checked by the build system (and therefore implied by the signature) or included in the sources (and therefore peer reviewed) downstream. If the user who initiated the build can specify arbitrary compiler flags, the verifier must validate those flags. For example, GCC's -D flag allows the user to overwrite arbitrary symbols, and therefore also to completely change the behavior of a binary. Similarly, if the user can specify a custom compiler, then the verifier must ensure that the "right" compiler was used. In general, the more validation the build process can perform, the better.

For a good example of binary provenance, see Debian's deb-buildinfo (*https://oreil.ly/WNUw_*) format. For more general advice, see the Reproducible Builds project's documentation (*https://oreil.ly/Y5VFW*). For a standard way to sign and encode this information, consider JSON Web Tokens (JWT) (*https://jwt.io*).

Code Signing

Code signing (*https://oreil.ly/f4gdr*) is often used as a security mechanism to increase trust in binaries. Use care when applying this technique, however, because a signature's value lies entirely in what it represents and how well the signing key is protected.

Consider the case of trusting a Windows binary, as long as it has any valid Authenticode signature. To bypass this control, an attacker can either buy (*https://oreil.ly/EiiiU*) or steal (*https://oreil.ly/j_0Co*) a valid signing certificate, which perhaps costs a few hundred to a few thousand dollars (depending on the type of certificate). While this approach does have security value, it has limited benefit.

To increase the effectiveness of code signing, we recommend that you explicitly list the signers you accept and lock down access to the associated signing keys. You should also ensure that the environment where code signing occurs is hardened, so an attacker can't abuse the signing process to sign their own malicious binaries. Consider the process of obtaining a valid code signature to be a "deployment" and follow the recommendations laid out in this chapter to protect those deployments.

Provenance-Based Deployment Policies

"Verify Artifacts, Not Just People" on page 309 recommends that the official build automation pipeline should verify what is being deployed. How do you verify that the pipeline is configured properly? And what if you want to make specific guarantees for some deployment environments that don't apply to other environments?

You can use explicit deployment policies that describe the intended properties of each deployment environment to address these concerns. The deployment environments can then match these policies against the binary provenance of artifacts deployed to them.

This approach has several benefits over a pure signature-based approach:

- It reduces the number of implicit assumptions throughout the software supply chain, making it easier to analyze and ensure correctness.
- It clarifies the contract of each step in the software supply chain, reducing the likelihood of misconfiguration.
- It allows you to use a single signing key per build step rather than per deployment environment, since you can now use the binary provenance for deployment decisions.

For example, suppose you have a microservices architecture and want to guarantee that each microservice can be built only from code submitted to that microservice's source repository. Using code signing, you would need one key per source repository, and the CI/CD system would have to choose the correct signing key based on the source repository. The disadvantage to this approach is that it's challenging to verify that the CI/CD system's configuration meets these requirements.

Using provenance-based deployment policies, the CI/CD system produces binary provenance stating the originating source repository, always signed with a single key. The deployment policy for each microservice lists which source repository is allowed. Verification of correctness is much easier than with code signing, because the deployment policy describes each microservice's properties in a single place.

The rules listed in your deployment policy should mitigate the threats to your system. Refer to the threat model you created for your system. What rules can you define to mitigate those threats? For reference, here are some example rules you may want to implement:

- Source code was submitted to version control and peer reviewed.
- Source code came from a particular location, such as a specific build target and repository.
- Build was through the official CI/CD pipeline (see "Verifiable Builds" on page 319).
- Tests have passed.
- Binary was explicitly allowed for this deployment environment. For example, do not allow "test" binaries in production.
- Version of code or build is sufficiently recent.[13]
- Code is free of known vulnerabilities, as reported by a sufficiently recent security scan.[14]

The in-toto framework (*https://in-toto.github.io*) provides one standard for implementing provenance policies.

Implementing policy decisions

If you implement your own engine for provenance-based deployment policies, remember that three steps are necessary:

1. Verify that the *provenance is authentic*. This step also implicitly verifies the integrity of the provenance, preventing an adversary from tampering with or forging it. Typically, this means verifying that the provenance was cryptographically signed by a specific key.
2. Verify that the *provenance applies to the artifact*. This step also implicitly verifies the integrity of the artifact, ensuring an adversary cannot apply an otherwise "good" provenance to a "bad" artifact. Typically, this means comparing a cryptographic hash of the artifact to the value found within the provenance's payload.
3. Verify that the *provenance meets all the policy rules.*

The simplest example of this process is a rule that requires artifacts to be signed by a specific key. This single check implements all three steps: it verifies that the signature

---

13 For a discussion on rollbacks to vulnerable versions, see "Minimum Acceptable Security Version Numbers" on page 195.

14 For example, you might require proof that Cloud Security Scanner (*https://oreil.ly/mrTi7*) found no results against your test instance running this specific version of the code.

itself is valid, that the artifact applies to the signature, and that the signature is present.

Let's consider a more complex example: "Docker image must be built from GitHub repo `mysql/mysql-server`." Suppose your build system uses key K_B to sign build provenance in a JWT format. In this case, the schema of the token's payload would be the following, where the subject, `sub`, is an RFC 6920 URI (*https://oreil.ly/_8zJm*):

```
{
    "sub": "ni:///sha-256;...",
    "input": {"source_uri": "..."}
}
```

To evaluate whether an artifact satisfies this rule, the engine needs to verify the following:

1. The JWT signature verifies using key K_B.

2. `sub` matches the SHA-256 hash of the artifact.

3. `input.source_uri` is exactly `"https://github.com/mysql/mysql-server"`.

Verifiable Builds

We call a build *verifiable* if the binary provenance produced by the build is trustworthy.[15] Verifiability is in the eye of the beholder. Whether or not you trust a particular build system depends on your threat model and how the build system fits into your organization's larger security story.

Consider whether the following examples of nonfunctional requirements are appropriate for your organization,[16] and add any requirements that meet your specific needs:

- If a single developer's workstation is compromised, the integrity of binary provenance or output artifacts is not compromised.

- An adversary cannot tamper with provenance or output artifacts without detection.

- One build cannot affect the integrity of another build, whether run in parallel or serial.

---

15 Recall that pure signatures still count as "binary provenance," as described in the previous section.

16 See "Design Objectives and Requirements" on page 44.

- A build cannot produce provenance containing false information. For example, the provenance should not be able to claim an artifact was built from Git commit abc...def when it really came from 123...456.

- Nonadministrators cannot configure user-defined build steps, such as a Makefile or a Jenkins Groovy script, in a way that violates any requirement in this list.

- A snapshot of all source artifacts is available for at least N months after the build, to allow for potential investigations.

- A build is reproducible (see "Hermetic, Reproducible, or Verifiable?" on page 321). This approach may be desirable even if it is not required by the verifiable build architecture, as defined in the next section. For example, reproducible builds may be useful to independently reverify the binary provenance of an artifact after discovering a security incident or vulnerability.

Verifiable build architectures

The purpose of a verifiable build system is to increase a verifier's trust in the binary provenance produced by that build system. Regardless of the specific requirements for verifiability, three main architectures are available:

Trusted build service
> The verifier requires that the original build has been performed by a build service that the verifier trusts. Usually, this means that the trusted build service signs the binary provenance with a key accessible only to that service.
>
> This approach has the advantages of needing to build only once and not requiring reproducibility (see "Hermetic, Reproducible, or Verifiable?" on page 321). Google uses this model for internal builds.

A rebuild you perform yourself
> The verifier reproduces the build on the fly in order to validate the binary provenance. For example, if the binary provenance claims to come from Git commit abc...def, the verifier fetches that Git commit, reruns the build commands listed in the binary provenance, and checks that the output is bit-for-bit identical to the artifact in question. See the following sidebar for more about reproducibility. While this approach may initially seem appealing because you trust yourself, it is not scalable. Builds often take minutes or hours, whereas deployment decisions often need to be made in milliseconds. This also requires the build to be fully reproducible, which is not always practical; see the sidebar for more information.

Rebuilding service
> The verifier requires that some quorum of "rebuilders" have reproduced the build and attested to the authenticity of the binary provenance. This is a hybrid of the two previous options. In practice, this approach usually means that each

rebuilder monitors a package repository, proactively rebuilds each new version, and stores the results in some database. Then, the verifier looks up entries in N different databases, keyed by the cryptographic hash of the artifact in question. Open source projects like Debian (*https://oreil.ly/zNZ7G*) use this model when a central authority model is infeasible or undesirable.

Hermetic, Reproducible, or Verifiable?

The concepts of reproducible builds and hermetic builds are closely related to verifiable builds. Terminology in this area is not yet standard,[17] so we propose the following definitions:

Hermetic

All inputs to the build are fully specified up front, outside the build process. In addition to the source code, this requirement applies to all compilers, build tools, libraries, and any other inputs that might influence the build. All references must be unambiguous, either as fully resolved version numbers or cryptographic hashes. Hermeticity information is checked in as part of the source code, but it is also acceptable for this information to live externally, such as in a Debian *.buildinfo* file (*https://oreil.ly/O7ElS*).

Hermetic builds have the following benefits:

- They enable build input analysis and policy application. Examples from Google include detecting vulnerable software that needs patching by using the Common Vulnerabilities and Exposures (CVE) database, ensuring compliance with open source licenses, and preventing software use that is disallowed by policy, such as a known insecure library.

- They guarantee integrity of third-party imports—for example, by verifying cryptographic hashes of dependencies or by requiring that all fetches use HTTPS and come from trustworthy repositories.

- They enable cherry-picking. You can fix a bug by patching the code, rebuilding the binary, and rolling it out to production without including any extraneous changes in behavior, such as behavior changes caused by a different compiler version. Cherry-picking significantly reduces the risk associated with emergency releases, which may not undergo as much testing and vetting as regular releases.

---

17 For example, the SRE book uses the terms *hermetic* and *reproducible* interchangeably. The Reproducible Builds project (*https://reproducible-builds.org*) defines *reproducible* the same way this chapter defines the term, but occasionally overloads *reproducible* to mean *verifiable*.

Examples of hermetic builds include Bazel (*https://bazel.build*) when run in sandboxed mode and npm (*https://www.npmjs.com*) when using *package-lock.json*.

Reproducible
Running the same build commands on the same inputs is guaranteed to produce bit-by-bit identical outputs. Reproducibility almost always requires hermeticity.[18]

Reproducible builds have the following benefits:

- *Verifiability*—A verifier can determine the binary provenance of an artifact by reproducing the build themselves or by using a quorum of rebuilders, as described in "Verifiable Builds" on page 319.

- *Hermeticity*—Nonreproducibility often indicates nonhermeticity. Continuously testing for reproducibility can help detect nonhermeticity early, thereby ensuring all the benefits of hermeticity described earlier.

- *Build caching*—Reproducible builds allow for better caching of intermediate build artifacts in large build graphs, such as in Bazel.

To make a build reproducible, you must remove all sources of nondeterminism and provide all information necessary to reproduce the build (known as the *buildinfo*). For example, if a compiler includes a timestamp in an output artifact, you must set that timestamp to a fixed value or include the timestamp in the buildinfo. In most cases, you must fully specify the full toolchain and operating system; different versions usually produce slightly different output. For practical advice, see the Reproducible Builds website (*https://reproducible-builds.org*).

Verifiable
You can determine the binary provenance of an artifact—information such as what sources it was built from—in a trustworthy manner. It is usually desirable (but not strictly required) for verifiable builds to also be reproducible and hermetic.

Implementing verifiable builds

Regardless of whether a verifiable build service is a "trusted build service" or a "rebuilding service," you should keep several important design considerations in mind.

---

18 As a counterexample, consider a build process that fetches the latest version of a dependency during the build but otherwise produces identical outputs. This process is reproducible so long as two builds happen at roughly the same time, but is not hermetic.

At a basic level, almost all CI/CD systems function according to the steps in Figure 14-4: the service takes in requests, fetches any necessary inputs, performs the build, and writes the output to a storage system.

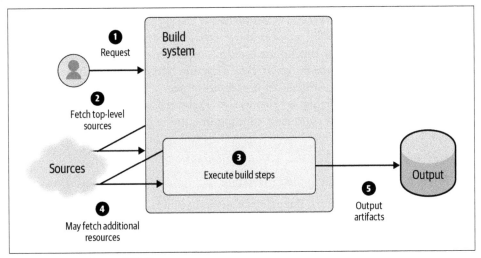

Figure 14-4. A basic CI/CD system

Given such a system, you can add signed provenance to the output relatively easily, as shown in Figure 14-5. For a small organization with a "central build service" model, this additional signing step may be sufficient to address security concerns.

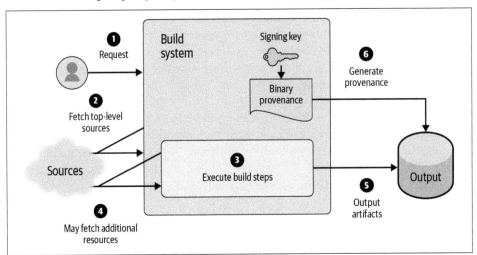

Figure 14-5. The addition of signing to an existing CI/CD system

As the size of your organization grows and you have more resources to invest in security, you will likely want to address two more security risks: untrusted inputs and unauthenticated inputs.

Untrusted inputs.   Adversaries can potentially use the inputs to the build to subvert the build process. Many build services allow nonadministrative users to define arbitrary commands to execute during the build process—for example, through the Jenkinsfile, *travis.yml*, the Makefile, or *BUILD*. This functionality is usually necessary to support the wide variety of builds an organization needs. However, from a security perspective, this functionality is effectively "Remote Code Execution (RCE) by design." A malicious build command running in a privileged environment could do the following:

- Steal the signing key.
- Insert false information in the provenance.
- Modify the system state, influencing subsequent builds.
- Manipulate another build that's happening in parallel.

Even if users are not allowed to define their own steps, compilation is a very complex operation that provides ample opportunity for RCE vulnerabilities.

You can mitigate this threat via privilege separation. Use a trusted orchestrator process to set up the initial known good state, start the build, and create the signed provenance when the build is finished. Optionally, the orchestrator may fetch inputs to address the threats described in the following subsection. All user-defined build commands should execute within another environment that has no access to the signing key or any other special privileges. You can create this environment in various ways —for example, through a sandbox on the same machine as the orchestrator, or by running on a separate machine.

Unauthenticated inputs.   Even if the user and build steps are trustworthy, most builds have dependencies on other artifacts. Any such dependency is a surface through which adversaries can potentially subvert the build. For example, if the build system fetches a dependency over HTTP without TLS, an attacker can perform a man-in-the-middle attack to modify the dependency in transit.

For this reason, we recommend hermetic builds (see "Hermetic, Reproducible, or Verifiable?" on page 321). The build process should declare all inputs up front, and only the orchestrator should fetch those inputs. Hermetic builds give much higher confidence that the inputs listed in the provenance are correct.

Once you've accounted for untrusted and unauthenticated inputs, your system resembles Figure 14-6. Such a model is much more resistant to attack than the simple model in Figure 14-5.

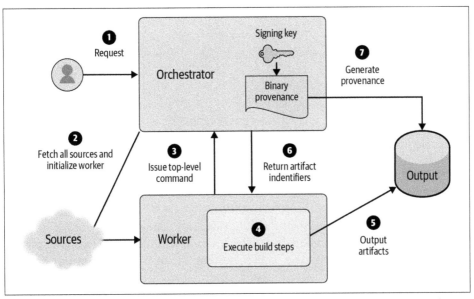

Figure 14-6. An "ideal" CI/CD design that addresses risks of untrusted and unauthenticated inputs

Deployment Choke Points

To "verify artifacts, not just people," deployment decisions must occur at proper choke points within the deployment environment. In this context, a *choke point* is a point through which all deployment requests must flow. Adversaries can bypass deployment decisions that don't occur at choke points.

Consider Kubernetes as an example for setting up deployment choke points, as shown in Figure 14-7. Suppose you want to verify all deployments to the pods in a specific Kubernetes cluster. The master node would make a good choke point because all deployments are supposed to flow through it. To make this a proper choke point, configure the worker nodes to accept requests only from the master node. This way, adversaries cannot deploy directly to worker nodes.[19]

---

19 In reality, there must be some way to deploy software to the node itself—the bootloader, the operating system, the Kubernetes software, and so on—and that deployment mechanism must have its own policy enforcement, which is likely a completely different implementation than the one used for pods.

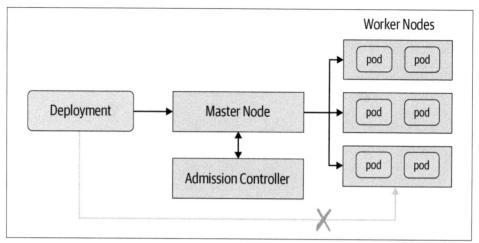

Figure 14-7. Kubernetes architecture—all deployments must flow through the master

Ideally, the choke point performs the policy decision, either directly or via an RPC. Kubernetes offers an Admission Controller (*https://oreil.ly/Bm04C*) webhook for this exact purpose. If you use Google Kubernetes Engine, Binary Authorization (*https://oreil.ly/YxiJX*) offers a hosted admission controller and many additional features. And even if you don't use Kubernetes, you may be able to modify your "admission" point to perform the deployment decision.

Alternatively, you can place a "proxy" in front of the choke point and perform the policy decision in the proxy, as shown in Figure 14-8. This approach requires config‐ uring your "admission" point to allow access only via the proxy. Otherwise, an adver‐ sary can bypass the proxy by talking directly to the admission point.

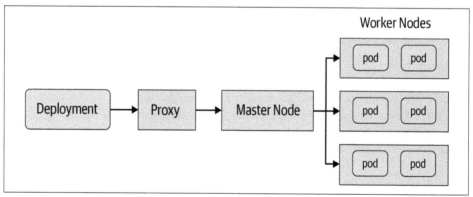

Figure 14-8. Alternative architecture using a proxy to make policy decisions

Post-Deployment Verification

Even when you enforce deployment policies or signature checks at deployment time, logging and post-deployment verification are almost always desirable, for the following reasons:

- *Policies can change*, in which case the verification engine must reevaluate existing deployments in the system to ensure they still comply with the new policies. This is particularly important when enabling a policy for the first time.

- The request might have been allowed to proceed because the decision service was unavailable. This *fail open* design is often necessary to ensure the availability of the service, especially when first rolling out an enforcement feature.

- An operator might have used a *breakglass mechanism* to bypass the decision in the case of an emergency, as described in the following section.

- Users need a way to *test* potential policy changes before committing them, to make sure that the existing state won't violate the new version of the policy.

- For reasons similar to the "fail open" use case, users may also want a *dry run* mode, where the system always allows requests at deployment time but monitoring surfaces potential problems.

- Investigators may need the information after an incident for *forensics* reasons.

The enforcement decision point must log enough information to allow the verifier to evaluate the policy after the deployment.[20] Logging of the full request is usually necessary but not always sufficient—if policy evaluation requires some other state, the logs must include that extra state. For example, we ran into this issue when implementing post-deployment verification for Borg: because "job" requests include references to existing "allocs" and "packages," we had to join three log sources—jobs, allocs, and packages—to get the full state necessary to make a decision.[21]

---

20 Ideally, the logs are highly reliable and tamper-evident, even in the face of outages or system compromise. For example, suppose a Kubernetes master receives a request while the logging backend is unavailable. The master can temporarily save the log to local disk. What if the machine dies before the logging backend comes back up? Or what if the machine runs out of space? This is a challenging area for which we're still developing solutions.

21 A Borg alloc (short for *allocation*) is a reserved set of resources on a machine in which one or more sets of Linux processes can be run in a container. Packages contain the Borg job's binaries and data files. For a complete description of Borg, see Verma, Abhishek et al. 2015. "Large-Scale Cluster Management at Google with Borg." *Proceedings of the 10th European Conference on Computer Systems*: 1–17. doi: 10.1145/2741948.2741964.

Practical Advice

We've learned several lessons over the years while implementing verifiable builds and deployment policies in a variety of contexts. Most of these lessons are less about the actual technology choices, and more about how to deploy changes that are reliable, easy to debug, and easy to understand. This section contains some practical advice that we hope you'll find useful.

Take It One Step at a Time

Providing a highly secure, reliable, and consistent software supply chain will likely require you to make many changes—from scripting your build steps, to implementing build provenance, to implementing configuration-as-code. Coordinating all of those changes may be difficult. Bugs or missing functionality in these controls can also pose a significant risk to engineering productivity. In the worst-case scenario, an error in these controls can potentially cause an outage for your service.

You may be more successful if you focus on securing one particular aspect of the supply chain at a time. That way, you can minimize the risk of disruption while also helping your coworkers learn new workflows.

Provide Actionable Error Messages

When a deployment is rejected, the error message must clearly explain what went wrong and how to fix the situation. For example, if an artifact is rejected because it was built from an incorrect source URI, the fix can be to either update the policy to allow that URI, or to rebuild from the correct URI. Your policy decision engine should give the user actionable feedback that provides such suggestions. Simply saying "does not meet policy" will likely leave the user confused and floundering.

Consider these user journeys when designing your architecture and policy language. Some design choices make providing actionable feedback for users very difficult, so try to catch these problems early. For example, one of our early policy language prototypes offered a lot of flexibility in expressing policies, but prevented us from supplying actionable error messages. We ultimately abandoned this approach in favor of a very limited language that allowed for better error messages.

Ensure Unambiguous Provenance

Google's verifiable build system originally uploaded binary provenance to a database asynchronously. Then at deployment time, the policy engine looked up the provenance in the database using the hash of the artifact as a key.

While this approach *mostly* worked just fine, we ran into a major issue: users could build an artifact multiple times, resulting in multiple entries for the same hash.

Consider the case of the empty file: we had literally millions of provenance records tied to the hash of the empty file, since many different builds produced an empty file as part of their output. In order to verify such a file, our system had to check whether *any* of the provenance records passed the policy. This in turn resulted in two problems:

- When we failed to find a passing record, we had no way to provide actionable error messages. For example, instead of saying, "The source URI was X, but the policy said it was supposed to be Y," we had to say, "None of these 497,129 records met the policy." This was a bad user experience.

- Verification time was linear in the number of records returned. This caused us to exceed our 100 ms latency SLO by several orders of magnitude!

We also ran into issues with the asynchronous upload to the database. Uploads could fail silently, in which case our policy engine would reject the deployment. Meanwhile, users didn't understand why it had been rejected. We could have fixed this problem by making the upload synchronous, but that solution would have made our build system less reliable.

Therefore, we strongly recommend making provenance unambiguous. Whenever possible, avoid using databases and instead *propagate the provenance inline with the artifact*. Doing so makes the overall system more reliable, lower latency, and easier to debug. For example, a system using Kubernetes can add an annotation that's passed to the Admission Controller webhook.

Create Unambiguous Policies

Similar to our recommended approach to an artifact's provenance, the policy that applies to a particular deployment should be unambiguous. We recommend designing the system so that only a single policy applies to any given deployment. Consider the alternative: if two policies apply, do both policies need to pass, or can just one policy pass? It's easier to avoid this question altogether. If you want to apply a global policy across an organization, you can do so as a meta-policy: implement a check that all of the individual policies meet some global criteria.

Include a Deployment Breakglass

In an emergency, it may be necessary to bypass the deployment policy. For example, an engineer may need to reconfigure a frontend to divert traffic from a failing backend, and the corresponding configuration-as-code change might take too long to deploy through the regular CI/CD pipeline. A breakglass mechanism that bypasses the policy can allow engineers to quickly resolve outages and promotes a culture of security and reliability (see Chapter 21).

Because adversaries may exploit the breakglass mechanism, all breakglass deployments must raise alarms and be audited quickly. In order to make auditing practical, breakglass events should be rare—if there are too many events, it may not be possible to differentiate malicious activity from legitimate usage.

Securing Against the Threat Model, Revisited

We can now map advanced mitigations to our previously unaddressed threats, as shown in Table 14-2.

Table 14-2. Advanced mitigations to complex threat examples

Threat	Mitigation
An engineer deploys an old version of the code with a known vulnerability.	The deployment policy requires the code to have undergone a security vulnerability scan within the last *N* days.
The CI system is misconfigured to allow requests to build from arbitrary source repositories. As a result, a malicious adversary can build from a source repository containing malicious code.	The CI system generates binary provenance describing what source repository it pulled from. The production environment enforces a deployment policy requiring provenance to prove that the deployed artifact originated from an approved source repository.
A malicious adversary uploads a custom build script to the CI system that exfiltrates the signing key. The adversary then uses that key to sign and deploy a malicious binary.	The verifiable build system separates privileges so that the component that runs custom build scripts does not have access to the signing key.
A malicious adversary tricks the CD system to use a backdoored compiler or build tool that produces a malicious binary.	Hermetic builds require developers to explicitly specify the choice of compiler and build tool in the source code. This choice is peer reviewed like all other code.

With appropriate security controls around your software supply chain, you can mitigate even advanced and complex threats.

Conclusion

The recommendations in this chapter can help you harden your software supply chain against various insider threats. Code reviews and automation are essential tactics for preventing mistakes and increasing attack costs for malicious actors. Configuration-as-code extends those benefits to configuration, which traditionally receives much less scrutiny than code. Meanwhile, artifact-based deployment controls, particularly those involving binary provenance and verifiable builds, bring protection against sophisticated adversaries and allow you to scale as your organization grows.

Together, these recommendations help ensure that the code you wrote and tested (following the principles in Chapters 12 and 13) is the code that's actually deployed in production. Despite your best efforts, however, your code probably won't always behave as expected. When that happens, you can use some of the debugging strategies presented in the next chapter.

CHAPTER 15

Investigating Systems

By Pete Nuttall, Matt Linton, and David Seidman
with Vera Haas, Julie Saracino, and Amaya Booker

Most systems eventually fail. Your ability to investigate a complex system relies on a number of factors: in addition to having access to adequate logs and information sources for debugging, you need proper expertise. You also need to design your logging systems with protection and access control in mind. In this chapter, we walk through debugging techniques and provide some strategies for what to do when you're stuck. We then discuss the differences between debugging a system issue and investigating a security concern, and examine tradeoffs to take into account when deciding which logs to retain. Finally, we look at how to keep these valuable sources of information secure and reliable.

In an ideal world, we would all build perfect systems, and our users would have only the best of intentions. In reality, you'll encounter bugs and need to conduct security investigations. As you observe a system running in production over time, you'll identify areas for improvement and places where you can streamline and optimize processes. All of these tasks require debugging and investigation techniques, and appropriate system access.

However, granting even read-only debugging access creates a risk that this access may be abused. To address this risk, you need proper security mechanisms in place. You also need to strike a careful balance between the debugging needs of developers and operations staff, and the security requirements of storing and accessing sensitive data.

In this chapter, we use the term *debugger* to mean a human who is debugging software problems—not GDB (the GNU Debugger) (*https://oreil.ly/Fl82Z*) or similar tools. Unless otherwise noted, we use the term "we" to refer to the authors of this chapter, not Google as a whole.

From Debugging to Investigation

> [T]he realization came over me with full force that a good part of the remainder of my life was going to be spent in finding errors in my own programs.
>
> —Maurice Wilkes, Memoirs of a Computer Pioneer (MIT Press, 1985)

Debugging has a bad reputation. Bugs surface at the worst of times. It can be hard to estimate when a bug will be fixed, or when a system will be "good enough" to let many people use it. For most people, it's more fun to write new code than to debug existing programs. Debugging can be perceived as unrewarding. However, it's necessary, and you may even find the practice enjoyable when viewed through the lens of learning new facts and tools. In our experience, debugging also makes us better programmers, and reminds us that sometimes we're not as smart as we think we are.

Example: Temporary Files

Consider the following outage, which we (the authors) debugged two years ago.[1] The investigation began when we received an alert that a Spanner database (*https://oreil.ly/ZYr1W*) was running out of storage quota. We went through the process of debugging, asking ourselves the following questions:

1. What caused the database to run out of storage?

   Quick triage indicated the problem was caused by an accumulation of many small files being created in Google's massive distributed filesystem, Colossus (*https://oreil.ly/dkocj*), which was likely triggered by a change in user request traffic.

2. What was creating all the tiny files?

   We looked at service metrics, which showed the files resulted from the Spanner server running low on memory. According to normal behavior, recent writes (updates) were buffered in memory; as the server ran low on memory, it flushed the data to files on Colossus. Unfortunately, each server in the Spanner zone had only a small amount of memory to accommodate updates. As a result, rather

---

1 Although the outage occurred in a large distributed system, people who have maintained smaller and self-contained systems will see a lot of similarities—for example, in outages involving a single mail server whose hard drive has run out of space!

---

than flushing a manageable number of larger, compressed files,[2] each server flushed many tiny files to Colossus.

3. Where was the memory being used?

   Each server ran as a Borg task (in a container), which capped the memory available to it.[3] To determine where within the kernel memory was used, we directly issued the `slabtop` command on the production machine. We determine that the directory entry (dentry) cache was the largest user of memory.

4. Why was the dentry cache so big?

   We made an educated guess that the Spanner database server was creating and deleting vast numbers of temporary files—a few for each flush operation. Each flush operation increased the size of the dentry cache, making the problem worse.

5. How could we confirm our hypothesis?

   To test this theory, we created and ran a program on Borg to reproduce the bug by creating and deleting files in a loop. After a few million files, the dentry cache had used all the memory in its container, confirming the hypothesis.

6. Was this a kernel bug?

   We researched expected behavior of the Linux kernel, and determined that the kernel caches the nonexistence of files—some build systems need this feature to ensure acceptable performance. In normal operation, the kernel evicts entries from the dentry cache when the container is full. However, because the Spanner server repeatedly flushed updates, the container never became full enough to trigger evictions. We addressed this issue by designating that temporary files didn't need to be cached.

The debugging process described here illustrates many of the concepts we discuss in this chapter. However, the most important takeaway from this story is that *we debugged this issue*—and you can, too! Solving and fixing the problem didn't require any magic; it just required slow and structured investigation. To break down the characteristics of our investigation:

---

2 Spanner stores data as a Log-Structured Merge (LSM) tree. For details on this format, see Luo, Chen, and Michael J. Carey. 2018. "LSM-Based Storage Techniques: A Survey." arXiv preprint arXiv:1812.07527v3 (*https://oreil.ly/DjWJn*).

3 For more on Borg, see Verma, Abhishek et al. 2015. "Large-Scale Cluster Management at Google with Borg." *Proceedings of the 10th European Conference on Computer Systems*: 1–17. doi:10.1145/2741948.2741964.

- After the system showed signs of degradation, we debugged the problem using existing logs and monitoring infrastructure.
- We were able to debug the issue even though it occurred in kernel space and code that the debuggers had not seen before.
- We'd never noticed the issue before this outage, even though it had likely been present for several years.
- No part of the system was broken. All parts were working as intended.
- The developers of the Spanner server were surprised that temporary files could consume memory long after the files had been deleted.
- We were able to debug the kernel's memory usage by using tools provided by the kernel developers. Even though we'd never used these tools before, we were able to make progress relatively quickly because we were trained and well practiced in debugging techniques.
- We initially misdiagnosed the bug as a user error. We changed our minds only after examining our data.
- By developing a hypothesis and then creating a way to test our theory, we confirmed the root cause before we introduced changes to the system.

Debugging Techniques

This section shares some techniques for systematic debugging.[4] Debugging is a skill that you can learn and practice. Chapter 12 of the SRE book offers two requirements for successful debugging:

- Know how the system is supposed to work.
- Be systematic: collect data, hypothesize causes, and test theories.

The first of these requirements is trickier. Take the canonical example of a system built by a single developer who suddenly leaves the company, taking all knowledge of the system with them. The system may continue to work for months, but one day it mysteriously breaks and no one can fix it. Some of the advice that follows can help, but there's no real substitute for understanding the system ahead of time (see Chapter 6).

---

4 You may also be interested in the blog post "What Does Debugging a Program Look Like?" (*https://oreil.ly/J2U1R*) by Julia Evans.

Distinguish horses from zebras

When you hear hoofbeats, do you first think of horses, or zebras? Instructors some-time pose this question to medical students learning how to triage and diagnose dis-eases. It's a reminder that most ailments are common—most hoofbeats are caused by horses, not zebras. You can imagine why this is helpful advice for a medical student: they don't want to assume symptoms add up to a rare disease when, in fact, the con-dition is common and straightforward to remedy.

In contrast, given a large enough scale, experienced engineers will observe both com-mon *and* rare events. People building computer systems can (and must) work to completely eliminate all problems. As a system grows in scale, and its operators elim-inate common problems over time, rare problems appear more frequently. To quote Bryan Cantrill (*https://oreil.ly/eYfUO*): "Over time, the horses are found; only the zebras are left."

Consider the very rare issue of memory corruption by bit flip. A modern error-correcting memory module has a less than 1% chance per year of encountering an uncorrectable bit flip that can crash a system.[5] An engineer debugging an unexpected crash probably won't think, "I bet this was caused by an extremely unlikely electrical malfunction in the memory chips!" However, at very large scale, these rarities become certainties. A hypothetical cloud service utilizing 25,000 machines might use memory across 400,000 RAM chips. Given the odds of a 0.1% yearly risk of uncor-rectable errors *per chip*, the scale of the service could lead to 400 occurrences annu-ally. People running the cloud service will likely observe a memory failure every day.

Debugging these kinds of rare events can be challenging, but it's achievable with the right kind of data. To provide one example, Google hardware engineers once noticed that certain RAM chips failed much more often than expected. Asset data allowed them to track the source of the failing DIMMs (memory modules), and they were able to trace the modules to a single provider. After extensive debugging and investi-gation, the engineers identified the root cause: an environmental failure in a clean room, in a single factory where the DIMMs were produced. This problem was a "zebra"—a rare bug visible only at scale.

As a service grows, today's strange outlier bug may become next year's routine bug. In the year 2000, memory hardware corruption was a surprise for Google (*https://oreil.ly/CicjH*). Today, such hardware failures are routine, and we plan for them with end-to-end integrity checking and other reliability measures.

---

5 Schroeder, Bianca, Eduardo Pinheiro, and Wolf-Dietrich Weber. 2009. "DRAM Errors in the Wild: A Large-Scale Field Study." *ACM SIGMETRICS Performance Evaluation Review* 37(1). doi:10.1145/2492101.1555372.

In recent years, we've encountered some other zebras:

- Two web search requests hashed to the same 64-bit cache key, causing results for one request to be served in place of the other.

- C++ converted an int64 to an int (only 32 bits), resulting in problems after 2^{32} requests (for more about this bug, see "Clean up code" on page 346).

- A bug in a distributed rebalancing algorithm was triggered only when the code ran simultaneously on hundreds of servers.

- Someone left a load test running for a week, causing performance to slowly degrade. We eventually determined that the machine was gradually suffering from memory allocation issues, leading to the degradation. We discovered this particular zebra because a normally short-lived test was left running for much longer than normal.

- Investigating slow C++ tests showed that the dynamic linker's loading time was superlinear in terms of the number of shared libraries loaded: at 10,000 shared libraries, it could take minutes to start running main.

When dealing with smaller, newer systems, expect horses (common bugs). When dealing with older, larger, and relatively stable systems, expect zebras (rare bugs)—operators have likely observed and fixed common bugs that surfaced over time. Issues are more likely to crop up in new parts of the system.

Data Corruption and Checksums

Memory may become corrupted for many reasons. Hardware problems, perhaps caused by environmental factors, are one cause. Software problems—for example, one thread writing while another reads—can also cause memory corruption. It is very dangerous for software engineers to think every weird bug is a hardware problem.

Modern DRAM provides several defenses against memory corruption:

- Error-correcting code (ECC) RAM corrects most corruptions.

- Detected, uncorrectable errors trigger a machine check exception, enabling the operating system to take action.

- An operating system can either panic or kill the process referencing corrupted memory. Either of these events prevents the system from using invalid memory contents.

Checksums are numbers derived from data for the purpose of detecting changes to the data. They can protect against unanticipated hardware and software failures. When using checksums, keep the following in mind:

- The tradeoff between the CPU cost of the checksum and the level of protection it provides
- Cyclic redundancy checks (CRCs) protect against single bit flips, while cryptographic hashes protect against human attackers. CRCs are much cheaper in terms of CPU time.
- The scope of the checksum

For example, imagine a client that sends a key and a value over the network to a server, which then stores the value on disk. A filesystem-level checksum only protects against filesystem or disk bugs. A checksum of the value generated by a client protects against network and server bugs. However, consider a bug where the client attempts to retrieve a value from the server. The client sends a key, but the buggy server reads the wrong value—and the checksum of the wrong value—from disk and returns those incorrect values to the client. Because the checksum's scope is limited to just the value, the checksum still passes, despite the bug. A better solution might include the key in both the value *and* the checksum. This solution would catch the case where the key and returned value do not match the checksum.

Set aside time for debugging and investigations

Both security investigations (to be discussed later) and debugging often take time—many hours of uninterrupted work. The temporary files scenario described in the previous section required somewhere between 5 and 10 hours of debugging. When running a major incident, give debuggers and investigators the space to focus by isolating them from the minute-by-minute response.

Debugging rewards slow, methodical, persistent approaches, in which people double-check their work and assumptions and are willing to dig deep. The temporary files problem also offers a negative example of debugging: the first responder initially diagnosed the outage as caused by user traffic and blamed poor system behavior on users. At the time, the team was in operational overload and experiencing pager fatigue due to nonurgent pages.

 Chapter 17 of the SRE workbook discusses reducing operational overload. Chapter 11 of the SRE book suggests keeping ticket and pager volume below two per shift to give engineers time to dig deep into issues.

Record your observations and expectations

Write down what you see. Separately, write down your theories, even if you've already rejected them. Doing so has several advantages:

- It introduces structure to the investigation and helps you remember the steps you took during your investigation. When you start debugging, you don't know how long it will take to solve the issue—resolution might take five minutes or five months.

- Another debugger can read your notes, understand what you observed, and quickly participate in or take over the investigation. Your notes can help teammates avoid duplicative work, and may inspire others to think of new avenues for investigation. For more on this topic, see "Negative Results Are Magic" in Chapter 12 of the SRE book.

- In the case of potential security issues, it can be helpful to keep a log of each access and investigation step. Later, you may need to prove (sometimes in a court of law) which actions were performed by the attacker and which were performed by investigators.

After you've written down what you observed, write down what you expected to observe and why. Bugs often lurk in the space between your mental model of the system and its actual implementation. In the temporary files example, the developers assumed that deleting a file removed all references to it.

Know what's normal for your system

Often, debuggers start debugging what is actually an expected system behavior. Here are a few examples from our experience:

- A binary called `abort` near the end of its `shutdown` code. New developers saw the `abort` call in the logs and started debugging the call, not noticing that the interesting failure was actually the reason for the call to `shutdown`.

- When the Chrome web browser starts, it attempts to resolve three random domains (such as `cegzaukxwefark.local`) to determine whether the network is illicitly tampering with DNS. Even Google's own investigation team has mistaken these DNS resolutions for malware trying to resolve a command-and-control server hostname.

Debuggers often need to filter out these normal events, even if the events look relevant or suspicious. Security investigators have the added problem of a steady level of background noise and active adversaries that may be trying to hide their actions. You often need to filter out routine noisy activity like automated SSH login brute forcing, authentication errors caused by users' mistyped passwords, and port scanning before you can observe more serious issues.

One way to understand normal system behavior is to establish a baseline of system behavior when you don't suspect any problems. If you have a problem already, you

---

may be able to infer your baseline by examining historical logs from before the problem began.

For example, in Chapter 1 we described a global YouTube outage caused by a change to a generic logging library. The change caused the servers to run out of memory (OOM) and fail. Because the library was widely used within Google, our post-outage investigation questioned whether the outage had affected the number of OOMs for all other Borg tasks. While logs suggested that we had many OOM conditions that day, we were able to compare that data against a baseline of data from the previous two weeks, which showed that Google has many OOM conditions *every* day. Although the bug was serious, it did not meaningfully affect the OOM metric for Borg tasks.

Beware of normalizing deviance from best practices. Often, bugs become "normal behavior" over time, and you no longer notice them. For example, we once worked on a server that had spent ~10% of its memory in heap fragmentation. After many years of asserting that ~10% was the expected and therefore acceptable amount of loss, we examined a fragmentation profile and quickly found major opportunities for saving memory.

Operational overload (*https://oreil.ly/L144H*) and alert fatigue can lead you to grow a blind spot, and thus normalize deviance. To address normalized deviance, we actively listen to newcomers to the team, and to facilitate fresh perspectives, we rotate people in and out of on-call rotations and response teams—the process of writing documentation and explaining a system to others can also prompt you to question how well you understand a system. Additionally, we use Red Teams (see Chapter 20) to test our blind spots.

Reproduce the bug

If possible, attempt to reproduce the bug outside of the production environment. This approach has two main advantages:

- You don't impact systems serving actual users, so you can crash the system and corrupt data as much as you want.
- Because you don't expose any sensitive data, you can involve many people in the investigation without raising data security issues. You can also enable operations that aren't appropriate with actual user data, and capabilities like extra logging.

Sometimes, debugging outside of the production environment isn't feasible. Perhaps the bug triggers only at scale, or you can't isolate its trigger. The temporary files example is one such situation: we couldn't reproduce the bug with a full serving stack.

Isolate the problem

If you can reproduce the issue, the next step is to isolate the problem—ideally, to the smallest subset of code that still manifests it. You can do this by disabling components or temporarily commenting out subroutines until the problem is revealed.

In the temporary files example, once we observed that the memory management was acting strangely on all servers, we no longer had to debug all components on every affected machine. For another example, consider a single server (out of a large cluster of systems) that suddenly starts introducing high latency or errors. This scenario is the standard test of your monitoring, logs and other observability systems: can you quickly find a single bad server among the many servers in your system? See "What to Do When You're Stuck" on page 344 for more information.

You can also isolate problems within code. To provide a concrete example, we recently investigated memory usage for a program with a very limited memory budget. In particular, we examined the memory mappings for thread stacks. Although our mental model assumed that all threads had the same stack size, to our surprise we found that different thread stacks had many different sizes. Some stacks were quite large and risked consuming a big chunk of our memory budget. The initial debugging scope included the kernel, glibc, Google's threading library, and all code that started threads. A trivial example based around glibc's pthread_create created thread stacks of the same size, so we could rule out the kernel and glibc as the sources of the different sizes. We then examined the code that started threads, and discovered that many libraries just picked a thread size at random, explaining the variation of sizes. This understanding enabled us to save memory by focusing on the few threads with large stacks.

Be mindful of correlation versus causation

Sometimes debuggers assume that two events that start at the same time, or that exhibit similar symptoms, have the same root cause. However, correlation does not always imply causation. Two mundane problems might occur at the same time but have different root causes.

Some correlations are trivial. For example, an increase in latency might lead to a reduction in user requests, simply because users are waiting longer for the system to respond. If a team repeatedly discovers correlations that in retrospect are trivial, there might be a gap in their understanding of how the system is supposed to work. In the temporary files example, if you know that the failure to delete files results in full disks, you won't be surprised by the correlation.

However, our experience has shown that investigating correlations is often useful—notably, correlations that occur at the start of outages. You can home in on likely causes by thinking, "X is broken, Y is broken, Z is broken; what's the common element among the three?" We've also had some success with correlation-based tooling.

For example, we deployed a system that automatically correlates machine problems with the Borg tasks running on the machine. As a result, we can often identify a suspicious Borg task causing a widespread problem. This kind of automated tooling produces much more effective, statistically stronger, and faster correlations than human observation.

Errors can also manifest during deployment—see Chapter 12 in the SRE book. In simple situations, the new code being deployed may have problems, but deployments can also trigger latent bugs in old systems. In these situations, debugging may erroneously focus on the new code being deployed, rather than the latent issues. Systematic investigation—determining what is happening, and why—helps in these cases. In one example we witnessed, the old code had much worse performance than the new code, which resulted in an accidental throttle on the system as a whole. When its performance improved, other parts of the system became overloaded instead. The outage was correlated with the new deployment, but the deployment was not the root cause.

Test your hypotheses with actual data

When debugging, it can be tempting to speculate about the root causes of issues before actually looking at the system. When it comes to performance issues, this tendency introduces blind spots, as the problems often lie in code the debuggers have not looked at in a long time. As an example, once we were debugging a web server that was running slowly. We assumed the problem lay in the backends, but a profiler (*https://oreil.ly/3YrvQ*) showed that the practice of logging every possible scrap of input to disk and then calling sync was causing vast amounts of delay. We discovered this only when we set aside our initial assumptions and dug into the system more deeply.

Observability is the property of being able to determine what your system is doing by examining its outputs. Tracing solutions like Dapper (*https://oreil.ly/9qDWj*) and Zipkin (*https://zipkin.io*) are very useful for this kind of debugging. Debugging sessions start with basic questions like, "Can you find a slow Dapper trace?"[6]

 It can be challenging for beginners to determine what tool is best for the job, or even what tools exist. Brendan Gregg's *Systems Performance* (Prentice Hall, 2013), which provides an exhaustive tour of tooling and techniques, is a fantastic reference for performance debugging.

---

6 These tools often require some setup; we will discuss them further in "What to Do When You're Stuck" on page 344.

Reread the docs

Consider the following guidance from the Python documentation (*https://oreil.ly/PudXU*):

> There are no implied relationships among the comparison operators. The truth of x==y does not imply that x!=y is false. Accordingly, when defining __eq__(), one should also define __ne__() so that the operators will behave as expected.

Recently, a Google team spent a good amount of time debugging an internal dashboard optimization. When they got stuck, the team reread the documentation and discovered a plainly written warning message that explained why the optimization had never worked at all. People were so used to the dashboard's slow performance, they failed to notice that the optimization was completely ineffective.[7] Initially, the bug seemed remarkable; the team thought it was an issue in Python itself. After they found the warning message, they determined that it wasn't a zebra, it was a horse— their code had never worked.

Practice!

Debugging skills stay fresh only if you use them often. You can speed up your investigations and keep the tips we've provided here fresh in your mind by staying familiar with relevant tools and logs. Regularly practicing debugging also provides the opportunity to script the common and tedious parts of the process—for example, automation to examine logs. To get better at debugging (or to stay sharp), practice, and keep the code you write during debugging sessions.

At Google, we formally practice debugging with regular large-scale disaster recovery tests (referred to as DiRT, or the Disaster Recovery Testing program)[8] and security penetration tests (see Chapter 16). Smaller-scale tests, involving one or two engineers in a room for an hour, are much easier to set up and are still quite valuable.

What to Do When You're Stuck

What should you do when you've been investigating an issue for days and still have no idea what caused the problem? Maybe it manifests only in the production environment, and you can't reproduce the bug without affecting live users. Maybe while mitigating the problem, you lost important debugging information when the logs rotated. Maybe the nature of the problem prevents useful logging. We once debugged an issue where a memory container ran out of RAM and the kernel issued a SIGKILL for all processes in the container, stopping all logging. Without logs, we couldn't debug the issue.

---

7 This is another example of normalized deviance, where people get used to suboptimal behavior!

8 See Krishnan, Kripa. 2012. "Weathering the Unexpected." *ACM Queue* 10(9). *https://oreil.ly/xFPfT*.

A key strategy in these situations is to improve the debugging process. Sometimes, using the methods for developing postmortems (as described in Chapter 18) may suggest ways forward. Many systems are in production for years or decades, so efforts to improve debugging are nearly always worthwhile. This section describes some approaches to improving your debugging methods.

Improve observability

Sometimes you need to see what a bit of code is doing. Is this code branch used? Is this function used? Could this data structure be large? Is this backend slow at the 99th percentile? What backends is this query even using? In these situations, you need better visibility into the system.

In some cases, methods like adding more structured logging to improve observability are straightforward. We once investigated a system that monitoring showed was serving too many 404 errors,[9] but the web server wasn't logging these errors. After adding additional logging for the web server, we discovered that malware was attempting to fetch erroneous files from the system.

Other debugging improvements take serious engineering effort. For example, debugging a complex system like Bigtable (*https://oreil.ly/31cv1*) requires sophisticated instrumentation. The Bigtable master is the central coordinator for a Bigtable zone. It stores the list of servers and tablets in RAM, and several mutexes protect these critical sections. As Bigtable deployments at Google grew over time, the Bigtable master and these mutexes became a scaling bottleneck. To get more visibility into possible problems, we implemented a wrapper around a mutex that exposes stats such as queue depth and the time the mutex is held.

Tracing solutions like Dapper and Zipkin are very useful for this kind of complex debugging. For example, suppose you have a tree of RPCs, with the frontend calling a server, which calls another server, and so on. Each RPC tree has a unique ID assigned at the root. Each server then logs traces about the RPCs it receives, sends, and so on. Dapper collects all traces centrally and joins them via ID. This way, a debugger can see all the backends touched by the user's request. We've found Dapper to be critical to understanding latency in distributed systems. Similarly, Google embeds a simple web server in nearly every binary to provide visibility into each binary's behavior. The server has debugging endpoints that provide counters, a symbolized dump of all the running threads, inflight RPCs, and so on. For more information, see Henderson (2017).[10]

---

9 404 is a standard HTTP error code for "file not found."

10 Henderson, Fergus. 2017. "Software Engineering at Google." arXiv preprint arXiv:1702.01715v2 (*https://oreil.ly/2-6pU*).

Observability is not a substitute for understanding your system. Nor is it a substitute for critical thinking when debugging (sadly!). Often, we've found ourselves frantically adding more logging and counters in an effort to see what the system is doing, but what's really going on becomes clear only when we've taken a step back and thought about the problem.

Observability is a large and quickly evolving topic, and it's useful for more than debugging.[11] If you're a smaller organization with limited developer resources, you can consider using open source systems or purchasing a third-party observability solution.

Take a break

Giving yourself a bit of distance from an issue can often lead to new insights when you return to the problem. If you've been working heads-down on debugging and hit a lull, take a break: drink some water, go outside, get some exercise, or read a book. Bugs sometimes make themselves evident after a good sleep. A senior engineer in our forensic investigation team keeps a cello in the team's lab. When he's truly stuck on a problem, it's common for him to retreat into the lab for 20 minutes or so to play; he then comes back reenergized and refocused (*https://oreil.ly/axc_Y*). Another investigator keeps a guitar handy, and others keep sketching and doodling pads in their desks so they can draw or create a silly animated GIF to share with the team when they need that mental realignment.

Make sure to also maintain good team communication. When you step aside to take a break, let the team know that you need a recharge and are following best practices. It's also helpful to document where you are in the investigation and why you're stuck. Doing so makes it easier for another investigator to pick up your work, and for you to return to the place where you left off. Chapter 17 has more advice on maintaining morale.

Clean up code

Sometimes you suspect there's a bug in a chunk of your code, but can't see it. Trying to generically improve code quality may help in this situation. As mentioned earlier in this chapter, we once debugged a bit of code that failed in production after 2^{32} requests because C++ was converting an `int64` into an `int` (only 32 bits) and truncating it. Although the compiler can warn you about such conversions using `-Wconversion` (*https://oreil.ly/BUPuH*), we weren't using the warning because our code had many benign conversions. Cleaning up the code enabled us to use the

---

11 For a comprehensive survey of the topic, see Cindy Sridharan's "Monitoring in the Time of Cloud Native" (*https://oreil.ly/n6-j9*) blog post.

compiler warning to detect more possible bugs and prevent new bugs related to conversion.

Here are some other tips for cleanup:

- Improve unit test coverage. Target functions where you suspect bugs may lie, or that have a track record of being buggy. (See Chapter 13 for more information.)
- For concurrent programs, use sanitizers (*https://oreil.ly/GJJq9*) (see "Sanitize Your Code" on page 267) and annotate mutexes (*https://oreil.ly/z1BQk*).
- Improve error handling. Often, adding some more context around an error is sufficient to expose the problem.

Delete it!

Sometimes bugs lurk in legacy systems, especially if developers haven't had time to get or stay familiar with the codebase or maintenance has lapsed. A legacy system might also be compromised or incur new bugs. Instead of debugging or hardening the legacy system, consider deleting it.

Deleting a legacy system can also improve your security posture. For example, one of the authors was once contacted (through Google's Vulnerability Reward Program, as described in Chapter 20) by a security researcher who had found a security issue in one of our team's legacy systems. The team had previously isolated this system to its own network, but hadn't upgraded the system in quite some time. Newer members of the team were unaware that the legacy system even existed. To address the researcher's discovery, we decided to remove the system. We no longer needed most of the functionality it provided, and we were able to replace it with a considerably simpler modern system.

 Be thoughtful when rewriting legacy systems. Ask yourself why your rewritten system will do a better job than the legacy system. Sometimes, you might want to rewrite a system because it's fun to add new code, and debugging old code is tedious. There are better reasons for replacing systems: sometimes requirements for the system change, and with a small amount of work, you can remove the old system. Alternatively, perhaps you've learned something from the first system and can incorporate this knowledge to make the second system better.

Stop when things start to go wrong

Many bugs are tricky to find because the source and its effects can be far apart in the system. We recently encountered an issue where network gear was corrupting internal DNS responses for hundreds of machines. For example, programs would perform a DNS lookup for the machine exa1, but receive the address of exa2. Two of our systems had different responses to this bug:

- One system, an archival service, would connect to exa2, the wrong machine. However, the system then checked that the machine to which it had connected was the expected machine. Since the machine names didn't match, the archival service job failed.

- Another system that collected machine metrics would collect metrics from the wrong machine, exa2. The system then triggered repairs on exa1. We detected this behavior only when a technician pointed out that they'd been asked to repair the fifth disk of a machine that didn't have five disks.

Of these two responses, we prefer the behavior of the archival service. When issues and their effects are far apart in the system—for example, when the network is causing application-level errors—having applications fail closed can prevent downstream effects (such as suspecting disk failure on the wrong system). We cover the topic of whether to fail open or fail closed in greater depth in Chapter 8.

Improve access and authorization controls, even for nonsensitive systems

It's possible to have "too many cooks in the kitchen"—that is, you may run into debugging situations where many people could be the source of a bug, making it difficult to isolate the cause. We once responded to an outage caused by a corrupted database row, and we couldn't locate the source of the corrupt data. To eliminate the possibility that someone could write to the production database by mistake, we minimized the number of roles that had access and required a justification for any human access. Even though the data was not sensitive, implementing a standard security system helped us prevent and investigate future bugs. Thankfully, we were also able to restore that database row from backup.

Collaborative Debugging: A Way to Teach

Many engineering teams teach debugging by working collectively on actual live issues in person (or over a videoconference). In addition to keeping experienced debuggers' skills fresh, collaborative debugging helps to build psychological safety for new team members: they have the opportunity to see the best debuggers on the team get stuck, backtrack, or otherwise struggle, which shows them that it's OK to be wrong and to have a hard time.[12] For more on security education, see Chapter 21.

---

12 See Julia Rozovsky's blog post "The Five Keys to a Successful Google Team" (*https://oreil.ly/gpxoL*) and the *New York Times* article "What Google Learned from Its Quest to Build the Perfect Team" (*https://oreil.ly/YJmwk*) by Charles Duhigg.

We've found that the following rules optimize the learning experience:

- Only two people should have laptops open:
  - A "driver," who performs actions requested by the others
  - A "note taker"
- Every action should be determined by the audience. Only the driver and the note taker are permitted to use computers, but they do not determine the actions taken. This way, participants don't perform solo debugging, only to present an answer without sharing their thought processes and troubleshooting steps.

The team collectively identifies one or more problems to examine, but no one in the room should know in advance how to solve the issues. Each person can request that the driver perform an action to troubleshoot the issue (for example, open a dashboard, look at logs, reboot a server, etc.). Since everyone is present to witness the suggestions, everyone can learn about tools and techniques that participants suggest. Even very experienced team members learn new things from these exercises.

As described in Chapter 28 of the SRE book, some teams also use "Wheel of Misfortune" simulation exercises. These exercises can either be theoretical, with verbal walk-throughs of problem solving, or practical, where the test giver induces a fault in a system. These scenarios also involve two roles:

- The "test giver," who constructs and presents the test
- The "test taker," who attempts to solve the problem, perhaps with the help of their teammates

Some teams prefer the safe environment of staged exercises, but practical Wheel of Misfortune exercises require nontrivial setup, whereas most systems always have a live issue to collectively debug. Regardless of the approach, it's important to maintain an inclusive learning environment where everyone feels safe to actively contribute.

Both collaborative debugging and Wheel of Misfortune exercises are excellent ways to introduce new techniques to your team and reinforce best practices. People can see how the techniques are useful in real-world situations, often for the trickiest of problems. Teams also get some practice debugging issues together, making them more effective when a real crisis occurs.

How Security Investigations and Debugging Differ

We expect every engineer to debug systems, but we advise that trained and experienced security and forensic specialists investigate system compromises. When the line between "bug investigation" and "security problem" is unclear, there's an opportunity for collaboration between the two sets of specialist teams.

A *bug investigation* often begins when a system experiences a problem. The investigation focuses on what happened in the system: what data was sent, what happened with that data, and how the service began acting contrary to its intent. *Security investigations* begin a little differently, and quickly pivot to questions like: What has the user who submitted that job been doing? What other activity is that user responsible for? Do we have a live attacker in the system? What will the attacker do next? In short, debugging is more code-focused, while a security investigation may quickly focus on the adversary behind an attack.

The steps we recommended previously for debugging issues may also be counterproductive during security investigations. Adding new code, deprecating systems, and so on may have unintended side effects. We've responded to a number of incidents where a debugger removed files that normally didn't belong on the system in the hopes of resolving errant behavior, and it turned out that those files had been introduced by the attacker, who was thus alerted to the investigation. In one case, the attacker even responded in kind by deleting the entire system!

Once you suspect that a security compromise has occurred, your investigation may also take on a new sense of urgency. The possibility that a system is being intentionally subverted raises questions that feel serious and pressing. What is the adversary after? What other systems may be subverted? Do you need to call law enforcement or regulators? Security investigations grow organically in complexity as the organization begins to address operational security concerns (Chapter 17 discusses this topic further). Experts from other teams, such as Legal, may get involved before you can begin your investigation. In short, the moment you suspect a security compromise is a good time to get help from security professionals.

Intersection of Security and Reliability: Recognizing a Compromise

During an investigation, you may come across many inconsistencies that are simply oddities in a system that should be corrected. However, if these inconsistencies start to add up, or you encounter an increasing number of inconsistencies that have no explanation, an adversary might be tampering with your systems. Here's a sample list of inconsistencies that might raise suspicions about a potential compromise:

- Logs and data necessary for debugging are missing, truncated, or corrupted.
- You began your investigation looking at system behavior, but find yourself developing your hypothesis around the actions of *an account* or *a user*.
- The system is behaving in ways that you can't explain as accidental. For example, your web server keeps spawning interactive shells when it appears to crash.
- Files have characteristics that seem abnormal for the file type (e.g., you find a file called *rick_roll.gif*, but it is 1 GB in size and appears to have ZIP or TAR headers).
- Files appear to have been intentionally hidden, misnamed in familiar ways (e.g., *explore.exe* on Windows), or otherwise obfuscated.

Deciding when to stop investigating and declare a security incident can be a difficult judgment call. Many engineers have a natural inclination to refrain from "making a scene" by escalating issues that aren't yet proven to be security-related, but continuing the investigation to the point of proof may be the wrong move. Our advice is to remember "horses versus zebras": the vast majority of bugs are, in fact, bugs, not malicious actions. However, *also* keep a vigilant eye open for those black and white stripes zipping by.

Collect Appropriate and Useful Logs

At their heart, logs and system crash dumps are both just information you can collect to help you understand what happened in a system and to investigate problems—both accidental and intentional.

Before you launch any service, it's important to consider the kinds of data the service will store on behalf of users, and the pathways to access the data. Assume that any action that leads to data or system access may be in scope for a future investigation, and that someone will need to audit that action. Investigating any service issue *or* security issue depends heavily on logs.

Our discussion here of "logs" refers to structured, timestamped records from systems. During investigations, analysts may also rely heavily on other sources of data, like core dumps, memory dumps, or stack traces. We recommend handling those systems as much like logs as possible. Structured logs are useful for many different business purposes, such as per-usage billing. However, we focus here on structured logs collected for security investigations—the information you need to collect now so it's available in the event of a future issue.

Design Your Logging to Be Immutable

The system you build to collect logs should be immutable. When log entries are written, it should be difficult to alter them (but not impossible; see "Take Privacy into Consideration" on page 352), and alterations should have an immutable audit trail. Attackers commonly erase traces of their activity on a system from all log sources as soon as they establish a solid foothold. A common best practice to counter this tactic is to write your logs remotely to a centralized and distributed log server. This increases the attacker's workload: in addition to compromising the original system, they also have to compromise the remote log server. Be sure to harden the log system carefully.

Before the age of modern computing, extra-critical servers logged directly to an attached line printer, like the one in Figure 15-1, which printed log records to paper as they were generated. In order to erase their traces, a remote attacker would have needed someone to physically remove paper from the printer and burn it!

Figure 15-1. A line printer

Take Privacy into Consideration

The need for privacy-preserving features is an increasingly important factor in the design of systems. While privacy is not a focus of this book, you will likely need to take into account local regulations and your organization's privacy policies when designing logging for security investigations and debugging. Be sure to consult with any privacy and legal colleagues in your organization on this topic. Here are some topics you may want to discuss:

Depth of logging

To be maximally useful for any investigation, logs need to be as complete as possible. A security investigation might need to examine every action a user (or an attacker using their account) performed inside a system, the host from which they logged in, and the exact times at which the events occurred. Agree on an organizational policy about what information is acceptable to log, given that many privacy-preserving techniques discourage retaining sensitive user data in logs.

Retention

For some investigations, it can be beneficial to retain logs for a long time. According to a 2018 study, it takes most organizations an average of about 200 days (*https://oreil.ly/vAunm*) to discover a system compromise. Insider threat investigations at Google have relied on operating system security logs going back several years. How long you can keep logs is an important discussion to have within your organization.

Access and audit controls

Many of the controls we recommend for protecting data also apply to logs. Be sure to protect logs and metadata just as you protect other data. See Chapter 5 for relevant strategies.

Data anonymization or pseudonymization

Anonymizing unnecessary data components—either as they're written or after a period of time—is one increasingly common privacy-preserving method for handling logs. You can even implement this functionality such that investigators and debuggers can't determine who a given user is, but can clearly build a timeline of that user's actions throughout their session for debugging purposes. Anonymization is tricky to get right. We recommend consulting privacy specialists and reading published literature on this topic.[13]

Encryption

You can also implement privacy-preserving logging using asymmetric encryption of data. This encryption method is ideal for protecting log data: it uses a nonsensitive "public key" that anyone can use to write data securely, but requires a secret (private) key to decrypt the data. Design options like daily key pairs can allow debuggers to obtain small subsets of log data from recent system activity, while preventing someone from obtaining large amounts of log data in aggregate. Be sure to carefully consider how you store keys.

---

13 See, e.g., Ghiasvand, Siavash, and Florina M. Ciorba. 2017. "Anonymization of System Logs for Privacy and Storage Benefits." arXiv preprint arXiv:1706.04337 (*https://oreil.ly/c_a0N*). See also Jan Lindquist's article on pseudonymization of personal data (*https://oreil.ly/W3OFr*) for General Data Protection Regulation (GDPR) compliance.

Determine Which Security Logs to Retain

Although security engineers would often prefer having too many logs to having too few, it pays to be a bit selective in what you log and retain. Storing an overabundance of logs can be costly (as discussed in "Budget for Logging" on page 357), and sifting through excessively large data sets can slow down an investigator and use a large amount of resources. In this section, we discuss some types of logs you may want to capture and retain.

Operating system logs

Most modern operating systems have built-in logging. Windows has Windows Event logs, while Linux and Mac have syslog and auditd logs. Many vendor-supplied appliances (such as camera systems, environmental controls, and fire alarm panels) have a standard operating system that also produces logs (such as Linux) under the hood. Built-in logging frameworks are useful for investigations, and using them requires almost no effort because they're often enabled by default or easily configured. Some mechanisms, like auditd, are not enabled by default for performance reasons, but enabling them can be an acceptable tradeoff in real-world use.

Host agents

Many companies choose to enable additional logging capabilities by installing a *host intrusion detection system* (HIDS) or *host agent* on workstations and servers.

Antivirus Software

Antivirus software scans files for patterns that indicate known malware (for example, a code sequence unique to a particular virus) and looks for suspicious behavior (for example, attempts to modify sensitive system files). Experts don't always agree on the value and use of antivirus software in a modern security setting.[14] We think that having antivirus protection deployed on every endpoint computer has become less useful over time as threats have grown more sophisticated. Additionally, if poorly authored, antivirus software can even introduce more security risk to the system.

Modern (sometimes referred to as "next-gen") host agents use innovative techniques aimed at detecting increasingly sophisticated threats. Some agents blend system and user behavior modeling, machine learning, and threat intelligence to identify previously unknown attacks. Other agents are more focused on gathering additional data about the system's operation, which can be useful for offline detection and debugging

---

14 See, e.g., Joxean Koret's presentation "Breaking Antivirus Software" (*https://oreil.ly/alqtv*) at 44CON 2014.

activities. Some, such as OSQuery (*https://osquery.io*) and GRR (*https://github.com/google/grr*), provide real-time visibility into a system.

Host agents always impact performance, and are often a source of friction between end users and IT teams. Generally speaking, the more data an agent can gather, the greater its performance impact may be because of deeper platform integration and more on-host processing. Some agents run as part of the kernel, while others run as userspace applications. Kernel agents have more functionality, and are therefore typically more effective, but they can suffer from reliability and performance issues as they try to keep up with operating system functionality changes. Agents that run as applications are much easier to install and configure, and tend to have fewer compatibility problems. The value and performance of host agents varies widely, so we recommend thoroughly evaluating a host agent before using it.

Application logs

Logging applications—whether vendor-supplied like SAP and Microsoft SharePoint, open source, or custom-written—generate logs that you can collect and analyze. You can then use these logs for custom detection and to augment investigation data. For example, we use application logs from Google Drive (*https://oreil.ly/Fhckk*) to determine if a compromised computer has downloaded sensitive data.

When developing custom applications, collaboration between security specialists and developers can ensure that the applications log security-relevant actions, such as data writes, changes in ownership or state, and account-related activity. As we mention in "Improve observability" on page 345, instrumenting your applications for logging can also facilitate debugging for esoteric security and reliability issues that would otherwise be difficult to triage.

Cloud logs

Increasingly, organizations are moving parts of their business or IT processes to cloud-based services, ranging from data in Software-as-a-Service (SaaS) applications to virtual machines running critical customer-facing workloads. All of these services present unique attack surfaces and generate unique logs. For example, an attacker can compromise the account credentials for a cloud project, deploy new containers to the project's Kubernetes cluster, and use those containers to steal data from the cluster's accessible storage buckets. Cloud computing models commonly launch new instances daily, which makes detecting threats in the cloud dynamic and complex.

When it comes to detecting suspicious activity, cloud services present advantages and disadvantages. Using services like Google's BigQuery, it's easy and relatively cheap to collect and store large amounts of log data, and even to run detection rules, directly in the cloud. Google Cloud services also offer built-in logging solutions like Cloud Audit Logs (*https://oreil.ly/XF4ta*) and Stackdriver Logging (*https://oreil.ly/6SUwV*).

On the other hand, because there are many kinds of cloud services, it can be hard to identify, enable, and centralize all the logs you need. Because it's easy for developers to create new IT assets in the cloud, many companies find it difficult to identify all of their cloud-based assets. Cloud service providers may also predetermine which logs are available to you, and these options may not be configurable. It's important to understand the limitations of your provider's logging and your potential blind spots.

Taking Inventory of Your Assets

While building the pipelines you need to investigate system problems, consider building a set of tools to use that data to identify your cloud assets, including the assets you might not know about. To provide an example for the latter case, integrating with your financial system to look for bills being paid to cloud providers may reveal system components that need further attention. In an article about Google's Beyond-Corp architecture (*https://oreil.ly/7JXZx*), we referenced a set of tools called the Device Inventory Service, which we leverage to discover assets that may belong to Google (or contain Google's data). Building a similar service and extending it to your cloud environments is one way to identify these types of assets.

A variety of commercial software, often itself based in the cloud, aims to detect attacks against cloud services. Most of the established cloud providers offer integrated threat detection services, such as Google's Event Threat Detection (*https://oreil.ly/yJdVl*). Many companies combine these built-in services with internally developed detection rules or third-party products.

Cloud access security brokers (CASBs) are a notable category of detection and prevention technology. CASBs function as intermediaries between end users and cloud services to enforce security controls and provide logging. For example, a CASB might prevent your users from uploading certain kinds of files, or log every file downloaded by a user. Many CASBs have a detection function that alerts the detection team about potentially malicious access. You can also integrate logs from the CASB into custom detection rules.

Network-based logging and detection

Since the late 1990s, the use of *network intrusion detection systems* (NIDSs) and *intrusion prevention systems* (IPSs) that capture and inspect network packets has been a common detection and logging technique. IPSs also block some attacks. For example, they may capture information about which IP addresses have exchanged traffic, along with limited information about that traffic, such as packet size. Some IPSs may have the ability to record the entire contents of certain packets, based on customizable criteria—for example, packets sent to high-risk systems. Others can also detect malicious activity in real time and send alerts to the appropriate team. Since these systems are very useful and have few downsides beyond cost, we highly recommend them for almost any organization. However, think carefully about who can effectively triage the alerts they generate.

Logs of DNS queries are also useful network-based sources. DNS logs enable you to see whether any computer at the company has resolved a hostname. For example, you might want to see whether any host on your network has performed a DNS query for a known malicious hostname, or you may want to examine previously resolved domains to identify every machine visited by an attacker that had control of your system. A security operations team might also use DNS "sinkholes" that falsely resolve known malicious domains so they can't be effectively used by attackers. Detection systems then tend to trigger a high-priority alert when users access a sink-holed domain.

You can also use logs from any web proxies used for internal or egress traffic. For example, you can use a web proxy to scan web pages for indicators of phishing or known vulnerability patterns. When using a proxy for detection, you'll also want to consider employee privacy and discuss the use of proxy logs with a legal team. Generally speaking, we recommend tailoring your detection as closely as possible to malicious content in order to minimize the amount of employee data you encounter while triaging alerts.

Budget for Logging

Debugging and investigative activities use resources. One system we worked on had 100 TB of logs, which were mostly never used. Because logging consumes a significant amount of resources, and logs are often monitored less frequently in the absence of problems, it can be tempting to underinvest in the logging and debugging infrastructure. To avoid this, we strongly recommend that you budget for logging in advance, taking into account how much data you may need to resolve a service issue or security incident.

Modern log systems often incorporate a relational data system (e.g., Elasticsearch or BigQuery) to quickly and easily query data in real time. The cost of this system grows along with the number of events it needs to store and index, the number of machines it needs to process and query the data, and the storage space required. When retaining data for long periods of time, it's therefore useful to prioritize logs from relevant data sources for longer-term storage. This is an important tradeoff decision: if an attacker is good at hiding their tracks, it may take you quite some time to discover that an incident has occurred. If you store only a week's worth of access logs, you may not be able to investigate an intrusion at all!

Intersection of Security and Reliability: Budgeting for Long-Term Log Storage

Your need to retain log data for long periods of time may come into conflict with your budget. What if you can't afford enough log storage and processing infrastructure to keep as many logs as you'd like? To balance the costs of storage against your retention needs, we recommend designing your logs to *degrade gracefully*, instead of halting log collection when you reach storage capacity.

Data summarization is an increasingly common method to implement graceful degradation. For example, you might build a log system that dedicates 90% of storage to full log retention, and reserves the remaining 10% for lower-fidelity summarizations of some data. To avoid having to reread and parse already written logs (which is computationally expensive), your system could write two log files at collection time: the first log contains full-fidelity data, while the second contains a summarization. As your storage reaches capacity, you can delete the larger logs to free up storage space, and retain the smaller files as longer-lived data. For example, you can produce both full packet captures and netflow data, deleting the captures after N days but keeping the netflow data for a year. The logs will then have much lower storage costs, but still provide key intelligence about the information that hosts communicate.

We also recommend the following investment strategies for security-focused log collection:

- Focus on logs that have a good signal-to-noise ratio. For example, firewalls routinely block many packets, most of which are harmless. Even malicious packets blocked by a firewall may not be worth paying attention to. Gathering logs for these blocked packets could use a tremendous amount of bandwidth and storage for almost no benefit.

- Compress logs whenever possible. Because most logs contain a lot of duplicated metadata, compression is typically very effective.

- Separate storage into "warm" and "cold." You can offload logs from the distant past to cheap offline cloud storage ("cold storage"), while retaining logs that are more recent or related to known incidents on local servers for immediate use ("warm storage"). Similarly, you might store compressed raw logs for a long time, but put only recent logs in the expensive relational database with full indexing.

- Rotate logs intelligently. Generally, it's best to delete the oldest logs first, but you may want to retain the most important log types longer.

Robust, Secure Debugging Access

To debug issues, you often need access to the systems and the data they store. Can a malicious or compromised debugger see sensitive information? Can a failure of a security system (and remember: all systems fail!) be resolved? You need to ensure that your debugging systems are reliable and secure.

Reliability

Logging is another way systems can fail. For example, a system can run out of disk space to store logs. Failing open in this example entails another tradeoff: the approach can make your entire system more resilient, but an attacker can potentially disrupt your logging mechanism.

Plan for situations where you might need to debug or repair the security systems themselves. Consider the tradeoffs necessary to make sure you don't lock yourself out of a system, but can still keep it secure. In this case, you might consider keeping a set of emergency-only credentials, offline in a secure location, that set off high-confidence alarms when used. As an example, a recent Google network outage (*https://oreil.ly/hxpj3*) caused high packet loss. When responders attempted to obtain internal credentials, the authentication system could not reach one backend and failed closed. However, emergency credentials enabled the responders to authenticate and fix the network.

Security

One system we worked on, used for phone support, allowed administrators to impersonate a user and to view the UI from their perspective. As a debugger, this system was wonderful; you could clearly and quickly reproduce a user's problem. However, this type of system provides possibilities for abuse. Debugging endpoints—from impersonation to raw database access—need to be secured.

For many incidents, debugging unusual system behavior need not require access to user data. For example, when diagnosing TCP traffic problems, the speed and quality of bytes on the wire is often enough to diagnose issues. Encrypting data in transit can protect it from any possible attempt by third parties to observe it. This has the fortunate side effect of allowing more engineers access to packet dumps when needed. However, one possible mistake is to treat metadata as nonsensitive. A malicious actor can still learn a lot about a user from metadata by tracking correlated access patterns —for instance, by noting the same user accessing a divorce lawyer and a dating site in the same session. You should carefully assess the risks from treating metadata as non-sensitive.

Also, some analysis *does* require actual data—for example, finding frequently accessed records in a database, and then figuring out why these accesses are common.

We once debugged a low-level storage problem caused by a single account receiving thousands of emails per hour. "Zero Trust Networking" on page 62 has more information about access control for these situations.

Conclusion

Debugging and investigations are necessary aspects of managing a system. To reiterate the key points in the chapter:

- *Debugging* is an essential activity whereby systematic techniques—not guesswork—achieve results. You can make debugging vastly easier by implementing tools or logging to provide visibility into the system. Practice debugging to hone your skills.

- *Security investigations* are different from debugging. They involve different people, tactics, and risks. Your investigation team should include experienced security professionals.

- *Centralized logging* is useful for debugging purposes, critical for investigations, and often useful for business analysis.

- *Iterate* by looking at some recent investigations and asking yourself what information would have helped you debug an issue or investigate a concern. Debugging is a process of continuous improvement; you will regularly add data sources and look for ways to improve observability.

- *Design for safety*. You need logs. Debuggers need access to systems and stored data. However, as the amount of data you store increases, both logs and debugging endpoints can become targets for adversaries. Design logging systems to collect information you'll need, but also to require robust permissions, privileges, and policies to obtain that data.

Both debugging and security investigations often depend on sudden insight and luck, and even the best debuggers are sometimes sadly left in the dark. Remember that chance favors the prepared: by being ready with logs, and a system for indexing and investigating them, you can take advantage of the chances that come your way. Good luck!

PART IV

Maintaining Systems

Organizations that are prepared to cope with uncomfortable situations have a better chance of dealing with a critical incident.

Even though it's impossible to plan for every scenario that might disrupt your organization, the first steps toward a comprehensive disaster planning strategy, as discussed in Chapter 16, are pragmatic and approachable. They include setting up an incident response team, prestaging your systems and people before an incident, and testing your systems and response plans—preparation steps that will also help equip you for crisis management, the subject of Chapter 17. When dealing with a security crisis, people with a variety of skills and roles will need to be able to collaborate and communicate effectively to keep your systems running.

In the wake of an attack, your organization will need to take control of recovery and deal with the aftermath, as discussed in Chapter 18. Some up-front planning during these stages will also help you to mount a thorough response, and learn from what happened to prevent reoccurrence.

To paint a more complete picture, we've included some chapter-specific contextual examples:

- Chapter 16 features a story about Google creating a response plan for how to handle a devastating earthquake in the San Francisco Bay Area.
- Chapter 17 tells the story of an engineer discovering that a service account they don't recognize has been added to a cloud project they haven't seen before.

- Chapter 18 discusses the tradeoffs between ejecting an attacker, mitigating their immediate actions, and making long-term changes when faced with an incident such as a large-scale phishing attack.

CHAPTER 16

Disaster Planning

By Michael Robinson and Sean Noonan
with Alex Bramley and Kavita Guliani

Because systems will inevitably experience reliability failures or security incidents, you need to be prepared to deal with them. Consequently, we recommend conducting disaster planning activities toward the end of the development cycle, after completing the implementation phase.

This chapter begins with disaster risk analysis—a necessary step for developing a flexible disaster response plan. We then walk through the steps of setting up an incident response team, and provide tips on how to identify prestaging activities that you can perform before a disaster occurs. We conclude with a deep dive about testing your organization before a disaster strikes and a few examples showing how Google prepared for some specific disaster scenarios.

Complex systems can fail in both simple and complex ways, ranging from unexpected service outages to attacks by malicious actors to gain unauthorized access. You can anticipate and prevent some of these failures through reliability engineering and security best practices, but in the long term, failure is almost unavoidable.

Instead of merely hoping that a system will survive a disaster or an attack, or that your staff will be able to mount a reasonable response, disaster planning ensures that you continuously work to improve your ability to recover from a disaster. The good news is, the first steps toward developing a comprehensive strategy are pragmatic and approachable.

Defining "Disaster"

It's rare that you become aware of a disaster only when it's in full swing. Rather than stumbling upon a building fully engulfed in flames, you're more likely to first see or smell smoke—some seemingly small indication that does not necessarily look like a disaster. The fire spreads gradually, and you don't realize the extremity of the situation until you're in the thick of it. Similarly, sometimes a small event—like the accounting error mentioned in Chapter 2—might trigger a full-scale incident response.

Disasters come in various forms:

- *Natural disasters*, including earthquakes, tornadoes, floods, and fires. These tend to be obvious, with varying degrees of impact to a system.

- *Infrastructure disasters*, such as component failures or misconfigurations. These are not always easily diagnosable, and their impact can range from small to large.

- *Service or product outages*, which are observable by customers or other stakeholders.

- *Degradations* of services operating near a threshold. These are sometimes difficult to identify.

- An *external attacker*, who may gain unauthorized access for an extended period of time before being detected.

- *Unauthorized disclosure of sensitive data.*

- *Urgent security vulnerabilities*, requiring you to immediately apply patches to correct new, critical vulnerabilities. These events are treated just like imminent security attacks (see "Compromises Versus Bugs" on page 390).

In this and the following chapter, we use the terms *disaster* and *crisis* interchangeably to mean any situation that may warrant declaring an incident and mounting a response.

Dynamic Disaster Response Strategies

The range of potential disasters is large, but designing flexible disaster response plans will enable you to adapt to rapidly changing situations. By thinking in advance about the possible scenarios you might encounter, you're already taking the first step in preparing for them. As with any skill set, you can hone your disaster response skills by planning, practicing, and iterating on procedures until they become second nature.

Incident response isn't like riding a bicycle. Without routine practice, it is difficult for responders to retain good muscle memory. Lack of practice can lead to fractured responses and longer recovery times, so it's a good idea to rehearse and refine your disaster response plans often. Well-practiced incident management skills let subject matter experts function naturally during response to incidents—if those skills are second nature, experts won't struggle to follow the process itself.

It's helpful to segment a response plan into phases such as immediate response, short-term recovery, long-term recovery, and resumption of operations. Figure 16-1 shows the general phases associated with disaster recovery.

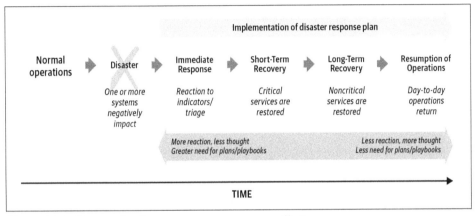

Figure 16-1. Phases of a disaster recovery response effort

The short-term recovery phase should include developing *exit criteria* for the incident—that is, the criteria for declaring that the incident response is complete. A successful recovery might mean restoring a service to a fully operational status, but the underlying solution may have a new design that provides the same level of service. The criteria may also require completely mitigating security threats identified by risk analysis.

When developing a strategy to address immediate responses, short- and long-term recovery, and the resumption of operations, your organization can prepare by doing the following:

- Performing an analysis of potential disasters that will either likely affect the organization or have significant impact
- Establishing a response team
- Creating response plans and detailed playbooks
- Configuring systems appropriately
- Testing your procedures and your systems
- Incorporating feedback from tests and evaluations

Disaster Risk Analysis

Conducting a disaster risk analysis is the first step toward determining an organization's most critical operations—operations whose absence would cause total disruption. Key operational functions include not only important core systems, but also their underlying dependencies, such as networking and application-layer components. Disaster risk analysis should identify the following:

- Systems that, if damaged or offline, could incapacitate operations. You can classify systems as mission-essential, mission-important, or nonessential.

- Resources—either technological or human—that you'll need in order to respond to an incident.

- Disaster scenarios that are likely to occur for each of your systems. The scenarios can be grouped by likelihood of occurrence, frequency of occurrence, and impact to operations (low, medium, high, or critical).

Although you may be able to intuitively conduct an assessment of your operations, a more formalized approach to risk assessment can avoid groupthink and highlight risks that aren't necessarily obvious. For a thorough analysis, we recommend ranking the risks facing your organization by using a standardized matrix that accounts for each risk's probability of occurrence and its impact to the organization. Appendix A provides a sample risk assessment matrix that both large and small organizations can tailor to the specifics of their systems.

Risk ratings provide a good rule of thumb about where to focus attention first. You should review your list of risks for potential outliers after ranking them—for example, an improbable event might rate as critical because of its potential impact. You might also want to solicit an expert to review the assessment to identify risks with hidden factors or dependencies.

Your risk assessment may vary depending on where your organization's assets are located. For example, a site in Japan or Taiwan should account for typhoons, while a site in the Southeastern US should account for hurricanes. Risk ratings may also change as an organization matures and incorporates fault-tolerant systems, like redundant internet circuits and backup power supplies, into its systems. Large organizations should perform risk assessments on both global and per-site levels, and review and update these assessments periodically as the operating environment changes. Equipped with a risk assessment that identifies which systems need protection, you're ready to create a response team prepared with tools, procedures, and training.

Setting Up an Incident Response Team

There are various ways to staff an incident response (IR) team. Organizations typically staff these teams in one of several ways:

- By creating a dedicated full-time IR team
- By assigning IR duties to individuals in addition to their existing job functions
- By outsourcing IR activities to third parties.

Because of budget and size constraints, many organizations rely on existing employees to wear two hats, with some employees performing their regular job duties as well as incident response when the need arises. Organizations with more complex needs may find staffing a dedicated IR team with internal employees worthwhile to ensure that responders are always available to respond, are appropriately trained, have the necessary system access, and have sufficient time to respond to a wide variety of incidents.

Regardless of which staffing model you implement, you can use the following techniques to create successful teams.

Identify Team Members and Roles

When preparing a response plan, you need to identify the core team of people who will respond to incidents and clearly establish their roles. While small organizations may have individual contributors from various teams or even a single team that responds to every incident, organizations with more resources might choose to have a dedicated team for each functional area—for example, a security response team, a privacy team, and an operational team focused on the reliability of public-facing sites.

You can also outsource some functions, while keeping other functions internal. For example, you might not have sufficient funding and workload to fully staff an in-house forensics team, so you might outsource that expertise while keeping your incident response team in house. A potential drawback to outsourcing is that external responders may not be immediately available. It's important to consider response time when determining which functions to keep in-house and which resources to outsource and call upon during an emergency.

You may need some or all of the following roles for an incident response:

Incident commander
   An individual who leads the response to an individual incident.

SREs (https://oreil.ly/IeMvF)
   People who can reconfigure an impacted system or implement code to fix a bug.

Public relations
> People who can respond to public inquiries or release statements to the media. These individuals frequently work with the communications lead to craft messages.

Customer support
> People who can respond to customer inquiries or proactively reach out to affected customers.

Legal
> An attorney who can provide counsel on legal matters such as applicable laws, statutes, regulations, or contracts.

Privacy engineers
> People who can address impact on technical privacy matters.

Forensic specialists
> People who can perform event reconstruction and attribution to determine what happened and how it occurred.

Security engineers
> People who can review the security impact of the incident and work with SREs or privacy engineers to secure a system.

When determining which roles will be staffed by in-house personnel, you may need to implement a rotational staffing model, where the IR team operates in shifts. It's critical to staff shifts during an incident in order to reduce fatigue and provide ongoing support during the incident. You can also adopt this model to provide flexibility as main job responsibilities evolve and flow over time. Keep in mind that these are roles, not individuals. An individual may hold multiple roles during an incident.

Avoid Single Points of Failure

Incidents do not respect meeting invitations, the standard workday, travel plans, or vacation schedules. While on-call rotations can increase your ability to respond to incidents, pay special attention to avoiding single points of failure. For example, executives should empower delegates who can approve emergency code fixes, configuration changes, and communication messages during incidents when you can't wait for someone's vacation travel to end. If your organization is multinational, appoint delegates across time zones.

After you determine which roles should be staffed internally, you can create an initial list of personnel to serve on the individual IR teams. Identifying these people in advance helps to clarify roles, responsibilities, and ownership during a response effort, and minimizes chaos and setup time. It's also helpful to identify a *champion* for your IR team—a person with enough seniority to commit resources and remove roadblocks. The champion can help assemble a team and work with senior leaders when there are competing priorities. Check out Chapter 21 for more information.

Establish a Team Charter

An IR team's charter should start with the team's *mission*—a single sentence describing the types of incidents they'll handle. The mission allows the reader to quickly understand what the team does.

The *scope* of the charter should describe the environment you work in, focusing on technologies, end users, products, and stakeholders. This section should clearly define the types of incidents the team will handle, which incidents should be handled by internally staffed resources, and which incidents should be assigned to outsourced teams.

Team Morale

When establishing a team charter—whether for a dedicated response team or a cross-functional virtual response team—be sure to consider if the scope and workload are appropriate. When people are overworked, their productivity may decrease; over time, they may even leave your organization. For a discussion of morale during incident response, see "Morale" on page 405.

To ensure that the IR team focuses on qualifying incidents, it is important that the organization's leadership and the IR champion agree on the scope. For example, while an IR team could certainly respond to individual customer inquiries about system firewall configurations and log enablement/verification, those tasks may be better suited for a customer support team.

Finally, it's important to define what *success* looks like for the team. In other words, how do you know when the IR team's job is done or can be declared done?

Establish Severity and Priority Models

Severity and priority models can assist an IR team in quantifying and understanding the gravity of incidents and the operational tempo needed to respond to them. You should use both models concurrently, as they're related.

A *severity model* allows the team to categorize incidents based on the severity of their impact on the organization. You might rank incidents on a five-point (0–4) scale, with 0 indicating the most severe incidents and 4 indicating the least severe incidents. You should adopt whatever scale best fits your organizational culture (colors, animals, etc.). For example, if you're using the five-point scale, unauthorized individuals on a network may qualify as a severity 0 incident, while temporary unavailability of security logs may be severity 2. When building the model, review any previously performed risk analyses so you can assign categories of incidents appropriate severity ratings. Doing so will ensure that not all incidents receive a critical or moderate severity rating. Accurate ratings will help incident commanders prioritize when multiple incidents are reported simultaneously.

A *priority model* defines how quickly personnel need to respond to incidents. This model builds upon your understanding of incident severity and can also use a five-point (0–4) scale, with 0 indicating high priority and 4 indicating low priority. Priority drives the tempo of the work required: an incident rated 0 merits immediate incident response, where team members respond to this incident before any other work. You can handle an incident with a rating of 4 with routine operational work. An agreed upon-priority model also helps keep various teams and operational leads in sync. Imagine one team treating an incident as priority 0, while a second team with a limited awareness of the total circumstances considers it a priority 2. The two teams will likely operate at a different tempo, delaying proper incident response.

Typically, once it's fully understood, the severity of an incident will remain fixed throughout the incident's lifecycle. Priority, on the other hand, may change throughout an incident. During the early phases of triaging and implementing a critical fix, the priority may be 0. After a critical fix is in place, you may lower the priority to 1 or 2 as the engineering teams perform cleanup work.

Define Operating Parameters for Engaging the IR Team

After you've established severity and priority models, you can define operating parameters to describe the day-to-day functioning of the incident response team. This becomes increasingly important when teams perform regular operational work in addition to incident response work, or when you need to communicate with virtual teams or outsourced teams. Operating parameters ensure that severity 0 and priority 0 incidents receive a timely response.

Operating parameters might include the following:

- The expected time it takes to initially respond to reported incidents—for example, within 5 minutes, 30 minutes, an hour, or the next business day
- The expected time it takes to perform an initial triage assessment and develop a response plan and operating schedule
- Service level objectives (SLOs) (*https://oreil.ly/MtL_o*), so team members understand when incident response should interrupt day-to-day work.

There are many ways to organize on-call rotations to ensure incident response work is properly load-balanced across a team or balanced according to regularly scheduled ongoing work. For a detailed discussion, refer to Chapters 11 and 14 of the SRE book, Chapters 8 and 9 of the SRE workbook, and Chapter 14 of Limoncelli, Chalup, and Hogan (2014).[1]

Develop Response Plans

Decision making during severe incidents may be challenging because responders are attempting to work quickly with limited information. Well-crafted response plans can guide responders, reduce wasted steps, and provide an overarching approach for how to respond to different categories of incidents. While an organization may have a company-wide incident response policy, the IR team needs to create a set of response plans covering the following subjects:

Incident reporting
How an incident is reported to the IR team.

Triage
A list of the IR team members who will respond to the initial report and start triaging the incident.

Service level objectives
A reference to the SLOs on how quickly the responders will act.

Roles and responsibilities
Clear definitions of the roles and responsibilities of the IR team participants.

Outreach
How to reach out to engineering teams and participants who may need to assist in incident response.

Communications
Effective communication during an incident does not happen without advance planning. You need to establish how to do each of the following:

- Inform leadership of an incident (for example, via email, text message, or phone call), and the information to include in these communications.
- Conduct intraorganization communication during an incident, including within and between response teams (standing up chat rooms, videoconferencing, email, secure IRC channels, bug tracking tools, and so on).

---

1 Limoncelli, Thomas A., Strata R. Chalup, and Christina J. Hogan. 2014. *The Practice of Cloud System Administration: Designing and Operating Large Distributed Systems.* Boston, MA: Addison-Wesley.

- Communicate with external stakeholders, such as regulators or law enforcement, when the situation requires it. You need to partner with the legal function and other departments of your organization to plan and support this communication. Consider keeping an index of contact details and communication methods for each external stakeholder. If your IR team grows large enough, you might automate those notification mechanisms as appropriate.

- Communicate incidents to support teams who interact with customers.

- Communicate with responders and leadership without tipping off an adversary if a communication system is unavailable, or if you suspect that a communication system is compromised.

Security and Reliability Risk: Communicating When Your Email or Instant Messaging System Is Compromised

Many incident response teams rely heavily on email or an instant messaging system when coordinating a response to an incident. Team members who are distributed across remote sites can look at communication threads to determine the current status of a response effort. Unfortunately, reliance on a single communication system can work against an IR team's efforts. For example:

- An adversary who has compromised an email or instant messaging server or a domain controller may choose to join the distribution group used to coordinate the response. The attacker can then follow the response effort and sidestep future detection efforts. Additionally, they may be able to learn the status of mitigation efforts and then pivot to systems that the IR team has declared clean.

- If the communication system is offline, the IR team may not be able to contact stakeholders or teams in other locations. This can add an appreciable delay to response effort coordination and the time it takes to bring your organization back online.

To avoid such an event from disrupting your ability to stand up an IR team, ensure that the communications section of your IR plan covers backup communication methods. We discuss the topic of operational security (OpSec) in more detail in "Operational Security" on page 394.

Every response plan should outline high-level procedures so a trained responder can act. The plan should contain references to sufficiently detailed playbooks that trained responders can use to carry out specific actions, and it might also be a good idea to outline the overarching approach for responding to particular classes of incidents. For example, when dealing with network connectivity issues, a response plan should contain a broadly defined summary of the areas to analyze and the troubleshooting steps to perform, and it should reference a playbook that contains specific instructions on how to access the appropriate network devices—e.g., logging into a router or firewall. Response plans might also outline the criteria for an incident responder to determine when to notify senior leadership of incidents and when to work with localized engineering teams.

Create Detailed Playbooks

Playbooks complement response plans and list specific instructions for how a responder should perform particular tasks from beginning to end. For example, playbooks might describe how to grant responders emergency temporary administrative access to certain systems, how to output and parse particular logs for analysis, or how to fail over a system and when to implement graceful degradation.[2] Playbooks are procedural in nature and should be frequently revised and updated. They are typically team-specific, which implies that the response to any disaster may involve multiple teams working through their own specific procedural playbooks.

Ensure Access and Update Mechanisms Are in Place

Your team should define a place to store documentation so that materials are available during a disaster. A disaster may impact access to documentation—for example, if company servers go offline—so make sure you have copies in a location that is accessible during an emergency, and that these copies stay up to date.

Systems get patched, updated, and reconfigured, and threat postures can change. You may discover new vulnerabilities, and new exploits will appear in the wild. Periodically review and update your response plans to make sure they're accurate and reflect any recent configuration or operational changes.

Good incident management requires frequent and robust information management. A team should identify a suitable system for tracking information about an incident and retaining incident data. Teams that handle security and privacy incidents may want a system that's tightly controlled by access on a need-to-know basis, while response teams that deal with service or product outages may want to create a system that is broadly accessible throughout the company.

Prestaging Systems and People Before an Incident

After you've performed risk analysis, created an IR team, and documented the appropriate procedures, you need to identify prestaging activities that you can perform before a disaster occurs. Make sure you consider prestaging that's relevant to every

---

2 These topics are described in Chapter 22 of the SRE book.

phase of the incident response lifecycle. Typically, prestaging involves configuring systems with defined logging retention, automatic responses, and clearly defined human procedures. By understanding each of these elements, a response team can eliminate gaps in coverage between sources of data, automated responses, and human responses. Response plans and playbooks (discussed in the previous section) describe much of what is required for human interactions, but responders also need access to appropriate tools and infrastructure.

To facilitate rapid response to incidents, an IR team should predetermine appropriate levels of access for incident response and establish escalation procedures ahead of time so the process to obtain emergency access isn't slow and convoluted. The IR team should have read access to logs for analysis and event reconstruction, as well as access to tools for analyzing data, sending reports, and conducting forensic examinations.

Configuring Systems

You can make a number of adjustments to systems before a disaster or incident to reduce an IR team's initial response time. For example:

- Build fault tolerance into local systems and create failovers. For more information on this topic, see Chapters 8 and 9.

- Deploy forensic agents, such as GRR (*https://github.com/google/grr*) agents or EnCase (*https://oreil.ly/7-gVj*) Remote Agents, across the network with logs enabled. This will aid both your response and later forensic analysis. Be aware that security logs may require a lengthy retention period, as discussed in Chapter 15 (the industry average for detecting intrusions is approximately 200 days, and logs deleted before an incident is detected cannot be used to investigate it). However, some countries, such as those in the European Union, have particular requirements about how long you can retain logs. When setting up a retention plan, consult your organization's attorney.

- If your organization commits backups to tape or other media, retain an identical set of the hardware and software used to create them so you can restore the backups in a timely fashion if the primary backup system is unavailable. You should also perform periodic restore drills to make sure your equipment, software, and procedures work correctly. IR teams should identify the procedures they'll use to work with individual domain teams (e.g., email teams or network backup teams) to test, verify, and perform data restoration during incidents.

- Have multiple fallback paths for access and recovery in emergencies. An outage that impacts your production network may be hard to recover from unless you have secure alternative pathways to access the network control plane. Similarly, if you discover a breach and aren't sure how widespread the compromise of your corporate workstations is, recovery will be much easier if you have a known safe set of air-gapped systems that you can still trust.

Training

IR team members should be trained on severity/priority models, the IR team's operating model, response times, and the locations of response plans and playbooks. You can read more about Google's approach to incident response in Chapter 9 of the SRE workbook.

Training requirements for incident response extend beyond the IR team, however. During emergencies, some engineers may respond without thinking about or realizing the consequences of their actions. To mitigate this risk, we recommend training the engineers who will assist the IR team on the various IR roles and their responsibilities. We use a system called Incident Management at Google (IMAG), which is based on the Incident Command System (*https://oreil.ly/LwmI6*). The IMAG framework assigns critical roles like incident commander, operational leads, and communications lead.

Train your employees to recognize, report, and escalate an incident. Incidents may be detected by engineers, customers/users, automated alerts, or an administrator. Separate, clear channels should exist for each party to report an incident, and company employees should be trained on how and when to escalate an incident to the IR team.[3] This training should support the organization's IR policy.

There should be a finite limit on the amount of time an engineer can grapple with an incident before escalation. The amount of time available for a first responder depends upon the level of risk the organization is prepared to accept. You might start with a 15-minute window, and adjust that window as necessary.

You should establish the criteria for decision making before the heat of the moment to ensure that responders choose the most logical course of action, rather than making a gut decision on the fly. First responders are frequently faced with the need to make immediate decisions about whether to take a compromised system offline or what containment method to use. For more discussion on this topic, see Chapter 17.

You should train engineers to understand that incident response can require addressing competing priorities that may appear to be mutually exclusive—for example, the need to maintain maximum uptime and availability while also preserving artifacts for forensic investigation. You should also train engineers to create notes about their

---

3 See Chapter 14 of the SRE book and the production-specific worked examples in Chapter 9 of the SRE workbook.

response activities, so they can later differentiate these activities from artifacts left by an attacker.

Processes and Procedures

By establishing a set of processes and procedures to follow before an incident occurs, you drastically reduce the response time and cognitive load for responders. For example, we recommend the following:

- Defining rapid procurement methods for hardware and software. You may need additional equipment or resources, such as servers, software, or fuel for generators, during emergencies.

- Establishing contract approval processes for outsourcing services. For smaller organizations, this may mean identifying outsourced capabilities such as forensic investigation services.

- Creating policies and procedures to preserve evidence and logs during security incidents and prevent log overwrites. For more details, see Chapter 15.

Testing Systems and Response Plans

Once you've created all the materials your organization needs to be prepared for an incident, as described in the preceding sections, it's essential to evaluate the effectiveness of those materials and improve upon any deficiencies you identify. We recommend testing from several perspectives:

- Evaluate automated systems to make sure they're operating correctly.

- Test processes to eliminate any gaps in the procedures and tools used by first responders and engineering teams.

- Train personnel who will respond during incidents to make sure they have the necessary skills to respond to a crisis.

You should run these tests on a periodic basis—annually, at a minimum—to ensure that your systems, procedures, and responses are dependable and applicable in case of an actual emergency.

Each component plays a vital role in returning a disaster-stricken system to an operational state. Even if your IR team is highly skilled, without procedures or automated systems, its ability to respond to a disaster will be inconsistent. If your technical procedures are documented but aren't accessible or usable, they'll likely never be implemented. Testing the resilience of each layer of the disaster response plan decreases those risks.

For many systems, you'll need to document the technical procedures for mitigating threats, audit the controls regularly (for example, quarterly or annually) to ensure they're still being implemented, and provide a list of fixes to engineers to correct any weaknesses you identify. Organizations just beginning their IR planning may want to investigate certifications around disaster recovery and business continuity planning for inspiration.

Auditing Automated Systems

You should audit all critical systems *and* dependent systems—including backup systems, logging systems, software updaters, alert generators, and communication systems—to make sure they're operating correctly. A full audit should ensure the following:

The backup system is operating correctly.
> Backups should be created correctly, stored in a safe location, stored for the appropriate amount of time, and stored with the correct permissions. Conduct data recovery and validation exercises periodically to ensure that you can retrieve and use the data from backups. For more information about Google's data integrity approach, see Chapter 26 of the SRE book.

Event logs (discussed in the previous chapter) are stored correctly.
> These logs allow responders to construct an accurate timeline when reconstructing events during forensic investigations. You should store event logs for a time period appropriate to the organization's level of risk and other applicable considerations.

Critical vulnerabilities are patched in a timely fashion.
> Audit both automatic and manual patch processes to reduce the need for human intervention and the likelihood of human errors.

Alerts are generated correctly.
> Systems generate alerts—email alerts, dashboard updates, text messages, etc.—when particular criteria are met. Validate each alert rule to make sure it fires correctly. Also, make sure to account for dependencies. For example, how are your alerts impacted if an SMTP server goes offline during a network outage?

Communication tools, such as chat clients, email, conference-call bridging services, and secure IRC, work as intended.
> Functioning communication channels are essential for response teams. You should also audit the failover capability of these tools and ensure that they retain the messages you'll need to write the postmortem.

Conducting Nonintrusive Tabletops

Tabletop exercises are incredibly valuable tools for testing documented procedures and evaluating the performance of response teams. These exercises can be starting points for evaluating end-to-end incident responses, and can also be useful when practical testing—for example, causing an actual earthquake—isn't feasible. The simulations can range from small to large in scope, and are typically nonintrusive: because they don't take a system offline, they don't disrupt production environments.

Similar to the Wheel of Misfortune exercises described in Chapter 15 of the SRE book, you can run a tabletop exercise by presenting participants with an incident scenario with various follow-up storyline variations. Ask participants to describe how they would respond to the scenario, and what procedures and protocols they would follow. This approach lets participants flex their decision-making skills and receive constructive feedback. The open structure of these exercises means that they can incorporate a wide range of participants, including these:

- Frontline engineers, following detailed playbooks to restore a crippled system to service
- Senior leadership, making business-level decisions with respect to operations
- Public relations professionals, coordinating external communications
- Lawyers, providing contextual legal guidance and helping craft public communications

The most important aspect of these tabletops is to challenge responders and provide an opportunity for everyone involved to practice the relevant procedures and decision-making processes before a real incident occurs.

Here are some of the key features to consider when implementing tabletop exercises:

Believability
> Tabletop scenarios should be believable—an engaging scenario motivates participants to follow along without suspending disbelief. For example, an exercise might posit that a user falls for a phishing attack, allowing an adversary to exploit a vulnerability on the user's workstation. You can base pivot points—the steps by which an attacker moves throughout a network—on realistic attacks and known vulnerabilities and weaknesses.

Details
> The person who crafts the tabletop scenario should research that scenario in advance, and the facilitator should be well versed in the details of the event and typical responses to the scenario. To aid believability, the creator of the tabletop can create artifacts that participants would encounter during a real incident, such as log files, reports from customers or users, and alerts.

Decision points

Much like a "choose your own adventure" story, a tabletop exercise should have decision points that help the plot unfold. A typical 60-minute tabletop exercise contains approximately 10–20 storyline decision points to engage the participants in decision making that affects the outcome of the exercise. For example, if tabletop participants decide to take a compromised email server offline, then the participants can't send email notifications for the rest of the scenario.

Participants and facilitators

Make tabletop exercises as interactive as possible. As the exercise unfolds, the facilitator may need to respond to the actions and commands executed by the responders. Rather than simply discussing how they would respond to an incident, participants should demonstrate how they would respond. For example, if an IR playbook calls for an incident responder to escalate a ransomware attack to a member of the forensics team for investigation and also to a member of the network security team to block traffic to a hostile website, the responder should carry out these procedures during the tabletop exercise. "Performing the response" helps the incident responder build muscle memory. The facilitator should familiarize themselves with the scenario in advance so they can improvise and nudge the responders in the right direction when needed. Again, the goal here is to enable participants to actively engage in the scenario.

Outcomes

Rather than leaving participants feeling defeated, a successful tabletop exercise should conclude with actionable feedback on what worked well and what didn't work so well. The participants and facilitator should be able to make concrete recommendations for areas of improvement for the incident response team. Where appropriate, participants should recommend changes to systems and policies to fix inherent weaknesses they find. To make sure that participants address these recommendations, create action items with specific owners.

Testing Response in Production Environments

While tabletop exercises are useful for simulating a range of incident scenarios, you need to test some incident scenarios, attack vectors, and vulnerabilities in a real-world production environment. These tests operate at the intersection of security and reliability by allowing IR teams to understand operational constraints, practice with real-world parameters, and observe how their responses affect production environments and uptime.

Single system testing/fault injection

Rather than testing an entire system end to end, you can break large systems into individual software and/or hardware components for testing. Tests can come in a variety of forms and can involve a single local component or a single component with organization-wide reach. For example, what happens when a malicious insider connects a USB storage device to a workstation and attempts to download sensitive content? Do the local logs track the local USB port activity? Are the logs sufficiently aggregated and escalated in a timely fashion, enabling a security team to respond quickly?

We particularly recommend that you conduct single-system testing by using fault injection. Building fault injection into your systems allows you to run targeted tests without disrupting the entire system. More importantly, fault injection frameworks allow individual teams to test their systems without involving their dependencies. As an example, consider the open source Envoy HTTP proxy, which is often used for load balancing. In addition to its many load-balancing features, the proxy supports a fault injection HTTP filter (*https://oreil.ly/rDsp_*), which you can use to return arbitrary errors for a percentage of traffic or to delay requests for a specific amount of time. Using this type of fault injection, you can test that your system handles time-outs correctly, and that time-outs don't lead to unpredictable behavior in production.

When you do find unusual behavior in production, a well-exercised fault injection framework can enable more structured investigation, where you can reproduce production issues in a controlled way. For example, imagine the following scenario: when a company's users attempt to access specific resources, the infrastructure checks all authentication requests using a single source. The company then migrates to a service that requires multiple authentication checks against various sources to obtain similar information. As a result, clients began to exceed the configured time-out for these function calls. The error handling within the caching component of the authentication library erroneously treats these time-outs as permanent (rather than temporary) failures, triggering many other small failures throughout the infrastructure. By using an established incident response framework of fault injection to inject latency in some of the calls, the response team can easily reproduce the behavior, confirm their suspicions, and develop a fix.

Human resource testing

While many tests address technical aspects of a system, tests should also consider personnel failures. What happens when specific personnel are unavailable or fail to act? Often, IR teams rely on individuals with strong institutional knowledge of the organization rather than following set processes. If key decision makers or managers are unavailable during a response, how will the rest of the IR team proceed?

Multicomponent testing

Working with distributed systems means that any number of dependent systems or system components might fail. You need to plan for multicomponent failures and create relevant incident response procedures. Consider a system that depends on multiple components, each of which you tested individually. If two or more components fail simultaneously, what parts of incident response must you handle differently?

A thought exercise might not be sufficient to test every dependency. When considering a service disruption in a security context, you need to consider security concerns in addition to failure scenarios. For example, when failovers occur, does the system respect existing ACLs? What safeguards ensure this behavior? If you're testing an authorization service, does the dependent service fail closed? For a deeper dive into this topic, see Chapter 5.

System-wide failures/failovers

Beyond testing single components and dependencies, consider what happens when your entire system fails. For example, many organizations run primary and secondary (or disaster recovery) datacenters. Until you fail over to operate from your secondary location, you can't be confident that your failover strategy will protect your business and security posture. Google regularly cycles power to entire datacenter buildings to test if the failure causes a user-visible impact. This exercise ensures both that services retain the ability to operate without a specific datacenter location, and that the technicians performing this work are well practiced in managing power-off/power-on procedures.

For services running on another provider's cloud infrastructure, consider what happens to your service if an entire availability zone or region fails.

Red Team Testing

In addition to announced testing, Google practices disaster preparedness exercises known as *Red Team* exercises: offensive testing performed by its Information Security Assurance organization. Similar to DiRT exercises (see "DiRT Exercise Testing Emergency Access" on page 384), these exercises simulate real attacks in order to test and improve detection and response capabilities, and to demonstrate the business impact of security issues.

A Red Team typically provides no advance notice to incident responders, with the exception of senior leadership. Because Red Teams are familiar with Google's infrastructure, their tests are much more productive than standard network penetration tests. Since these exercises occur internally, they provide an opportunity to balance between fully external attacks (where the attacker is outside of Google) and internal attacks (insider risk). Additionally, Red Team exercises supplement security reviews by testing security end to end, and by testing human behavior through attacks like phishing and social engineering. For a deeper exploration of Red Teams, see "Special Teams: Blue and Red Teams" on page 465.

Evaluating Responses

When responding to both live incidents and test scenarios, it's important to create an effective feedback loop so you don't fall victim to the same situations repeatedly. Live incidents should require postmortems with specific action items; you can similarly create postmortems and corresponding action items for testing. While testing can be both a fun exercise and an excellent learning experience, the practice does require some rigor—it's important to track a test's execution, and to critically evaluate its impact and how people throughout your organization respond to the test. Performing an exercise without implementing the lessons you learn from it is merely entertainment.

When evaluating your organization's responses to incidents and tests, consider the following best practices:

- Measure the responses. Evaluators should be able to identify what worked well and what did not. Measure the amount of time it took to implement each stage of the response so you can identify corrective measures.

- Write blameless postmortems and focus on how you can improve the systems, procedures, and processes.[4]

- Create feedback loops for improving existing plans or developing new plans as needed.

- Collect artifacts and feed them back into signal detection. Make sure you address any gaps you identify.

- So that you can perform forensic analysis and address gaps, make sure you save the appropriate logs and other relevant material—especially when conducting security exercises.

- Evaluate even "failed" tests. What worked, and what do you need to improve?[5]

- As discussed in "Special Teams: Blue and Red Teams" on page 465, implement color teams to ensure that your organization acts on the lessons you learn. You may need a hybrid Purple Team to make sure that the Blue Team addresses the vulnerabilities exploited by a Red Team in a timely fashion, thereby preventing attackers from leveraging the same vulnerabilities repeatedly. You can think of Purple Teams like regression testing for vulnerabilities.

---

4 See Chapter 15 of the SRE book.

5 See Chapter 13 of the SRE book.

Google Examples

To make the concepts and best practices described in this chapter more concrete, here are a few real-world examples.

Test with Global Impact

In 2019, Google conducted a test of the response to a major earthquake in the San Francisco Bay Area. The scenario included components to simulate the impact on the physical plant and its facilities, transportation infrastructure, networking components, utilities and power, communication, business operations, and executive decision making. Our goal was to test Google's response to a large disruption and the impact on global operations. Specifically, we tested the following:

- How would Google provide immediate first aid to individuals injured during the earthquake and multiple aftershocks?
- How would Google provide help to the public?
- How would employees escalate information to Google's leadership? In the event of communication disruption—for example, a downed cellular network or disrupted LAN/MAN/WAN—how would Google disseminate information to employees?
- Who would be available for on-site response if employees had conflicts of interest—for example, if employees needed to take care of their family members and homes?
- How would unpassable secondary roadways impact the region? How would the overflow impact primary roadways?
- How would Google provide assistance to employees, contractors, and visitors who were stranded on Google's campuses?
- How could Google evaluate the damage to its buildings, which might include broken pipes, sewage issues, broken glass, loss of power, and broken network connections?
- If locally affected teams could not initiate a transfer of authority/responsibility, how would SREs and various engineering teams outside the geographic area take control over systems?
- How could we enable leadership outside the affected geographic area to continue with business operations and making business-related decisions?

DiRT Exercise Testing Emergency Access

Sometimes we can test the robustness of both reliability and security operations simultaneously. During one of our annual Disaster Recovery Training (DiRT) exercises,[6] SREs tested the procedure and functionality of breakglass credentials:[7] could they gain emergency access to the corporate and production networks when standard ACL services were down? To add a security testing layer, the DiRT team also looped in the signals detection team. When SREs engaged the breakglass procedure, the detection team was able to confirm that the correct alert fired and that the access request was legitimate.

Industry-Wide Vulnerabilities

In 2018, Google received early notice of two vulnerabilities in the Linux kernel, which underpins much of our production infrastructure. By sending specially crafted IP fragments and TCP segments, either SegmentSmack (CVE-2018-5390 (*https://oreil.ly/MMhA7*)) or FragmentSmack (CVE-2018-5391 (*https://oreil.ly/cwl3J*)) could cause a server to perform expensive operations. By using large amounts of both CPU and wall-clock time, this vulnerability could allow an attacker to obtain a significant scale boost beyond a normal denial-of-service attack—a service that could normally cope with a 1 Mpps attack would fall over at approximately 50 Kpps, a 20× reduction in resilience.

Disaster planning and preparation enabled us to mitigate this risk in two dimensions: technical aspects and incident management aspects. On the incident management front, the looming disaster was so significant that Google assigned a team of incident managers to work on the problem full time. The team needed to identify the affected systems, including vendor firmware images, and enact a comprehensive plan to mitigate the risk.

On the technical front, SREs had already implemented defense-in-depth measures for the Linux kernel. A runtime patch, or *ksplice*, that uses function redirection tables to make rebooting a new kernel unnecessary can address many security issues. Google also maintains kernel rollout discipline: we regularly push new kernels to the entire fleet of machines with a target of less than 30 days, and we have well-defined mechanisms to increase the rollout speed of this standard operating procedure if necessary.[8]

---

6 See Kripa Krishnan's article "Weathering the Unexpected" (*https://oreil.ly/cn_il*) and her USENIX LISA15 presentation "10 Years of Crashing Google" (*https://oreil.ly/ZRZAI*).

7 A breakglass mechanism can bypass policies to allow engineers to quickly resolve outages. See "Breakglass" on page 67.

8 Chapter 9 discusses additional design approaches that prepare your organization to respond to incidents quickly.

If we'd been unable to fix the vulnerability using a ksplice, we could have performed an emergency rollout at speed. However, in this case, it was possible to address the two affected functions in the kernel—`tcp_collapse_ofo_queue` and `tcp_prune_ofo_queue`—with a kernel splice. SREs were able to apply the ksplice to production systems without adversely affecting the production environment. Because the rollout procedure was already tested and approved, SREs quickly obtained VP approval to apply the patch during a code freeze.

Conclusion

When contemplating how to spin up disaster recovery tests and plans from scratch, the sheer volume of possible approaches can seem overwhelming. However, you can apply the concepts and best practices in this chapter even at a small scale.

As a starting point, identify your most important system or a piece of critical data, and then identify how you would respond to various disasters that affect it. You need to determine how long you can operate without a service and the number of people or other systems that it impacts.

From this first important step, you can expand your coverage piece by piece into a robust disaster preparedness strategy. From an initial strategy of identifying and preventing the sparks that start a fire, you can work your way up to responding to that inevitable eventual blaze.

CHAPTER 17

Crisis Management

By Matt Linton
with Nick Soda and Gary O'Connor

Once your systems are running, you'll want to keep those systems up, even when malicious actors are attacking your organization. The reliability of your systems is a measure of how well your organization can withstand a security crisis, and reliability directly impacts the happiness of your users.

This chapter starts by clarifying how to recognize a crisis, followed by a detailed plan of how to take command and maintain control of an incident—a topic that includes deep-dives into operational security and forensics. Communications are a critical but often overlooked part of crisis management. We guide you through some communication-related pitfalls to avoid and provide examples and templates. Finally, we walk through a sample crisis scenario to demonstrate how the pieces of incident response fit together.

Incident response is critical for both reliability and security incidents. Chapter 14 of the SRE book and Chapter 9 of the SRE workbook explore incident response as it relates to reliability outages. We use the same methodology—the Incident Management at Google (IMAG) framework—to respond to security incidents.

Security incidents are inevitable. A common maxim in the industry states that "There are only two types of companies: those that know they've been compromised, and those that don't know." The outcome of a security incident depends upon how well your organization prepares, and also how well you respond. To achieve a mature security posture, your organization needs to institute and practice an incident response (IR) capability, as discussed in the previous chapter.

In addition to the familiar pressures of ensuring that unauthorized parties can't access your systems and that your data stays where it should, IR teams today face new and difficult challenges. As the security industry trends toward greater transparency[1] and a need for increased openness with users, this expectation poses a unique challenge for any IR team accustomed to operating away from the spotlight of public attention. Additionally, regulations like the EU's General Data Protection Regulation (GDPR) (*https://eugdpr.org*) and service contracts with security-conscious customers continually push the boundaries of how quickly investigations must begin, progress, and complete. Today, it's not unusual for a customer to ask for a notification of a potential security problem within 24 hours (or less) of initial detection.

Incident notification has become a core feature of the security domain, alongside technological advances such as easy and ubiquitous use of cloud computing, widespread adoption of "bring your own device" (BYOD) policies in the workplace, and the Internet of Things (IoT). Such advances have created new challenges for IT and security staff—for example, limited control over and visibility into all of an organization's assets.

Is It a Crisis or Not?

Not every incident is a crisis. In fact, if your organization is in good shape, relatively few incidents should turn into crises. Once an escalation occurs, a responder's first step in assessing the escalation is *triage*—using the knowledge and information available to them to make educated and informed assumptions about the severity and potential consequences of the incident.

Triage is a well-established skill in the emergency medical community. An emergency medical technician (EMT) arriving on the scene of a vehicle accident will first make sure there are no immediate risks of further injury to anyone at the scene, and then perform triage. For example, if a bus has collided with a car, a few pieces of information are already logically available. The people in the car may have sustained serious injuries, because a collision with a heavy bus can inflict a great deal of damage. A bus can hold many passengers, so there may be multiple injuries to passengers. It's unlikely that any dangerous chemicals are present, because neither vehicle would typically carry them. Within the first minute of arriving, the EMT knows that they'll need to call for more ambulances, possibly alert a critical care unit, and call the fire department to free any trapped occupants from the smaller vehicle. They probably don't need a hazardous materials cleanup crew.

---

1 See, e.g., Google's Transparency Report (*https://oreil.ly/vQNR3*).

Your security response team should use these same assessment methods to triage incidents as they come in. As a first step, they must estimate the potential severity of the attack.

Triaging the Incident

When triaging, the engineer assigned to investigate must gather basic facts to help decide whether the escalation is one of the following:

- An error (i.e., a false positive)
- An easily correctable problem (an opportunistic compromise, perhaps)
- A complex and potentially damaging problem (such as a targeted compromise)

They should be able to triage predictable problems, bugs, and other straightforward issues using predetermined processes. Larger and more complex issues, such as targeted attacks, will likely require an organized and managed response.

Every team should have preplanned criteria to help determine what constitutes an incident. Ideally, they should identify what kinds of risks are severe versus acceptable in their environment before an incident happens. The response to an incident will depend on the type of environment where the incident happened, the state of the organization's preventative controls, and the sophistication of its response program. Consider how three organizations might respond to the same threat—a ransomware attack:

- *Organization 1* has a mature security process and layered defenses, including a restriction that permits only cryptographically signed and approved software to execute. In this environment, it's highly unlikely that well-known ransomware can infect a machine or spread throughout the network. If it does, the detection system raises an alert, and someone investigates. Because of the mature processes and layered defenses, a single engineer can handle the issue: they can check to make sure no suspicious activity has occurred beyond the attempted malware execution, and resolve the issue using a standard process. This scenario doesn't require a crisis-style incident response effort.

- *Organization 2* has a sales department that hosts customer demos in a cloud environment, where people who want to learn about the organization's software install and manage their test instances. The security team notices that these users tend to make security configuration mistakes that result in system compromises. So that these compromises don't require manual intervention from a human responder, the security team establishes a mechanism to automatically wipe and replace compromised cloud test instances. In this case, a ransomware worm would also not require much forensics or incident response attention. Although

Organization 2 doesn't prevent the ransomware from executing (as in Organization 1's case), Organization 2's automated mitigation tools can contain the risk.

- *Organization 3* has fewer layered defenses and limited visibility into whether its systems are compromised. The organization is at much greater risk of the ransomware spreading across its network and may not be able to respond quickly. In this case, a large number of business-critical systems may be affected if the worm spreads, and the organization will be severely impacted, requiring significant technical resources to rebuild the compromised networks and systems. This worm presents a serious risk for Organization 3.

While all three organizations are responding to the same source of risk (a ransomware attack), the differences in their layered defenses and level of process maturity affect the potential severity and impact of the attack. While Organization 1 may need to simply initiate a playbook-driven response, Organization 3 may face a crisis that requires coordinated incident management. As the likelihood that an incident will pose a serious risk to the organization increases, so does the likelihood that it will require an organized response by many participants.

Your team can perform some basic assessments to determine whether an escalation requires a standard playbook-driven approach or a crisis management approach. Ask yourself the following questions:

- What data do you store that might be accessible to someone on that system? What is the value or criticality of that data?
- What trust relationships does the potentially compromised system have with other systems?
- Are there compensating controls that an attacker would also have to penetrate (and that seem intact) in order to take advantage of their foothold?
- Does the attack seem to be commodity opportunistic malware (e.g., Adware), or does it appear more advanced or targeted (e.g., a phishing campaign seemingly crafted with your organization in mind)?

Think through all the relevant factors for your organization, and determine the highest likely level of organizational risk given those facts.

Compromises Versus Bugs

IR teams have long been tasked with responding to suspected intrusions and compromises. But what about software and hardware bugs, a.k.a. security vulnerabilities? Do you treat a newly discovered security vulnerability in your systems as a compromise that has yet to be discovered?

Software bugs are inevitable, and you can plan for them (as explained in Chapter 8). Good defensive practices remove or limit the potential negative consequences of vulnerabilities before they begin.[2] If you plan well and implement in-depth defenses with additional layers of security, you shouldn't need to handle vulnerability remediation the same way you handle incidents. That said, it may be appropriate to manage complicated or large-impact vulnerabilities with incident response processes, which can help you organize and respond quickly.

At Google, we typically treat vulnerabilities that carry extreme risk as incidents. Even if a bug isn't actively being exploited, a particularly severe one can still introduce extreme risk. If you're involved in fixing the vulnerability before it's publicly disclosed (these efforts are often called *coordinated vulnerability disclosures*, or CVDs), operational security and confidentiality concerns may warrant a heightened response . Alternatively, if you're hurrying to patch systems after a public disclosure, securing systems that have complex interdependencies may require urgent effort, and it may be difficult and time-consuming to deploy fixes.

Some examples of particularly risky vulnerabilities include Spectre and Meltdown (CVE-2017-5715 and 5753), glibc (CVE-2015-0235), Stagefright (CVE-2015-1538), Shellshock (CVE-2014-6271), and Heartbleed (CVE-2014-0160).

Coordinated Vulnerability Disclosure

There are many interpretations of what *CVD* means. The emergent ISO standard 29147:2018 (*https://oreil.ly/GBGam*) provides some guidance. At Google, we generally define CVD as a process in which a team must maintain a careful balance between the amount of time it may take the vendor to issue security patches, the needs and wishes of the person who finds or reports the bug, and the needs of the user base and customers.

Taking Command of Your Incident

Now that we've discussed the process of triage and risk assessment, the next three sections assume a "big one" has happened: you've identified or suspect a targeted compromise, and you need to perform full-fledged incident response.

---

2 In one of our design reviews at Google, an engineer suggested that "There are two kinds of software developers: those who sandboxed Ghostscript, and those who should have sandboxed Ghostscript."

The First Step: Don't Panic!

Many responders associate a serious incident escalation with a rising sense of panic and an adrenaline rush. Emergency responders in the fire, rescue, and medical fields are warned in basic training not to run at the scene of an emergency. Not only does running risk making the problem worse by increasing the likelihood of an accident on the scene, it also instills a sense of panic in the responder and the public. In a similar fashion, during a security incident, the extra few seconds you gain by rushing are quickly eclipsed by the consequences of a failure to plan.

Although the SRE and security teams at Google perform incident management similarly, there is a difference between beginning a crisis management response for a security incident and for a reliability incident such as an outage. When an outage occurs, the on-call SRE prepares to step into action. Their goal is to quickly find the errors and fix them to restore the system to a good state. Most importantly, the system is not conscious of its actions and won't resist being fixed.

In a potential compromise, the attacker may be paying close attention to actions taken by the target organization and work against the responders as they try to fix things. It can be catastrophic to attempt to fix the system without first completing a full investigation. Because typical SRE work doesn't carry that risk, an SRE's usual response is to fix the system first and then document what they learned from the failure. For example, if an engineer submits a change list (CL) that breaks production, an SRE might take immediate action to revert the CL, making the problem go away. Once the problem is fixed, the SRE will begin investigating what happened. A security response instead requires the team to complete a full investigation into what happened prior to attempting to correct things.

As a security incident responder, your first task is to take control of your emotions. Take the first five minutes of an escalation to breathe deeply, allow any feelings of panic to pass, remind yourself that you need a plan, and begin thinking through the next steps. While the desire to react immediately is strong, in practice, postmortems rarely report that a security response would have been more effective if staff had responded five minutes sooner. It's more likely that some additional planning up front will add greater value.

Beginning Your Response

At Google, once an engineer decides that the issue they're facing is an Incident, we follow a standard process. That process, called Incident Management at Google, is fully described in Chapter 9 of the SRE workbook, along with case studies of outages and events where we've applied this protocol. This section describes how you can use IMAG as a standard framework to manage a security compromise.

First, a quick refresher: as mentioned in the previous chapter, IMAG is based on a formal process called the Incident Command System (ICS) (*https://oreil.ly/4cLxY*), which is used by fire, rescue, and police agencies around the world. Like ICS, IMAG is a flexible response framework that is lightweight enough to manage small incidents, but capable of expanding to encompass large and wide-ranging issues. Our IMAG program is tasked with formalizing processes to ensure maximum success in three key areas of incident handling: command, control, and communications.

The first step in managing an incident is to take *command*. In IMAG, we do this by issuing a declaration: "Our team is declaring an incident involving X, and I am the incident commander (IC)." Explicitly saying "this is an incident" may seem simple and perhaps unnecessary, but being explicit in order to avoid misunderstandings is a core principle of both command and communications. Beginning your incident with a declaration is the first step in aligning everyone's expectations. Incidents are complex and unusual, involve high amounts of tension, and happen at high speed. Those involved need to focus. Executives should be notified that teams might ignore or bypass normal processes until the incident is contained.

After a responder takes command and becomes the IC, their job is to keep *control* of the incident. The IC directs the response and ensures people are moving forward toward specific goals at all times, so that the chaos and uncertainty around a crisis doesn't throw teams off track. In order to maintain control, the IC and their leads must constantly maintain excellent *communications* with everyone involved.

Google uses IMAG as a general-purpose response framework for all sorts of incidents. All on-call engineers (ideally) are trained in the same set of fundamentals and taught how to use them to scale and professionally manage a response. While the focus of SRE and security teams may differ, ultimately, having the same framework for response enables both groups to seamlessly interoperate under stress, when working with unfamiliar teams may be at its most difficult.

Establishing Your Incident Team

Under the IMAG model, once an Incident is declared, the person declaring the incident either becomes the incident commander or selects an IC from among the other available staff. Regardless of which route you take, make this assignment explicit in order to avoid misunderstandings among responders. The person designated the IC must also explicitly acknowledge that they accept the assignment.

Next, the IC will assess what actions need to be taken immediately, and who can fill those roles. You'll likely need some skilled engineers to initiate the investigation. Large organizations may have a dedicated security team; very large organizations might even have a dedicated incident response team. A small organization may have one dedicated security person, or someone who handles security part time alongside other operational responsibilities.

Regardless of the size or makeup of the organization, the IC should locate staff who know the potentially affected systems well and deputize these individuals into an incident response team. If the incident grows larger and requires more staff, it's helpful to assign a few leaders to head up certain aspects of the investigation. Nearly every incident needs an *operations lead* (OL): the tactical counterpart and partner to the IC. While the IC focuses on setting the strategic goals needed to make progress on the incident response, the OL focuses on meeting those goals and determining how to do so. Most of the technical staff performing investigations, fixing and patching systems, and so on should report to the OL.

Some other lead roles you may need to fill include the following:

Management liaison

> You may need someone to make tough calls on the spot. Who from your organization can decide to shut down a revenue-generating service if necessary? Who can decide to send staff home or revoke the credentials of other engineers?

Legal lead

> Your incident may raise legal questions that you'll need help answering. Do your employees have an enhanced expectation of privacy? For example, if you think someone downloaded malware via their web browser, do you need extra permissions to examine their browser history? What if you think they downloaded malware via their personal browser profile?

Communications lead

> Depending on the nature of the incident, you may need to communicate with your customers, regulators, etc. A professional who is skilled at communicating could be a vital addition to your response team.

Operational Security

In the context of crisis management, *operational security (OpSec)* refers to the practice of keeping your response activity secret. Whether you are working on a suspected compromise, an insider abuse investigation, or a dangerous vulnerability whose existence could lead to widespread exploitation if publicized, you'll likely have information that you need to keep secret, at least for a limited amount of time. We strongly recommend that you establish an OpSec plan today—before you ever have an incident—so that you don't have to come up with this plan in a rush at the last minute. Once a secret is lost, it's hard to regain.

The IC is ultimately responsible for ensuring that rules around confidentiality are set, communicated, and followed. Every team member asked to work on an investigation should be briefed on what to expect. You may have specific rules for how to handle data, or expectations around which communication channels to use. For example, if you suspect your email server is within scope of a breach, you might prohibit employees from emailing one another about the breach in case an attacker can see those conversations.

As a best practice, we recommend that your IC document specific guidance for each incident response team member. Each team member should review and acknowledge these guidelines before starting work on the incident. If you don't clearly communicate confidentiality rules to all relevant parties, you risk an information leak or premature disclosure.

In addition to protecting the response activity from your attacker, a good OpSec plan addresses how the response can proceed without further exposing the organization. Consider an attacker who compromises one of your employee's accounts and is trying to steal other passwords from memory on a server. They'd be delighted if a system administrator logged into the affected machine with administrative credentials during their investigation. Plan ahead for how you'll access data and machines without providing your attacker additional leverage. One way to accomplish this is to deploy remote forensic agents to all your systems in advance. These software packages maintain an access path for authorized responders from your company to obtain forensic artifacts without risking their own accounts by logging into the system.

The consequences of cluing in an attacker that you've discovered their attack can be high. A determined attacker who wants to persist beyond your investigation may go quiet. This deprives you of valuable insight into the extent of their compromise and can cause you to miss one (or more) of their footholds. And an attacker who has accomplished their objective and does not want to stay quiet may respond to your discovery by destroying as much of your organization as they can on their way out the door!

The following are some common OpSec mistakes:

- Communicating about or documenting the incident in a medium (such as email) that enables the attacker to monitor response activities.

- Logging into compromised servers. This exposes potentially useful authentication credentials to the attacker.

- Connecting to and interacting with the attacker's "command and control" servers. For example, don't try to access an attacker's malware by downloading it from a machine you're using to perform your investigation. Your actions will stand out in the attacker's logs as unusual and could warn them of your investigation. Also, don't perform port scanning or domain lookups for the attacker's machines (a common mistake made by novice responders).

- Locking accounts or changing passwords of affected users before your investigation is complete.

- Taking systems offline before you understand the full scope of the attack.

- Allowing your analysis workstations to be accessed with the same credentials an attacker may have stolen.

Consider the following good practices in your OpSec response:

- Conduct meetings and discussions in person where possible. If you need to use chat or email, use new machines and infrastructure. For example, an organization facing a compromise of unknown extent might build a new temporary cloud-based environment and deploy machines that differ from its regular fleet (e.g., Chromebooks) for responders to communicate. Ideally, this tactic provides a clean environment to chat, document, and communicate outside of the attacker's view.

- Wherever possible, ensure that your machines have remote agents or key-based access methods configured. This allows you to collect evidence without revealing login secrets.

- Be specific and explicit about confidentiality when asking people to help—they may not know particular information is supposed to be kept confidential unless you tell them.

- For each step of your investigation, consider the conclusions a shrewd attacker may draw from your actions. For example, an attacker who compromises a Windows server may notice a sudden rush of group policy tightening and conclude that they've been discovered.

When Your Tools Try to Be Helpful

Many modern communication and collaboration tools (e.g., email and chat clients, or collaborative document editors) try to be helpful by automatically detecting patterns that seem like internet content and creating links. Some tools even connect to those remote links and cache the content they find so they can display that content faster if it's requested. For example, writing "example.com" in a spreadsheet or email or chat window may result in content being downloaded from that site without any further interaction on your part.

Ordinarily this behavior is helpful, but if you're trying to practice good operational security while collecting data about your attacker, these tools can betray you by automatically talking to the attacker's infrastructure in easily observable ways.

If several analysts are sharing information in a private chat forum that automatically fetches content, something like the following may appear in an attacker's logs:

```
10.20.38.156 - - [03/Aug/2019:11:30:40 -0700] "GET /malware_c2.gif HTTP/
1.1" 206 36277 "-" "Chatbot-LinkExpanding 1.0"
```

If your attacker is paying attention, this is a pretty obvious signal that you've discovered their *malware_c2.gif* file.

Get in the habit of always writing out domains and other network-based indicators in ways that your tools will not match and autocomplete, even when you're not investigating an incident. Writing example.com as example[dot]com as a matter of routine will make a slipup during an investigation much less likely.

Trading Good OpSec for the Greater Good

There's one glaring exception to the general advice of keeping your incident response a secret: if you're faced with an imminent and clearly identifiable risk. If you suspect a compromise to a system so critical that vital data, systems, or even lives may be at risk, extreme measures may be justified. In the case of a vulnerability or bug that's being managed as an incident, sometimes that bug may be so easily exploited and so widely known (e.g., Shellshock[3]) that turning off or entirely disabling the system might be the best way to protect it. Doing so will, of course, make it obvious to your attacker and others that something is amiss.

Security and Reliability Tradeoff: Imminent Risk

You might have to endure product downtime and user anger in order to accomplish longer-term security and reliability objectives. In early 2019, Apple responded to a publicly disclosed, easily exploitable privacy bug in Facetime by turning off all access to the Facetime servers until it had deployed fixes. This day-long outage for a popular service was widely recognized in the security industry as the right course of action. In this case, Apple chose protecting its users from an easily exploitable issue over guaranteeing service availability.

These sorts of big decisions and organizational tradeoffs aren't likely to be solely made by the incident commander, except in extremely risky situations (e.g., shutting off a control system for a power grid to prevent a catastrophe). Typically, executives within the organization make such calls. However, the IC is the resident expert in the room when those decisions are debated, and their advice and security expertise are critical. At the end of the day, much of an organization's decision making in a crisis isn't about making the *right* call; it's about making the *best possible* call from among a range of suboptimal choices.

---

3 Shellshock (*https://oreil.ly/8eDCJ*) was a remote exploit so simple to deploy that within a few days of its publication, millions of servers were already being actively attacked.

The Investigative Process

Investigating a security compromise involves attempting to backtrack through each phase of the attack to reconstruct the attacker's steps. Ideally, your IR team (composed of any engineers assigned to the job) will attempt to maintain a tight loop of effort among multiple tasks.[4] This effort focuses on identifying all the affected parts of the organization and learning as much as possible about what happened.

Digital forensics refers to the process of figuring out all of the actions an attacker may have taken on a device. A forensic analyst (the engineer performing forensics—ideally, someone with special training and experience) analyzes all the parts of the system, including available logs, to try to determine what happened. The analyst may perform some or all of the following investigative steps:

Forensic imaging

Making a secure read-only copy (and checksum) of any data storage devices attached to a compromised system. This preserves the data in a known state at the exact time the copy is taken, without accidentally overwriting or damaging the original disk. Court proceedings often need forensic images of original disks as evidence.

Memory imaging

Making a copy of a system's memory (or in some cases, the memory of a running binary). Memory can contain many pieces of digital evidence that may be useful during an investigation—for example, process trees, executables that were running, and even passwords to files that attackers may have encrypted.

File carving

Extracting a disk's contents to see if you can recover certain file types, especially those that may have been deleted—for example, logs the attacker tried to delete. Some operating systems don't zero the contents of files when they're deleted. Instead, they only unlink the filename and mark the disk area as free for later reuse. As a result, you may be able to recover data an attacker attempted to remove.

Log analysis

Investigating events relating to the system that appear in logs, whether on the system itself or from other sources. Network logs may show who talked to the system and when; logs from other servers and desktops may show other activities.

---

4 This tight loop of effort has a minimal delay between steps, such that no one is unable to do their part because they're waiting on someone else to complete their part.

Malware analysis

Performing analysis on tools used by attackers to determine what those tools do, how they work, and what systems the tools might communicate with. The data from this analysis is usually fed back to teams doing forensic and detection work to provide better insight about potential indications that a system has been compromised.

In digital forensics, the relationships between events are as important as the events themselves.

Much of the work a forensic analyst does to obtain artifacts contributes to the goal of building a *forensic timeline*.[5] By collecting a chronologically ordered list of events, an analyst can determine correlation and causation of attacker activity, proving *why* these events happened.

Example: An Email Attack

Let's consider a fictional scenario: an unknown attacker has successfully compromised an engineer's workstation by sending a malicious attachment via email to a developer, who unwittingly opened it. This attachment installed a malicious browser extension onto the developer's workstation. The attacker, leveraging the malicious extension, then stole the developer's credentials and logged in to a file server. Once inside the server, the attacker proceeded to collect confidential files and copy them to their own remote server. Eventually, the developer detected the compromise when reviewing their installed browser extensions and reported the breach to security.

As an incident responder, your first instinct may be to lock the developer's account right away—but remember the operational security concerns mentioned earlier. You should always start your investigation with a hands-off approach, until you know enough about the attack to make informed decisions about how to react. At the beginning of the investigation, you have very little information. You know only that a malicious browser extension exists on the developer's machine.

Your first step is always to remain calm and not to panic. Next, declare that an incident is in progress and engage an operations lead to conduct a deeper investigation. From here, the OL should build a team to answer the following questions:

- How did the backdoor get installed?
- What are the capabilities of the backdoor?

---

5 A forensic timeline is a list of all the events that happened on a system, ideally centered on the events related to an investigation, ordered by the time at which those events occurred.

- On what other browsers in the organization does this backdoor exist?
- What did the attacker do on the developer's system?

We refer to these initial questions as *pivot points*: as you answer each question, new questions arise. For example, once the response team discovers that the attack progressed to a file share, that file share becomes the subject of a new forensic investigation. The investigation team must subsequently answer the same set of questions for the file share and any new leads that follow. As the team identifies each of the attacker's tools and techniques, they process the information to determine where to target any additional investigations.

Sharding the investigation

If you have enough personnel available to staff multiple efforts simultaneously (see "Parallelizing the Incident" on page 401), consider splitting your effort into three tracks, each tasked with a major piece of the investigation. For example, your OL might separate their makeshift team into three groups:

- A *Forensics* group to investigate systems and identify which ones the attacker has touched.
- A *Reversing* group to study suspicious binaries, determining the unique fingerprints that serve as indicators of compromise (IOCs).[6]
- A *Hunting* group to search all systems for those fingerprints. This group notifies the Forensics group any time they identify a suspect system.

Figure 17-1 shows the relationships between the groups. The OL is responsible for keeping a tight feedback loop between these teams.

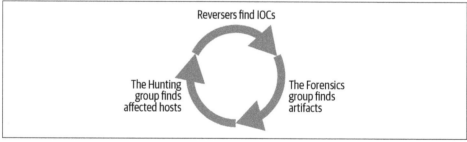

Figure 17-1. The relationship between investigative groups

---

6 Malware reversing is rather specialized work, and not all organizations have someone skilled in this practice.

Eventually, the rate at which you discover new leads will slow down. At this point, the IC decides it's time to move on to remediation. Have you learned all there is to learn? Probably not. But you may have learned all you need to know to successfully remove the attacker and protect the data they're after. It can be tough to determine where to draw this line because of all the unknowns involved. Making this decision is a lot like knowing when to stop microwaving a bag of popcorn: when the interval between pops noticeably increases, you should move along before the entire bag burns. Prior to remediating, a lot of planning and coordination needs to happen. Chapter 18 covers this in much more detail.

Digital Forensics at Scale

While this chapter's description of forensic analysis explains the basics, the topic of performing forensics at scale or in difficult environments like cloud deployments (where you may not have the tools you're used to, or your tools may work differently than normal) is a broad one. A series of forensic blog posts from Google (*https://oreil.ly/YGbtX*) covers these topics in more depth.

Keeping Control of the Incident

Once an incident is declared and your team members are assigned responsibilities, the IC's job is to keep the effort running smoothly. This task involves predicting the needs of the response team, and addressing those needs before they become problems. To be effective, the IC should devote all of their time to controlling and managing the incident. If, as IC, you find yourself jumping in to check logs, performing quick forensics tasks, or otherwise involving yourself with operations, it's time to step back and reassess your priorities. If no one is at the helm of the ship, it's guaranteed to veer off course or even crash.

Parallelizing the Incident

Ideally, a practiced IR team can *parallelize* the incident by breaking down all the pieces of the incident response process and running them simultaneously, to the greatest extent possible. If you anticipate an unassigned task or a piece of information you'll need during the incident lifecycle, assign someone to complete the task or prepare for the work. For example, you might not yet be ready to share your forensic findings with law enforcement or a third-party firm that will aid in your investigation, but if you plan to share your findings in the future, your raw investigation notes won't be helpful. Assign someone to prepare a redacted and shareable list of indicators as your investigation proceeds.

It may seem counterintuitive to begin preparations to clean up your environment during the early stages of your forensic investigation, but if you have available staff, it's a great time to assign this task. IMAG allows you to create custom roles at any time, so you assign someone the *remediation lead* (RL) role at any point during the incident. The RL can begin studying the areas of confirmed compromise as the ops team discovers them. Armed with this information, the RL can create a plan to clean up and fix these compromised areas later. When the ops team completes their investigation, the IC will already have the cleanup plan in place. At this point, rather than deciding next steps on the spot, they can initiate the next phase of work. Similarly, if you have the staff available, it's never too early to assign someone to begin the postmortem.

To borrow a programming construct, an IC's role in a large incident looks like a set of steps through a `while` loop:

```
(While the incident is still ongoing):
  1. Check with each of your leads:
    a. What's their status?
    b. Have they found new information that others may need to act upon?
    c. Have they hit any roadblocks?
    d. Do they need more personnel or resources?
    e. Are they overwhelmed?
    f. Do you spot any issues that may pop up later or cause problems?
    g. How's the fatigue level of each of your leads? Of each team?
  2. Update status documents, dashboards, or other information sources.
  3. Are relevant stakeholders (executives, legal, PR, etc.) informed?
  4. Do you need any help or additional resources?
  5. Are any tasks that could be done in parallel waiting?
  6. Do you have enough information to make remediation and cleanup
     decisions?
  7. How much time does the team need before they can give the next
     set of updates?
  8. Is the incident over?
Loop to beginning.
```

The *OODA loop* is another relevant framework for incident-related decision making: a pattern where the responder should *observe, orient, decide*, and *act*. This is a helpful mnemonic for reminding yourself to consider new information carefully, think about how it applies to the big picture for your incident, decide on a course of action with intent, and only then take action.

Handovers

No human can work nonstop on a single problem for long periods of time without experiencing problems. Most of the time, the crises we encounter take time to resolve. Smoothly passing work back and forth between responders is a must and helps to build a culture of security and reliability (see Chapter 21).

Fighting a large forest fire is physically and emotionally demanding and can take days, weeks, or even months. To fight such a fire, the California Department of Forestry and Fire Protection breaks it into "areas" and assigns an incident commander to each one. The IC for a given area establishes a long-term objective for their area and short-term goals to progress toward the objective. They split their available resources into shifts so that while one team works, another team rests and is ready to relieve the first team when they're exhausted.

When the crews working on the fire are nearing their limits, the IC collects status updates from all the team leads and assigns new team leads to replace them. The IC then briefs the new team leads on the overall objective, their assignment, specific goals they are expected to accomplish, resources available, safety hazards, and any other relevant information. Then the new team leads and their staff take over from the previous shift's staff. Each incoming lead communicates quickly with the outgoing lead to ensure they didn't miss any relevant facts. The fatigued crew can now rest while the firefighting continues.

Security incident response is not as physically demanding as fighting fires, but your team will experience similar emotional and stress-related exhaustion. It's crucial to have a plan to hand their work off to others when necessary. Eventually, a tired responder will start to make mistakes. If worked hard enough for long enough, your team will make more mistakes than they are correcting—a phenomenon often referred to as the *law of diminishing returns* (*https://oreil.ly/_1_iU*). Staff fatigue isn't just a matter of treating your team kindly; fatigue can cripple your response through errors and low morale. To avoid overwork, we recommend limiting shifts (including IC shifts) to no more than 12 continuous hours.

If you have a large staff and want to accelerate your response, consider splitting your response team into two smaller groups. These teams can staff your response 24 hours a day until the incident is resolved. If you don't have a large staff, you might need to accept the risk of a slower response so your staff can go home and rest. While small teams can work extra-long hours in "hero mode," this mode is unsustainable and yields lower-quality results. We recommend that you use hero mode very sparingly.

Consider an organization with teams in the Americas, Asia-Pacific, and European regions. This kind of organization can staff a "follow-the-sun" rotation so that fresh responders continually cycle on the incident according to a schedule, as depicted in Figure 17-2. A smaller organization might have a similar schedule, but with fewer locations and more time between rotations, or perhaps a single location with half the operations staff working night shifts to keep the response going while the others rest.

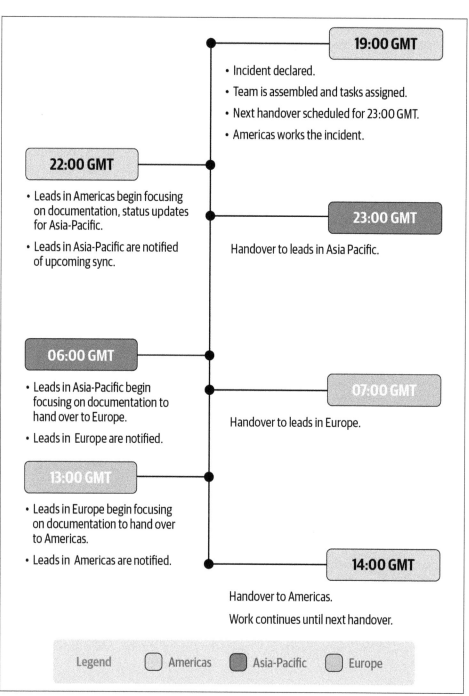

Figure 17-2. Follow-the-sun rotation

The IC should prepare for an incident handover ahead of time. Handovers include updating tracking documentation, evidence notes and files, and any other written records kept during the shift. Arrange handover logistics, time, and method of communication in advance. The meeting should begin with a summary of the current incident state and direction of the investigation. You should also include a formal handover from each lead (ops, comms, etc.) to their corresponding replacement.

The information you should communicate to the incoming team depends on the incident. At Google, we've found it consistently helpful for the IC of the outgoing team to ask themselves, "If I weren't handing this investigation over to you, what would I spend the next 12 hours working on?" The IC of the incoming relief team should have an answer to this question before the handover meeting ends.

For example, a handover meeting agenda might look something like this:

1. [Outgoing IC] Delegate one person to take notes, preferably from the incoming team.
2. [Outgoing IC] Summarize current status.
3. [Outgoing IC] Outline the tasks the IC would do over the next 12 hours if they weren't handing off the incident.
4. [All attendees] Discuss the issue.
5. [Incoming IC] Outline the tasks you expect to handle during the next 12 hours.
6. [Incoming IC] Establish time(s) of next meeting(s).

Morale

During any major incident, the IC needs to maintain team morale. This responsibility is often overlooked, but is critical. Incidents can be stressful, and each engineer will respond differently to these high-pressure situations. Some rise to the challenge and participate enthusiastically, while others find the combination of intense effort and ambiguity deeply frustrating, and would like nothing more than to leave the scene of the incident and go home.

As an IC, don't forget that motivating, encouraging, and keeping track of the general emotional state of your team are key factors in achieving a positive incident outcome. Here are some tips for maintaining morale in the midst of a crisis:

Eat

As your response team pushes itself to make progress, hunger will invariably strike. This decreases the team's effectiveness and can put people on edge. Plan in advance to take breaks and bring in food whenever possible. This helps keep the team happy and focused when you need them to be.

Sleep

The law of diminishing returns applies to humans, too. Your staff will become less effective over time as exhaustion sets in and each member passes their own peak fatigue point. After this point, it's possible that continued work will result in more mistakes than progress, setting the incident response back. Keep watch for fatigue in your responders, and be sure that they are allowed rest periods as needed. Leaders may even need to intervene to ensure that people who don't recognize their own need for rest still take breaks.

Destress

When the opportunity presents itself—for example, if the team is waiting for a file array to finish rebuilding and can't make parallel progress—gather everyone together for a destressing activity. Several years ago, during a particularly large and lengthy incident at Google, the response team took a one-hour break to smash a failed hard drive using a hammer and some liquid nitrogen. Years later, the team involved recalls that activity as a highlight of the response.

Watch for burnout

As an IC, you should actively watch for signs of burnout in your team (and yourself). Is a critical engineer starting to become more cynical and defeatist? Are staff expressing fears that the challenge is unwinnable? This may be the first time they've had to handle a major incident, and they may have a lot of fears. Talk with them frankly and make sure they understand your expectations and how they can meet those expectations. If a team member needs a break and you have someone to replace them, offer a relief period.

Lead by example

A realistic but positive outlook openly expressed by a leader goes a long way toward setting your team's expectations around their success. This kind of outlook encourages the team and makes them feel like they can achieve their goal. Additionally, members of a response team may be skeptical that taking time for self-care (e.g., eating and sleeping adequately) is truly encouraged until they see the IC or OL openly doing so as a best practice.

Communications

Of all the technical issues involved in incident response, communication remains the most challenging. Even in the best of circumstances, effective communication with coworkers and others outside your immediate group can be difficult. When subjected to stress, tight deadlines, and the high stakes of a security incident, these difficulties can intensify and quickly lead to a delayed or missed response. Here are a few major communications challenges you might encounter, and tips for managing them.

Many excellent books cover the topic of communications thoroughly. For a deeper understanding of communications, we recommend Nick Morgan's *Can You Hear Me?* (Harvard Business Review Press, 2018) and Alan Alda's *If I Understood You, Would I Have This Look on My Face?* (Random House, 2017).

Misunderstandings

Misunderstandings between the responders will likely make up the bulk of your communication problems. People who are used to working together may make assumptions about things that haven't been said. People who are not used to working together may use unfamiliar jargon, acronyms that mean different things to different teams, or assume a common frame of reference that isn't actually common.

For example, take the phrase "We can turn the service back on when the attack is mitigated." To the product team, this may mean that as soon as the attacker's tools are deleted, the system is safe to use. To the security team, this may mean that the system isn't safe to use until a complete investigation has concluded that the attacker is no longer able to exist in, or return to, the environment.

When you find yourself handling an incident, as a rule of thumb, it's helpful to always *be explicit and overcommunicate*. Explain what you mean when you ask for something or set an expectation, even if you think the other person ought to know what you mean. In the example from the previous paragraph, it couldn't hurt to say, "We can turn the service back on when we are confident that all paths back in have been fixed, and that the attacker is no longer able to access our systems." Keep in mind that the responsibility of communicating usually belongs to the communicator —only they can make sure the people they're communicating with receive the intended message.

Hedging

Hedging is another common communication mistake. When people are expected to give advice in a stressful situation but aren't feeling confident, they often tend to add qualifiers to their statements. Avoiding expressing certainty about an uncertain situation by saying something like "We're pretty sure we found all the malware" might feel safer, but hedging often muddies the situation and leads to uncertainty among decision makers. Again, being explicit and overcommunicating is the best remedy here. If your IC asks if you've identified all the attacker's tools, "We're pretty sure" is a weak answer. It would be better to answer, "We are sure about our servers, NAS, email, and file shares, but aren't feeling confident about our hosted systems because we have less log visibility there."

Meetings

To make progress on an incident, you'll need to get people together to coordinate their efforts. Regular, rapid syncs with key players in the incident response are a particularly effective way to maintain control and visibility of everything that's happening. The IC, the OL, a company attorney, and a few key executives might meet every two or four hours to make sure the team can quickly adapt to any new developments.

We recommend aggressively limiting attendees of these meetings. If you have a room or videoconference full of people, and only a handful are speaking while the rest listen or check email, your invite list is too large. Ideally, the incident leads should attend these meetings while everyone else works on tasks that need to be completed. Once the meeting ends, the leads can update their respective teams.

While meetings are often a necessary part of working together, improperly managed meetings risk derailing your progress. We strongly recommend that an IC open every meeting with a set agenda they've planned in advance. This may seem like an obvious step, but it can be easy to forget during the adrenaline rush and stress of an ongoing incident. Here's an example agenda used at Google for a security incident kickoff meeting:

1. [IC] Delegate one person to take notes.
2. [IC] All attendees introduce themselves, starting with the IC:
   a. Name
   b. Team
   c. Role
3. [IC] Rules of engagement:
   a. Do you need to take confidentiality into account?
   b. Are there specific operational security concerns to consider?
   c. Who owns making decisions? Who should be included in decision-making processes? Who should *not* be included?
   d. Let your lead know if you're switching tasks/finished doing something.
4. [IC] Describe current status: what problem are we solving?
5. [All] Discuss the issue.
6. [IC] Summarize actions and owners.
7. [IC] Ask the group:
   a. Are there any more resources we need?
   b. Are there any other groups we need to involve?
   c. What roadblocks are there?

8. [IC] Establish time of next sync meeting and expected attendance:

   a. Who is required?

   b. Who is optional?

And here's one for an in-progress sync meeting:

1. [IC] Delegate one person to take notes.

2. [IC or ops lead] Summarize current status.

3. [IC] Receive updates from each attendee/thread of activity.

4. [IC] Discuss next steps.

5. [Ops lead] Assign tasks, and get each person to repeat what they think they're going to do.

6. [IC] Establish time(s) of next meeting(s).

7. [Ops lead] Update action tracker.

In both example agendas, the IC assigns a note taker. Through experience, we've learned that a note taker is essential for keeping your investigation on track. Leads are busy dealing with all the issues that arise in the meeting and won't have the bandwidth to take good notes. During an incident, you often forget items you *think* you'll remember. These notes also become invaluable when writing your postmortem. Keep in mind that if the incident has any legal ramifications, you'll want to consult with your legal team on the best way to manage this information.

Keeping the Right People Informed with the Right Levels of Detail

Figuring out the right level of detail to communicate is a major challenge for incident communications. Multiple individuals at multiple levels will need to know *something* related to the incident, but for OpSec reasons, they likely cannot or should not know *all* the details. Be aware that employees who are only vaguely aware of the incident are likely to engage in gap-filling.[7] Rumors among employees can quickly become erroneous and damaging when relayed outside the organization.

A long-running investigation may involve frequent updates with different levels of detail to the following people:

Executives and senior leadership
    They should receive brief, succinct updates on progress, roadblocks, and potential consequences.

---

7 If an individual doesn't have access to the actual information, they're inclined to make something up.

The IR team
> This team requires up-to-date information about the investigation.

Organizational personnel not involved in the incident
> Your organization may need to decide what to tell personnel. If you tell all staff about the incident, you may be able to solicit their assistance. On the other hand, these people may spread information further than you intended. If you don't tell organizational personnel about an incident but they find out anyway, you may need to deal with the rumor mill.

Customers
> Customers may be legally entitled to be informed of the incident within a set period of time, or your organization may choose to voluntarily notify them. If a response involves shutting off services visible to customers, they may have questions and demand answers.

Legal/justice system participants
> If you escalated the incident to law enforcement, they may have questions and may begin requesting information you didn't originally intend to share.

To help manage all these demands without constantly distracting the IC, we recommend appointing a *communications lead* (CL). The core job of the CL is to stay informed about the incident as it unfolds and to prepare comms to the relevant stakeholders. The key responsibilities of the CL include the following:

- Working with sales, support, and other internal partner teams to answer any questions they may have.
- Preparing briefs for executives, legal, regulators, and others with oversight roles.
- Working with press and PR to ensure that people have the right information to make accurate and timely statements about the incident when necessary. Ensure that people outside of the response team don't make conflicting statements.
- Keeping constant and careful watch on the spread of information about the incident, so the incident staff respect any "need to know" guidelines.

The CL will want to consider reaching out to domain experts, external crisis communication consultants, or anyone else they need to help manage information related to the incident with minimal delay.

Putting It All Together

This section ties together the contents of this chapter by walking through a hypothetical response to a compromise that an organization of any size might encounter. Consider a scenario where an engineer discovers that a service account they don't recognize has been added to a cloud project they haven't seen before. At noon, they escalate their concerns to the security team. After a preliminary investigation, the security team determines that an engineer's account has likely been compromised. Using the advice and best practices presented earlier, let's walk through how you might respond to such a compromise from beginning to end.

Triage

The first step in your response is to triage. Start with a worst-case assumption: the security team's suspicions are correct that the engineer's account is compromised. An attacker using privileged access to view sensitive internal information and/or user data would be a serious security breach, so you declare an incident.

Declaring an Incident

As the incident commander, you notify the rest of the security team of the following:

- An incident has occurred.
- You will be assuming the role of IC.
- You'll need additional support from the team to investigate.

Communications and Operational Security

Now that you've declared the incident, other people in the organization—executives, legal, etc.—need to know an incident is in progress. If the attacker compromised your organization's infrastructure, emailing or chatting with these people may be risky. Follow operational security best practices. Suppose your contingency plan calls for using an organization credit card to register a business account in a cloud-based environment not associated with your organization, and to create accounts for each person involved in the incident. To create and connect to this environment, you use freshly rebuilt laptops not connected to your organization's management infrastructure.

Using this new environment, you call your executives and key legal staff to advise them on how to obtain a secure laptop and a cloud account so they can participate via email and chats. Since all the current responders are local to the office, you use a nearby meeting room to discuss the particulars of the incident.

Beginning the Incident

As the IC, you need to assign engineers to investigate, so you ask an engineer on the security team with forensics experience to be the operations lead. Your new OL starts their forensic investigation immediately and recruits other engineers as needed. They begin by collecting logs from the cloud environment, focusing on the time period when the service account credentials in question were added. After confirming that the credentials were added by the engineer's account during a time period when the engineer was definitely out of the office, the forensics team concludes that the account has been compromised.

The forensics team now pivots from investigating only the suspect account to investigating all other activities around the time the account was added. The team decides to collect all the system logs relating to the compromised account, as well as that engineer's laptop and workstation. The team determines that this investigation could take a single analyst quite some time, so they decide to add more staff and distribute the effort.

Your organization doesn't have a large security team, so you don't have enough skilled forensic analysts to adequately distribute the forensic task. However, you do have system administrators who understand their systems well and who can help analyze logs. You decide to assign these sysadmins to the forensics team. Your OL contacts them via email with a request to "discuss a few things" over a phone call, and briefs them fully during that call. The OL asks the sysadmins to collect all logs related to the compromised account from any system in the organization, while the forensics team analyzes the laptop and desktop.

By 5 p.m. it's clear that the investigation is going to last much longer than your team can continue working. As the IC, you correctly anticipate that your team will become fatigued and start to make mistakes before they can resolve the incident, so you need to come up with a handover or continuity plan. You notify your team that they have four hours to complete as much analysis of the logs and hosts as possible. During this time, you keep leadership and legal up to date and check in with the OL to see if their team needs additional help.

At the 9 p.m. team sync, the OL reveals that their team has found the attacker's initial entry point: a very well-crafted phishing email to the engineer, who was tricked into running a command that downloads the attacker's backdoor and establishes a persistent remote connection.

Handover

By the 9 p.m. team sync, many of the engineers working on the problem have been at work for 12 hours or longer. As a diligent IC, you know that continuing to work at this pace is risky, and that the incident will require a lot more effort. You decide to hand off some of the work. While your organization doesn't have a full security team outside of the main San Francisco office, you have an engineering office in London with some senior staff.

You tell your team to take the next hour to finish documenting their findings while you contact the London team. A senior engineer in the London office is appointed as the next IC. As the outgoing IC, you brief the replacement IC on everything you've learned so far. After receiving ownership rights on all the incident-related documentation and making sure that the London team understands the next step, the London IC acknowledges that they are in charge until 9:00 PST the next morning. The San Francisco team is relieved and sent home to rest. Overnight, the London team continues the investigation, focusing on analyzing the backdoor scripts and actions performed by the attacker.

Handing Back the Incident

At 9:00 the next morning, the San Francisco and London teams hold a handover sync. Overnight, the London team made lots of progress. They determined that the script run on the compromised workstation installed a simple backdoor, enabling the attacker to log in from a remote machine and start looking around the system. Noticing that the engineer's shell history included logins to cloud service accounts, the adversary took advantage of the saved credentials and added their own service account key to the list of administrative tokens.

After doing so, they took no further action on the workstation. Instead, cloud service logs show that the attacker interacted directly with the service APIs. They uploaded a new machine image and launched dozens of copies of that virtual machine in a new cloud project. The London team hasn't yet analyzed any of the running images, but they audited all credentials in all existing projects and confirmed that the malicious service account and API tokens they know about are the only credentials that can't be verified as legitimate.

With this update from the London team, you acknowledge the new information and confirm that you are taking over as the IC. Next, you distill the new information and provide a concise update to executive leaders and legal. You also brief your team on the new findings.

Although you know that the attacker had administrative access to production services, you don't yet know whether user data was at risk or affected. You give your forensics team a new high-priority task: look at all other actions the attacker may have taken against existing production machines.

Preparing Communications and Remediation

As your investigation proceeds, you decide that it's time to parallelize a few more components of your incident response. If the attacker potentially accessed your organization's user data, you may need to inform users. You also need to mitigate the attack. You choose a colleague who is a strong technical writer to be the communications lead (CL). You ask one of the system admins who isn't working on forensics to become the remediation lead (RL).

In collaboration with the organization's attorney, the CL drafts a blog post that explains what happened and the potential customer impact. Although there are many blanks (such as "*<fill this in>* data was *<fill this in>*"), having the structure ready and approved ahead of time helps you to communicate your message much faster when you know the full details.

Meanwhile, the RL makes a list of every resource the organization knows to have been affected by the attacker, along with proposals for how to clean up each resource. Even if you know that the engineer's password wasn't exposed in the initial phishing email, you'll need to change their account credentials. To be on the safe side, you decide to guard against backdoors that you haven't yet found but that may appear later. You make a copy of the engineer's important data and then erase their home directory, creating a new one on a freshly installed workstation.

As your response progresses, your team learns that the attacker didn't access any production data—to everyone's great relief! The additional VMs the attacker launched appear to be a swarm of coin mining servers that mine digital currency and direct the funds to the attacker's virtual wallet. Your RL notes that you can delete these machines, or you can snapshot and archive the machines if you wish to report the incident to law enforcement later on. You can also delete the project the machines were created in.

Closure

Around mid-afternoon, your team has run out of leads. They've searched every resource the malicious API keys may have touched, built their mitigation document, and confirmed that the attacker didn't touch any sensitive data. Fortunately, this was an opportunistic coin mining exercise and the attacker wasn't interested in any of your data—just a lot of compute capability on someone else's bill. Your team decides that it's time to execute your remediation plan. After checking in with legal and leadership to ensure that the decision to close out the incident has their approval, you signal the team that it's time to act.

Freed from their forensic tasks, the operations team now divides up the tasks from the remediation plan and completes them as quickly as possible, ensuring that the attacker is shut off quickly and completely. They then spend the rest of the afternoon writing down their observations for a postmortem. Finally, you (the IC) hold an outbrief, where everyone on the team has the opportunity to discuss how the incident went. You clearly communicate that the incident is closed and no longer requires an emergency response. Your last task before everyone goes home to rest is to brief the London team so they also know that the incident is completed.

Conclusion

Incident management, when scaled, becomes its own art that is distinct and separate from general project management and smaller incident response work. By focusing on processes, tools, and proper organizational structures, it's possible to staff a team that can effectively respond to any crisis at the speed today's market requires. Whether you're a small organization whose engineers and core team become a temporary response team as needed, a giant-scale organization with response teams across the globe, or anything in between, you can apply the best practices described in this chapter to effectively and efficiently respond to a security compromise. Parallelizing your incident response and forensic work and professionally managing the team using ICS/IMAG will help you respond scalably and reliably to any incidents that arise.

CHAPTER 18

Recovery and Aftermath

*By Alex Perry, Gary O'Connor, and Heather Adkins
with Nick Soda*

To avoid service disruptions for your users, you need to be able to quickly recover from security- and reliability-related incidents. However, there's a key difference when you are recovering from a security incident: your attacker. A persistent attacker can leverage ongoing access to your environment or reengage at any moment, even while you're executing a recovery.

In this chapter, we take a deep dive into what people designing, implementing, and maintaining systems need to know about recovering from attacks. The people performing recovery efforts often aren't security professionals—they're the people who build the affected systems and operate them every day. The lessons and examples in this chapter highlight how to keep your attacker at bay while you're recovering. We walk through the logistics, timeline, planning, and initiation of the recovery phases. We also discuss key tradeoffs, like when to disrupt an attacker's activity versus allowing them to remain on your systems so you can learn more about them.

If your organization experiences a serious incident, will you know how to recover? Who performs that recovery, and do they know what decisions to make? Chapter 17 of the SRE book and Chapter 9 of the SRE workbook discuss practices for preventing and managing service outages. Many of those practices are also relevant to security, but recovering from security attacks has unique elements—particularly when the incident involves an active malicious attacker (see Chapter 2). For this reason, while this chapter provides a general outline for handling many kinds of recovery efforts, we place a particular emphasis on what recovery engineers need to know about security attacks.

As we discuss in Chapters 8 and 9, systems built according to good design principles can be resilient against attack and easily recoverable. This is true whether the system is a single compute instance, a distributed system, or a complex multitiered application. To facilitate recovery, a well-built system must also be integrated with crisis management tactics. As discussed in the previous chapter, effective crisis management entails a delicate balance between continuing to deter an attacker while restoring any injured assets to a known (potentially improved) good state. This chapter describes the nuanced considerations that good recovery checklists incorporate to achieve these goals.

In our experience, recovery engineers are often the people who design, implement, and maintain these systems every day. During an attack, you may need to call in security specialists for particular roles, such as performing forensic activities, triaging security vulnerabilities, or making nuanced decisions (see Chapter 17), but recovering systems to a known good state requires the expertise that comes from working with the system every day. A partnership between incident coordination and recovery efforts allows security specialists and recovery engineers to bidirectionally share information to restore the system.

Recovering from security attacks often involves a far more ambiguous environment than preplanned playbooks can accommodate.[1] An attacker can change their behavior mid-attack, and recovery engineers can make mistakes or discover unanticipated characteristics or details about their systems. This chapter presents a dynamic approach to recovery that aims to match the flexibility of your attacker.

The act of recovery can also be a powerful tool to jump-start improvements to your security posture. Recovery takes the form of both short-term tactical mitigations and long-term strategic improvements. We close this chapter with some ways to think about the continuum between a security incident, recovery, and the quiet period before the next incident.

Recovery Logistics

As discussed in the previous chapter, a well-managed incident benefits from a parallelized response. Parallelization is especially beneficial during recovery. The individuals working on the recovery effort should be different from the people investigating the incident, for several reasons:

---

1 The topic of recovery from security incidents is well covered in many resources, such as NIST SP 800-184 (*https://oreil.ly/7N8mr*), the Guide for Cybersecurity Event Recovery. The NIST guide emphasizes the need to plan ahead by creating robust recovery checklists for all types of anticipated events well in advance of an event. It also provides instructions on testing these plans. It is a good general reference, but you may find that implementing its rigid advice during a time of crisis proves challenging.

- The investigation phase of an incident is often time-consuming and detailed, requiring focus for long periods of time. During prolonged incidents, investigation teams often need a break by the time the recovery effort begins.

- The recovery phase of an incident may begin while your investigation is still ongoing. As a result, you'll need separate teams that can work in parallel, feeding information to each other.

- The skills required for performing the investigation may be different from the skills required for the recovery effort.

When preparing for a recovery and considering your options, you should have a formalized team structure in place. Depending on the scope of the incident, this team can be as small as a single individual or as large as your whole organization. For more complicated incidents, we recommend creating coordination mechanisms like formal teams, frequent meetings, shared documentation repositories, and peer reviews. Many organizations model recovery team operations on their existing Agile development processes by using sprints, Scrum teams, and tight feedback loops.

On Roles and Responsibilities

The topics we cover in this chapter are applicable to organizations of all sizes, from a few people working on an open source project to small businesses and large companies. While we often refer to teams and formalized roles, these concepts are adaptable to any scale.

For example, when we discuss setting up a formalized team structure, that structure could be an internal team of employees who each agree to take on one or more roles, or you could adapt the model by outsourcing some aspects of recovery to a third party—for example, by hiring a contractor to rebuild a system. Since recovery efforts often involve many parts of an organization, some of which may not normally handle crisis response, adaptability is especially important.

A well-organized recovery from a complex incident may look like a carefully choreographed ballet performance,[2] with the actions of different individuals working on the recovery all affecting each other. It's important that the dancers in the recovery ballet avoid stepping on one another's feet. As such, you should clearly define roles for preparing, reviewing, and executing your recovery, making sure that everyone understands the operational risks and that participants communicate face-to-face frequently.

---

2 Or a *Three Stooges* sketch if you don't have a well-documented plan!

As the incident progresses, the incident commander (IC) and operations lead (OL) should appoint a remediation lead (RL) to begin planning the recovery, as described in Chapter 17. The RL should coordinate closely with the IC on a recovery checklist to ensure that the recovery effort aligns with the rest of the investigation. The RL is also responsible for assembling a team of individuals with relevant expertise and building out the recovery checklist (discussed in "Recovery Checklists" on page 428).

At Google, the teams that perform recovery are the teams that build and run the systems day to day. These individuals include SREs, developers, system administrators, helpdesk personnel, and relevant security specialists that manage routine processes like code audits and configuration reviews.

Information management and communication during recovery are vital components of a successful response. Raw incident trails, scratch notes, recovery checklists, new operational documentation, and information about the attack itself will be important artifacts. Be sure that this documentation is available to recovery teams but inaccessible to the attacker; use something like an air-gapped computer for storage. For example, you might use a combination of information management tools like bug tracking systems, cloud-based collaboration tools, whiteboards, and even notecards taped to a wall. Make sure those tools are outside the broadest potential scope of the attacker's compromise of your systems. Consider starting with notecards, and adding an independent service provider once you're sure no recovery team members' machines are compromised.

Good information management is another key aspect of ensuring a smooth recovery. Use resources that everyone can access and update in real time as issues arise or as checklist items are completed. If your recovery plan is only accessible to your remediation lead, this will be a roadblock to fast execution.

As you restore your systems, it's also important to keep reliable notes about what happened during recovery. If you make a mistake along the way, your audit trail will help you fix any issues. Assigning dedicated note takers or documentation specialists can be a good idea. At Google, we leverage technical writers to optimize information management during our recovery efforts. We recommend reading Chapter 21, which discusses further organizational aspects.

Recovery Timeline

The best time to start the recovery phase of an incident varies greatly depending on the nature of the investigation. If the affected infrastructure is mission-critical, you may choose to recover from an attack almost immediately. This is often the case when recovering from denial-of-service attacks. Alternatively, if your incident involves an attacker who has full control of your infrastructure, you may begin planning recovery almost immediately but execute the plan only when you fully understand what the attacker has done. The recovery processes we discuss in this chapter apply to any recovery timeline: while the investigation is still ongoing, after the investigation phase of an incident concludes, or during both of these phases.

Having enough information about the incident and understanding the scope of the recovery will inform which route to take. Typically, by the time you spin up a recovery operation, the investigation team has begun a postmortem document (perhaps in the form of preliminary raw notes), which the recovery team updates as they proceed. The information in this document will inform the recovery team's planning phase (see "Planning the Recovery" on page 421), which should be completed before initiating the recovery (see "Initiating the Recovery" on page 429).

As the initial plan may evolve over time, planning for and executing the recovery may overlap. However, *you shouldn't begin recovery efforts without some sort of plan*. Likewise, we recommend creating recovery checklists before proceeding with your recovery. Your post-recovery actions (see "After the Recovery" on page 435) should begin as soon as the recovery effort is complete. Allowing too much time to lapse between these two phases can lead you to forget the details of your earlier actions, or postpone work on necessary medium- and long-term fixes.

Planning the Recovery

The goal of your recovery effort is to mitigate an attack and return your systems to their normal routine state, applying any necessary improvements along the way. Complex security events often require parallelizing incident management and setting up structured teams to execute on different parts of the incident.

The recovery planning process will rely on the information the investigation team discovers, and it's important that you carefully plan your recovery before you take action. In these cases, you should begin planning for recovery as soon as you have sufficient baseline information about what the attacker has done. The following sections describe some preparation best practices and common pitfalls to avoid.

Scoping the Recovery

How you define recovery for your incident will vary depending on the type of attack you've encountered. For example, it may be relatively straightforward to recover from a minor issue such as ransomware on a single machine: you simply reinstall the system. However, you'll need a combination of multiple recovery strategies and skill sets from across your organization to recover from a nation-state actor with presence across your whole network who has exfiltrated sensitive data. Keep in mind that the effort required for recovery may not be proportional to the severity or sophistication of the attack. An organization unprepared for a simple ransomware attack may end up with many compromised machines and need to mount a resource-intensive recovery effort.

To initiate recovery from a security incident, your recovery team needs to have a complete list of the systems, networks, and data affected by the attack. They also need sufficient information about the attacker's tactics, techniques, and procedures (TTPs) to identify any related resources that may be impacted. For example, if your recovery team discovers that a configuration distribution system has been compromised, this system is in scope for recovery. Any systems that received configurations from this system may also be in scope. The investigation team therefore needs to determine if the attacker modified any configurations, and whether those configs were pushed to other systems.

As mentioned in Chapter 17, ideally, the IC assigns someone to maintain action items in a mitigation doc for a formal postmortem (discussed in "Postmortems" on page 436) early in the investigation. The mitigation doc and subsequent postmortem will identify steps to address the root cause of the compromise. You need enough information to prioritize action items and classify them as either short-term mitigations (such as patching known vulnerabilities) or strategic long-term changes (such as changing build processes to prevent use of vulnerable libraries).

To understand how to protect these assets in the future, you should examine each directly or indirectly impacted asset in conjunction with your attacker's behaviors. For example, if your attacker was able to exploit a vulnerable software stack on a web server, your recovery will require understanding the attack so you can patch the hole in any other systems running the package. Similarly, if your attacker gained access by phishing the account credentials of a user, your recovery team needs to plan a way to stop another attacker from doing the same thing tomorrow. Take care to understand what assets an attacker may be able to leverage for a future attack. You might consider making a list of the attacker's behaviors and possible defenses for your recovery effort, as we did in Chapter 2 (see Table 2-3). You can use this list as operational documentation to explain why you're introducing certain new defenses.

Assembling a list of compromised assets and short-term mitigations requires a tight loop of communication and feedback involving your postmortem notes, the investigation teams, and the incident commander. Your recovery team will need to learn about new investigation findings as soon as possible. Without efficient exchange of information between the investigation and recovery teams, attackers can bypass mitigation efforts. Your recovery plan should also make room for the possibility that your attacker is still present and watching your actions.

Recovery Considerations

As you're designing the recovery phase of the incident, you may run into several open-ended questions that are difficult to answer. This section covers some common pitfalls and ideas about how you can balance trade-offs. These principles will feel familiar to security specialists who often handle complex incidents, but the information is relevant to anyone participating in recovery efforts. Before you make a decision, ask yourself the following questions.

How will your attacker respond to your recovery effort?

Your mitigation and recovery checklist (see "Recovery Checklists" on page 428 and "Examples" on page 437) will include severing any connection your attacker has to your resources and ensuring they can't return. Implementing this step is a delicate balancing act requiring near-perfect knowledge of the attack and a solid plan to execute the ejection. A mistake can lead to your attacker taking additional actions that you may not anticipate or have visibility into.

Consider this example: during an incident, your investigation team discovers that an attacker has compromised six systems, but the team can't determine how that initial attack began. It's even unclear how your attacker got access to any of your systems in the first place. Your recovery team creates and enacts a plan to rebuild those six compromised systems. In this scenario, the recovery team is acting without full knowledge of how the attack began, how the attacker will respond, or whether the attacker is still active on other systems. An attacker who is still active will be able to see from their position in another compromised system that you've taken those six systems offline, and may proceed to destroy the rest of the infrastructure that remains accessible.

In addition to compromising your systems, attackers can also eavesdrop on email, bug tracking systems, code changes, calendars, and other resources that you'll probably want to use to coordinate your recovery. Depending on the severity of the incident and the type of compromise you're recovering from, you may want to conduct your investigation and recovery using systems that aren't visible to the attacker.

Consider a recovery team that's coordinating over an instant messaging system while one of the team member's accounts is compromised. The attacker, who is also logged in and watching the chat, can see all the private communications while recovery is happening—including any known elements of the investigation. The attacker might even be able to infer information the recovery team doesn't know. Your attacker might use this knowledge to compromise even more systems in a different way, bypassing all visibility the investigation team may have. In this scenario, the recovery team should have set up a new instant messaging system and deployed new machines —for example, inexpensive Chromebooks—for responder communication.

These examples may seem extreme, but they illustrate a very simple point: there's a human on the other side of the attack who is reacting to your incident response. Your recovery plan should consider what actions that human may take after learning of your plans. You should seek to fully understand the attacker's access and take action to minimize the risk of further harm.

 Today, security incident responders generally agree that you should wait until you have a full understanding of an attack before ejecting the attacker. This prevents the attacker from observing your mitigations and helps you to respond defensively.

While this is good advice, apply it carefully. If your attacker is doing something dangerous already (such as taking sensitive data or destroying systems), you may choose to act before you have a complete picture of their actions. If you choose to eject the attacker before you have full knowledge of their intent and the scope of the attack, you're entering into a game of chess. Prepare accordingly, and know the steps you need to take to reach checkmate!

If you're handling a complex incident, or if an active attacker is interacting with your systems, your recovery plan should include tight integration with the investigation team to ensure that the attacker is not regaining access to your systems or working around your mitigations. Make sure to inform the investigation team of your recovery plans—they should be confident that your plans will stop the attack.

Is your recovery infrastructure or tooling compromised?

In the early stages of recovery planning, it's important to determine what infrastructure and tooling you need to conduct your response and ask your investigation team whether they believe these recovery systems are compromised. Their answer will determine whether or not you can perform a safe recovery, and what additional remediation steps you may need to prepare for a more complete response.

For example, imagine that an attacker has compromised several laptops on your network and the configuration server that governs their setup. In this case, you need a remediation plan for the configuration server before you can rebuild any compromised laptops. Similarly, if an attacker has introduced malicious code into your custom backup restoration tool, you need to find their changes and restore the code to normal before recovering any data.

More importantly, you must consider how you will recover assets—whether systems, applications, networks, or data—that are located on infrastructure currently under the attacker's control. Recovering an asset while the attacker has control of the infrastructure can lead to a repeat compromise from the same attacker. A common recovery pattern in these situations is to set up a "clean" or "safe" version of the asset, such as a clean network or system, that's isolated from any compromised versions. This may mean completely replicating your entire infrastructure, or at least key parts of it.

To return to our example of a compromised configuration server, you may choose to create a quarantined network and rebuild this system with a fresh operating system install. You can then manually configure the system so that you can bootstrap new machines from it without introducing any attacker-controlled configurations.

What variants of the attack exist?

Suppose your investigation team reports that an attacker has exploited a buffer over-flow vulnerability against your web serving infrastructure. While the attacker gained access to only a single system, you know that 20 other servers are running the same flawed software. When planning your recovery, you should address the one system that's known to be compromised, but also consider two other factors: whether the other 20 servers are also compromised, and how you will mitigate the effects of the vulnerability for all of these machines in the future.

Repeating Risks

Imagine that a large ship needs to hold its position at sea. The ship drops anchor and inadvertently hooks onto an undersea cable, which isn't strong enough and breaks. While the risk of a vessel snagging an undersea cable is small, the effects can be cata-strophic, having a huge impact on intercontinental network capacity—and this risk exists for all the undersea cables in the world, not just the one that happened to have been hooked by that one errant ship. A network outage of this type should trigger an analysis of the broader category of risk. For example, future capacity planning should incorporate this newly discovered category of outages to ensure sufficient redundant capacity.

It's also worth considering if your systems are susceptible (in the short term) to varia-tions of the type of attack that you're currently experiencing. In the buffer overflow example, your recovery planning should look for any related software vulnerabilities in the infrastructure—either a related vulnerability class, or the same vulnerability in another piece of software. This consideration is especially important in custom-built code or where you're using shared libraries. We cover several options for testing for variants, such as fuzzing, in Chapter 13.

If you're using open source or commercial software and testing variants is beyond your control, hopefully the people who maintain the software have themselves con-sidered possible attack variants and implemented the necessary protections. It's worth checking for available patches for other parts of your software stack and including a broad series of upgrades as part of your recovery.

Will your recovery reintroduce attack vectors?

Many recovery methods seek to restore affected resources to a known good state. This effort may rely on system images, source code stored in repositories, or configurations. A key consideration for your recovery should be whether your recovery actions will reintroduce attack vectors that make your system vulnerable, or regress any durability or safety progress you have made. Consider a system image that contains vulnerable software allowing an attacker to compromise the system. If you reuse this system image during recovery, you will reintroduce the vulnerable software.

This form of vulnerability reintroduction is a common pitfall in many environments —including modern cloud computing and on-premise environments—that rely on "golden images" that commonly consist of whole system snapshots. It's important to update these golden images and delete compromised snapshots before the systems come back online, either at the source or immediately after install.

If your attacker was able to modify parts of your recovery infrastructure (for example, the configurations stored in a source code repository), and you restore the system using these compromised settings, you'll set your recovery back by persisting the attacker's changes. Restoring your system to a good state may require going far back in time to avoid such a regression. This also means you'll need to think carefully about the attack timeline: when did the attacker make modifications, and how far back do you need to go to revert their changes? If you can't determine the exact time the attacker made a modification, you may need to rebuild large parts of your infrastructure in parallel from scratch.

When recovering systems or data from traditional backups (such as tape backups), you should consider whether your system also backed up your attacker's modifications. You should either destroy or quarantine any backups or data snapshots that contain evidence of your attacker for later analysis.

What are your mitigation options?

Following good practices for resilient design in your systems (see Chapter 9) can help you to recover quickly from security incidents. If your service is a distributed system (as opposed to a monolithic binary), you can apply security fixes to individual modules relatively quickly and easily: you can perform an "in-place" update to a flawed module without introducing significant risk to the surrounding modules. Similarly, in cloud computing environments, you can establish mechanisms to shut down compromised containers or virtual machines and rapidly replace them with known good versions.

However, depending on the assets that your attacker has compromised (such as machines, printers, cameras, data, and accounts), you may find that you are left with a number of less than ideal mitigation choices. You might have to decide which option is the least bad, and incur varying degrees of technical debt for the short-term gain of permanently ejecting the attacker from your systems. For example, to block an attacker's access, you may choose to manually add a deny rule to the live configuration of a router. To prevent the attacker from seeing the change you're making, you might bypass normal procedures for having such changes peer reviewed and tracked in a version control system. In this situation, you should disable automatic rule pushes until you add the new firewall rules to the canonical version of the configuration. You should also set a reminder to reenable those automatic rule pushes at some point in the future.

When deciding whether to accept technical debt during your short-term mitigations to eject the attacker, ask yourself the following questions:

- How quickly (and when) can we replace or remove these short-term mitigations? In other words, how long will this technical debt be in place?

- Is the organization committed to maintaining the mitigation for the duration of its lifetime? Are the teams that own the new technical debt willing to accept that debt and pay it off later, through improvements?

- Will the mitigation affect the uptime of our systems, and will we exceed our error budgets?[3]

- How can people in the organization recognize this mitigation as short term? Consider tagging the mitigation as technical debt to be removed later so that its status is visible to anyone else working on the system. For example, add comments to code and descriptive commit or push messages so that anyone who relies on the new functionality knows it might change or disappear in the future.

- How can a future engineer with no domain expertise regarding the incident prove that the mitigation is no longer necessary, and that they can remove it without creating risk?

- How effective will the short-term mitigation be if left in place for a long time (either accidentally or through circumstance)? Imagine an attacker has compromised one of your databases. You decide to keep the database online while you sanitize and migrate the data to a new system. Your short-term mitigation is to isolate the database on a separate network. Ask yourself: What will the effect be if that migration takes six months instead of the intended two weeks? Will people in the organization forget that the database was compromised and accidently reconnect it to safe networks?

---

3 Error budgets are described in Chapter 3 of the SRE book.

- Has a domain expert identified the loopholes in your answers to the preceding questions?

Recovery Checklists

Once you've figured out the scope of the recovery, you should lay out your options (as discussed in "Initiating the Recovery" on page 429) and carefully consider the trade-offs you need to make. This information forms the basis of your recovery checklist (or several checklists, depending on the complexity of your incident). Every recovery effort you make should leverage routine and tested practices. Thoroughly documenting and sharing your recovery steps makes it easier for the people involved in the incident response to collaborate and advise on the recovery plan. A well-documented checklist also enables your recovery team to identify areas of effort that you can parallelize and helps you coordinate the work.

As shown in the template recovery checklist in Figure 18-1, each item on the checklist maps to an individual task and the corresponding skills required for its completion.[4] Individuals on your recovery team can claim tasks based on their skills. The incident commander can then be confident that all checked-off recovery steps have been completed.

Your checklist should contain all the relevant details, such as specific tools and commands to use for the recovery. That way, when you start your cleanup efforts, all the team members will have clear, agreed-upon guidance about what tasks need to be completed, and in what order. The checklist should also account for any cleanup steps or rollback procedures you'll need in case the plan fails. We'll use the template checklist in Figure 18-1 in the worked examples at the end of the chapter.

---

4 How you implement a "hands off keyboard" briefing is up to you, but the main thrust of the exercise is to have the full attention and participation of the audience. During an incident, it can be tempting for responders to constantly keep an eye on running scripts or status dashboards. To execute nuanced and complex recovery, it's important to have everyone's full attention during briefings so everyone is on the same page.

INSTRUCTIONS:

- Highlight in GREEN when COMPLETED.
- Highlight in ORANGE TO-DO items.
- Highlight in RED if task cannot be completed; it must be replaced with an equivalent action.
- Highlight in BLUE if task will not be completed because it is operationally risky and we need to make adjustments.

Incident commander

- Give a "hands off keyboards" briefing.
- Provide an overview of tasks and constraints.
- Notify everyone involved of the exact time remediation will begin.

In order of operations, the remediation lead initiates execution of the following:

1. [Team name #1]: Description of task
   a. Detailed commands or steps
2. [Team name #2]: Description of task
   a. Detailed commands or steps
3. [Team name #3]: Description of task
   a. Detailed commands or steps
4. [Team name #4]: Description of task
   a. Detailed commands or steps

Figure 18-1. Checklist template

Initiating the Recovery

After a security incident, the safe and reliable recovery of your system relies heavily on effective processes, such as carefully constructed checklists. Depending on the type of incident you are managing, you will need to consider effective technical options. The goal of your mitigation and recovery effort is to eject the attacker from your environment, ensure they can't return, and make your system more secure. Chapter 9 covers principles for designing recovery options into a system ahead of time. This section covers the practical realities of executing recovery with these principles in mind, and the pros and cons of making certain decisions.

Isolating Assets (Quarantine)

Isolation (also referred to as a *quarantine*) is a very common technique for mitigating the effects of an attack. A classic example is antivirus software that moves a malicious binary into a quarantine folder, where file permissions prevent anything else on the system from reading or executing the binary. Quarantine is also commonly used to isolate a single compromised host. You can quarantine a host either at the network level (for example, by disabling the switch port) or on the host itself (for example, by disabling networking). You can even quarantine entire networks of compromised machines using network segmentation—many DoS response strategies move services away from affected networks.

> ## BeyondCorp
>
> At Google, the Zero Trust concept of our BeyondCorp architecture (*https://oreil.ly/jGrvI*) lets us easily mitigate incidents by using isolation. By default, architectures like BeyondCorp amplify quarantine and isolation techniques during attack mitigation.
>
> BeyondCorp mandates that we trust assets only after we've validated their security posture and they're approved to talk to corporate services. As a result, there is little trust between assets. This creates a natural isolation boundary that prevents common attacker techniques like *lateral movement* (the movement between two machines on the network). Access to services is well defined via proxy infrastructure and strong credentials, which can be revoked at any time.

Isolating assets can also be useful if you need to leave compromised infrastructure running. Consider a scenario in which one of your critical databases has been compromised. Because of its importance, you need to keep the database online during mitigation—perhaps this database is mission-critical and will take several weeks to rebuild, and your organization doesn't want to shut down its entire business for that long. You may be able to curtail the attacker's influence by isolating the database on a network of its own and placing restrictions on what network traffic it can send and receive (to/from the internet and to the rest of your infrastructure).

A word of warning: leaving compromised assets online is a pernicious form of technical debt. If you don't address this debt in a timely fashion and leave them online for longer than intended, these compromised assets can incur substantial damage. This may happen for several reasons: because this is the only copy of the quarantined data (no backups), because there are challenges to replacing the quarantined asset, or because people simply forget about the compromised assets during the hustle and bustle of an incident. In a worst-case scenario, someone new to your organization (or the incident) may even unquarantine a compromised resource!

Consider ways you can mark these assets as compromised, such as using highly visible stickers on the devices, or keeping an up-to-date list of MAC addresses of quarantined systems and monitoring for whether these addresses appear on your network. Stickers proactively aim to avoid reuse, while the address list enables fast reactive removal. Be sure your recovery checklist and postmortem cover whether any quarantined assets are safely and permanently remediated.

System Rebuilds and Software Upgrades

Consider the following conundrum: you've discovered an attacker's malware on three systems and are entering into the recovery phase of the incident. To eject the attacker, do you delete the malware and leave the systems running, or do you reinstall the systems? Depending on the complexity and criticality of your systems, you may have to consider the tradeoffs between these options. On the one hand, if the affected systems are mission-critical and difficult to rebuild, you may be tempted to delete the attacker's malware and move on. On the other hand, if the attacker has installed multiple types of malware and you don't know about all of them, you may end up missing the opportunity for a comprehensive cleanup. Typically, reinstalling systems from scratch with known good images and software is the best solution.[5]

If you've operated your environment using reliable and secure design principles, rebuilding your systems or upgrading software should be relatively straightforward. Chapter 9 provides some tips on knowing the state of your system, including host management and firmware.

For example, if you're using a system with hardware-backed boot verification that follows a cryptographic chain of trust up through the operating system and applications (Chromebooks are a good example), then restoring your systems is simply a matter of power cycling, which returns the system to a known good state. Automated release systems like Rapid (as discussed in Chapter 8 of the SRE book) can also provide a reliable and predictable way to apply software updates during recovery. In cloud computing environments, you can rely on instantaneous container and software releases to replace any compromised systems with a safe standard image.

If you are entering the recovery phase of an incident without mechanisms like source code control systems, or standard system images to manage configurations or systems using known good versions, consider introducing such mechanisms as part of your short-term recovery plan. There are open source options for managing system builds, such as Bazel (*https://bazel.info*); configurations, such as Chef (*https://chef.io*); and application integration and deployment, such as Helm (*https://helm.sh*) for Kubernetes. Adopting new solutions in a short time frame may seem daunting at first, and when setting up these solutions, you may need to make a rough first pass at the correct configuration. If figuring out the right configuration will entail time and effort at the expense of other important technical work, you may need to refine your configuration later. Make sure you carefully consider the technical debt you're accumulating in exchange for short-term security wins, and have a plan to improve the setup of such new systems.

Data Sanitization

Depending on the scope of your incident, you should confirm that your attacker hasn't tampered with your source code, binaries, images, and configurations, or the

---

5 Depending on the sophistication of the attacker and depth of the attack, you may need to consider reinstalling the BIOS and reformatting the hard drive, or even replacing the physical hardware. Recovery from UEFI rootkits, for example, can be hard, as described in the ESET Research whitepaper on LoJax (*https://oreil.ly/ ZxFQj*).

systems you use to build, manage, or release them. One common technique for sanitizing your system ecosystem is to obtain known good copies from their original source (such as open source or commercial software providers), backups, or uncompromised version control systems. Once you have a known good copy, you can perform checksum comparisons of the versions you want to use against known good states and packages. If your old good copies are hosted on compromised infrastructure, make sure you have high confidence that you know when the attacker began tampering with your systems, and be sure to review your data sources.

Strong binary provenance of where your code comes from (as discussed in Chapter 14) makes recovery more straightforward. Imagine that you discover your attacker has introduced malicious code into the glibc library used on your build system. You need to identify all the binaries built during the "at risk" time frame, where those binaries were deployed, and any dependencies they have. When performing this examination, clearly mark the known compromised code, libraries, and binaries. You should also create tests that will prevent you from reintroducing vulnerable or backdoored code. These precautions will ensure that others on your recovery team don't inadvertently use compromised code during the recovery or accidently reintroduce vulnerable versions.

You should also check to see if your attacker tampered with any application-level data, such as records in a database. As discussed in Chapter 9, ensuring strong cryptographic integrity of your backups increases your confidence in those backups, and allows you to be sure that any comparisons you need to make against potentially compromised live data are accurate. Reconciling changes made by an attacker may also be quite complex and require you to build special tooling. For example, in order to make use of partial restore, you may need custom tools to splice files or records obtained from backups into your production systems, while also performing a simultaneous integrity check. Ideally, you should build and test these tools when developing your reliability strategy.

Recovery Data

Recovery processes often rely on tools that support a range of operations, such as rollbacks, restores, backups, hermetic rebuilds, and transaction playbacks. "Persistent data" on page 208 discusses securely storing data used for these operations.

Many of these tools have parameters that trade speed of progress against data safety. We don't recommend changing those parameters from their defaults unless the tools are regularly tested against realistic production-scale workloads. Testing, staging, or (even worse) mocks do not exercise infrastructure systems realistically. For example, it's difficult to realistically simulate the delay it takes for memory caches to fill up or for load-balancing estimators to stabilize outside of realistic production conditions. Those parameters vary by service, and since the delay is usually visible in monitoring data, you should tune those settings between incidents. Dealing with a tool that misbehaves when you're trying to recover from a hostile security attack is as challenging as facing a new attacker.

You may already have monitoring in place to detect significant data loss due to software errors. It's also possible that your attacker avoided triggering these alerts. Even so, it's always worth reviewing these logs: the data may identify an inflection point where an attack started. If the metrics reveal such a point, you now have an independent lower bound of how many backups to skip.

An in-place restore of an insufficiently old backup could reactivate any compromises that were backed up during the incident. If it took a while to detect the intrusion, your oldest "safe" backup may have already been overwritten. If so, data remediation may be your only option.

A restored backup can contain desirably modified data interspersed with corrupted data. This corruption may be caused by a malicious change (by the attacker) or a random event (such as a tape going bad or a hard drive failure). Tools that rebuild data tend to focus on recovery from either random damage or malicious damage, but not both. It's important to understand which functionality your recovery and rebuild tools provide, along with the limitations of the approach. Otherwise, the results of data recovery may not match your expectations. Using routine integrity procedures —for example, verifying recovered data against known good cryptographic signatures —will help here. Ultimately, redundancy and testing are the best defenses against random events.

Credential and Secret Rotation

It's common for attackers to hijack existing accounts used within your infrastructure to impersonate legitimate users or services. For example, attackers carrying out a password phishing attack might try to obtain the credentials for an account they can use to log in to your systems. Similarly, through techniques like pass-the-hash,[6] attackers can obtain and reuse credentials, including credentials for administrator accounts. Chapter 9 discusses another scenario: the compromise of the SSH *authorized_keys* file. During recovery, you often need to rotate credentials for your system, user, service, and application accounts via methods such as key rotation (e.g., of the keys used in SSH authentication). Depending on what your investigation reveals, ancillary devices such as network devices and out-of-band management systems, as well as cloud-based services like SaaS applications, may also be in scope.

---

6 Pass-the-hash (*https://oreil.ly/ZhNsa*) is a technique that allows an attacker to replay credentials stolen locally from a machine (NTLM or LanMan hashes) over the network to log in to other systems, without needing the user's clear-text password.

Your environment may have other secrets that need attention, such as keys used for encryption of data at rest and cryptographic keys used for SSL. If your frontend web serving infrastructure is compromised or potentially accessible by an attacker, you may need to consider rotating your SSL keys. If you don't take action after an attacker steals your keys, they might use the keys to perform a man-in-the-middle attack. Similarly, if the encryption key for records in your database is on a compromised database server, the safest path forward is to rotate the keys and reencrypt the data.

Cryptographic keys are often used for application-level communications, as well. If the attacker had access to systems where such application-level keys are stored, you'll want to rotate the keys. Carefully consider where you store API keys, such as the keys you use for cloud-based services. Storing service keys in source code or local configuration files is a common vulnerability:[7] if your attacker has access to these files, they can gain access to other environments later on. As part of your recovery, you should determine if these files were available to the attacker (although it may not be possible to prove they were accessed) and rotate such service keys conservatively and often.

Depending on the scenario, credential rotation can require careful execution. In the case of a single phished account, it may be a simple task to ask the user to change their password and move on. However, if an attacker had access to a wide variety of accounts, including administrator accounts, or you don't know precisely which accounts they may have compromised, you may have to rotate the credentials of all users. When creating your recovery checklists, be sure to lay out the order in which to reset the accounts, prioritizing administrator credentials, known compromised accounts, and accounts that grant access to sensitive resources. If you have a large number of system users, you may need to disrupt all users with a single one-time event.

Seize the Opportunity

One-time credential rotations in large organizations often cause significant business disruptions. Imagine asking thousands of people to take action at the same time. Single sign-on (SSO) services and centralized authentication systems can ease the impact of rotating credentials by simplifying the actions users need to take during the recovery phase. However, introducing complex systems like SSO during incident recovery may be time-consuming and expensive, and therefore less viable for short-term mitigation.

---

7 Storing cloud service keys in local files and source code is not considered a best practice. For a recent systematic study of exposed service keys in GitHub, see Meli, Michael, Matthew R. McNiece, and Bradley Reaves. 2019. "How Bad Can It Git? Characterizing Secret Leakage in Public GitHub Repositories." *Proceedings of the 26th Annual Networked and Distributed Systems Security Symposium. https://oreil.ly/r65fM.*

Modern identity and access solutions that leverage the cloud are becoming more attractive and let you add two-factor authentication relatively quickly. Using two-factor authentication in your environment—especially for less-protected entry points like access to email—is a quick win. Two-factor authentication can also provide an added benefit: you'll know if an attacker is still attempting to log in to accounts. These attempted logins will look like account login failures.

To improve your security posture, your long-term mitigation roadmap might explore a cloud-based two-factor authentication service during short-term mitigation, and also incorporate more systematic changes, like adopting FIDO-based security keys (which we discuss in Chapter 7).

Another complication with credential rotation arises if your organization has weak handling practices: an attack and mitigation may make the situation worse. Suppose your company makes use of a centralized system, such as an LDAP database or Windows Active Directory, to manage employee accounts. Some of these systems store a history of passwords (usually, hashed and salted). Typically, systems retain password history so you can compare new passwords to older ones, and prevent users from reusing passwords over time. If an attacker has access to all the hashed passwords and a way to crack those passwords,[8] they might be able to infer patterns in the way users update their passwords. For example, if a user uses a year in each password (*password2019*, *password2020*, and so on), the attacker may be able to predict the next password in the sequence. This can be dangerous when password changes are part of your remediation strategy.

If you have access to security specialists, it's a good idea to consult them when creating your recovery plan. These specialists can perform threat modeling and offer advice on how to improve your credential handling practices. They may recommend obviating the need for complex password schemes by adopting two-factor authentication.

After the Recovery

Once you've ejected the attacker and completed your recovery, the next step is to transition out of the incident and consider the long-term impacts of what happened. If you experienced a minor incident like the compromise of a single employee

---

8 The safest way to store passwords is by using a salted key derivation function specifically designed for password hashing, such as scrypt (*https://oreil.ly/m5mge*) or Argon2 (*https://oreil.ly/_yS2Q*). Unlike still common approaches to password hashing like salted SHA-1, these functions provide protection against common password recovery attacks ranging from prepopulated lookup tables to low-cost specialized hardware. Even when using a strong password hash, it's best practice to make sure that the hashes themselves are encrypted at rest using a well-protected key to add another hurdle for a potential adversary.

account or a single system, the recovery phase and aftermath may be relatively straightforward. If you experienced a more serious incident with a larger impact, the recovery and aftermath phases may be extensive.

In the aftermath of Operation Aurora in 2009, Google set out to make systematic and strategic changes to its environment. We made some of these changes overnight, while others—such as BeyondCorp and our work with the FIDO alliance to institute widespread adoption of two-factor authentication using security keys[9]—required more time. Your postmortem should distinguish between what you can achieve in the short term versus the long term.

Postmortems

It's good practice for the teams working on an incident to keep notes about their work, which you can later integrate into the official *postmortem*. Every postmortem should feature a list of action items that address the underlying problems you found during the incident. A strong postmortem covers technology issues that the attacker exploited, and also recognizes opportunities for improved incident handling. Additionally, you should document the time frames and efforts associated with these action items, and decide which action items belong to short-term versus long-term roadmaps. We cover blameless postmortems in detail in Chapter 15 of the SRE book, but here are some additional security-focused questions to consider:

- What were the main contributing factors to the incident? Are there variants and similar issues elsewhere in the environment that you can address?
- What testing or auditing processes should have detected these factors earlier? If they don't already exist, can you build such processes to catch similar factors in the future?
- Was this incident detected by an expected technology control (such as an intrusion detection system)? If not, how can you improve the detection systems?
- How quickly was the incident detected and responded to? Is this within an acceptable range of time? If not, how can you improve your response time?
- Was important data protected sufficiently enough to deter an attacker from accessing it? What new controls should you introduce?
- Was the recovery team able to use tools—including source versioning, deployment, testing, backup, and restoration services—effectively?

---

9 For more on Google's work to implement security keys for itself and users, see Lang, Juan et al. 2016. "Security Keys: Practical Cryptographic Second Factors for the Modern Web." *Proceedings of the 20th International Conference on Financial Cryptography and Data Security*: 422–440. *https://oreil.ly/bL9Fm*.

- What normal procedures—such as normal testing, deployment, or release processes—did the team bypass during the recovery? What remediation may you need to apply right now?
- Were any changes made to infrastructure or tools as a temporary mitigation that you now need to refactor?
- What bugs did you identify and file during the incident and recovery phases that you now need to address?
- What best practices exist in the industry and among peer groups that could have aided you during any phase of preventing, detecting, or responding to the attack?

We recommend laying out a clear set of action items with explicit owners, sorted in order of short-term and long-term initiatives. Short-term initiatives are typically straightforward, don't take long to implement, and address issues that are relatively small in scope. We often call these action items "low-hanging fruit" because you can identify and address them easily. Examples include adding two-factor authentication, lowering the time to apply patches, or setting up a vulnerability discovery program.

Long-term initiatives will likely fold into your larger program strategy for improving the security posture of your organization. These action items are typically more fundamental to the way your systems and processes work—for example, starting a dedicated security team, deploying backbone encryption, or altering operating system choices.

In an ideal world, the full incident lifecycle—from compromise all the way to security posture improvements—will complete before the next incident happens. However, keep in mind that the period of routine steady state after the last incident is also the routine state preceding the next incident. This lull in incident activity is your opportunity to learn, adapt, identify new threats, and prepare for the next incident. The last part of this book focuses on improving and maintaining your security posture during these lulls.

Examples

The following worked examples show the relationship between a postmortem, the buildout of recovery checklists, and the execution of recovery, as well as how long-term mitigations roll into a larger security program plan. These examples don't cover all considerations of incident response; instead, we focus on how to make tradeoffs between ejecting the attacker, mitigating their immediate actions, and making long-term changes.

Compromised Cloud Instances

Scenario: A web-based software package used by your organization to serve user traffic from virtual machines (VMs) in a cloud provider's infrastructure has a common software vulnerability. An opportunistic attacker using vulnerability scanning tools discovers your vulnerable web servers and exploits them. Once the attacker takes over the VMs, they use them to launch new attacks.

In this case, the remediation lead uses notes from the investigation team to determine that the team needs to patch the software, redeploy the virtual machines, and shut down the compromised instances. The RL also determines that the short-term mitigation should discover and address related vulnerabilities. Figure 18-2 offers a hypothetical recovery checklist for this incident. For brevity, we excluded specific commands and execution steps—items that your actual recovery checklists should include.

INSTRUCTIONS:

- Highlight in GREEN when COMPLETED.
- Highlight in ORANGE TO-DO items.
- Highlight in RED if task cannot be completed; it must be replaced with an equivalent action.
- Highlight in BLUE if task will not be completed because it is operationally risky and adjustments need to be made.

Incident commander:
- Give a "hands off keyboards" briefing.
- Provide an overview of tasks and constraints.
- Notify all people involved of the exact time remediation will begin.

The remediation lead initiates execution of the following, in order:
1. Security specialists (or security-focused SREs or developers): Set up vulnerability scanning.
   a. *This section should include specific details of setting up vulnerability scanning of other software used on the cloud instances to see if you need to apply additional fixes.*
2. Web developer team: Patch vulnerable software.
   a. *This section should include specific details of where vulnerable software is sourced from, which versions should be deployed, and the steps (or commands) to do so.*
3. SRE team: Deploy new cloud instances (in parallel with compromised instances).
   a. *This section should include specific instructions for how to deploy clean cloud instances with the upgraded software installed by default. Once tested and validated, they should be configured to serve user traffic again.*
4. SRE team: Disable compromised cloud instances.
   a. *This section should include specific steps of how to shut down compromised cloud instances, and either archive them permanently or delete them so they can't be reused.*

Figure 18-2. Checklist for recovery: compromised cloud instance

After recovery is complete, the incident postmortem—which was collaboratively developed by everyone working on the incident—identifies the need for a formal vulnerability management program to proactively discover and patch known issues in a timely manner. This recommendation is rolled into the long-term strategy for improving the organization's security posture.

Large-Scale Phishing Attack

Scenario: Over a seven-day period, an attacker launches a password phishing campaign against your organization, which doesn't use two-factor authentication. 70% of your employees fall for this phishing attack. The attacker uses the passwords to read your organization's email and leaks sensitive information to the press.

As the IC in this scenario, you're faced with a number of complexities:

- The investigation team determines that the attacker has not yet tried to access any system other than email using the passwords.
- Your organization's VPN and related IT services, including the management of your cloud systems, use independent authentication systems from your email service. However, many employees share passwords between services.
- The attacker has stated that they will take more action against your organization in the coming days.

Working with the remediation lead, you have to juggle the tradeoffs between ejecting the attacker quickly (by removing their access to email) and ensuring that the attacker can't access any other systems in the meantime. This recovery effort requires precise execution, for which Figure 18-3 offers a hypothetical checklist. Again, we omit the exact commands and procedures for the purpose of brevity, but your real checklist should include these details.

INSTRUCTIONS:
- Highlight in GREEN when COMPLETED.
- Highlight in ORANGE TO-DO items.
- Highlight in RED if task cannot be completed; it must be replaced with an equivalent action.
- Highlight in BLUE if task will not be completed because it is operationally risky and adjustments need to be made.

Incident commander
- Give a "hands off keyboards" briefing.
- Provide an overview of tasks and constraints.
- Notify all people involved of the exact time remediation will begin.

The remediation lead initiates execution of the following, in order:
1. System administrators/SREs: Implement infrastructure for two-factor authentication for email.
   a. *This section should include specific details of how to enroll all employees in two-factor authentication for email.*
2. Email SREs: Lock email accounts.
   a. *This section should include specific details of how to lock the email accounts of employees until they are reset and use two-factor authentication. Due to the ongoing activity of the attacker, you may choose to lock all the accounts at once rather than providing employees with a rolling window.*
3. IT staff (such as Helpdesk): Enact adoption of two-factor authentication and password resets.
   a. *This section should include specific details of how IT staff should help users change their email, VPN, and cloud-based passwords, and begin using two-factor authentication for email. Depending on the size of the organization, this step might involve an all-hands staff meeting.*
4. System administrators/SREs: Adopt two-factor authentication for VPN and cloud systems.
   a. *This section should include specific details for implementing two-factor authentication for email, VPN, and cloud services.*

Figure 18-3. Checklist for recovery: large-scale phishing attack

Once recovery is complete, your formal postmortem highlights the need for the following:

- More widespread use of two-factor authentication on critical communication and infrastructure systems
- An SSO solution
- Education for employees about phishing attacks

Your organization also notes the need for an IT security specialist to advise you about standard best practices. This recommendation is rolled into the long-term strategy for improving your organization's security posture.

Targeted Attack Requiring Complex Recovery

Scenario: Unbeknownst to you, an attacker has been able to access your systems for over a month. They stole the SSL keys used to protect communications with your customers over the web, inserted a backdoor into your source code to siphon $0.02 from every transaction, and are monitoring the emails of executives in your organization.

As the IC, you are faced with a number of complexities:

- Your investigation team is unclear how the attack began, or how the attacker is continuing to access your systems.
- Your attacker can monitor the activities of executives and the incident response team.
- Your attacker can modify source code and deploy it to production systems.
- Your attacker has access to infrastructure where SSL keys are stored.
- Encrypted web-based communications with customers are potentially compromised.
- Your attacker has stolen money.

We won't provide a detailed set of example recovery checklists for this rather complex attack, but will instead focus on one very important aspect of the incident: the need to parallelize recovery. Working with the RL, you'll need to create a recovery checklist for each of these problems so you can better coordinate recovery steps. During this time, you'll also need to stay connected to your investigation team, which is learning more about the attacker's past and current actions.

For example, your effort may require some or all of the following recovery teams (you can probably think of others, as well):

Email team
> This team will sever the attacker's access to the email system and ensure they cannot reenter. The team may need to reset passwords, introduce two-factor authentication, and so on.

Source code team
> This team will determine how to sever access to source code, sanitize affected source code files, and redeploy the sanitized code to production systems. To carry out this work, the team needs to know when the attacker changed the source code in production and whether safe versions exist. This team also needs to make sure the attacker has not made changes to the persistent version control history, and cannot make additional source code changes.

SSL keys team

This team will determine how to safely deploy new SSL keys to the web serving infrastructure. To carry out this work, the team needs to know how the attacker gained access to the keys and how to prevent unauthorized access in the future.

Customer data team

This team will determine what customer information the attacker potentially had access to and whether you need to perform remediation, such as customer password changes or session resets. This remediation team may also be closely tied to any additional concerns raised by customer support, legal, and related staff.

Reconciliation team

This team will look at the implications of the $0.02 siphoned from every transaction. Do you need to append records in the database to accommodate long-term financial recording? This team may also be closely tied to any additional concerns raised by finance and legal staff.

In complex incidents such as these, it's often necessary to make less-than-ideal choices during recovery. For example, consider the team that needs to sever access to your company's email. They may have a few options, such as turning off the email system, locking all accounts, or bringing up a new email system in parallel. Each of these options will incur some impact to the organization, will likely alert the attacker, and may not necessarily address how the attacker gained access in the first place. The recovery and investigation teams need to work together closely to find a path forward that suits the situation.

Conclusion

Recovery is a distinct and crucial step in your incident response process that requires a dedicated team of specialists who know their domain well. There are many aspects to consider when planning your recovery: How will your attacker react? Who performs what actions, and when? What do you say to your users? Your recovery process should be parallelized, carefully planned, and regularly synced with your incident commander and investigative team. Your recovery effort should always have the end goal of ejecting your attacker, remediating the compromise, and improving the overall security and reliability of your systems. Each compromise should yield lessons that enable you to improve the long-term security posture of your organization.

Organization and Culture

While the engineering practices highlighted in this book will help your organization build secure and reliable systems, your efforts will be effective only if your entire organization is invested in a culture of security and reliability. Culture is a powerful and unique defining component of every organization, and you should not underestimate its role in your ability to institute change.

Part V of this book focuses on cultural aspects of implementing the approaches presented thus far. Chrome was one of the first products at Google to have a dedicated security team, actively promoting a security-centric culture. We start with a case study of that team, focusing on its role in Chrome's popularity and success. In Chapter 20, we posit that everyone in an organization is responsible for security and reliability. The role of security specialists should be to implement security-specific technologies that require specialist knowledge, and to devise best practices, policies, and training. Chapter 21 rounds out the book with a discussion of strategies for fostering a healthy culture of security and reliability.

CHAPTER 19

Case Study: Chrome Security Team

By Parisa Tabriz
with Susanne Landers and Paul Blankinship

In the early days of Google, security work—including product-focused security—was entirely centralized. Chrome was one of the first products to build out a security-focused organization, to tackle the unique challenges of building a secure, modern web browser. This case study describes the evolution of Chrome's security team, the core principles it developed, and some concrete ideas about how to scale security across an organization.

Background and Team Evolution

In 2006, a team was formed at Google with the aim of building an open source Windows browser, in less than two years, that would be more secure, faster, and more stable than the alternatives in the market. This was an ambitious goal and presented unique security challenges:

- Modern web browsers have similar complexity to an operating system, and much of their functionality is considered security-critical.

- Client-side and Windows software were different from most of Google's existing product and system offerings at the time, so limited transferable security expertise was available within Google's central security team.

- Since the project intended to begin and remain predominantly open source, it had unique development and operational requirements and could not rely on Google's corporate security practices or solutions.

This browser project ultimately launched as Google Chrome in 2008. Since then, Chrome has been credited as redefining the standard for online security (*https://oreil.ly/Rb6TJ*) and has become one of the world's most popular browsers.

Over the past decade, Chrome's security-focused organization has gone through four rough stages of evolution:

Team v0.1

Chrome did not formally establish a security team before its official launch in 2008, but relied on expertise distributed within the engineering team, along with consulting from Google's central security team and third-party security vendors. The initial launch was not without security flaws—in fact, a number of critical buffer overflows (*https://oreil.ly/GxjAV*) were discovered within the first two weeks of public availability! Many of the initial launch bugs fit the pattern of flaws that result from developers under time pressure trying to ship C++ code that's optimized for performance. Bugs also existed in the implementation of the browser application and web platform. Discovering bugs, fixing them, writing tests to prevent regressions, and eventually designing them away is part of the normal process of a maturing team.

Team v1.0

A year after the public beta release, with actual usage of the browser beginning to grow, a dedicated Chrome security team was created. This initial security team, composed of engineers from Google's central security team and new hires, leveraged best practices and norms established at Google and also brought in new perspectives and experiences from outside the organization.

Team v2.0

In 2010, Chrome launched a Vulnerability Reward Program (VRP) (*https://oreil.ly/cMY8z*) to recognize contributions from the larger security research community. The overwhelming response to the VRP announcement provided a useful incubator in the early days of the security team. Chrome was originally based on WebKit—an open source HTML rendering engine that previously hadn't seen much security scrutiny—so one of the team's first missions was to respond to the huge influx of external bug reports. At the time, Chrome's engineering team was very lean and not yet familiar with all of the WebKit codebase, so the security team found that the most expedient approach to getting a vulnerability resolved was often to just dive in, build up expertise on the codebase, and fix many of the bugs themselves!

These early decisions ended up having a big impact on the team's culture going forward. It established the security team not as isolated consultants or analysts, but instead as a hybrid engineering team of security experts. One of the strongest advantages of this hybrid approach is in the unique and practical insights it provides about how to incorporate secure development into the day-to-day processes of every engineer working on Chrome.

Team v3.0

By 2012, Chrome usage had grown further, as had the team's ambitions—and the attention from attackers. To help scale security across the growing Chrome project, the core security team established, socialized, and published a set of core security principles (*https://oreil.ly/aeU6_*).

In 2013, after bringing on an engineering manager and hiring more engineers dedicated to security, the team held an offsite meeting to reflect on their work, define a team mission, and brainstorm about the larger security problems they wanted to tackle, along with potential solutions. This mission-defining exercise resulted in a statement that articulated the shared purpose of the team: to provide Chrome users with the most secure platform possible to navigate the web, and generally advance security on the web.

At that 2013 offsite session, to brainstorm in an inclusive way, everyone wrote their ideas down on Post-it notes. The team collectively clustered ideas to identify themes, which resulted in establishing a few evergreen focus areas of work. These focus areas include the following:

Security reviews

The security team regularly consults with other teams to help design and assess the security of new projects and review security-sensitive changes to the codebase. Security reviews are a shared team responsibility and help promote knowledge transfer. The team scales this work by writing documentation, hosting security training, and serving as owners (*https://oreil.ly/t4EoT*) for the security-critical parts of Chrome's code.

Bug finding and fixing

With millions of lines of security-critical code and hundreds of developers around the world constantly making changes, the team invests in a range of approaches to help everyone find and fix bugs as quickly as possible.

Architecture and exploit mitigation

Recognizing that you can never prevent all security bugs, the team invests in secure design and architecture projects to minimize the impact of any single bug. Since Chrome is available across popular desktop and mobile operating systems (for example, Microsoft Windows, macOS, Linux, Android, and iOS), which are themselves continually evolving, this requires ongoing OS-specific investments and strategies.

Usable security

However confident the team can be that Chrome software and the systems used to build it are invulnerable to attack, they still need to take into account how and when users (who are, after all, fallible) themselves make security-sensitive decisions. Given the wide range of digital literacy among browser users, the team invests in helping users make safe decisions as they browse the web—making security more *usable*.

Web platform security
Beyond Chrome, the team works on advancing security for developers who are building web apps so that it's easier for anyone to build safe experiences on the web.

Identifying accountable leads for each focus area, and later dedicated managers, helped establish a more scalable team organization. Importantly, the focus area leads embraced agility, team-wide information sharing, and project swarming or collaboration, so that no individual or focus area became siloed from other focus areas.

Finding and retaining great people—individuals who care about the team's mission and core principles and collaborate well with others—is critical. Everyone in the team contributes to hiring, interviewing, and providing ongoing growth-oriented feedback to their teammates. Having the right people is more important than any organizational detail.

In terms of actually finding candidates, the team has heavily leveraged its personal networks, and constantly works to nurture and grow those networks with people from diverse backgrounds. We've also converted a number of interns to full-time employees. Occasionally, we've reached out cold to individuals who have spoken at conferences or whose published work shows they care about the web and building products to work at scale. One advantage of working in the open is that it means we can point prospective candidates to details of our team's efforts and recent accomplishments on the Chromium developer wiki (*https://www.chromium.org*) so they can quickly understand more about the team's work, challenges, and culture.

Importantly, we have pursued and considered individuals who were *interested* in security, but whose expertise or accomplishments were in other areas. For example, we hired one engineer who had an accomplished SRE background, cared deeply about the mission of keeping people safe, and was interested in learning about security. This diversity of experience and perspectives is broadly recognized as a key factor in the team's success.

In the following sections, we share more insights into how Chrome's core security principles have been applied in practice. These principles remain as relevant to Chrome today (ca. 2020) as they did when first written in 2012.

Security Is a Team Responsibility

One of the key reasons that Chrome has such a strong security focus is that we've embraced security as a core product principle and established a culture where security is considered a team responsibility.

Although the Chrome security team has the privilege of focusing almost entirely on security, team members recognize they can never own security for all of Chrome. Instead, they make an effort to build security awareness and best practices into the daily habits and processes of everyone working on the product. System design conventions aim to make the easy, fast, and well-lit path the secure path as well. This has often required additional work up front but has resulted in more effective partnerships in the long term.

One example of this in practice is the way the team approaches security bugs. All engineers, including security team members, fix bugs and write code. If security teams only find and report bugs, they may lose touch with how hard it is to write bug-free code or fix bugs. This also helps mitigate the "us" versus "them" mentality that sometimes arises when security engineers don't contribute to traditional engineering tasks.

As the team grew beyond its early days of vulnerability firefighting, it worked to develop a more proactive approach to security. This meant investing time in building and maintaining a fuzzing infrastructure and tooling for developers that made it faster and easier to identify changes that introduced bugs and to revert or fix them. The faster a developer can identify a new bug, the easier it is to fix, and the less impact it has on end users.

In addition to creating useful tooling for developers, the team creates positive incentives for engineering teams to do fuzzing. For example, it organizes annual fuzzing contests with prizes and creates fuzzing tutorials (*https://oreil.ly/alX7Q*) to help any engineer learn how to fuzz. Organizing events and making it easier to contribute helps people realize they don't need to be a "security expert" to improve security. The Chrome fuzzing infrastructure started small—a single computer under an engineer's desk. As of 2019, it supports fuzzing across Google and the world.[1] In addition to fuzzing, the security team builds and maintains secure base libraries (e.g., the safe numerics library), so that the default way for anyone to implement changes is the safe way.

Security team members often send peer bonuses (*https://oreil.ly/ahPxg*) or positive feedback to individuals or their managers when they notice someone modeling

---

1 Google open sourced ClusterFuzz (*https://oreil.ly/3PrQI*), the fuzzing backend for its OSS-Fuzz service (*https://oreil.ly/mIjbw*), in early 2019.

strong security practices. Since security work sometimes goes unnoticed or is not visible to end users, taking extra effort to recognize it directly or in a way that's aligned with career goals helps set up the positive incentives for better security.

Independent of tactics, if organizations don't already hold the position that security is a core value and shared responsibility, more fundamental reflection and discussion are needed to prove the importance of security and reliability to an organization's core goals.

Help Users Safely Navigate the Web

Effective security should not depend on the expertise of any end user. Any product with a large-scale user base needs to carefully balance usability, capability, and other business constraints. In most cases, Chrome aims to make security nearly invisible to the user: we update transparently, we bias toward safe defaults, and we continually try to make the safe decision the easy decision and help users avoid unsafe decisions.

During the Team v3.0 phase, we collectively acknowledged that we had a cluster of open problems with usable security—problems that stem from humans interacting with software. For example, we knew users were falling victim to social engineering and phishing attacks, and we had concerns about the effectiveness of Chrome's security warnings. We wanted to tackle these problems, but we had limited human-centered software expertise in the team. We decided that we needed to strategically hire for more usable security expertise and serendipitously connected with an internal candidate who was interested in a new role.

At the time, this candidate was on the research scientist job ladder, from which Chrome had no precedent for hiring. We convinced leadership to hire the candidate, despite early reservations, by underscoring how the candidate's academic expertise and diverse perspectives were actually an asset to the team and necessary to augment its existing skill set. Partnering closely with the user experience (UX) team, with which security had occasionally been at odds in the past, this new addition to our team went on to establish Chrome's usable security focus area. Eventually, we hired additional UX designers and researchers to help us more deeply understand users' security and privacy needs. We learned that security experts, given their high comprehension of the way computer systems and networks work, are often blind to many of the challenges users face.

Speed Matters

User safety depends on quickly detecting security flaws and delivering fixes to users before attackers can exploit them. One of Chrome's most important security features is fast, automatic updates. From early days, the security team worked closely with technical program managers (TPMs), who established Chrome's release process (*https://oreil.ly/J1Vao*) and managed the quality and reliability of each new release. Release TPMs measure the rates of crashes, ensure timely fixes for high-priority bugs, roll releases forward carefully and incrementally, push back on engineers when things are going too fast, and hustle to get reliability- or safety-improving releases out to users as fast as is reasonable.

Early on, we used the Pwn2Own (*https://oreil.ly/5PwMU*) and later Pwnium (*https://oreil.ly/bQthO*) hacking contests as forcing functions to see if we could actually release and deploy critical security fixes in under 24 hours. (We can.) This required strong partnership and a significant amount of help and buy-in from the release TPM team, and though we demonstrated the capability, we've rarely needed to use it, thanks to Chrome's investment in defense in depth.

Design for Defense in Depth

No matter how fast the team is able to detect and fix any single security bug in Chrome, these bugs are bound to occur, particularly when you consider the security shortcomings of C++ and the complexity of a browser. Since attackers are continually advancing their capabilities, Chrome is continually investing in developing exploit mitigation techniques and an architecture that helps avoid single points of failure. The team has created a living color-by-risk component diagram (*https://oreil.ly/ssfOj*) so anyone can reason about Chrome's security architecture and various layers of defense to inform their work.

One of the best examples of defense in depth in practice is the ongoing investment in sandboxing capabilities. Chrome initially launched with a multiprocess architecture and sandboxed renderer processes. This prevented a malicious website from taking over a user's whole computer, which was a significant advancement in browser architecture for the time. In 2008, the largest threat from the web was a malicious web page using a browser compromise to install malware on the user's machine, and the Chrome architecture successfully brought that problem under control.

But computer usage evolved, and with the popularization of cloud computing and web services, more and more sensitive data has moved online. This means that cross-website data theft could be as important a target as compromise of the local machine. It wasn't clear when the focus of attacks would shift from "renderer compromise that installs malware" to "renderer compromise that steals cross-site data," but the team knew the incentives were there to make the move inevitable. With that realization, in 2012 the team embarked on Site Isolation (*https://oreil.ly/_mfzd*), a project to advance the state of sandboxing to isolate individual sites.

Originally, the team predicted the Site Isolation project would take a year to complete, but we were off by more than a factor of five! Estimation mistakes like this tend to put a bull's-eye on a project's back from upper management—and with good reason. The team regularly articulated to leadership and various stakeholders the defense-in-depth motivation for the project, its progress, and the reasons why it was more work than first anticipated. Team members also demonstrated a positive impact on overall Chrome code health, which benefited other parts of Chrome. All of this gave the team additional cover to defend the project and communicate its value to senior stakeholders over the years until its eventual public launch. (Coincidentally, Site Isolation partially mitigates speculative execution vulnerabilities (*https://oreil.ly/EBJb9*), which were discovered in 2018.)

Since defense-in-depth work is less likely to result in user-visible changes (when done right), it's even more important for leadership to proactively manage, recognize, and invest in these projects.

Be Transparent and Engage the Community

Transparency has been a core value for the Chrome team since the start. We do not downplay security impact or bury vulnerabilities with silent fixes, because doing so serves users poorly. Instead, we provide users and administrators with the information they need to accurately assess risk. The security team publishes how it handles security issues (*https://oreil.ly/pA9ba*), discloses all vulnerabilities fixed in Chrome and its dependencies—whether discovered internally or externally–and, whenever possible, lists every fixed security issue in its release notes (*https://oreil.ly/C-_Qm*).

Beyond vulnerabilities, we share quarterly summaries (*https://oreil.ly/teoUI*) about what we're doing with the public and engage with users via an external discussion mailing list (*security-dev@chromium.org*) so that anyone can send us ideas, questions, or participate in ongoing discussions. We actively encourage individuals to share their work at conferences or security gatherings or via their social networks. We also engage with the larger security community via Chrome's Vulnerability Reward Program and security conference sponsorship. Chrome is more secure thanks to the contributions of many people who don't identify as being part of the team, and we do our best to acknowledge and reward those contributions by ensuring proper attribution and paying out monetary rewards.

Across Google, we organized an annual offsite meeting to connect the Chrome security team with the central security team and other embedded teams (for example, Android's security team). We also encourage the security enthusiasts across Google to do 20% of their work on Chrome (and vice versa), or find opportunities to collaborate with academic researchers on Chromium projects.

Working in an open environment allows the team to share its work, accomplishments, and ideas, and to get feedback or pursue collaborations beyond the confines of Google. All of this contributes to advancing the common understanding of browser and web security. The team's multiyear effort to increase HTTPS adoption, described in Chapter 7, is one example of how communicating changes and engaging with a larger community can lead to ecosystem change.

Conclusion

The team working on Chrome identified security as a core principle in the early stages of the project, and scaled its investment and strategy as the team and user base grew. The Chrome security team was formally established just a year after the browser's launch, and over time its roles and responsibilities became more clearly defined. The team articulated a mission and a set of core security principles, and established key focus areas for its work.

Promoting security as a team responsibility, embracing transparency, and engaging with communities outside of Chrome helped to create and advance a security-centric culture. Aiming to innovate at speed led to a dynamic product and the ability to respond with agility to a changing landscape. Designing for defense in depth helped to protect users from one-off bugs and novel attacks. Considering the human aspects of security, from the end-user experience to the hiring process, helped the team expand its understanding of security and address more complex challenges. A willingness to meet challenges head-on and learn from mistakes enabled the team to work toward making the default path the secure one as well.

CHAPTER 20

Understanding Roles and Responsibilities

By Heather Adkins, Cyrus Vesuna, Hunter King,
Felix Gröbert, and David Challoner
with Susanne Landers, Steven Roddis, Sergey Simakov,
Shylaja Nukala, Janet Vong, Douglas Colish, Betsy Beyer,
and Paul Blankinship

This chapter addresses the question of who should work on security. We challenge the common myth that security is a topic that only experts should handle. Instead, we argue that *everyone* is responsible for security, though you may need a security specialist in some instances. We also address the role of security experts in a world where security is tightly integrated into the lifecycle of systems, and therefore handled by other types of professionals. Finally, we conclude with a look at some of the specialist options available to support an organization, especially as it grows over time.

As this book emphasizes many times, building systems is a *process*, and the processes for improving security and reliability rely on people. This means that building secure and reliable systems involves tackling two important questions:

- Who is responsible for security and reliability in the organization?
- How are security and reliability efforts integrated into the organization?

The answer to these questions is highly dependent on your organization's objectives and culture (the topic of the next chapter). The following sections lay out some high-level guidance for how to think about these questions, and offer insight into how Google has approached them over time.

Who Is Responsible for Security and Reliability?

Who works on security and reliability in a given organization? We believe that security and reliability should be integrated into the lifecycle of systems; therefore, they're everyone's responsibility. We'd like to challenge the myth that organizations should place the burden for these concerns solely on dedicated experts.

If reliability and security are delegated to an isolated team of people who can't mandate that other teams make security-related changes, the same failures will happen repeatedly. Their task may start to feel Sisyphean—repetitive and unproductive.

We encourage organizations to make reliability and security the responsibility of *everyone*: developers, SREs, security engineers, test engineers, tech leads, managers, project managers, tech writers, executives, and so on. That way, the nonfunctional requirements described in Chapter 4 become a focus for the whole organization throughout a system's entire lifecycle.

A System Security and Reliability Analogy

Modern cars offer a good analogy for the way security and reliability are embedded into system design and delivery. Almost every component of a car incorporates both security and reliability in some way. Seats are designed to handle a crash, a windshield needs to crack safely, and headlights are angled to avoid blinding oncoming traffic. Seat belts must withstand being latched thousands of times. The windshield has to repel all types of weather, and the headlights must always turn on when you need them. A car's digital systems must be similarly hardened. Everyone who plays a part in building the car must do this work—not just safety and reliability experts.

The Roles of Specialists

If everyone is responsible for security and reliability, then you might wonder: what exactly is the role of a security specialist or reliability expert? According to one school of thought, the engineers building a given system should primarily focus on its core functionality. For example, developers might focus on building a set of critical user journeys for a mobile phone–based app. Complementing the work of the developer team, a security-focused engineer will look at the app from the perspective of an attacker aiming to undermine its safety. A reliability-focused engineer can help understand the dependency chains and, based on these, identify what metrics should be measured that will lead to happy customers and an SLA-compliant system. This division of labor is common in many development environments, but it's important that these types of roles work together rather than in isolation.

To expand on this idea further, depending on the complexity of a system, an organization may need people with specialized experience to make nuanced judgment calls. Since it's not possible to build an absolutely secure system that's resilient against every attack, or a system that is perfectly reliable, advice from experts can help steer development teams. Ideally, this guidance should be integrated into the development lifecycle. This integration can take multiple forms, and security and reliability specialists should work directly with developers or other specialists that consult at each stage of the lifecycle to improve systems.[1] For example, security consultation can happen in multiple stages:

- A *security design review* at the outset of a project to determine how security is integrated
- *Ongoing security audits* to make sure a product is built correctly per security specifications
- *Testing* to see what vulnerabilities an independent person can find

---

Security and Reliability Risk Evaluation

Nuanced security and reliability advice can be helpful in making judgment calls about risk. For example, suppose developers working on a project haven't had time to build in a desired security protection or think about graceful degradation, but need to launch the product or system soon. A security engineer and an SRE can help the organization understand what might happen if it's launched in its current state. Will adversaries be able to attack a vulnerable system? Will the global system go down if user traffic for a certain country is higher than expected? What is the likelihood that either of these events will happen? Is the organization equipped with temporary mitigations for potential issues that might arise? Experienced security engineers and SREs can offer valuable advice in these situations.

---

1 The development arc described in Chapter 18 of the SRE workbook demonstrates the value that an experienced SRE offers throughout the entire product lifecycle.

Security experts should be responsible for implementing security-specific technologies that require specialist knowledge. Cryptography is the canonical example: "don't roll your own crypto" is a common industry catchphrase meant to discourage enterprising developers from implementing their own solutions. Cryptography implementations, whether in libraries or hardware, should be left to experts. If your organization needs to provide secure services (such as a web service over HTTPS), use industry-accepted and verified solutions instead of attempting to write your own encryption algorithm. Specialist security knowledge can also be required to implement other types of highly complex security infrastructure, such as custom authentication, authorization, and auditing (AAA) systems, or new secure frameworks to prevent common security vulnerabilities.

Reliability engineers (such as SREs) are best positioned to develop centralized infrastructure and organization-wide automation. Chapter 7 of the SRE book discusses the value and evolution of horizontal solutions, and shows how critical software that enables product development and launches can evolve into a platform.

Finally, specialists in security and reliability can devise best practices, policies, and training tailored to your organization's workflows. These tools should empower developers to adopt best practices and implement effective security and reliability practices. A specialist should aim to build a brain trust of knowledge for the organization by constantly educating themselves on developments in the industry and generating broader awareness (see "Culture of Awareness" on page 476). In creating awareness, a specialist can help the organization become more secure and reliable in an iterative way. For example, Google has SRE- and security-focused educational programs that provide a baseline level of knowledge to all new hires in these specific roles. In addition to making the course material available company-wide, we also offer employees many self-study courses on these topics.

Understanding Security Expertise

Anyone who has tried to hire security professionals into their organization knows that the task can be challenging. If you're not a security specialist yourself, what should you look for when hiring one? Medical professionals provide a good analogy: most have a general understanding of the fundamentals of human health, but many specialize at some point. In the medical field, family doctors or general practitioners are typically responsible for primary care, but more serious conditions may call for a specialist in neurology, cardiology, or some other area. Similarly, all security professionals tend to command a general body of knowledge, but they also tend to specialize in a few specific areas.

Before you hire a security specialist, it's important to know the types of skills your organization will need. If your organization is small—for example, if you're a startup or an open source project—a generalist may cover many of your needs. As your organization grows and matures, its security challenges may become more complex and require increased specialization. Table 20-1 presents some key milestones in Google's early history that needed corresponding security expertise.

Table 20-1. Security expertise needed at key milestones in Google's history

Company milestones	Expertise needed	Security challenges
Google Search (1998) *Google Search provides users with the ability to find publicly available information.*	General	Search query log data protection Denial-of-service protection Network and system security
Google AdWords (2000) *Google AdWords (Google Ads) enables advertisers to show ads on Google Search and other products.*	General Data security Network security Systems security Application security Compliance and audit Anti-fraud Privacy Denial of service Insider risk	Financial data protection Regulatory compliance Complex web applications Identity Account abuse Fraud and insider abuse
Blogger (2003) *Blogger is a platform that allows users to host their own web pages.*	General Data security Network security Systems security Application security Content abuse Denial of service	Denial of service Platform abuse Complex web applications
Google Mail (Gmail) (2004) *Gmail is Google's free webmail system, with advanced features available via a paid GSuite account.*	General Privacy Data security Network security Systems security Application security Cryptography Anti-spam Anti-abuse Incident response Insider risk Enterprise security	Protecting highly sensitive user content at rest and in transit Threat models involving highly capable external attackers Complex web applications Identity systems Account abuse Email spam and abuse Denial of service Insider abuse Enterprise needs

Certifications and Academia

Some security experts seek to earn certifications in their field of interest. Security-focused industry certifications are offered by institutions worldwide, and can be good indicators of someone's interest in developing relevant skills for their career and their ability to learn key concepts. These certifications typically involve a standardized knowledge-based test. Some certifications require a minimum amount of classroom, conference, or job experience. Nearly all expire after a certain amount of time, or require certificants to refresh minimum requirements.

These standardized testing mechanisms may not necessarily attest to someone's aptitude for success in a security role at your organization, so we recommend taking a balanced approach to assessing security specialists, considering all of their qualifications in totality: their practical experience, certifications, and personal interest. While certifications may speak to someone's ability to pass exams, we have seen credentialed professionals who've had difficulty applying their knowledge to solving problems. At the same time, early career candidates, or those coming to the field from other specialist roles, may use certifications to upgrade their knowledge quickly. With a keen interest in the field, or practical experience with open source projects (instead of workplace experience), such early career candidates may be able to add value quickly.

Because security experts are increasingly in demand, many industries and universities have been developing and evolving security-focused academic programs. Some institutions offer general security-focused degrees that cover many security domains. Other degree programs concentrate on a specific security domain (which is common for doctoral students), and some offer a blended curriculum that focuses on the overlap between cybersecurity issues and domains such as public policy, law, and privacy. As with certifications, we recommend considering a candidate's academic achievements in the context of their practical experience and your organization's needs.

For example, you might want to bring on an experienced professional as your first security hire, and then hire early career talent once the team is established and can offer mentorship. Alternatively, if your organization is working on a niche technical problem (such as securing self-driving cars), a new PhD graduate with deep knowledge in that specific research area but little work experience might fit the role nicely.

Integrating Security into the Organization

Knowing when to start working on security is more of an art than a science. Opinions on this topic are plentiful and varied. However, it's generally safe to say that the sooner you start thinking about security, the better off you'll be. In more concrete terms, we've observed certain conditions over the years that are likely to trigger organizations (including our own) to start building a security program:

- When an organization begins to handle data of a personal nature, such as logs of sensitive user activity, financial information, health records, or email

- When an organization needs to build highly secure environments or custom technologies, such as custom security features in a web browser

- When regulations require adherence to a standard (such as Sarbanes-Oxley, PCI DSS, or GDPR) or a related audit[2]
- When an organization has contractual requirements with customers, especially around breach notification or minimum security standards
- During or after a compromise or data breach (ideally, before)
- As a reaction to the compromise of a peer operating in the same industry

In general, you'll want to start working on security far before any of these conditions are met, and especially before a data breach! It's far simpler to implement security before, rather than after, such an event. For example, if your company plans to launch a new product that accepts online payments, you may want to consider a specialty vendor for that functionality. Vetting a vendor and ensuring that they have good data handling practices will take time.

Imagine that you launch with a vendor that doesn't integrate the online payment system securely. A data breach could incur regulatory fines, loss of customer trust, and a hit to productivity as your engineers reimplement the system correctly. Many organizations cease to exist after such incidents.[3]

Similarly, imagine that your company is signing a new contract with a partner that has additional data handling requirements. Hypothetically, your legal team may advise you to implement those requirements before signing the contract. What might happen if you delay those extra protections and suffer a breach as a result?

Related questions often arise when considering the cost of a security program and the resources your company can invest in the program: how expensive is implementing security, and can the company afford it? While this chapter can't cover this very complex topic deeply, we'll emphasize two main takeaways.

First off, for security to be effective, it must be carefully balanced with your organization's other requirements. To put this guideline in perspective, we can make Google nearly 100% safe from malicious actors by turning off our datacenters, networks, computing devices, and so on. While doing so would achieve a high level of safety, Google would no longer have customers and would disappear into the annals of failed companies. Availability is a core tenet of security! In order to craft a reasonable

---

2 The Sarbanes-Oxley Act of 2002 (the Public Company Accounting Reform and Investor Protection Act) sets standards for public US companies regarding their accounting practices, and includes information security topics. The Payment Card Industry Data Security Standard sets minimum guidelines around protecting credit card information; compliance is required for anyone doing payment processing of this kind. The General Data Protection Regulation is an EU regulation concerned with the handling of personal data.

3 A few notable cases of organizations that went out of business or filed for bankruptcy after breaches are Code Spaces (*https://oreil.ly/Oj9ng*) and the American Medical Collection Agency (*https://oreil.ly/BcR9C*).

security strategy, you need to understand what the business requires to operate (and in the case of most companies, what it takes to earn a profit). Find the right balance between the requirements of your business and adequate security controls.

Secondly, security is everyone's responsibility. You can reduce the cost of some security processes by distributing it among the teams affected the most. For example, consider a company that has six products, each staffed with a product team and protected by 20 firewalls. In this scenario, one common approach is to have a central security team maintain the configuration of all 120 firewalls. This setup requires the security team to have extensive knowledge of six different products—a recipe for eventual reliability issues or delays in system changes, all of which can increase the cost of your security program. An alternative approach is to assign responsibility to the security team for operating an automated configuration system that accepts, validates, approves, and pushes firewall changes proposed by the six product teams. This way, each product team can efficiently propose minor changes for review and scale the configuration process. These kinds of optimizations can save time and even improve system reliability by catching errors early without human involvement.

Because security is such an integral part of an organization's lifecycle, nontechnical areas of the organization also need to consider security early on. For example, boards of directors often examine the security and privacy practices of the entities they oversee. Lawsuits in the aftermath of data breaches, such as the shareholder suit against Yahoo! in 2017, are driving this trend.[4] When preparing your roadmap for security, be sure to consider these types of stakeholders in your process.

Finally, it's important to create processes for maintaining a constant understanding of the current issues you need to address, along with their priorities. When treated as a continuous process, security requires an ongoing assessment of the risks the business is facing. In order to iterate defense-in-depth security controls over time, you need to incorporate risk assessment into your software development lifecycle and security practices. The next section discusses some practical strategies for doing so.

Embedding Security Specialists and Security Teams

Over the years, we've seen many companies experiment with where to embed security specialists and security teams inside their organizations. The configurations have ranged from fully embedded security specialists inside product teams (see Chapter 19) to fully centralized security teams. Google's central security team is organizationally configured as a hybrid of both options.

---

4 In the US, executives and boards of directors are increasingly being held accountable for security in their organizations. The Concord Law School at Purdue University has written a good article (*https://oreil.ly/wl7Yn*) on this trend.

Many companies also have different accountability arrangements for decision making. We've seen Chief Information Security Officers (CISOs) and other leadership roles responsible for security report to just about every C-level executive: the CEO, CFO, CIO, or COO, the general counsel for the company, a VP of Engineering, and even the CSO (Chief Security Officer, usually responsible also for physical security). There is no right or wrong configuration, and the choice your organization makes will be highly dependent on what's most effective for your security efforts.

The rest of this section offers some details on configuration options that we've had success with over the years. While we're a big technology company, many of these components also work well in small or medium-sized organizations. However, we imagine this configuration may not work well for a financial company or a public utility, where accountability for security may have different stakeholders and drivers. Your mileage may vary.

Example: Embedding Security at Google

At Google, we first built out a central security organization that operates as a peer to product engineering. The head of this organization is a senior leader within engineering (a VP). This creates a reporting structure in which security is seen as an engineering ally, but also allows the security team sufficient independence to raise issues and resolve disputes without conflicts of interest other leaders may have. This is similar to the way the SRE organization at Google maintains separate reporting chains from product development teams.[5] In this way, we create an open and transparent engagement model that focuses on improvements. Otherwise, you risk having a team with the following characteristics:

- Unable to raise serious issues because launches are overprioritized
- Seen as a blocking gate that needs to be circumvented organizationally via silent launches
- Slowed down by insufficient documentation or code access

Google's central security team relies on standard processes like ticketing systems to interact with the rest of the organization when teams need to request a design review, an access control change, and so on. For a sense of how this workflow functions, see "Google's Smart System for Intake" on page 464.

As Google has grown, it has also become useful to embed a "security champion" within individual product engineering peer groups. The security champion becomes the gateway to facilitate collaboration between the central security team and the product team. When starting out, this role is ideal for senior engineers with good

---

5 See Chapter 31 in the SRE book.

standing in the organization and an interest or a background in security. These engineers also become the technical leads for product security initiatives. As product teams become more complex, this role is assigned to a senior decider, such as a director or VP—this person can make tough calls (such as balancing launches versus security fixes), acquire resources, and resolve conflicts.

In the security champion model, it's important to establish and agree upon an engagement process and responsibilities. For example, the central team may continue to perform design reviews and audits, set organization-wide security policies and standards, build safe application frameworks (see Chapter 13), and devise common infrastructure such as least privilege methods (see Chapter 5). Distributed security champions are key stakeholders for these activities, and should help decide how these controls will work in their product teams. The security champions also drive the implementation of policies, frameworks, infrastructure, and methods within their respective product teams. This organizational configuration requires a tight communication loop through team charters, cross-functional meetings, mailing lists, chat channels, and so on.

Because of Google and Alphabet's large size, in addition to a central security team and distributed security champions, we also have special decentralized security teams for more complex products. For example, the Android security team sits within the Android engineering organization. Chrome has a similar model (see Chapter 19). This means the Android and Chrome security teams are responsible for the end-to-end security of their respective products, which includes deciding on product-specific standards, frameworks, infrastructure, and methods. These specialized security teams run the product security review process and have special programs to harden the products. For example, the Android security team has worked to harden the media stack (*https://oreil.ly/rME44*) and has benefited from an integrated security and engineering approach.

In all of these models, it's important for the security team to be open and approachable. In addition to a security review process, during which developers can receive help from subject matter experts, engineers need timely and consistent feedback on security-related issues throughout the project lifecycle. We address a number of cultural issues around these interactions in Chapter 21.

Google's Smart System for Intake

In many organizations, a ticket queue is the only communication channel to the security team. The "one size fits most" nature of tickets typically results in a lot of back and forth in order to extract relevant information. To help our teams save time, we built a smart system as our ticket queue frontend to automate away as much of the consulting process as possible.

Instead of providing a simple form or forms as input into our queue, we built a system with a dynamic questionnaire. As the user describes their request, the system automatically asks common security-related questions, and provides warnings and recommendations to educate them about risky decisions. These guiding questions help the user determine whether they are using a memory-safe language, applying a vetted templating system/framework, handling sensitive data, or modifying a critical system. After the user fills out the form, the system is able to identify an explicit problem and create a ticket to automatically route to the correct user or team. Then a security engineer can quickly parse the inherently structured information and relevant data, and help the user.

Since security work constantly evolves and the questionnaire won't cover all use cases, the intake form allows users to bypass sections and choose an "other" option if their request doesn't directly map to a defined workflow. To prevent users from defaulting to the "other" option, we explicitly say that this option is for one-off requests that are time-sensitive.

One key feature of the expert system is its ability to evolve and grow with the organization. If a large number of users skip our questionnaire, we know our expert system needs tweaking. Security engineers periodically examine the sections users most often bypass, and either add new question paths or modify overly burdensome question segments. The goal is to encourage users to focus on the main security questions they need to think about.

Building this system helped us accomplish the following:

- Let the user self-serve, and self-educate themselves in the process.
- Save time for meaningful and productive collaboration in providing a recommendation.
- Dramatically improve the overall speed of understanding the problem and providing a recommendation.
- Greatly increase the overall number of tickets successfully closed per week.
- Improve the quality of the information in tickets.

Special Teams: Blue and Red Teams

Security teams are often tagged using colors to denote their role in securing an organization.[6] All of these color-coded teams work toward the common goal of improving the security posture of the company.

---

6 This color scheme is derived from the US military (*https://oreil.ly/nuNjO*).

Blue Teams are primarily responsible for assessing and hardening software and infrastructure. They're also responsible for detection, containment, and recovery in the event of a successful attack. Blue Team members can be anyone in an organization who works on defending it, including the people who build secure and reliable systems.

Red Teams run offensive security exercises: end-to-end attacks that simulate realistic adversaries. These exercises reveal weaknesses in an organization's defenses and test its ability to detect and defend against attacks.

Typically, Red Teams focus on the following:

A specific goal
> For example, a Red Team might seek to exploit customer account data (or more specifically, to find and exfiltrate to a safe destination some customer account data that is available in your environment). Such exercises are very similar to the way adversaries operate.

Surveillance
> The aim is to determine whether your detection methods can detect reconnaissance by an adversary. Surveillance can also serve as a map for future goal-based engagements.

Targeted attacks
> The aim is to demonstrate the feasibility of exploiting security issues that are supposedly theoretical and very unlikely to be exploited. As a result, you can determine which issues merit building a defense.

Before starting a Red Team program, be sure to obtain buy-in from parts of the organization that might be affected by these exercises, including legal and executives. This is also a good time to define boundaries—for example, Red Teams should not access customer data or disrupt production services, and they should use approximations for data theft and service outages (e.g., by compromising only the data of test accounts). These boundaries need to strike a balance between conducting a realistic exercise and establishing a timing and scope that your partner teams are comfortable with. Of course, your adversaries won't respect these boundaries, so Red Teams should pay extra attention to key areas that are not well protected.

Some Red Teams share their attack plans with the Blue Team, and work very closely with them to get fast and comprehensive insight into the detection situation. This relationship can even be formalized with a Purple Team that bridges the two.[7] This can be useful if you are conducting many exercises and want to move fast, or if you

---

7 For more on Purple Teams, see Brotherston, Lee, and Amanda Berlin. 2017. *Defensive Security Handbook: Best Practices for Securing Infrastructure.* Sebastopol, CA: O'Reilly Media.

want to distribute Red Team activity among product engineers. This configuration can also inspire the Red Team to look in places it might not otherwise consider. The engineers that design, implement, and maintain systems know the system best, and usually have an instinct for where the weaknesses are.

Detecting Red Teams

If your Red and Blue Teams choose not to share information with each other, be sure to establish a protocol for what to do when the Blue Team detects the Red Team. Imagine this scenario: a Red Team successfully breaches your customer database. The Blue Team detects them and executes emergency response procedures, resulting in notifications to your executives, legal team, and regulators! A good protocol for deescalation after detection will prevent this sort of confusion.

Red Teams are not vulnerability scanning or penetration testing teams. *Vulnerability scanning teams* look for predictable and known weaknesses in software and configurations that can be automatically scanned for. *Penetration testing teams* focus more on finding a large set of vulnerabilities and the testers trying to exploit them. Their scope is narrower, focused on a particular product, infrastructure component, or process. As these teams mostly test prevention aspects and some detection aspects of an organization's security defense, their typical engagement lasts days.

In contrast, Red Team engagements are goal-oriented and typically last weeks. Their goals are specific targets, such as intellectual property or customer data exfiltration. They are broadly scoped and use any means necessary to attain their goals (within safety limits) by traversing product, infrastructure, and internal/external boundaries.

Given time, good Red Teams can attain their goals, often without being detected. Rather than viewing a successful Red Team attack as a judgment of a poor or ineffective business unit, use this information to better understand some of your more complex systems in a blameless way.[8] Use Red Team exercises as an opportunity to better learn how these systems are interconnected and how they share trust boundaries. Red Teams are designed to help bolster threat models and build defenses.

---

8 Do so by building on a culture of blameless postmortems, as described in Chapter 15 of the SRE book.

Because they don't exactly mirror the behavior of external attackers, Red Team attacks aren't a perfect test of your detection and response capabilities. This is especially true if the Red Team is staffed by internal engineers who have existing knowledge about the systems they're attempting to penetrate.

You also can't feasibly conduct Red Team attacks frequently enough to provide a real-time view of your vulnerability to attacks or statistically significant metrics for your detection and response teams. Red Teams are meant to find the rare edge cases that normal testing cannot. All caveats aside, regularly conducting Red Team exercises is a good way to understand your security posture end to end.

You can also leverage Red Teams to teach the people who design, implement, and maintain systems about the adversarial mindset. Embedding these people directly into the attack team—for example, via a small-scoped project—will give them firsthand insight into how attackers scrutinize a system for possible vulnerabilities and work around defenses. They can inject this knowledge into their team's development process later on.

Engaging with a Red Team helps you better understand your organization's security posture and develop a roadmap for implementing meaningful risk reduction projects. By understanding the implications of your current risk tolerance, you can determine whether you need to make adjustments.

External Researchers

Another way to examine and improve your security posture is to work closely with outside researchers and enthusiasts who find vulnerabilities in your systems. As we mentioned in Chapter 2, this can be a useful way to get feedback about your systems.

Many companies work with outside researchers by establishing *Vulnerability Reward Programs (VRPs)*, also colloquially referred to as *bug bounty programs*. These programs offer rewards in exchange for responsibly disclosing vulnerabilities about your system, which may or may not come in cash form.[9] Google's first VRP, started in 2006, offered a T-shirt and a simple thank you message on our public-facing web page. Through reward programs, you can expand the hunt for security-related bugs outside of your immediate organization and engage with a larger number of security researchers.

---

9 See Google researcher sirdarckcat's blog post on rewards (*https://oreil.ly/Lgtv3*) for a more philosophical outlook.

Before starting a VRP, it's a good idea to first cover the basics of finding and addressing regular security issues that thorough reviews and basic vulnerability scanning can find. Otherwise, you end up paying external people to find bugs that your own teams could have easily detected. This is not the intended purpose of VRPs. It also has the downside that more than one researcher (*https://oreil.ly/6qBkN*) may report the same issue to you.

Knowing how to set up a bug bounty program requires a little bit of legwork up front. If you choose to run a bug bounty program, you can follow these basic steps:

1. Determine whether your organization is ready for this program.

   a. Scope the areas of your system to target. For example, you might not be able to target corporate systems.

   b. Determine payout levels and set aside funds for payouts.[10]

2. Consider whether you want to run an in-house bug bounty program or hire an organization that specializes in these programs.

3. If running your own, set up a process for bug intake, triage, investigation, validation, follow-up, and fixes. In our experience, you can estimate this process to take approximately 40 hours for each serious issue, excluding fixes.

4. Define a process for making payments. Remember that reporters may be located all over the world, not just in your home country. You will need to work with your legal and finance teams to understand any constraints that may exist on your organization.

5. Launch, learn, and iterate.

Every bug bounty program faces some likely challenges, including the following:

The need to fine-tune the firehose of issues being reported
   Depending on your industry reputation, the attack surface, payout amounts, and the ease of finding bugs, you may be fielding an overwhelming number of reports. Understand up front what level of response will be required from your organization.

Poor report quality
   A bug bounty program can become burdensome if most of your engineers are chasing down basic issues or nonissues. We have found this is especially true for web services, since many users have misconfigured browsers and "find" bugs that aren't actually bugs. Security researchers are less likely to be in this pool, but sometimes it's hard to discern a bug reporter's qualifications up front.

---

10 For further reading, see sirdarckcat's post about vulnerability pricing (*https://oreil.ly/11Q2P*).

Language barriers

A vulnerability researcher may not necessarily report a bug to you in your native language. Tools for language translation can be helpful here, or your organization may have someone who understands the language used by the reporter.

Vulnerability disclosure guidelines

The rules for disclosing vulnerabilities are not generally agreed upon. Should the researcher go public with what they know, and if so, when? How long should the researcher give your organization to fix the bug? What types of findings will be rewarded, and what types won't? There are many differing opinions about the "right" methods to use here. Here are some suggestions for further reading:

- The Google security team has written a blog post (*https://oreil.ly/t_FP9*) on responsible disclosure.[11]

- Project Zero, an internal vulnerability research team at Google, has also written a blog post (*https://oreil.ly/oDjT-*) on data-driven updates to disclosure policy.

- The Oulu University Secure Programming Group provides a useful collection of vulnerability disclosure publications (*https://oreil.ly/qILyu*).

- The International Standards Organization (ISO) provides recommendations (*https://oreil.ly/kRc5Z*) for vulnerability disclosure.

Be prepared to address issues researchers report to you in a timely manner. Also be aware that they may find issues that have been actively exploited by a malicious actor for some period of time, in which case you may also have a security breach to address.

Conclusion

Security and reliability are created by the quality or absence of processes and practices. People are the most important drivers of these processes and practices. Effective employees are able to collaborate across roles, departments, and cultural boundaries. We live in a world where the future is unknowable and our adversaries are unpredictable. At the end of the day, ensuring that everyone in your organization is responsible for security and reliability is the best defense!

---

11 sirdarckcat has also written a post about vulnerability disclosure (*https://oreil.ly/iQn3z*).

Building a Culture of Security and Reliability

By Heather Adkins
with Peter Valchev, Felix Gröbert, Ana Oprea,
Sergey Simakov, Douglas Colish, and Betsy Beyer

Imagine a new employee joining your organization. Is that employee aware of the importance of security and reliability, and how they are prioritized among other organizational objectives? Do employees know what role they play in ensuring that systems can withstand errors coming from a bad push or malicious adversaries?

This chapter outlines aspects of a healthy culture of security and reliability. We also touch on how you can affect organizational culture by choosing good practices when it's time to make changes. Finally, we provide insights into how to influence leadership and teams across the organization to build buy-in for security and reliability.

We share some practices here that we've found useful at Google and elsewhere, but keep in mind that no two organizations are exactly the same—you'll need to adapt these techniques to the culture of your organization. You will also find that it's likely not possible to adopt all of these strategies. This chapter is meant to be a guide and reference for continuous consideration. It's worth noting that at Google, we don't practice the recommendations we cover here perfectly every day, but rather seek to improve in each approach as part of building our overall culture.

Effective security and reliability flourish when organizations embrace their importance by building a culture around these fundamentals. Organizations that explicitly design, implement, and maintain the culture they seek to embody achieve success by making culture a team effort—the responsibility of everyone, from the CEO and their leadership team, to technical leaders and managers, to the people who design, implement, and maintain systems.

Imagine this scenario: just last week, the CEO told your entire organization that getting the next Big Deal was critical to the future of the company. This afternoon, you found evidence of an attacker on the company's systems, and you know these systems will have to be taken offline. Customers are going to be angry, and the Big Deal may be at risk. You also know that your team may get blamed for not applying security patches last month, but a lot of people were on vacation and everyone is under tight deadlines for the Big Deal. What kinds of decisions does your company culture support employees making in this situation? A healthy organization with a strong security culture would encourage employees to report the incidents immediately despite the risk of delaying the Big Deal.

Suppose that at the same time you're investigating the malicious interloper, the frontend development team accidently pushes a significant change intended for staging to the live production system. The error takes the company's revenue stream offline for over an hour, and customers are overwhelming the support helpline. The trust of your customer base is quickly eroding. A culture of reliability would encourage employees to redesign the process that allowed an accidental frontend push, so that teams can manage the needs of customers and the risk of missing or delaying the Big Deal.

In these situations, cultural norms should encourage blameless postmortems to uncover patterns of failure that can be fixed, thereby avoiding harmful conditions in the future.[1] Companies with healthy cultures know that getting hacked once is very painful, but getting hacked twice is even worse. Similarly, they know that 100% is never the right reliability target; using tools like error budgets[2] and controls around safe code pushes can keep users happy by striking the right balance between reliability and velocity. Finally, companies with a healthy security and reliability culture know that in the long term, customers appreciate transparency when incidents inevitably occur, and that hiding such incidents can erode user trust.

This chapter describes some patterns and anti-patterns for building a culture of security and reliability. While we hope that this information will be helpful to organizations of all shapes and sizes, culture is a unique element of an organization, crafted in the context of its particular challenges and features. No two organizations will have the same culture, and not all of the advice we provide here may be applicable to everyone. This is a chapter meant to provide a range of ideas on the topic of culture, but it's unlikely that every organization will be able to adopt all of the practices we

---

1 See Chapter 15 of the SRE book.

2 This is discussed in Chapter 3 of the SRE book.

discuss. The somewhat idealized view we present here won't be wholly practical in real-world situations. At Google too, we don't get culture right all the time, and we're constantly seeking to improve upon the status quo. We hope that from among the wide range of viewpoints and options presented here, you'll find some that may work in your environment.

Defining a Healthy Security and Reliability Culture

Like healthy systems, a healthy team culture can be explicitly designed, implemented, and maintained. Throughout this book, we've focused on the technical and process components of building healthy systems. Design principles for building healthy cultures exist as well. In fact, culture is a core component of designing, implementing, and maintaining secure and reliable systems.

Culture of Security and Reliability by Default

As we discuss in Chapter 4, it's often tempting to delay considering security and reliability until the later stages of a project's lifecycle. This postponement appears to accelerate initial velocity, but it does so at the expense of sustained velocity and a potentially increased cost of retrofits. Over time, these retrofits can increase technical debt or be applied inconsistently, leading to failure. To illustrate this point, imagine that when buying a car, you had to separately seek out a seat belt vendor, someone to review the safety of the car's windshield, and an inspector to validate the airbags. Addressing safety and reliability concerns only *after* manufacturing a car would place a high burden on the consumer, who may not be in the best position to assess whether the solutions implemented are sufficient. It could also lead to inconsistent practices between any two manufactured cars.

This analogy reflects the need for systems to be *secure and reliable by default*. When security and reliability choices are made throughout the lifecycle of a project, it's easier to maintain consistency. Also, when these are integrated parts of the system, they can become invisible to the consumer. To return to the car analogy: consumers don't need to give much thought to safety mechanisms like seat belts, windshields, or rearview cameras to trust that they do the right thing.

Organizations with healthy cultures of by-default security and reliability encourage employees to discuss such topics early in the project lifecycle—for example, during the design stage—and throughout each iteration of implementation. As products mature, their security and reliability will continue to mature organically as well; this is formalized into the software development lifecycle.

Such a culture makes it easier for people designing, maintaining, and implementing systems to incorporate the themes of security and reliability automatically and transparently. For example, you can introduce automation for continuous builds, sanitizers, vulnerability discovery, and testing. Application frameworks and common libraries can help developers avoid common vulnerabilities like XSS and SQL injection. Guidance around choosing the appropriate programming languages or programming language features can help avoid memory corruption errors. This kind of automatic security aims to reduce friction (such as slow code audits) and errors (bugs not spotted during review), and should be relatively transparent to developers. As systems mature within these security and reliability constructs, ideally, employees will increasingly trust these implementations.

We provide some insight into the evolution of creating a culture of security and reliability by default at Google in Chapters 12, 13, and 19.

Culture of Review

When a strong review culture is in place, everyone is encouraged to think ahead of time about their role in approving changes. This can bolster the ongoing security and reliability properties of the system by ensuring that changes take these special considerations into account. Peer reviews to ensure the security and reliability features of a system apply in a variety of change scenarios, such as these:

- Multi-party authorization reviews for access or changes to maintain least privilege (see Chapter 5)

- Peer reviews to ensure that code changes are appropriate and of high quality, including security and reliability considerations (see Chapter 12)

- Peer reviews of configuration changes before they are pushed to production systems (see Chapter 14)

Building such a culture requires a broad understanding across the organization about the value of the reviews and how to carry them out.

Change review practices should be documented to set clear expectations about what will happen during the review. For example, for peer code reviews, you might document the organization's engineering practices related to code review and educate all new developers about these expectations.[3] When requiring peer review for multi-party authorization schemes (as described in Chapter 5), document when access will be granted and under what conditions it might be refused. This establishes a common cultural set of expectations across the organization, so that only valid approval requests will succeed. Similarly, you should set expectations that if an approver

---

3 Google's practices for code reviews are documented in the Code Review Developer Guide (*https://oreil.ly/ mnPdJ*). For additional background on Google's code review process and culture, see Sadowski, Caitlin et al. 2018. "Modern Code Review: A Case Study at Google." *https://oreil.ly/IfFJ1*.

denies a request, the reasons are understandable based on the documented policy, to avoid hard feelings between people and creating an "us versus them" mentality.

The corollary to documentation is to educate reviewers so they understand the baseline expectations for being a reviewer. This education can happen early on, during onboarding to the organization or a project. Consider onboarding new reviewers through an apprenticeship scheme, in which a more experienced or calibrated reviewer also looks over the change.

A culture of review requires everyone to participate in the review processes. While owners are responsible for ensuring the overall direction and standards of their respective areas, they too should be individually held accountable for the changes they initiate. No one should be able to opt out of a review simply because they have a senior role or don't want to participate. The owner of a code tree isn't exempt from having their code and configuration changes reviewed. In the same way, system owners aren't exempted from participating in multi-party authorization for logins.

Reducing Friction

Consider establishing lightweight review options that enable a quicker change process for minor changes. As we state in Chapter 14, reviews are effective only if they're mandatory. However, reviews need not be burdensome. A minor configuration change or a multi-party authorization request to temporarily access a nonsensitive resource doesn't have to require a heavyweight process. Be sure to have clearly established guidelines about what needs a lightweight review and what needs a heavyweight one, so developers and reviewers have the same expectations.

By choosing the right workflow tooling, you can also help reduce friction for developers—tools that make it easy to initiate changes, provide diffs for reviewers, and have automation support for small changes can decrease friction.[4]

Ensure that reviewers have the context necessary to make decisions, and have the option to decline or redirect a review if they lack enough context to accurately assess whether the change is safe. This is especially important when reviewing the security and reliability properties of an access request, such as multi-party authorization, or changes to code snippets with safety implications. If the reviewer is not familiar with the kinds of pitfalls to look out for, then the review will not act as a sufficient control. Automated checks can assist with building this context. For example, in Chapter 13 we discussed how Google uses Tricorder (*https://oreil.ly/rdYsN*) to automatically

---

4 A 2018 study of the modern code review process at Google (*https://oreil.ly/9FhBV*) found that developers valued the low-friction workflows provided by their tooling.

raise security issues for developers and reviewers in the presubmit phase of code changes.

Culture of Awareness

When members of an organization are aware they have security and reliability responsibilities, and know how to carry them out, they can be effective in achieving good outcomes. For example, an engineer may need to take extra steps to keep their account secure because they access sensitive systems. Someone whose job entails frequent communication with external parties may receive more phishing emails. An executive may be at higher risk when they travel to certain parts of the world. Organizations with healthy cultures build awareness of these kinds of conditions and reinforce it through educational programs.

Awareness and education strategies are key to building a strong security culture. These initiatives should strive to be lighthearted and fun so that learners are interested in the content. People retain different types of information at different rates depending on how that information is conveyed, their existing familiarity with the material, and even personal factors like age and background. In our experience, many learners have a higher retention rate with interactive methods of learning like hands-on labs than with passive learning methods like watching a video. When building awareness, optimize for the best learning experience by carefully considering what types of information you want people to retain and how you want them to learn.

Google takes several approaches to educating employees about security and reliability. On a broad scale, we provide mandatory annual training for all employees. We then reinforce these messages through specialty programs for certain roles. Here are some tactics we've found useful over years of implementing these programs at Google:

Interactive talks

Talks that encourage audience participation can be a way of relaying complex information in a compelling way. For example, at Google, sharing top root causes and mitigations for significant security and reliability incidents has helped our employees better understand why we focus on these topics. We've found that these types of interactive discussions also encourage people to raise issues they find, from suspicious activity on their workstations to buggy code that could take systems down. This practice helps people feel like they're part of the team that makes the organization more reliable and secure.

Games

Gamifying security and reliability is another way to build awareness. These methods tend to scale more effectively to larger organizations, which may be better able to give players flexibility around when they take the training and an option to retake it if they want. Our XSS game (*https://xss-game.appspot.com*)

(shown in Figure 21-1) has been quite successful in teaching developers about this common web application vulnerability.

Figure 21-1. A security training game

Reference documentation

Reading documentation may have a lower retention rate for learning than methods like hands-on exercises, but we've found that it's critically important to provide developers with strong documentation they can reference when needed. As we note in Chapter 12, reference documentation is important because it's difficult to keep the numerous nuances of security and reliability in one's mind simultaneously. For guidance on common security problems, Google maintains a set of internal security best practices that engineers can search for answers to problems as they arise.[5] All documentation should have clear ownership and be kept up to date or deprecated when it's not relevant anymore.

Awareness campaigns

It can be hard to notify developers about recent security and reliability issues and developments. To tackle this, Google publishes weekly engineering advice in a one-page format (Figure 21-2 shows an example). These "Testing on the Toilet" (*https://oreil.ly/cO_P8*) episodes are distributed to restrooms throughout all Google offices. While initially aimed at improving testing, the program also

---

5 For example, Google maintains a set of best practices for cross-site scripting (*https://oreil.ly/qYpj8*).

occasionally features security and reliability topics. A flyer posted in an unavoidable location is a good way to present tips and provide inspiration.[6]

Testing on the Toilet Presents... Security in the Stall   October 10, 2017

Avoid Inline Event Handlers in HTML

October is Security & Privacy Month. It includes a Security Fixit, which focuses on protecting our code from common web vulnerabilities, including XSS (cross-site scripting). Learn more about getting involved at the Security Fixit site.

A common anti-pattern in web applications is the use of inline event handlers, such as `onclick` or `onload`. You can easily introduce them in your markup, like this:

```
<body onload="prepareBunnyRace()">
  <b onclick="runBunniesRun()">Make the bunnies run!</b>
</body>
```

Why are inline event handlers bad?

- They can lead to XSS bugs because their contents require tricky escaping; getting it wrong can allow an attacker to inject malicious scripts into your page.
- Their contents are not compiled or covered by checkers such as JS Conformance, making it easier to write bad or insecure code; this pattern violates the JavaScript style guide.
- They prevent your application from adopting Content Security Policy, a new web standard to provide defense-in-depth against script injection, which requires all scripts to come from trusted sources.
- They mix document structure and behavior, which is strongly discouraged by the HTML style guide because it increases the cost of maintaining your markup.

Luckily, most instances of inline event handlers in your HTML are easy to refactor into safer and cleaner alternatives. The best way is to add event handlers in JavaScript: move the handlers to the JS file that contains the rest of your client-side code:

```
<body>                              goog.events.listen(document, 'DOMContentLoaded', () => {
  <b id="bunnyRunner">                prepareBunnyRace();
    Make the bunnies run!             goog.events.listen(document.getElementById('bunnyRunner'),
  </b>                                  'click', () => { runBunniesRun(); });
</body>                             });
```

Figure 21-2. An episode of Testing on the Toilet

Just-in-time notifications

Especially during procedural steps (like checking in code or upgrading software), you may want to remind people of good security and reliability practices. Showing just-in-time notifications to people in these situations can help them make better risk decisions. At Google, we have experimented with showing pop-ups and hints in the moment—for example, when employees are upgrading software from an untrusted repository or trying to upload sensitive data to unapproved

---

6 A recent study on the use of the Testing-on-the-Toilet program at Google showed that the program increased developer awareness. See Murphy-Hill, Emerson et al. 2019. "Do Developers Learn New Tools on the Toilet?" *Proceedings of the 41st International Conference on Software Engineering. https://oreil.ly/ZN18B. (https://oreil.ly/ZN18B)*

cloud storage systems. When users see alerts in real time when it matters, they can make better decisions for themselves and avoid mistakes.[7] On a related note, as we discuss in Chapter 13, presenting developers with presubmit security and reliability hints helps them make better choices when developing code.

Culture of Yes

Over time, organizations can develop a conservative risk culture, especially if security breaches or reliability issues have led to revenue loss or other bad outcomes. In an extreme form, this mindset can lead to a *culture of no*: the inclination to avoid risky changes and the negative consequences they might entail. When perpetuated in the name of security or reliability, a culture of no can cause an organization to stagnate, and even fail to innovate. We've found that healthy organizations have a way to work through the challenge of saying "yes" when taking advantage of an opportunity requires some amount of risk—that is, to take risks deliberately. To embrace risk in this way, you typically need to be able to assess and measure it.

As a concrete example, in Chapter 8 we describe the approach used to secure Google App Engine, a platform that proposed running third-party unverified code. In this situation, Google's security team could have judged the launch as too risky. After all, running arbitrary untrusted code is a fairly well-known security risk. You don't know, for instance, if the third party managing the code might be malicious and try to escape from the platform's execution environment and compromise your infrastructure. To address this risk, we embarked on an ambitious collaboration between the product and security teams to produce a layered, hardened system, which allowed us to launch a product that would have otherwise seemed too dangerous. This kind of collaboration made it easier to build additional security into the platform over time, since there was an established base of trust between the teams.

> ## Balancing Accountability and Risk Taking
>
> The inclination to say no to risky changes can also stem from an individual's fear of making the wrong call. In the context of design reviews and code audits, this tendency can be especially challenging, since it's not possible for humans performing manual reviews to find every single security or reliability problem. If people think they are the only line of defense against a risky change, they may be less inclined to embrace risk.

---

7 This topic is closely related to *nudging*, a method of changing behavior by subtly encouraging people to do the right thing. Nudge theory was developed by Richard Thaler and Cass Sunstein, who were awarded a Nobel Prize in Economics for their contribution to behavioral economics. For more information, see Thaler, Richard H., and Cass R. Sunstein. 2008. *Nudge: Improving Decisions About Health, Wealth, and Happiness.* New Haven, CT: Yale University Press.

> Organizations that embrace risk defend against this pressure by adopting design strategies for elements such as least privilege, resiliency, and testing. These layered approaches lift the burden of being perfect off of individuals' shoulders. If someone makes a mistake during review, other checks and balances can prevent disaster.

Another approach to embracing risk is to use error budgets (*https://oreil.ly/gd3MY*), which allow for failures up to a certain limit. Once the organization reaches a predetermined maximum limit, teams are expected to collaborate to reduce risk to normal levels. Because the error budget maintains an emphasis on security and reliability throughout the product's lifecycle, innovators have the freedom to introduce a certain number of risky changes.

Culture of Inevitably

No system is perfect, and any system may eventually fail. At some point, your organization will likely experience a service outage or a security incident. Embracing this inevitability can help teams have the appropriate frame of mind to build secure and reliable systems and respond to failures.[8] At Google, we assume failure can happen at any time—not because we aren't diligent about proactive measures or because we lack confidence in our systems, but because we know that real-world systems can never be 100% secure and reliable.

Chapter 16 discusses the need to prepare for the inevitable. Teams that embrace a culture of inevitability dedicate time to prepare for disasters so they can respond effectively. They talk openly about the possibilities for failure and set time aside to simulate these scenarios. Incident response skills are effective only when you use them regularly, so it's a good idea to use exercises such as tabletops, Red Team attacks, hands-on recovery tests, and disaster role playing (*https://oreil.ly/hyDi_*) to test and refine your organization's processes. Organizations that embrace the inevitable also study any failures that do occur, including within their peer groups. Internally, they use blameless postmortems—discussed in Chapter 18 of this book and in Chapter 15 of the SRE book—to reduce the fear of failure and build confidence that repeated events will be unlikely. They also make use of after-action reports published by other organizations, both within and outside of their industry. These reports provide a broader understanding of failure scenarios that may be relevant to the organization.

---

8 Dave Rensin, Director of Customer Reliability Engineering at Google, considers this topic in greater detail in his talk "Less Risk Through Greater Humanity" (*https://oreil.ly/ZrWkS*).

Culture of Sustainability

In order to sustain the reliability and security features of a system in the long term, your organization must ensure that efforts to improve them are made continuously—and dedicate sufficient resources (staff and time) to the task. Sustainability requires building the means to handle outages, security incidents, and other emergencies on an ongoing basis, using clearly defined processes.

To maintain this effort, teams must be able to balance the time spent on reactive work versus proactive investments that will pay off over the long term. To recall our example of the California Department of Forestry and Fire Protection from Chapter 17, effective teams allocate the burden of hard work across many people's shoulders so that no one person is saddled with excessive responsibility.

Organizations with a *culture of sustainability* measure the workloads necessary to handle operational work (for example, incident response[10]) as well as the investments required to make improvements over time.[11] They consider stress, burnout, and morale in their planning, adding sufficient resources to sustain long-term efforts or deferring work where necessary through prioritization. They avoid the need for heroics by setting up repeatable and predictable processes for handling emergencies and rotating the staff who handle emergencies regularly. They also proactively handle morale issues by surfacing individuals' concerns and continuously motivating people.

---

9 The final report of the Columbia Disaster Investigation Board is preserved on the NASA website (*https://oreil.ly/ew-BA*) for the general public to read. Chapter 7 in particular focuses on the culture of safety at NASA and its impact on the disaster. We've found that the report's findings can often be extrapolated to organizational culture in other types of engineering organizations.

10 See Chapter 29 of the SRE book.

11 See Chapter 32 of the SRE book.

Sustainable Reliability and Security Culture at Google

Google has many moving parts and a correspondingly complex adversary landscape, which necessitates large teams of dedicated SREs and operational security personnel. These teams operate in "follow the sun" shifts in order to avoid stress and burnout, and are designed to be staffed accordingly. They spend only a portion of their time doing operational work and the rest making infrastructure improvements. We also designate dedicated development resources for long-term initiatives. There's an intended virtuous circle in this work because these initiatives strive to automate away toilsome operational work, improving morale and freeing people to spend more time on mentally challenging problems.

The linchpin of the sustainability effort at Google, however, is the way we manage the health of our people. Managers are trained to focus on building and maintaining healthy teams, which includes addressing negative impacts of the work. These principles are encoded in our culture as part of Project Oxygen (*https://oreil.ly/9cZK1*).

Having a culture of sustainably also means knowing that sometimes exceptional circumstances can cause temporary deviations from expected workloads, and having good processes to handle those deviations. For example, if multiple business-critical systems haven't met their SLOs for a long period of time, or a serious security breach results in an extraordinary response effort, you may need an "all hands on deck" effort to get things back on track. During this time, teams may be entirely devoted to operational work and improving security or reliability. While you might have to defer all other organizational work, you may also have to deviate from best practices.

In healthy organizations, such extraordinary disruptions of normal business operations should be rare. When navigating these situations, the following considerations can help maintain a culture of sustainability once the situation is resolved:

- When operating outside of normal operations, be sure to clarify that the situation is temporary. For example, if you require all developers to manually supervise the changes they push to production (instead of only using automated systems), this might cause a lot of toil and unhappiness in the long term. Make clear that you expect the situation to return to normal soon, and give an idea of when that will happen.

- Have a dedicated group on standby that has an understanding of the risk landscape and the authority to make decisions quickly. For example, this group might grant exceptions to standard security and reliability procedures. This will reduce friction in execution, while giving the organization some assurance that safety mechanisms are still in place. Have a way to flag the times you had to bypass or overturn best practices, and be sure to address those one-offs later.

- When the event is complete, be sure that your postmortem reviews the reward system that may have led to the emergency. Sometimes, cultural issues like prioritizing feature launch over reliability or security features can lead to a build-up of technical debt. Addressing such issues proactively going forward will help the organization return to a cadence of sustainability.

Changing Culture Through Good Practice

Affecting organizational culture can be difficult, especially if the team or project you're working on is well established. It's not uncommon for an organization to want to make security and reliability improvements, but find that cultural obstacles stand in the way. Counterproductive cultures exist for many reasons: leadership approaches, starvation of resources, and more.

A common element of resistance to change—the kind of change necessary for security and reliability improvements—is fear. Change can conjure images of chaos, greater friction, loss of productivity and control, and increased risk. In particular, the topic of friction frequently surfaces in relation to new reliability and security controls. New access checks, processes, and procedures can be interpreted as interfering with developer or operational productivity. When organizations face tight deadlines and high expectations to deliver, either self-imposed or driven by management, fear of these new controls can heighten concerns. However, in our opinion, the belief that security and reliability improvements have to create friction is a myth. If you implement change with certain cultural considerations in mind, we believe these changes can actually improve everyone's experience.

This section discusses some technical strategies to introduce change that may be useful even in the most difficult cultures. You may not be the CEO or a leader in your organization, but every developer, SRE, and security professional is an instrument of change in their own sphere of influence. By making conscious choices about how you design, implement, and maintain systems, it is possible to have a positive effect on your organization's culture; by choosing certain strategies, you may find that over time you can turn the tide by building trust and goodwill.

The advice we give in this section is based on that goal—but culture is something developed over a long period of time, and it's highly dependent on the people and situations involved. When trying out some of the strategies outlined here in your organization, you may find they meet with only limited success, and some strategies may not work at all. Some cultures are static and resistant to change. Yet having a healthy culture that values security and reliability can be just as important as how you design, implement, and maintain your systems, so the fact that your efforts might not always work shouldn't stop you from trying.

Align Project Goals and Participant Incentives

It takes hard work to build trust, but it's quite easy to lose it. In order for people who design, implement and maintain systems to collaborate across multiple roles, they need to share a common reward system.

On a technical level, the reliability and safety of a project can be evaluated regularly through observable metrics like SLOs (*https://oreil.ly/m9rU1*) and threat modeling (for examples, see Chapters 2 and 14). On a process and people level, you should make sure that career advancement opportunities reward security and reliability. Ideally, individuals should be evaluated according to high-level documented expectations. These shouldn't be just a set of checkboxes to tick—they should highlight themes and goals that individuals should aspire to meet. For example, the entry-level Google software engineering job ladder specifies that engineers should master at least one common skill outside of core coding, like adding monitoring to their services or writing security tests.

Aligning project goals with your organization's strategy without aligning participant incentives might result in an unfriendly culture, whereby the people focused on improving the security and reliability of your products are not the ones who tend to get promoted. Since financial rewards regularly correlate to seniority, it's only fair to keep the employees who contribute to happy users happy by aligning project incentives to the reward system.

Reduce Fear with Risk-Reduction Mechanisms

Have you ever found yourself wanting to make a significant change, such as a rollout of new software or a new control, only to find that the organization pushes back because of the perceived risk? You can inspire confidence in your organization by making good deployment choices. We discuss many of these concepts Chapter 7, but it's worth specifically noting the impact of culture here. Here are some strategies you might want to try:

Canaries and staged rollouts
> You can reduce fear by slowly rolling out substantial changes through small canary groups of users or systems. That way, the blast radius of an ill-fated change is small if something goes wrong. Also consider going one step further, and implementing all changes via staged rollouts and canaries (see Chapter 16 in the SRE workbook). In practice, this approach has numerous benefits. For example, in Chapter 19 we discuss how the staged release cycle for Chrome balances the competing needs of speedy updates and reliability. Over time, Chrome's staged releases have fostered its reputation as a secure browser. We've also found that by making staged rollouts part of a routine change process, over time, an organiza-

tion comes to expect that care and diligence are applied to all changes—which builds confidence in change and reduces fear.

Dogfood

By showing users that you're not afraid of your own changes, you can instill confidence in the stability and productivity impact of any particular change. *Dogfooding* (or "eating your own dogfood") involves adopting a change before that change affects others. This is especially important if you're affecting the systems and processes that impact people's daily lives. For example, if you're rolling out a new least privilege mechanism such as multi-factor authorization, adopt the stricter control within your own team before you require all employees to implement the change. At Google, before we roll out new endpoint security software, we test it on some of our most discerning users (the security team) first.

Trusted testers

Inviting people in your organization to help test a change early in a project's lifecycle can reduce fear of future change. This approach lets stakeholders see a change before it becomes final, which allows them to raise concerns early. These newly open lines of communication give them a direct channel to deliver feedback if something goes wrong. Showing a willingness to gather feedback during testing phases can reduce silos between parts of your organization. It's important to make clear to the testers that you trust the feedback they're giving, and to make use of their feedback so they know they're heard. You can't always address every piece of feedback—not all of it will be valid or actionable—but by explaining your decisions to your tester population, you can build a strong coalition of trust.

Opt in before mandatory

A corollary to the dogfood and trusted tester strategies is making a new control optional before it becomes mandatory. This gives teams the opportunity to adopt changes on their own timeline. Complicated changes, such as new authorization controls or testing frameworks, have a cost; it can take time for an organization to fully adopt such changes, and you often need to balance these changes against other priorities. If teams know they have time to implement changes at their own pace, they may be less resistant to doing so.

Progressive stringency

If you have to put into effect a strict new policy for reliability or security, consider whether you can ratchet up the stringency over time: perhaps you can first introduce a lower-level control that has less impact before teams fully adopt a more stringent one with a heavier burden. For example, suppose you want to add least privilege controls that require employees to justify their access to certain data. Users who don't justify the access appropriately will be locked out of the system. In this scenario, you could start by having the developer team integrate the justification framework (such as a library) into the system, but keep end user justifications optional. Once you deem the system to be performant and secure, you could require justifications to access data without locking out users who fail to meet the established criteria. Instead, the system could provide detailed error messages when a user enters an inaccurate justification, providing a feedback loop to train users and improve use of the system. After a period of time, when metrics show a high success rate for proper justifications, you can make the stringent control that locks users out of the system mandatory.

Make Safety Nets the Norm

Reliability and security improvements often require you to remove long-relied-upon resources that don't measure up to the new safety standards you're introducing. For example, imagine you want to change how people in your organization use Unix root privileges (or similar highly privileged access), perhaps by implementing new proxy systems (see Chapter 3). Fear of substantial changes like these is natural. After all, what if a team suddenly loses access to a resource that's mission-critical? What if the change results in downtime?

You can reduce fear of change by providing safety nets like breakglass procedures (discussed in Chapter 5) that allow users to bypass a new stringent control. These emergency procedures should be used sparingly, however, and subjected to a high level of audit; they should be viewed as a last resort, not a convenient alternative. When implemented properly, breakglass procedures can provide nervous teams with the assurance that they can adopt a change or react to an incident without completely losing control or productivity. For example, suppose you have a staged rollout procedure that requires a long canary process, which you've implemented as a safety mechanism to prevent reliability issues. You can provide a breakglass bypass mechanism to make the push happen immediately if absolutely necessary. We discuss these types of situations in Chapter 14.

Increase Productivity and Usability

A fear of increased friction can make organizational changes with regard to security and reliability difficult. If people view new controls that slow down development and innovation as counterproductive, they may assume that their adoption will have a negative impact on the organization. For this reason, it's often important to think carefully about the adoption strategy for new initiatives: consider the amount of time necessary to incorporate the change, whether the change might slow down productivity, and whether the benefit outweighs the cost of making the change. We've found that the following techniques help decrease friction:

Build transparent functionality

In Chapters 6 and 12, we discuss relieving developers of the responsibility for security and reliability by using secure-by-construction APIs, frameworks, and libraries. Making the secure choice the default choice helps developers do the right thing without placing a heavy burden on them. This approach reduces friction over time because developers not only see the benefits of having secure and reliable systems, but also recognize your intent to keep these initiatives simple and easy. We've found this can build trust between teams over time.

Focus on usability

A focus on usability positively affects a culture of security and reliability.[12] If a new control is easier to use than what it's replacing, it can create positive incentives for change.

In Chapter 7, we talk about how we focused on usability when rolling out security keys for two-factor authentication. Users found that touching a security key to authenticate was much easier than typing in one-time passwords generated by hardware tokens.

As an added bonus, the enhanced security of these keys allowed us to require less frequent password changes.[13] We performed a risk analysis on this topic, considering tradeoffs in usability, security, and auditability. We found that security keys negate the efficacy of password theft by a remote attacker. When combined with monitoring to detect suspected compromise of passwords,[14] and enforcement of password changes in such an event, we were able to balance security and usability.

There are other opportunities where security and reliability features can deprecate old or unwanted processes and increase usability. Taking advantage of these opportunities can build user confidence and trust in security and reliability solutions.

---

12 Usable solutions for security and privacy have long been recognized as key to successful deployment of technology controls. For a flavor of what these conversations look like, you might be interested in exploring the proceedings of SOUPS (*https://oreil.ly/8bTuI*), a conference dedicated to usable security and privacy.

13 Studies have shown that users make poor choices that put their passwords at risk. For more information on the adverse effects of user password choices, see Zhang, Yinqian, Fabian Monrose, and Michael K. Reiter. 2010. "The Security of Modern Password Expiration: An Algorithmic Framework and Empirical Analysis." *Proceedings of the 17th ACM Conference on Computer and Communications Security*: 176–186. *https://oreil.ly/NbfFj*. Standards and compliance regimes are also considering these effects. For example, NIST 800-63 (*https://oreil.ly/q2Bgw*) has been updated to require a password change only when there is suspicion that it has been compromised.

14 Password Alert is a Chrome browser extension that alerts when a user has typed their Google or GSuite password into a malicious website.

Self-registration and self-resolution

    Self-registration and self-resolution portals empower developers and end users to address security and reliability issues directly, without gating on a central team that may be overloaded or slow. For example, Google uses deny and allow lists to control which applications can run on the systems that employees use. This technology is effective in preventing execution of malicious software (such as viruses).

    The downside is that if an employee wants to run software not already on the allow list, they need to seek approval. To reduce friction for exception requests, we developed a self-help portal called Upvote (*https://github.com/google/upvote*) that enables users to get approval for acceptable software quickly. In some cases, we can automatically determine a piece of software to be safe and approve it. If we can't automatically approve the software, we give the user an option to have it approved by a set number of peers.

    We've found social voting to be a satisfactory control. It's not perfect—sometimes employees approve software that's not necessarily business-related, such as video games—but this approach has had a high rate of effectiveness in preventing malware from being executed on our systems. And since it does not gate on a central team, friction for the control is kept very low.

Overcommunicate and Be Transparent

When advocating for change, the means of communication can influence outcomes. As we discuss in Chapters 7 and 19, good communication is key to building buy-in and confidence in success. Giving people information and clear insight into how change is happening can reduce fear and build trust. We've found the following strategies to be successful:

Document decisions

    When making a change, clearly document why it's happening, what success looks like, how the change will be rolled back if operating conditions deteriorate, and who to talk to in case of concerns. Make sure that you clearly communicate why you're making the change, especially if it directly affects employees. For example, every Production Excellence SLO at Google requires a documented rationale. Since the SRE organization is measured against these SLOs, it's important that SREs understand the meaning behind them.[15]

---

15 Production Excellence reviews are carried out periodically on SRE teams by senior SRE leaders, assessing them on a number of standard measures and providing feedback and encouragement. An SLO of 99.95% might be accompanied by a rationale such as, "We previously wanted to reach a 99.99% success rate, but found this target to be unrealistic in practice. We have not discovered a negative impact on developer productivity at 99.95%."

Create feedback channels

Make communication bidirectional by creating feedback channels through which people can raise concerns. This could be a feedback form, a link to your bug tracking system, or even a simple email address. As we mention in the discussion of trusted testers (see "Reduce Fear with Risk-Reduction Mechanisms" on page 484), giving partners and stakeholders a more direct involvement in a change can lessen fear.

Use dashboards

If you're making a complex change across multiple teams or parts of the infrastructure, use dashboards to show clear expectations of what you need people to do and provide feedback on how well they're doing. Dashboards are also helpful in showing the big picture of a rollout and keeping the organization in sync on progress.

Write frequent updates

If a change takes a long time (some changes at Google have taken several years), assign someone to write frequent (for example, monthly) stakeholder updates outlining progress. This will build confidence—especially in leadership—that the project is progressing and that someone has a watchful eye on the health of the program.

Build Empathy

You can't understand someone until you've walked a mile in their shoes.
—Unknown

People begin to understand the challenges others face when they understand the ins and out of performing their role. Cross-team empathy is especially important when it comes to reliability and security properties of the system, since (as discussed in Chapter 20) these responsibilities should be shared across the organization. Building empathy and understanding can help reduce fear in the face of necessary changes.

In Chapter 19, we outline a few techniques for building cross-team empathy—in particular, how teams can share responsibilities for writing, debugging, and fixing code. Similarly, the Chrome security team runs fixits not only to improve the security of the product, but also as a cross-organization team-building activity. Ideally, teams consistently share responsibilities from square one.

Job shadowing or job swapping is another approach to building empathy that doesn't require permanent organizational top-down changes. These engagements can range from a few hours (which tend to be less formal exercises) to several months (which may require management buy-in). By inviting others to experience your team's work, you can signal that you're willing to tear down organizational silos and build common understanding.

Google's SRE Security Exchange Program allows an SRE to shadow another SRE or security engineer for a week. At the end of the exchange, the SRE writes a report with improvement recommendations for both their home team and the host team. When conducted in the same office, this program requires a very low investment but provides many benefits in terms of knowledge sharing across the organization. Google's Mission Control program (*https://oreil.ly/MSlrf*) encourages people to join the SRE organization for six months, during which time they learn how to think like an SRE and respond to emergencies. In doing so, they directly see the impact of software changes initiated in partner organizations. A parallel program known as Hacker Camp encourages people to join the security team for six months, where they can work on security reviews and response efforts.

Programs like these may begin as small experiments with one or two engineers, and grow over time if successful. We've found that this type of job swapping both builds empathy and inspires exciting new ideas about how to solve challenges. Bringing in these new perspectives and building goodwill between teams helps grease the cogs of change.

Finally, building in mechanisms to say thank you—from simple emails to more elaborate forms—reinforces the positive impact that people have on one another and sets the right incentives. At Google, we've long had a culture of peer bonuses—small amounts of cash that don't cost the company a lot of money, but build large amounts of goodwill. A cash-free version of this called Kudos allows Googlers to formally recognize each other in digital form that's visible to everyone. Some of our offices have also experimented with thank-you postcards.

Convincing Leadership

If you work in a large organization, getting buy-in for reliability and security changes you want to make may be a challenge. Since many organizations are incentivized to spend their limited resources on revenue-generating or mission-forward efforts, it can be tough to get buy-in for improvements that are seen as happening behind the scenes.

This section explores some strategies we've used at Google, or seen used elsewhere, to get buy-in from leadership for security and reliability changes. As with the guidance given elsewhere in this chapter, your mileage may vary. Some of these strategies will be effective, while others won't be. Just as every organization's culture is unique, so is every leader and leadership team. It's worth repeating our previous advice here: just because you think one of these strategies won't work doesn't necessarily mean you shouldn't try it. The results just might surprise you.

Understand the Decision-Making Process

Suppose you want to make a fairly substantial change to your organization's custom frontend web-serving infrastructure to include DDoS protection; for example, referencing the benefits outlined in Chapter 10. You know this will vastly improve the reliability and security of the system, but it also requires multiple teams to incorporate new libraries or restructure code. Integrating and testing this change properly could take months. Given the high cost but positive impact, who in your organization would make the decision to move forward, and how would they make that decision? Understanding the answers to these questions is key to knowing how to influence leadership.

Here, the term *leadership* loosely applies to the people who make decisions, whether those decisions are around direction setting, resource allocation, or resolving conflicts. In short, these are the people who are perceived to have authority and accountability. They are the people you want to influence, so you need to figure out who they are. If you work in a large company, they could be VPs or other senior people in management. Smaller organizations, such as startups and nonprofits, often consider the CEO to be the senior decider. In an open source project, this could be the project's founder or top contributor.

The answer to the question "Who is the decider for this change?" can be tricky to determine. The authority to make decisions may indeed lie with someone typically considered to be at the top of the leadership hierarchy or in an obvious gatekeeping role, such as a lawyer or risk officer. But depending on the nature of the change you're proposing, the decision might also reside in a tech lead, or even with you. The decider may not be a single person; it could be a set of stakeholders across the organization from different departments such as legal, press relations, engineering, and product development.

Sometimes the authority to make a decision resides loosely within a group of people or, in the extreme form, within a whole community. For example, in Chapter 7 we describe how the Chrome team participated in increasing HTTPS usage on the internet. In this situation, the decision to make a directional change was made within the community, and required building an industry-wide consensus.

Determining who is a decider for a change may take some sleuthing, especially if you are new to an organization, or if there are no existing processes telling you how to get something done. However, you can't skip this step. Once you understand who the deciders are, you then should seek to understand the pressures and demands that they face. These might stem from their own management, boards of directors, or shareholders, and can even take the form of external influences like customer expectations. It's important to understand these pressures so you can understand where your proposed changes fit in. To return to our earlier example of adding DDoS protection to the frontend web-serving infrastructure, where would that change fit in relative to leadership's priorities?

Build a Case for Change

As we've mentioned already in this chapter, resistance to change can stem from fear or perception of friction, but in many cases it can also stem from not understanding the reason for a change. When faced with many priorities, decision makers and stakeholders have the difficult task of choosing between different goals that they would like to achieve. How will they know your change is valuable? It's important to understand the challenges decision makers face when building a case for your change. These are some of the steps in a successful case-building process:[16]

Gather data

You know that a change needs to be made. How did you come to that conclusion? It's important to have data to back up your proposed change. For example, if you know that building automated test frameworks into the build process will save developers time, can you demonstrate how much time this change will save? If you're advocating for continuous builds because the practice creates incentives for developers to fix errors, can you show how continuous builds save time in the release processes? Conduct research and user studies to produce data-rich reports complete with graphs, charts, and anecdotal stories from users; then summarize this data in a way that decision makers can digest. For example, if you want to drive down the time it takes your team to patch security vulnerabilities or address reliability configuration issues, consider creating a dashboard that tracks progress for each of the engineering teams. Showing those dashboards to the leaders of those areas can encourage individual teams to hit targets. Be mindful of the investments you'll need to make to gather high-quality, relevant data.

Educate others

Security and reliability issues can be hard to understand unless you're connected to them every day. Get the word out through talks and information sessions. At Google, we use Red Team postmortems (see Chapter 20) to educate leaders at a high level about the kinds of risks we're facing. While Red Teams were not originally created as an educational effort, they can raise awareness within all levels of the company. This has been beneficial in convincing teams to maintain their SLOs for remediating vulnerabilities.

---

16 For a practical example of how we successfully built a case for change, see "Example: Increasing HTTPS usage" on page 136.

Align incentives

Using the data you've gathered and your knowledge of the pressures deciders face, you may be able to address other concerns in their sphere of influence. In our earlier DDoS example, making the proposed change to the framework would provide a security benefit, but a more reliable website would also potentially help increase sales. This could be a strong argument to present to the company's leadership. For a real-world example, Chapter 19 discusses how rapid releases of Chrome get security fixes to users faster, with the additional benefit of quick deployment for reliability fixes and new features. This is great for users and product development stakeholders alike. Don't forget to discuss how you're reducing the fear and friction that may accompany a change—as mentioned earlier in this chapter, Google's rollout of security keys allowed us to eliminate unpopular password change policies and reduce end-user friction for two-factor authentication, which were powerful arguments for change.

Find allies

Chances are, you're not the only person who knows that a change you're proposing would be beneficial. Finding allies and convincing them to support your change can add weight to your argument, especially if those people are organizationally close to the decision makers. Allies can also test your assumptions about a change. Perhaps they know of different data-based arguments, or understand the organization in a way that you don't. This type of peer review can bolster the strength of your argument.

Observe industry trends

If you're adopting a change that other organizations have already adopted, you may be able to rely on their experiences to convince your leadership. Do your research—articles, books, public talks at conferences, and other materials may demonstrate how and why an organization took up a change. There may be additional data points you can use directly in building your case for change. You could even consider bringing in expert speakers to address your leadership on specific topics and industry trends.

Change the zeitgeist

If you can change the way people think about your problem over time, it may be easier to convince decision makers later on. This applies especially when you need broad consensus for a change. We discuss this dynamic briefly in the HTTPS case study in Chapter 7, where the Chrome team and others in the industry changed developer behavior over a long period of time, to the point where HTTPS as a default became the norm.

Pick Your Battles

If your organization is facing many reliability and security challenges, constant advocacy can create fatigue and resistance to additional change. It's important to pick your battles carefully: prioritize initiatives that have a chance of succeeding and know when to stop advocating for lost causes. This shows leadership and decision makers that you're tackling the most important issues.

Lost causes—that is, proposals you have to shelve—have value too. Even when you can't successfully advocate for change, having data that supports your ideas and allies that back your plan, and educating people about the problem, can be valuable. At some point, your organization may be ready to tackle a challenge you've already studied. If you already have a plan waiting in the wings, teams can move faster.

Escalations and Problem Resolution

Despite best efforts, sometimes the need to make decisions on a security or reliability change can rise to the surface in an explosive way. Perhaps a serious outage or security breach means that you quickly need more resources and staffing. Or perhaps two teams have differing opinions on how to solve a problem, and the natural course of decision making isn't working. In these types of situations, you may need to seek resolution from the management chain. When dealing with escalations, we recommend the following guidelines:

- Form a group of colleagues, mentors, tech leads, or managers to provide input on the situation from both sides. It's usually a good idea to walk through the situation with someone with an unbiased view before deciding to escalate.

- Have the group summarize the situation and proposed decision options for management. Keep this summary as concise as possible. Maintain a strictly factual tone, and include links to any relevant supporting data, conversations, bugs, designs, etc. Make the potential impact of each option as clear as possible.

- Share the summary with your own team's leadership to ensure further alignment on possible solutions. For example, multiple issues might require simultaneous escalation. You may want to either merge escalations or emphasize other aspects of corresponding situations.

- Schedule a session to present the situation to all affected management chains and designate appropriate decision makers in each chain. The decision makers should then make a formal decision or meet separately to discuss the issue.

As a concrete example, sometimes security issues at Google need to be escalated when an unresolvable disagreement arises between the product team and the security reviewer about the best course of action. In this case, an escalation is initiated within the security team. At that point, the two senior leaders within the organizations negotiate a compromise or decide to implement one of the options suggested by the security team or the product team. Because we integrate these escalations into our normal company culture, escalations aren't seen as confrontational.

Conclusion

Just as you design and manage systems, you can design, implement, and maintain the culture of an organization over time to support security and reliability goals. Reliability and security efforts should be considered just as carefully as engineering efforts. There are important cultural elements of engineering that, when taken in aggregate, or even on their own, can contribute to more robust systems.

Security and reliability improvements can inspire fear or concern about increased friction. There are strategies for addressing these fears and helping achieve buy-in from the people these changes affect. Making sure that your goals are well aligned with stakeholders—including leadership—is key. Focusing on usability and demonstrating empathy for users can encourage people to adopt change more readily. Making a small investment in thinking about how others perceive change may lead to greater success in convincing them that your changes are sound.

As we stated in the opening to this chapter, no two cultures are the same, and you'll need to adapt the strategies we've outlined to your own organization. In doing so, you will also find that you likely can't implement all of these strategies. It may be useful to pick and choose the areas your organization most needs to address, and improve those over time—which is the way Google approaches constant improvement over the long term.

Conclusion

We wrote this book because we believe there is a significant overlap in the technologies and practices that protect systems and keep them reliable, and that organizations should integrate the concepts of security and reliability throughout the process of designing, implementing, and maintaining systems. Whereas traditionally they have been treated as separate disciplines, our view is that security and reliability are inherent properties of a system, and they are therefore the responsibility of everyone involved in the project lifecycle. Many technology shifts are well underway that we believe will inspire organizations to take this view.

This technology revolution—what some have deemed the Fourth Industrial Revolution—is altering the world as we know it. This shift is being felt not only by consumers, in the form of more sophisticated products, but also by the developers who are producing these products. Organizations are increasingly reliant on technology, even if it's not the core of their business. For example, we're seeing systems that let surgeons perform surgery on patients located on the opposite side of the world. Scientists are using autonomous flying vehicles to survey archaeological sites, study the effects of soil erosion, and protect endangered species. Robots are being deployed to perform dangerous work in space and at nuclear disaster sites.

The expanding connectedness of technology means we are growing more dependent on the reliability of those solutions. As we extend our data surfaces to third parties, we need confidence that it's safe to do so. The trust we build with people is based on the reliability and security of the technologies on which we choose to run our infrastructure. This is true for organizations of any size, from a three-person open source project that thousands of other projects rely upon to a large multinational corporation selling a product to a global user base.

The complexity of modern systems, and the velocity at which they are developed, means that safety and reliability need to be integrated from a product's inception for maximum effectiveness. Seeing security and reliability as inherent properties of a system is not only natural but critical in today's automated, connected, and complex technological landscape.

It's no surprise, then, that within the broader community, DevOps and DevSecOps are driving the conversations around the sustainability of systems. However, the notion of an integrated security and reliability model will take time to evolve and become a natural part of the ecosystem. Many development lifecycles and organizations are functionally centered around the division of labor between teams responsible for the development, testing, security, reliability, and operation of a system. This model will need to transform to meet the demands of the technology shifts we are seeing.

In writing this book, we brought together teams from across Google—from developers to SREs to security engineers. This collaboration reflects the interactive spirit Google relies on to secure its systems and make them increasingly reliable. At Google, we make security and reliability concerns part of the product development process, and encourage people with different experiences and skills to work together and listen to the perspective that others bring. Because the people are as important as the systems themselves, we recommend investing thoughtfully in how you design your teams and structure their responsibilities and incentives. People need to agree on common requirements before they debate technical solutions for which consensus might be difficult to achieve. Don't underestimate the investment required to build trust and ensure you're all speaking a common language.

For those who are passionate about security and reliability, we conclude with the following advice: your ability to work across knowledge domains and embed expertise in the right places is key to your organization's success. Security and reliability need to be an integrated part of the entire computing environment. All these pieces must work together in harmony to solve problems. No checklist or silver-bullet advice we could give can compensate for your own ability to help your organization flex and grow as the nature of the security and reliability challenges it faces evolves.

As we come to the end of this book, we anticipate that it will mark the beginning of many important conversations. We hope you will join in this discussion too, by participating in communities with other professionals and sharing your stories. In this dialogue, we encourage you to honor the many viewpoints that different roles bring to the table, support the search for solutions, and share what has worked for you. We're confident that this conversation will help all of us in our effort to create secure and reliable systems.

A Disaster Risk Assessment Matrix

For a thorough disaster risk analysis, we recommend ranking the risks facing your organization by using a standardized matrix that accounts for each risk's probability of occurrence and its potential impact to the organization. Table A-1 is a sample risk assessment matrix that both large and small organizations can tailor to the specifics of their systems.

To use the matrix, assess the values appropriate for each of the columns of probability and impact. As we emphasize in Chapter 16, these values are likely dependent on what your organization does, its infrastructure, and where it is located. An organization operating out of Los Angeles, CA, in the US may have a higher likelihood of experiencing an earthquake than an organization operating out of Hamburg, Germany. If your organization has offices in many locations, you may even want to do a risk assessment per location.

Once you've calculated the probability and impact values, multiply them to determine the rank of each risk. The resulting values can be used to order the risks from highest to lowest, which serves as a guide for prioritization and preparation. A risk that ranks 0.8 will likely require more immediate attention than risks that have a value of 0.5 or 0.3. Be sure to develop response plans for the most critical risks your organization faces.

Table A-1. Sample disaster risk assessment matrix

Theme	Risk	Probability of occurrence within a year	Impact to organization if risk occurs	Ranking	Names of systems impacted by risk
		Almost never: 0.0 *Unlikely: 0.2* *Somewhat unlikely : 0.4* *Likely: 0.6* *Highly likely: 0.8* *Inevitable :1.0*	*Negligible: 0.0* *Minimal: 0.2* *Moderate: 0.5* *Severe : 0.8* *Critical: 1.0*	*Probability x impact*	
Environmental	Earthquake				
	Flood				
	Fire				
	Hurricane				
Infrastructure reliability	Power outage				
	Loss of internet connectivity				
	Authentication system down				
	High system latency/ infrastructure slowdown				
Security	System compromise				
	Insider theft of intellectual property				
	DDos/DoS attack				
	Misuse of system resources— e.g., cryptocurrency mining				
	Vandalism/ website defacement				
	Phishing attack				
	Software security bug				
	Hardware security bug				
	Emerging serious vulnerability, e.g., Meltdown/Spectre, Heartbleed				

Index

revocation mechanism (see explicit revocation mechanism)

risk

    classifying access based on, 63

    reliability versus security design considerations, 4

risk analysis, 366, 499

risk assessment

    disaster risk assessment matrix, 499

    understanding adversaries, 32-33

risk ratings, 366

risk reduction, reducing fear with, 484-486

risk taking, balancing accountability with, 479

RL (remediation lead), 402, 413, 420

role separation, 162

roles and responsibilities, 455-470

    Blue and Red Teams, 465-468

    embedding security at Google, 463-465

    embedding security specialists and security teams, 462

    external researchers, 468-470

    integrating security into the organization, 460-470

    recovery and, 419

    security/reliability as everyone's responsibility, 456-460

    security/reliability risk evaluation, 457

    specialists' roles, 456

    understanding security expertise, 458

rollbacks

    deny lists, 194

    firmware/hardware-centric constraints, 199

    minimum acceptable security version numbers, 195-198

    rotating signing keys, 198

    security/reliability tradeoffs, 192-200

rollouts

    incremental, 258

    legacy conversions, 259

    staged, 484

    strategy for, 258

rotation of keys (see key rotation)

RPCs (see remote procedure calls)

RSA, 19, 151

S

safe proxies (case study), 37-42

    Google Tool Proxy, 40-42

    in production environments, 37-40

SafeHtml, 115, 254

SafeSql, 115

safety nets, 486

same-origin policy, 110

sandboxing, 147, 149, 451

sanitizing code, 267

sanitizing data, 431

scalable revocation, 203

scope, of IR team charter, 369

secrets

    dangers of including in code, 311

    rotation of, 433-435

        (see also key rotation)

security (generally)

    as emergent property of system design, 46

    integrating into the organization, 460-470

    reliability and (see intersection of security and reliability; tradeoffs, reliability/security)

security boundaries

    defined, 106

    small TCBs and strong security boundaries, 108

    threat models and, 109

    understandability and, 105-111

security by design, xxv

security champions, 463

security changes (see change, designing for)

security experts (see security specialists)

security investigations (see investigating systems)

security logs

    application logs, 355

    cloud logs, 355

    determining which security logs to retain, 354-357

    host agents, 354

    network-based logging and detection, 356

    operating system logs, 354

security posture, changes to, 132-135

security risks, 4, 53

security specialists

    certifications and academia, 459

    embedding into the organization, 462

    hiring, 458

    role of, 456

security teams, 462

    (see also Blue Teams; Chrome security team; Red Teams)

About the Editors

Heather Adkins is an 18-year Google veteran and founding member of the Google security team. As Senior Director of Information Security, she has built a global team responsible for maintaining the safety and security of Google's networks, systems, and applications. She has an extensive background in systems and network administration with an emphasis on practical security and has worked to build and secure some of the world's largest infrastructure. She now focuses her time primarily on the defense of Google's computing infrastructure and working with industry to tackle some of the greatest security challenges.

Betsy Beyer is a Technical Writer for Google in NYC specializing in Site Reliability Engineering. She coauthored *Site Reliability Engineering: How Google Runs Production Systems* and *The Site Reliability Workbook: Practical Ways to Implement SRE* (O'Reilly). En route to her current career, Betsy studied international relations and English literature, and she holds degrees from Stanford and Tulane.

Paul Blankinship manages the technical writing team for Google's Security and Privacy Engineering group, and has helped develop Google's internal security and privacy policies. In addition to his career as a technical writer, he is an actively performing musician in the San Francisco Bay Area.

Piotr Lewandowski is a Senior Staff Site Reliability Engineer and has spent the past nine years improving the security posture of Google's infrastructure. As the Production Tech Lead for security, he is responsible for harmonious collaboration between the SRE and security organizations. In his previous role, he led a team responsible for the reliability of Google's critical security infrastructure. Before joining Google, he built a startup, worked at CERT Polska, and got a degree in computer science from Warsaw University of Technology.

Ana Oprea specializes in security, SRE, and planning and strategy for Google's technical infrastructure—a role that follows naturally from her previous experience as a software developer, technical consultant, and network admin. Having worked and studied in Germany, France, and Romania, she accounts for different cultural approaches when facing any challenge.

Adam Stubblefield is a Distinguished Engineer and the Area Tech Lead for security at Google. Over the past eight years, he's helped build much of Google's core security infrastructure. Adam has a PhD in computer science from Johns Hopkins University.

Colophon

The animal on the cover of *Building Secure and Reliable Systems* is a Chinese water dragon (*Physignathus cocincinus*), a species of agamid lizard found in parts of Southeast Asia, including Cambodia, Laos, Vietnam, Thailand, and China. They are also commonly known as Asian, Thai, or green water dragons. This species of lizard typically lives in warm, humid climates near permanent sources of standing water such as rivers, swamps, and rain forests.

Chinese water dragons can grow up to three feet long, and they range in color from bright to dark green. Males are typically larger and more vivid in color, with yellow, orange, or even pinkish coloring on their throats. These lizards have high horn scales down their heads and backs all the way to the base of their long and finely pointed tails, which make up almost 70% of their total body length and can be used for balance as well as defense against predators. They feed on insects, fish, birds, and small rodents, and may also eat vegetation or eggs.

Like many reptiles, Chinese water dragons have a small shiny spot at the top of their head called a *parietal* or *pineal eye* (also known colloquially as a "third eye"). This is thought to help reptiles like water dragons thermoregulate by sensing changes in light. Though they spend much of their time climbing trees, Chinese water dragons are also excellent swimmers—when startled, they will drop from the branches into the water and can stay submerged for up to 25 minutes. They can also run bipedally!

The Chinese water dragon is categorized as a vulnerable species by the International Union for Conservation of Nature. Many of the animals on O'Reilly covers are endangered; all of them are important to the world.

The cover illustration is by Karen Montgomery, based on a black-and-white engraving from *Histoire Naturelle*. The cover fonts are Gilroy Semibold and Guardian Sans. The text font is Adobe Minion Pro; the heading font is Adobe Myriad Condensed; and the code font is Dalton Maag's Ubuntu Mono.

O'REILLY®

There's much more
where this came from.

Experience books, videos, live online
training courses, and more from O'Reilly
and our 200+ partners—all in one place.

Learn more at oreilly.com/online-learning

9 781492 083122